BARRON'S
STUDENTS' #1 CHOICE

PASS KEY

TO THE

TOEFL® iBT

TEST OF ENGLISH AS A FOREIGN LANGUAGE
INTERNET-BASED TEST

1/25/17 MAY 2006

Sixth Edition

Pamela J. Sharpe, Ph.D.

BARRON'S EDUCATIONAL SERIES, INC.

428
TOEFL
Sharpe

To my former students
at home and abroad

All inquiries should be addressed to:
Barron's Educational Series, Inc.
250 Wireless Boulevard
Hauppauge, New York 11788
www.barronseduc.com

Library of Congress Catalog Card No. 2006045865
ISBN-10: 0-7641-7919-5
ISBN-13: 978-0-7641-7919-8

Library of Congress Cataloging-in-Publication Data

Sharpe, Pamela J.
    Pass key to the TOEFL iBT / Pamela J. Sharpe.—6th ed.
    Rev. ed. of: Pass key to the TOEFL, 5th ed. 2004.
      p.   cm.
    ISBN-13: 978-0-7641-7919-8 (book & audio compact disks)
    ISBN-10: 0-7641-7919-5 (book & audio compact disks)
    1. Test of English as a Foreign Language—Study guides.   2. English
language—Textbooks for foreign speakers.   3. English language—
Examinations—Study guides.   I. Title.

PE1128.S523   2006
428′.0076—dc22   2006045865

ACKNOWLEDGMENTS

With affection and appreciation, I acknowledge my indebtedness to the friends, family, and colleagues who have been part of the TOEFL team for so many years.

The late Dr. Jayne Harder, former Director of the English Language Institute at the University of Florida for initiating me into the science of linguistics and the art of teaching English as a second language;

Robert and Lillie Sharpe, my parents for their assistance in typing and proofreading previous editions and for their enthusiastic encouragement throughout my career;

The late Dr. Tom Clapp, former Dean of Continuing Education at the University of Toledo for the maturity and confidence that I gained during our marriage because he believed in me;

Carole Berglie, former Editor at Barron's Educational Series for her guidance in seeing the first edition of the manuscript through to publication;

Marcy Rosenbaum, Project Editor at Barron's Educational Series for her invaluable insights and wise counsel during every stage of development and production;

Debby Becak, Production Manager at Barron's Educational Series for the creative suggestions and designs, large and small, that have improved every chapter;

Bob O'Sullivan, Managing Editor at Barron's Educational Series for making important decisions at critical times during the project;

Mark Miele, Editorial Director at Barron's Educational Series for consulting on the project and for providing indispensable advice on legal questions;

Carlos Moreno, Carlos Moreno Photography for the photographs that provided the TOEFL-like context for the audio questions;

Joan Franklin, President, and John Rockwell, Editor, at Cinema Sound for casting and directing the talented voices and bringing the script to life;

Sara Black, Copy Editor for her constructive criticism and helpful corrections throughout the manuscript;

Kathy Telford, Proofreader at Proofreaders Plus for her attention to the important details, her positive approach to errors, and her friendship;

Dennis Oliver, Professor at Estrella Mountain Community College for coauthoring the *Glossary of Campus Vocabulary*;

Erin Osterman Fitzgerald, Legal Assistant for securing the reprint permissions and organizing the legal files;

David John Osterman, Technology Consultant for helping me to transform my office for the 21st century;

John T. Osterman, my husband—a special thank you for the unconditional love and the daily interest in and support for my writing career, as well as for checking my math in the evaluation tables. Each revision of this book is better than the last, and every new and revised year with John is the best year of my life.

PERMISSIONS

BRIEF TABLE OF CONTENTS

TIMETABLE FOR THE TOEFL® iBT

Test Section	Questions	Time
Reading	3–5 passages with 12–14 questions	60–100 minutes
Listening	2–3 conversations with 5 questions each 4–6 lectures with 6 questions each	60–90 minutes
BREAK		5–10 minutes
Speaking	2 independent tasks 4 integrated tasks	20 minutes
Writing	1 integrated task 1 independent task	20 minutes 30 minutes

Note: The tests in this book contain three reading passages, three conversations, and six lectures *or* five reading passages, two conversations, and four lectures because that is the standard length for an official TOEFL. Every official test includes either reading or listening material that is being field-tested for future use. There is no tutorial on the new iBT.

1

ORIENTATION

TO THE STUDENT: HOW TO USE THIS BOOK TO SUCCEED

A STUDY PLAN

Welcome to *Barron's Pass Key to the TOEFL® iBT, 6th Edition.* Do you know what a pass key is? A pass key is a master key, a key that opens every door. This book and the audio CDs were designed to help you prepare for the iBT®—the Internet-Based TOEFL. After you have succeeded on the TOEFL, other doors will open for you. But first you need a pass key to unlock the TOEFL.

Barron's Pass Key to the TOEFL® iBT, 6th Edition is the concise version of the classic book, *Barron's How to Prepare for the TOEFL® iBT, 12th Edition.* Small enough to carry in your backpack, book bag, or even a purse, this convenient book can always be in the right place when you have a few minutes to study—on the bus, while you wait for an appointment, or on break at work or school.

This concise version, *Pass Key to the TOEFL® iBT, 6th Edition,* can be used to prepare for the Internet-Based TOEFL® iBT. To make this book less expensive and more convenient to carry with you, we have included three model tests in the book and we have selected two of those model tests for the compact disks. The larger version of this book, *Barron's How to Prepare for the TOEFL® iBT, 12th Edition,* includes a detailed review of academic skills that you will need to develop, as well as four more model tests for a total of seven model tests. The 10 CDs that supplement the larger book provide the audio for all seven model tests. The CD-ROM that supplements the larger book includes both the audio and the visuals for the model tests on computer screens.

Ideally, you would use the two versions of this book for two different purposes. You would use this book, *Pass Key to the TOEFL® iBT, 6th Edition*, to take the best advantage of your time while you are away from your computer or when you don't want to carry heavy materials. You would use the larger version of the book, *Barron's How to Prepare for the TOEFL® iBT, 12th Edition*, and the CD-ROM that supplements it, to study academic skills, practice taking additional model tests, and simulate the experience of taking the TOEFL® iBT on the computer.

Whether you decide to use this book alone or in combination with the larger version, study thoughtfully, and take the TOEFL with confidence. It may well be the most important examination of your academic career. And this book can be a pass key to your success.

STEPS TO SUCCESS

This book is easy to use. More than one million Barron's students have succeeded on the TOEFL. You can be successful too, by following twelve steps.

➤ 1. Inform yourself about the test.

Read the answers to "FAQs—Frequently Asked Questions About the TOEFL® iBT" in this chapter. Then, if you cannot find a copy locally, visit the TOEFL web site at **www.ets.org/toefl** to download a copy of the *TOEFL Information and Registration Bulletin*. Research demonstrates that students who know what to expect will perform better on an examination.

➤ 2. Invest time in your study plan.

Be realistic about how much time you need to prepare for the TOEFL. Choose a syllabus from the choices in this chapter. Use distributed practice—two hours every day for four months will give you better results than twelve hours every day for forty days, even though you will be studying 120 hours for both schedules.

➤ 3. Develop study habits.

The study habits explained at the end of this chapter will help you succeed on the TOEFL and after the TOEFL when you are admitted to a college or university, or when you continue your professional training to keep your licenses current. Successful students understand the value of these habits.

➤ 4. Evaluate your strengths and weaknesses.

Take the Pretest, Model Test 1 in Chapter 2 and check your answers using the Explanatory or Example Answers in Chapter 7. Which sections of the TOEFL were easier for you? Which were more difficult? Plan to spend more time on the sections on which you received lower scores.

➤ 5. Master academic skills.

Chapter 3 contains ten of the academic skills that you will need to complete the tasks on the TOEFL® iBT. Read the strategies, complete the practice activities, and check your answers. If this chapter is difficult for you, it may be a good idea to refer to the larger version of this book, *Barron's How to Prepare for the TOEFL® iBT, 12th Edition*. The larger version includes forty academic skills.

➤ 6. Improve English proficiency.

Chapter 4 will show you how your English proficiency is tested on the TOEFL. Review important language problems and identify strategies for the language skill that corresponds to each section—Reading, Listening, Speaking, and Writing. Take the quizzes and check your answers. Although you need to know more English than it is possible to include in one chapter, this review will help you apply the English you know to the test situation. You will improve your English proficiency as measured by the TOEFL.

➤ 7. Understand the directions.

Take the time to read and understand the directions for each problem in Chapter 4 and each section on the model tests. If you already understand what to do in order to complete a certain type of question, you will not have to spend as much valuable time reading and analyzing the directions when you take the official TOEFL.

➤ 8. Check your progress.

After you finish the work in Chapters 3 and 4, you will be ready to check your progress. Take the first Progress Test, Model Test 2 in Chapter 5 and check your answers using the Explanatory or Example Answers in Chapter 7. You should begin to see how the academic skills are used on the new TOEFL® iBT.

➤ 9. Practice taking model tests.

Students who have an opportunity to take at least one model test will almost always increase their scores significantly on the official TOEFL test. Experience is a great teacher. This book provides you with three model tests for practice. In order to take advantage of the experience, you should always follow the test directions carefully and time each section. Take each model test without stopping for a break until you finish the Reading and Listening sections. Then take a five-minute break and work without stopping until you complete the Speaking and Writing sections. By simulating the test conditions, you will become familiar with the way that it feels to take the TOEFL and you will be able to concentrate on the questions instead of trying to figure out what is going to happen next. You will also learn to pace yourself so that you can finish each section within the time limits. Remember, you should not try to memorize the questions on the model tests. You will find similar questions on the official TOEFL, but you will not find exactly the same questions. Try to improve your skills, not your memory.

➤ 10. Estimate your TOEFL score.

Chapter 8 gives you a method for estimating your TOEFL score from scores on the model tests in this book. If you do not have a teacher or a reliable grader to evaluate your speaking and writing sections, you may want to consider using one of the services listed at the end of the chapter. You need to know how your speaking and writing will factor into the total score.

➤ 11. Maintain a positive attitude.

Throughout the book, you will find advice for staying positive and motivated. Most of it can be found under the heading "Advisor's Office." Take the time to read the suggestions and think about them. Other successful students have benefited from the same advice.

➤ 12. Take the test when you are ready.

Some students try to succeed on the TOEFL before they are ready. Be realistic about your study schedule. If you are not scoring very well on the model tests and the estimates of your TOEFL scores are below the minimum for you to achieve your goal, you should reconsider your registration date. Knowing when to take the test is part of a successful study plan. If you give yourself the time you need and if you follow the study plan using this book, you will reach your goal. In the future, you will not be asked whether you took the TOEFL a month earlier or later but you *will* be asked to produce the required score. You can do it! Take the test when you are ready.

TO THE TEACHER: RECOMMENDATIONS AND RESOURCES

PERSPECTIVES

In the Middle Ages, a man approached two stonemasons and asked them what they were doing. The first stonemason replied, "I am laying stones." The other answered, "I am building a cathedral."

I have been teaching TOEFL preparation classes since 1970 and writing TOEFL materials since 1975. As I go into my classes, I ask myself: Am I teaching TOEFL prep or am I helping students achieve their career goals? As I prepare each new edition of my books, I ask myself: Am I writing TOEFL preparation books or am I making tools that will help students succeed on the TOEFL and *after* the TOEFL? It is a very different perspective and inspires in a different way.

Certainly, we have seen many changes in the TOEFL across the decades. Often Educational Testing Service has revised the TOEFL in an effort to keep pace with changes in our ESL/EFL teaching paradigms, and occasionally the revisions in the TOEFL have produced changes in our teaching paradigms in something referred to as a *washback effect.*

This is probably the most challenging time in TOEFL preparation that I have experienced because the Internet-Based TOEFL (iBT) is more than a revision. It is a completely different kind of test, which requires a new approach to learning. Our students will have to demonstrate their ability to integrate the language skills by completing tasks similar to those that they will be expected to accomplish in academic settings. They will have to speak and write at high levels of proficiency.

Eventually, I believe that the changes on the TOEFL will be beneficial for our students and for us, their teachers. During the initial transition period, however, it could be difficult to plan appropriate lessons and adjust our teaching styles.

TEACHING TIPS

These ideas work for me. I invite you to try some of them in your classes.

➤ 1. Begin with a positive message.

It can be very simple. For instance, "The highest tower is built one brick at a time." If you put a new message in the same place every time—on an overhead or on the board—students will learn to look for it when they come into the room. Music serves the same purpose. It sets a positive mood for the session.

➤ 2. Write three important goals for the class so that students can see them.

Three goals are manageable for one class session. When they are visible, they keep us all on track. At the end of the class, referring to the goals gives everyone a sense of progress and closure for the day.

➤ 3. Arrange for model tests to be taken in a lab or at home on the honor system.

Your time with students is too valuable for you to spend four hours proctoring each model test. That would add up to twelve hours of class time for all of the model tests in this book.

➤ 4. Allow students to grade the Reading and Listening sections of their model tests.

If students take responsibility for grading the objective sections of their model tests, and for referring to the explanatory answers, you will save hours that you would have had to use doing routine clerical tasks. If the students take the model tests on the computer, the scoring for these sections will be done automatically; if they are using the book, the answer key is printed in Chapter 7. This will afford you the time you need to concentrate on answering questions.

➤ 5. Ask students to write their questions on note cards and bring them to class.

When students refer to the explanatory answers, many questions are resolved for them without asking the teacher. If students write down their questions, sometimes the answer becomes apparent to them at this stage. The questions that they bring to class are really worth discussion. If you have them on cards, you can prepare your answers for the question-and-answer session at the beginning of the next class. You always have the answer!

➤ 6. When several students have the same question, prepare a short presentation.

When the question is repeated, it gives us an indication of what our students need to know. By using their questions for class preparation, we show that we are teaching people, not subjects.

➤ 7. Make overheads of test questions and show the students how you choose an answer.

Let the students "listen in" on your thought processes as you decide why answers are incorrect and which answer choice is correct. Use the explanatory answers in the book to help you. For example, you might say, "I know that A is not correct because the professor did not include this research in his lecture. Choice B looks possible, but it is not complete. The choice leaves out the second part of the answer. That means it must be either Choice C or D. I know that D is not correct because the professor said that there were three types, not two. It must be Choice C." Modeling *how* to think helps students *learn* to think when they see similar test items.

➤ 8. Use class time to teach and practice academic skills.

Make overheads of material from Chapter 3 and go over it in class. Take the quizzes in class, using "Think, Answer, Compare, Discuss." Students have time to think and respond to each answer independently, and then they compare their answers to the correct answer and discuss why that choice is a good one.

➤ 9. Focus on speaking and writing in class.

Provide many good models of responses to speaking and writing questions in class. Show students how to use the checklists to evaluate speaking and writing.

➤ 10. Assign speaking tasks and writing tasks as homework.

Have students turn in tapes and essays. If you have voice mail and choose to use it for homework assignments, students can phone you and leave a one-minute response to a speaking task. Spend grading time on these important sections. Bring samples of good work to class—good organization, good openings, good support statements, good closings. Catch your students doing something good and use it as an example.

11. Provide counseling and encouragement as part of the class routine.

Ideally, one minute at the end of class can be used for a pep talk, a cheer, or a success story about a former student. This is one of my favorite cheers: T-O-E-F-L. We're making progress. We're doing well. T-O-E-F-L. I also like to stand by a poster at the door when students are leaving my class. The last thing they see is the affirmation on the poster: "I know more today than I did yesterday. I am preparing. I will succeed." Some students want a handshake, a high five, or a hug. Others just smile and say good-bye. Some hang by the door, and I know that they need to talk. Every excellent TOEFL prep teacher I know is also a very good counselor. You probably are, too.

RESOURCES

Several resources for teachers are listed in Chapter 8. Four syllabus options are listed in the next section. It is also worthwhile to read the "Steps to Success" for students printed on the previous pages. The most frequently asked questions (FAQs) are answered at the end of this chapter. If I can be of help to you or your students, please contact me by visiting my web site at *www.teflprep.com*.

SYLLABUS OPTIONS

A *syllabus* is a "study plan." There are four options from which to choose. The estimated number of hours for each option is the minimum time that is required to complete the plan.

The Standard Syllabus requires 16 weeks and 80 hours of your time. It is the best option because it allows you to study about 5 hours each week, and you can build in some review if you need it.

The Accelerated Syllabus also requires 80 hours, but it is possible to complete it in half the number of weeks by making a commitment to studying about ten hours each week. *Accelerated* means "fast." This calendar does not include time for review.

The Abbreviated Syllabus should be chosen only when you cannot find the time in your schedule to follow one of the other calendars.

Abbreviated means "shorter." This calendar does not allow you to complete all the study materials in the larger book. This concise version, *Barron's Pass Key to the TOEFL® iBT, 6th Edition*, contains only the material in the abbreviated syllabus.

The Individualized Syllabus is often chosen when you have already taken the TOEFL and you are very sure which sections will be most difficult for you when you take it again. This calendar allows you to concentrate on one or two sections without repeating information that you have already mastered on other sections.

Standard Syllabus — 16 Weeks/80 Hours
Text book: *Barron's How to Prepare for the TOEFL® iBT, 12th Edition*

Week	Topic	Reference Pages	Class Hours
1	Orientation		5 hours
	How to Use This Book to Succeed		
	Study Habits		
	Frequently Asked Questions		
	Model Test 1: Pretest—With Explanatory Answers		
	Academic Skills—With Activities		
2	Taking Notes		5 hours
3	Paraphrasing		5 hours
4	Summarizing		5 hours
5	Synthesizing		5 hours
6	Model Test 2: Progress Test— With Explanatory Answers		5 hours
	Review of TOEFL Sections— With Quizzes and Glossaries		
7	Reading		5 hours
8	Listening		5 hours
9	Speaking		5 hours
10	Writing		5 hours
	Model Tests—With Explanatory Answers		
11	Model Test 3: Progress Test		5 hours
12	Model Test 4: Progress Test		5 hours
13	Model Test 5: Progress Test		5 hours
14	Model Test 6: Progress Test		5 hours
15	Model Test 7: Progress Test		5 hours
16	Individualized Review		5 hours

Accelerated Syllabus — 8 Weeks/80 Hours
Text book: *Barron's How to Prepare for the TOEFL® iBT, 12th Edition*

Week	Topic	Reference Pages	Class Hours
1	Orientation		5 hours
	How to Use This Book to Succeed		
	Study Habits		
	Frequently Asked Questions		
	Model Test 1: Pretest—With Explanatory Answers		
	Academic Skills—With Activities		
2	Taking Notes		10 hours
	Paraphrasing		
3	Summarizing		10 hours
	Synthesizing		
4	Model Test 2: Progress Test— With Explanatory Answers		10 hours
	Review of TOEFL Sections— With Quizzes and Glossaries		
	Reading		
	Listening		
5	Speaking		10 hours
	Writing		
6	Model Tests—With Explanatory Answers		
	Model Test 3—Progress Test		10 hours
	Model Test 4—Progress Test		
7	Model Test 5—Progress Test		10 hours
	Model Test 6—Progress Test		
8	Model Test 7—Progress Test		15 hours
	Individualized Review		

Abbreviated Syllabus — 4 Weeks/40 Hours
Text book: *Barron's Pass Key to the TOEFL® iBT, 6th Edition*

Week	Topic	Reference Pages	Class Hours
1	Orientation		5 hours
	Frequently Asked Questions		
	Model Test 1: Pretest— With Explanatory Answers		
	Academic Skills		
	Taking Notes		2 hours
	Paraphrasing		2 hours
	Summarizing		2 hours
	Synthesizing		2 hours
2	Model Test 2: Progress Test— With Explanatory Answers		5 hours
	Review of TOEFL Sections and Glossaries		
	Reading		3 hours
	Listening		3 hours
	Speaking		3 hours
	Writing		3 hours
3	Model Test 3: Progress Test— With Explanatory Answers		5 hours
4	Individualized Review		5 hours

Individualized Syllabus — Variable Weeks/Hours

Week	Topic	Reference Pages	Class Hours
1	Orientation		4 hours
	Frequently Asked Questions		
	Model Test 1: Pretest		
2	Group and Individual Assignments		As needed

Both *Barron's How to Prepare for the TOEFL, 12th Edition* and *Barron's Pass Key to the TOEFL, 6th Edition,* are designed to support self-study. After analyzing the Pretest, the teacher can assign individualized review by selecting the chapters and pages that focus on the most challenging sections of the test for each student. It is often helpful to divide the class into groups of students who have similar patterns of error on the Pretest. Model tests provide a process for monitoring individual progress and redirecting student effort. *Barron's Practice Exercises for the TOEFL, 5th Edition,* is an additional resource for individual practice.

FAQs—FREQUENTLY ASKED QUESTIONS ABOUT THE TOEFL® iBT

The TOEFL is the Test of English as a Foreign Language. Almost one million students from 180 countries register to take the TOEFL every year at test centers throughout the world. Some of them do not score well because they do not understand enough English. Others do not score well because they do not understand the examination. The following questions are frequently asked by students as they prepare for the TOEFL.

TOEFL PROGRAMS

➤ What is the purpose of the TOEFL?

Since 1963, the TOEFL has been used by scholarship selection committees of governments, universities, and agencies such as Fulbright, the Agency for International Development, AMIDEAST, and Latin American Scholarship Programs as a standard measure of the English proficiency of their candidates. Some professional licensing and certification agencies also use TOEFL scores to evaluate English proficiency. The admissions committees of more than 4500 colleges and universities in the United States, Canada, Australia, Great Britain, and many other countries worldwide require foreign applicants to submit TOEFL scores along with transcripts and recommendations in order to be considered for admission.

➤ When was the Internet-Based TOEFL (iBT) launched?

The Internet-Based TOEFL (iBT), also called the Next Generation TOEFL, was launched on September 24, 2005, in the United States. The following month, it was administered in Canada, Germany, Italy, and France. The iBT is being introduced throughout the world in phases during 2006.

➤ When will the iBT be introduced in my country?

Five months before the test is introduced in a new area, notices will be published. To see a schedule of times and test centers, visit the TOEFL web site or check the *TOEFL® iBT Registration and Information Bulletin* on the TOEFL web site at *www.ets.org/toefl*. A revised timeline is continuously updated on the TOEFL web site.

➤ When and where will the iBT be offered?

Eventually, more than fifty test dates will be scheduled. Times during mornings, afternoons, and evenings will be available on both week-days and weekends.

➤ When will the CBT and the PBT be discontinued?

The Computer-Based TOEFL (CBT) and the Paper-Based TOEFL (PBT) will be discontinued in each country when the Internet-Based TOEFL is introduced.

➤ Which language skills are tested on the TOEFL?

Computer-Based TOEFL	Paper-Based TOEFL	Internet-Based TOEFL
Listening	Listening	Listening
Structure	Structure	Speaking
Reading	Reading	Reading
Writing	Test of Written English	Writing

➤ Does the TOEFL have a Speaking section?

The Internet-Based TOEFL includes a Speaking section with six questions. If the Paper-Based TOEFL must be used in a remote area, it will also contain a Speaking section.

➤ Why was the Structure section removed from the new TOEFL?

Grammar is now tested as part of the other sections. It is important to use good grammar in the Speaking and the Writing sections.

➤ Will the TOEFL® iBT writing topics be published?

Not at this time. However, many of the topics that were previously published for the Computer-Based TOEFL are similar to the types of topics found on the independent writing task for the iBT.

➤ Is it possible to take the iBT without the Speaking or the Writing sections?

The Speaking section and the Writing section are required on the Internet-Based TOEFL. You must take all sections of the TOEFL in order to receive a score.

➤ Is the Internet-Based TOEFL more difficult than previous TOEFL formats?

Although the Reading and Listening sections contain longer passages, the questions are not very different from those on previous TOEFL formats. However, most students find the Speaking and Writing sections more challenging. That is why it is a good idea to practice, using this book.

REGISTRATION

➤ How do I register for the TOEFL?

You can register for the Internet-Based TOEFL online, by mail, or by telephone.

Online   *www.ets.org/toefl* for testing worldwide
Phone   1-800-GO-TOEFL (1-800-468-6335) for testing in the United States and Canada
1-443-751-4862 for testing outside the United States and Canada

Mail   ETS-TOEFL iBT Registration Office, P.O. Box 6152, Princeton, NJ 08541-6152 USA
            Regional Registration Centers worldwide (addresses listed in the *TOEFL® iBT Registration and Information Bulletin*)

➤ Where can I find a free TOEFL® iBT Registration and Information Bulletin?

This important bulletin includes the information that you will need to register for the TOEFL. It can be downloaded free from the TOEFL web site *www.ets.org/toefl*. In addition, all Regional Registration Centers have paper copies of the bulletin, or it can be found at many libraries, universities, and educational counseling centers around the world. It is also possible to order a bulletin from Educational Testing Service, but the shipping can take as long as eight weeks.

➤ Where are the Regional Registration Centers?

Eight Regional Registration Centers (RRCs) are planned to support the test sites and counseling centers in their region. They will be listed on the web site soon.

➤ Will my registration be confirmed?

Your registration number can be printed when you register online, or you can receive your number by e-mail, if you prefer.

➤ When should I register for the TOEFL?

You must register at least seven days before the test date. Because test centers fill rapidly during desirable times, it is a good idea to register several months in advance. You may choose as many as four test centers for the same date so that you have a greater probability of completing your registration. If you are taking the TOEFL as part of the application process for college or university admission, you should plan to take the test early enough for your score to be received by the admission office before the application deadline.

➤ May I change the date or cancel my registration?

To receive a refund, you must reschedule or cancel three full days before your test date. For example, if your test is on Friday, you must call to cancel your registration on Monday. You will be charged a $40 fee for this service.

➤ What are the fees for the TOEFL® iBT?

The fee for the test administration, including four score reports is $140 U.S.

➤ How may I pay the fees?

You may pay by credit card, e-check from bank accounts in the United States, money order, or the current exchange rate for the U.S. dollar in one of the following currencies: Australian dollar, British pound, Canadian dollar, Danish krone, Euro, Hong Kong dollar, Japanese yen, New Zealand dollar, Norwegian kroner, Singapore dollar, Swedish krona, Swiss franc.

TEST ADMINISTRATION

➤ How will the TOEFL® iBT be administered?

The TOEFL will be offered on a schedule of dates in a network of test centers throughout the world. Most areas will have between thirty and forty administrations every year. The room in which the TOEFL is administered is usually a computer lab. You will be assigned a seat. If you are late, you will probably not be admitted.

➤ Where can I take the TOEFL?

The TOEFL web site at *www.ets.org/toefl* lists test centers and schedules.

➤ In what room will the test be offered?

The room may be a computer lab or a language laboratory. It may be a classroom with about fifteen computers at least four feet apart.

➤ What should I take with me to the test room?

You are not permitted to take anything with you when you enter the test room. No cell phones, paper, dictionaries, pens, or pencils are allowed. The test supervisor will give you a headset, paper, and pencils.

➤ What kind of identification is required?

In the United States, only your valid passport will be accepted for admission to the TOEFL. In other countries, your valid passport is still the best identification, but if you do not have a passport, you may refer to the TOEFL web site for special directions. Your photograph will be taken at the test center and reproduced on all official score reports, along with your signature. Be sure to use the same spelling and order of your name on your registration materials, the test center log that you will sign when you enter and leave the test area, the forms on the computer screens, and any correspondence that you may have with the TOEFL office. You should also use the same spelling on applications for schools and documents for agencies that will receive your score reports. Even a small difference can cause serious delays or even denial of the applications.

➤ How long is the testing session?

The TOEFL® iBT takes about four hours to administer, including the time required for giving directions and the break between the Listening and the Speaking sections.

EXAMINATION

➤ What kinds of questions are found on the iBT?

The majority of the questions on the iBT are multiple choice. Some other types of questions are also on the iBT. These questions have special directions on the screen. You will have many examples of them in the model tests in this book.

➤ Are all of the TOEFL® iBT tests the same?

Unlike the Computer-Based TOEFL (CBT), which presented questions based on your responses to previous questions, the iBT is a linear test. That means that on the same form, all of the test questions are the same.

➤ Why are some of the Reading and Listening sections longer?

The test developers include experimental questions for either the Reading or the Listening section on most TOEFL forms. You must do your best on all the questions because you will not know which questions are experimental and which are test questions that will be scored. For example, you may be taking the iBT with someone who has experimental questions in Reading, but you may have experimental questions in Listening. For this reason, your friend's test may have a longer Reading section, and your test may have a longer Listening section. The experimental questions may be at the beginning, middle, or end of the section.

➤ May I choose the order of the sections on my TOEFL?

You may not choose the order. Reading, Listening, Speaking, and Writing are tested in that order on the TOEFL, with a ten-minute break between the Listening and Speaking.

➤ What kinds of questions are found on the iBT?

Most of the questions are multiple choice, but some questions have special directions on the screen. You will have examples of the most frequently tested items in Chapter 4 in this book.

➤ May I take notes?

You are permitted to take notes and use them to answer the questions on the iBT. You will be given paper for that purpose when you enter the test room. Your notes will be collected and shredded after the test.

➤ May I change an answer?

On the Listening section, you can change your answer by clicking on a new answer. You can change your answer as many times as you wish until you click on the **Confirm Answer** button. On the Reading section, you can change your answer by clicking on the new answer. You can change your answer as many times as you wish, and you can go back to previous answers on the same reading passage. When you begin a new reading passage, you may not return to the previous passage to change answers. On the Speaking section, you will be cued with a beep to begin and end speaking. Everything that you say during the recording time will be submitted. You cannot change an answer. On the Writing section, you can revise your essays as much as you wish until the clock indicates that no time is remaining. If you submit your essays before time is up, you cannot return to them. The CD-ROM that supplements the larger book will provide you with practice in choosing and changing answers on the computer screen.

➤ If I am not sure of an answer, should I guess?

If you are not sure of an answer, you should guess. The number of incorrect answers is not subtracted from your score. First, eliminate all the possibilities that you know are NOT correct. Then, if you are almost sure of an answer, guess that one. If you have no idea of the correct answer for a question, choose one letter and use it for your "guess answer" throughout the entire examination. The "guess answer" is especially useful for finishing a section quickly.

➤ Why do some of the TOEFL tests have additional questions?

Some of the tests include questions that are being field-tested for use in future TOEFL administrations. These tests have more questions, but your answers to the additional field-test questions are not calculated as part of your score.

➤ What if I cannot hear the audio for the Listening section?

You will receive your own headphones with a microphone attached. Before the Listening section begins, you will have an opportunity to adjust the volume yourself. Be careful to adjust the volume when you are prompted to do so. If you wait until the test begins, you may not be able to adjust it. If there is a problem with your headset, raise your hand, and ask the test supervisor to provide you with another headset.

➤ What can I do if there is a problem during the test?

If there is a problem with the Internet connection or the power that supplies the computers, and if the test must be discontinued, everyone who is taking the test at that site is entitled to a refund or a free test on another date. This does not happen very often.

➤ What if I have a personal problem during the test?

If you become ill or you are being disturbed by the behavior of another person in the room, tell your test supervisor immediately. If you think that your score may be affected by the problem, ask the supervisor to file an Irregularities Report.

➤ Are breaks scheduled during the TOEFL?

A 10-minute break is scheduled between the Listening and the Speaking sections.

➤ How often may I take the iBT?

You may take the TOEFL as many times as you wish to score to your satisfaction. Although there were restrictions on when you could take the Computer-Based TOEFL (CBT), you can take the iBT more than once each month if you choose to do so.

➤ If I have already taken the TOEFL, how will the previous scores affect my new score?

TOEFL scores are valid for two years. If you have taken the TOEFL more than once but your first score report is more than two years ago, the first score will not be reported. If you have taken the TOEFL more than once in the past two years, a report will be sent for the test date that you request.

➤ May I keep my test?

You cannot save your test to a disk or send it to an e-mail address. If you try to do so, the TOEFL office may take legal action. There are examples of the official TOEFL test questions on the web site at *www.ets.org/toefl*.

➤ What happens to someone who cheats on the iBT?

Entering the room with false identification, tampering with the computer, using a camera, giving or receiving help, or trying to remove test materials or notes is considered cheating. Do not cheat. In spite of opportunity, knowledge that others are doing it, the desire to help a friend, or fear that you will not make a good score, *do not cheat*. On the TOEFL, cheating is a very serious matter. If you are discovered, you will be dismissed from the room, your score will be canceled, and you may not be able to take the test again on a future date.

SCORE REPORTS

➤ How is the Speaking section scored?

Trained raters listen to each of the speaking responses and assign them a number 0–4. The scores for all six responses are averaged and converted to a total section score 0–30.The raters grade the Speaking section using checklists similar to those printed in this book.

➤ How is the Writing section scored?

Trained raters read your essays and assign them a number 0–5. If there is disagreement about your score, a team leader will also read your essays. The scores for each essay are combined and converted to a section score 0–30. Raters grade the Writing section using checklists similar to those printed in this book.

➤ How is the total TOEFL score calculated?

The iBT has converted section scores for each of the four sections. The range for each section score is 0–30. When the scores for the four sections are added together, the total score range will be 0–120.

➤ How do I interpret my score?

You cannot pass or fail the TOEFL. Each school or agency will evaluate the scores according to its own requirements. Even at the same university, the requirements may vary for different programs of study, levels of study (graduate or undergraduate), and degrees of responsibility (student or teaching assistant). Many universities are setting minimum requirements for each section. The following range of requirements is typical of admissions policies for North American universities. This assumes, of course, that the applicant's documents other than English proficiency are acceptable.

Reading	19–21
Listening	17–21
Speaking	20–23
Writing	20–25
TOTAL	76–90

To be certain of the requirements for your school or agency, contact them directly.

➤ How do the scores compare on the iBT, CBT, and PBT formats?

The following chart compares TOEFL scores on the three most recent formats—the Internet-Based TOEFL (iBT), the Computer-Based TOEFL (CBT), and the Paper-Based TOEFL (PBT). More detailed charts are posted on the web site maintained by Educational Testing Service at *www.ets.org*.

iBT	CBT	PBT
111–120	273–300	640–677
96–110	243–272	590–639
79–95	213–242	550–589
65–78	183–212	513–549
53–64	153–182	477–512
41–52	123–152	437–476
30–40	93–122	397–436
19–29	63–92	347–396
6–18	23–62	311–346
0–5	0–22	310

➤ When can I see my scores?

You will be able to see your score report online fifteen business days after the test date. Score reports will be mailed to you and to the schools and agencies that you designate on the day they are posted online. You are entitled to five copies of your test results, including one copy for you and four official score reports.

➤ May I cancel my scores?

After you view your estimated score on the screen, you will be given the option to report or cancel your scores. If you choose to report your scores, you will then choose four institutions or agencies to receive score reports. All of this is arranged by responding to questions on the computer screen. If you do not want your scores to be reported, click on cancel when this option appears on the screen.

➤ How can I send additional score reports?

If you need more than four score reports, which are provided as part of your test fee, you may order more at $17 each. Order online or mail in the order form that you will find in your *TOEFL® iBT Registration and Information Bulletin.* Reports are sent in four days when you order them online. Allow at least two weeks for mail orders.

➤ Is there a direct correspondence between proficiency in English and a TOEFL score?

There is not always a direct correspondence between proficiency in English and a score on the TOEFL. Many students who are proficient in English are not proficient in how to approach the examination. That is why it is important to prepare by using this book.

➤ Can I estimate my TOEFL score before I take the official test?

To estimate your TOEFL score, after you complete each of the three model tests, use the score estimates in Chapter 8 of this book. If you complete Model Tests 1–7 on the CD-ROM that supplements the larger version of this book, you will see an estimate of your TOEFL score on the screen.

➤ Will I succeed on the TOEFL?

You will receive from your study what you give to your study. The information is here. Now, it is up to you to devote the time and the effort. More than one million students have succeeded by using *Barron's How to Prepare for the TOEFL.* You can be successful, too.

STUDY HABITS

A habit is a pattern of behavior that is acquired through repetition. Research indicates that it takes about twenty-one days to form a habit. The following study habits are characteristic of successful students. Be successful! Form these habits now. They will help you on the TOEFL and after the TOEFL.

➤ Accept responsibility.

Successful students understand that the score on the TOEFL is their responsibility. It doesn't happen because of luck. It is the result of their own efforts. Take responsibility for your TOEFL score. Don't leave it to chance.

- Don't rely on luck.
- Work diligently.

➤ Get organized.

You will need a place to study where you can concentrate. Try to find a quiet place where you can arrange your study materials and leave them until the next study session. If that is not practical, then find a bag that you can use to store all your materials so that you can have everything you need when you go to the library or another place to study. Don't use the bag for anything else. This will save time because you will not be looking for everything in different areas of your house or room, and you will not be trying to find TOEFL preparation material among other things in the bag. You are less likely to lose important notes.

- Find a study area.
- Keep your materials in one place.

➤ Set realistic goals.

Be honest about your preparation. Students who are just beginning to learn English are not prepared to take the TOEFL. Give yourself the time you need to prepare. By setting an unrealistic goal, for example, to finish preparing with this book in one week, you will probably be very disappointed. Even advanced students need time to learn academic skills and review language skills as well as to take model tests.

- Evaluate your English.
- Set a goal that you can achieve.

➤ Make a plan.

It is not enough to have a goal, even a realistic goal. Successful students also have a plan to accomplish a goal. What are you going to do to achieve the goal you have set? You will need to have time and resources. What are they? To help you make your plan, look at the options for a syllabus on pages 9–10.

- Dedicate time and resources.
- Select a syllabus.

➤ Establish priorities.

The pretest on pages 33–108 in this book will be helpful to you when you set priorities. By analyzing your strengths and weaknesses on the test, you will know which sections of the test will be the most difficult and which will be easy for you. You will also know which problems within each section require the most study. By focusing on those sections and problems, you can set priorities and use your time wisely.

- Take the pretest.
- Analyze your strengths and weaknesses.

➤ Manage time.

How do you spend time? Clearly, a certain amount of your time should be spent sleeping or relaxing. That is important to good health. However, you should think about how much time you spend worrying or procrastinating. That is not a healthy way to spend time. Successful students have a schedule that helps them manage their time. Preparing for the TOEFL is written down on the schedule. TOEFL preparation is planned for on a regular basis just like a standing appointment. If it is written down, it is more probable that you will give it the time necessary to achieve your goal. When you start to worry, use that energy to do something positive. Learn to use time while you are waiting for an appointment or commuting on public transportation to study. Even a five-minute review will help you.

- Schedule study time.
- Use unscheduled time well.

➤ Learn from mistakes.

If you knew everything, you wouldn't need this book. Expect to make mistakes on the quizzes and on the model tests. Read the explanatory answers, and learn from your mistakes. If you do this, you will be less likely to make those mistakes again on the official TOEFL.

- Study the explanatory answers.
- Review your errors.

➤ Stay motivated.

It is easy to begin with enthusiasm, but it is more difficult to maintain your initial commitment. How do you stay motivated? To keep their energy up, some students give themselves some incentives. Without small rewards along the way, it may be more difficult to stay motivated. Just be sure that the reward doesn't take more time than the study. Remember, an incentive is supposed to keep you moving, not slow you down.

- Give yourself small incentives.
- Keep moving.

➤ Choose to be positive.

Your attitude will influence your success on the TOEFL examination. To be successful, you must develop patterns of positive thinking. To help develop a positive attitude, memorize the following sentences and bring them to mind after each study session. Bring them to mind when you begin to have negative thoughts:

I know more today that I did yesterday.
I am preparing.
I will succeed.

Remember, some tension is normal and good. Accept it. Use it constructively. It will motivate you to study. But don't panic or worry. Panic will cause loss of concentration and poor performance. Avoid people who panic and worry. Don't listen to them. They will encourage negative thoughts.

> You know more today than you did yesterday.
> You are preparing.
> You will succeed.

There is more advice for success in the "Advisor's Office" throughout the book. Please read and consider the advice as you continue your TOEFL preparation.

2

MODEL TEST 1: PRETEST

READING SECTION

The Reading section tests your ability to understand reading passages like those in college textbooks. The passages are about 700 words in length.

This is the short format for the Reading section. On the short format, you will respond to three passages. After each passage, you will answer 12–14 questions about it.

Most questions are worth 1 point, but the last question in each passage is worth more than 1 point.

You will have 60 minutes to read all of the passages and answer the questions. You may take notes while you read, but notes are not graded. You may use your notes to answer the questions. Some passages may include a word or phrase that is underlined in blue. Click on the word or phrase to see a glossary definition or explanation.

Choose the best answer for multiple-choice questions. On the official TOEFL® iBT, follow the directions on the page or on the screen for computer-assisted questions. Click on **Next** to go to the next question. Click on **Back** to return to the previous question. You may return to previous questions for all of the passages in the same reading part, but after you go to the next part, you will not be able to return to passages in a previous part. Be sure that you have answered all of the questions for the passages in each part before you click on **Next** at the end of the passage to move to the next part.

You can click on **Review** to see a chart of the questions you have answered and the questions you have not answered in each part. From this screen, you can return to the question you want to answer in the part that is open.

A clock on the screen will show you how much time you have to complete the Reading section.

PART I

Reading 1 "Beowulf"

Historical Background

→ The epic poem *Beowulf*, written in Old English, is the earliest existing Germanic epic and one of four surviving Anglo-Saxon manuscripts. Although *Beowulf* was written by an anonymous Englishman in Old English, the tale takes place in that part of Scandinavia from which Germanic tribes emigrated to England. Beowulf comes from Geatland, the southeastern part of what is now Sweden. Hrothgar, king of the Danes, lives near what is now Leire, on Zealand, Denmark's largest island. The *Beowulf* epic contains three major tales about Beowulf and several minor tales that reflect a rich Germanic oral tradition of myths, legends, and folklore.

→ The *Beowulf* warriors have a foot in both the Bronze and Iron Ages. Their mead-halls reflect the wealthy living of the Bronze Age Northmen, and their wooden shields, wood-shafted spears, and bronze-hilted swords are those of the Bronze Age warrior. However, they carry iron-tipped spears, and their best swords have iron or iron-edged blades. Beowulf also orders an iron shield for his fight with a dragon. Iron replaced bronze because it produced a blade with a cutting edge that was stronger and sharper. The Northmen learned how to forge iron in about 500 B.C. Although they had been superior to the European Celts in bronze work, it was the Celts who taught them how to make and design iron work. Iron was accessible everywhere in Scandinavia, usually in the form of "bog-iron" found in the layers of peat in peat bogs.

The *Beowulf* epic also reveals interesting aspects of the lives of the Anglo-Saxons who lived in England at the time of the anonymous *Beowulf* poet. The Germanic tribes, including the Angles, the Saxons, and the Jutes, invaded England from about A.D. 450 to 600. By the time of the *Beowulf* poet, Anglo-Saxon society in England was neither primitive nor uncultured. A

→ Although the *Beowulf* manuscript was written in about A.D. 1000, it was not discovered until the seventeenth century. B Scholars do not know whether *Beowulf* is the sole surviving epic from a flourishing Anglo-Saxon literary period that produced other great epics or whether it was unique even in its own time. C Many scholars think that the epic was probably written sometime between the late seventh century and the early ninth century. If they are correct, the original manuscript was probably lost during the ninth-century Viking invasions of Anglia, in which the Danes destroyed the Anglo-Saxon monasteries and their great libraries. However, other scholars think that the poet's favorable attitude toward the Danes must place the epic's composition after the Viking invasions and at the start of the eleventh century, when this *Beowulf* manuscript was written.

→ The identity of the *Beowulf* poet is also uncertain. D He apparently was a Christian who loved the pagan heroic tradition of his ancestors and blended the values of the pagan hero with the Christian values of his own country and time. Because he wrote in the Anglian dialect, he probably was either a monk in a monastery or a poet in an Anglo-Saxon court located north of the Thames River.

Appeal and Value

Beowulf interests contemporary readers for many reasons. First, it is an outstanding adventure story. Grendel, Grendel's mother, and the dragon are marvelous characters, and each fight is unique, action-packed, and exciting. Second, Beowulf is a very appealing hero. He is the perfect warrior, combining extraordinary strength, skill, courage, and loyalty. Like Hercules, he devotes his life to making the world a safer place. He chooses to risk death in order to help other people, and he faces his inevitable death with heroism and dignity. Third, the *Beowulf* poet is interested in the psychological aspects of human behavior. For example, the Danish hero's welcoming speech illustrates his jealousy of Beowulf. The behavior of Beowulf's warriors in the dragon fight reveals their cowardice. Beowulf's attitudes toward heroism reflect his maturity and experience, while King Hrothgar's attitudes toward life show the experiences of an aged nobleman.

Finally, the *Beowulf* poet exhibits a mature appreciation of the transitory nature of human life and achievement. In Beowulf, as in the major epics of other cultures, the hero must create a meaningful life in a world that is often dangerous and uncaring. He must accept the inevitability of death. He chooses to reject despair; instead, he takes pride in himself and in his accomplishments, and he values human relationships.

1. According to paragraph 1, which of the following is true about *Beowulf*?

   Ⓐ It is the only manuscript from the Anglo-Saxon period. ⌖
   Ⓑ The original story was written in a German dialect. ✕
   Ⓒ The author did not sign his name to the poem. ⌖
   Ⓓ It is one of several epics from the first century. ⌖

   Paragraph 1 is marked with an arrow [➔].

2. The word <u>which</u> in the passage refers to

   Ⓐ tale
   Ⓑ Scandinavia
   Ⓒ manuscripts
   Ⓓ Old English

3. Why does the author mention "bog-iron" in paragraph 2?

  Ⓐ To demonstrate the availability of iron in Scandinavia
  Ⓑ To prove that iron was better than bronze for weapons
  Ⓒ To argue that the Celts provided the materials to make iron
  Ⓓ To suggest that 500 B.C. was the date that the Iron Age began

  Paragraph 2 is marked with an arrow [➔].

4. Which of the sentences below best expresses the information in the highlighted statement in the passage? The other choices change the meaning or leave out important information.

  Ⓐ Society in Anglo-Saxon England was both advanced and cultured.
  Ⓑ The society of the Anglo-Saxons was not primitive or cultured.
  Ⓒ The Anglo-Saxons had a society that was primitive, not cultured.
  Ⓓ England during the Anglo-Saxon society was advanced, not cultured.

5. The word <u>unique</u> in the passage is closest in meaning to

  Ⓐ old
  Ⓑ rare
  Ⓒ perfect
  Ⓓ weak

6. According to paragraph 4, why do many scholars believe that the original manuscript for *Beowulf* was lost?

  Ⓐ Because it is not like other manuscripts
  Ⓑ Because many libraries were burned
  Ⓒ Because the Danes were allies of the Anglo-Saxons
  Ⓓ Because no copies were found in monasteries

  Paragraph 4 is marked with an arrow [➔].

7. In paragraph 4, the author suggests that *Beowulf* was discovered in the

    Ⓐ first century
    Ⓑ ninth century
    Ⓒ eleventh century
    Ⓓ seventeenth century

    Paragraph 4 is marked with an arrow [➜].

8. Why does the author of this passage use the word "apparently" in paragraph 5?

    Ⓐ He is not certain that the author of *Beowulf* was a Christian.
    Ⓑ He is mentioning facts that are obvious to the readers.
    Ⓒ He is giving an example from a historical reference.
    Ⓓ He is introducing evidence about the author of *Beowulf*.

    Paragraph 5 is marked with an arrow [➜].

9. The author compared the Beowulf character to Hercules because

    Ⓐ they are both examples of the ideal hero
    Ⓑ their adventures with a dragon are very similar
    Ⓒ the speeches that they make are inspiring
    Ⓓ they lived at about the same time

10. The word <u>exhibits</u> in the passage is closest in meaning to

    Ⓐ creates
    Ⓑ demonstrates
    Ⓒ assumes
    Ⓓ terminates

11. The word <u>reject</u> in the passage is closest in meaning to

    Ⓐ manage
    Ⓑ evaluate
    Ⓒ refuse
    Ⓓ confront

12. Look at the four squares [■] that show where the following sentence could be inserted in the passage.

   Moreover, they disagree as to whether this *Beowulf* is a copy of an earlier manuscript.

   Where could the sentence best be added?

   Click on a square [■] to insert the sentence in the passage.

13. **Directions:** An introduction for a short summary of the passage appears below. Complete the summary by selecting the THREE answer choices that mention the most important points in the passage. Some sentences do not belong in the summary because they express ideas that are not included in the passage or are minor points from the passage. ***This question is worth 2 points.***

   Beowulf is the oldest Anglo-Saxon epic poem that has survived to the present day.

   -
   -
   -

Answer Choices

A The Northmen were adept in crafting tools and weapons made of bronze, but the Celts were superior in designing and working in iron.

B In the Viking invasions of England, the Danish armies destroyed monasteries, some of which contained extensive libraries.

C King Hrothgar and Beowulf become friends at the end of their lives, after having spent decades opposing each other on the battlefield.

D The poem chronicles life in Anglo-Saxon society during the Bronze and Iron Ages when Germanic tribes were invading England.

E Although *Beowulf* was written by an anonymous poet, probably a Christian, about 1000 A.D., it was not found until the seventeenth century.

F *Beowulf* is still interesting because it has engaging characters, an adventurous plot, and an appreciation for human behavior and relationships.

PART II

Reading 2 "Thermoregulation"

→ Mammals and birds generally maintain body temperature within a narrow range (36–38°C for most mammals and 39–42°C for most birds) that is usually considerably warmer than the environment. Because heat always flows from a warm object to cooler surroundings, birds and mammals must counteract the constant heat loss. This maintenance of warm body temperature depends on several key adaptations. The most basic mechanism is the high metabolic rate of endothermy itself. Endotherms can produce large amounts of metabolic heat that replace the flow of heat to the environment, and they can vary heat production to match changing rates of heat loss. Heat production is increased by such muscle activity as moving or shivering. In some mammals, certain hormones can cause mitochondria to increase their metabolic activity and produce heat instead of ATP. This **nonshivering thermogenesis (NST)** takes place throughout the body, but some mammals also have a tissue called **brown fat** in the neck and between the shoulders that is specialized for rapid heat production. Through shivering and NST, mammals and birds in cold environments can increase their metabolic heat production by as much as 5 to 10 times above the minimal levels that occur in warm conditions.

→ Another major thermoregulatory adaptation that evolved in mammals and birds is insulation (hair, feathers, and fat layers), which reduces the flow of heat and lowers the energy cost of keeping warm. Most land mammals and birds react to cold by raising their fur or feathers, thereby trapping a thicker layer of air. Ⓐ Humans rely more on a layer of fat just beneath the skin as insulation; goose bumps are a vestige of hair-raising left over from our furry ancestors. B Vasodilation and vasoconstriction also regulate heat exchange and may contribute to regional temperature differences within the animal. C For example, heat loss from a human is reduced when arms and legs cool to several degrees below the temperature of the body core, where most vital organs are located. D

→ Hair loses most of its insulating power when wet. Marine mammals such as whales and seals have a very thick layer of insulation fat called blubber, just under the skin. Marine mammals swim in water colder than their body core temperature, and many species spend at least part of the year in nearly freezing polar seas. The loss of heat to water occurs 50 to 100 times more rapidly than heat loss to air, and the skin temperature of a marine mammal is close to water temperature. Even so, the blubber insulation is so effective that marine mammals maintain body core temperatures of about 36–38°C with metabolic rates about the same as those of land mammals of similar size. The flippers or tail of a whale or seal lack insulating blubber, but countercurrent heat exchangers greatly reduce heat loss in these extremities, as they do in the legs of many birds.

→ Through metabolic heat production, insulation, and vascular adjustments, birds and mammals are capable of astonishing feats of thermoregulation. For example, small birds called chickadees, which weigh only 20 grams, can remain active and hold body temperature nearly constant at 40°C in environmental temperatures as low as −40°C—as long as they have enough food to supply the large amount of energy necessary for heat production.

Many mammals and birds live in places where thermoregulation requires cooling off as well as warming. For example, when a marine mammal moves into warm seas, as many whales do when they reproduce, excess metabolic heat is removed by vasodilation of numerous blood vessels in the outer layer of the skin. In hot climates or when vigorous exercise adds large amounts of metabolic heat to the body, many terrestrial mammals and birds may allow body temperature to rise by several degrees, which enhances heat loss by increasing the temperature gradient between the body and a warm environment.

→ Evaporative cooling often plays a key role in dissipating the body heat. If environmental temperature is above body temperature, animals gain heat from the environment as well as from metabolism, and evaporation is the only way to keep body temperature from rising rapidly. Panting is important in birds and many mammals. Some birds have a pouch richly supplied with blood vessels in the floor of the mouth; fluttering the pouch increases evaporation. Pigeons can use evaporative cooling to keep body temperature close to 40°C in air temperatures as high as 60°C, as long as they have sufficient water. Many terrestrial mammals have sweat glands controlled by the nervous system. Other mechanisms that promote evaporative cooling include spreading saliva on body surfaces, an adaptation of some kangaroos and rodents for combating severe heat stress. Some bats use both saliva and urine to enhance evaporative cooling.

Glossary
ATP: energy that drives certain reactions in cells
mitochondria: a membrane of ATP

14. According to paragraph 1, the most fundamental adaptation to maintain body temperature is

  Ⓐ the heat generated by the metabolism
  Ⓑ a shivering reflex in the muscles
  Ⓒ migration to a warmer environment
  Ⓓ higher caloric intake to match heat loss

Paragraph 1 is marked with an arrow [→].

15. Based on information in paragraph 1, which of the following best explains the term "thermogenesis"?

   Ⓐ Heat loss that must be reversed
   Ⓑ The adaptation of brown fat tissue in the neck
   Ⓒ The maintenance of healthy environmental conditions
   Ⓓ Conditions that affect the metabolism

   Paragraph 1 is marked with an arrow [➜].

16. Which of the sentences below best expresses the information in the highlighted statement in the passage? The other choices change the meaning or leave out important information.

   Ⓐ An increase in heat production causes muscle activity such as moving or shivering.
   Ⓑ Muscle activity like moving and shivering will increase heat production.
   Ⓒ Moving and shivering are muscle activities that increase with heat.
   Ⓓ When heat increases, the production of muscle activity also increases.

17. The word minimal in the passage is closest in meaning to

   Ⓐ most recent
   Ⓑ most active
   Ⓒ newest
   Ⓓ smallest

18. In paragraph 2, the author explains the concept of vasodilation and vasoconstriction by

   Ⓐ describing the evolution in our ancestors
   Ⓑ giving an example of heat loss in the extremities
   Ⓒ comparing the process in humans and animals
   Ⓓ identifying various types of insulation

   Paragraph 2 is marked with an arrow [➜].

19. The word <u>regulate</u> in the passage is closest in meaning to

    Ⓐ protect
    Ⓑ create
    Ⓒ reduce
    Ⓓ control

20. According to paragraph 3, why do many marine animals require a layer of blubber?

    Ⓐ Because marine animals have lost their hair during evolution
    Ⓑ Because heat is lost in water twice as fast as it is in air
    Ⓒ Because dry hair does not insulate marine animals
    Ⓓ Because they are so large that they require more insulation

    Paragraph 3 is marked with an arrow [➜].

21. The word <u>those</u> in the passage refers to

    Ⓐ marine animals
    Ⓑ core temperatures
    Ⓒ land mammals
    Ⓓ metabolic rates

22. Why does the author mention chickadees in paragraph 4?

    Ⓐ To discuss an animal that regulates heat very well
    Ⓑ To demonstrate why chickadees have to eat so much
    Ⓒ To mention an exception to the rules of thermoregulation
    Ⓓ To give a reason for heat production in small animals

    Paragraph 4 is marked with an arrow [➜].

23. In paragraph 6, the author states that evaporative cooling is often accomplished by all of the following methods EXCEPT

    Ⓐ by spreading saliva over the area
    Ⓑ by urinating on the body
    Ⓒ by panting or fluttering a pouch
    Ⓓ by immersing themselves in water

    Paragraph 6 is marked with an arrow [➜].

24. The word <u>enhance</u> in the passage is closest in meaning to

    Ⓒ simplify
    Ⓓ improve
    Ⓔ replace
    Ⓕ interrupt

25. Look at the four squares [■] that show where the following sentence could be inserted in the passage.

The insulating power of a layer of fur or feathers mainly depends on how much still air the layer traps.

Where could the sentence best be added?

Click on a square [■] to insert the sentence in the passage.

26. **Directions:** An introduction for a short summary of the passage appears below. Complete the summary by selecting the THREE answer choices that mention the most important points in the passage. Some sentences do not belong in the summary because they express ideas that are not included in the passage or are minor points from the passage. *This question is worth 2 points.*

Thermoregulation is the process by which animals control body temperatures within healthy limits.

●

●

●

(Answer choices are on next page.)

Answer Choices

A Although hair can be a very efficient insulation when it is dry and it can be raised, hair becomes ineffective when it is submerged in cold water.

B Some animals with few adaptations for thermoregulation migrate to moderate climates to avoid the extreme weather in the polar regions and the tropics.

C Mammals and birds use insulation to mitigate heat loss, including hair and feathers that can be raised to trap air as well as fat or blubber under the skin.

D Some birds have a special pouch in the mouth, which can be fluttered to increase evaporation and decrease their body temperatures by as much as 20°C.

E Endotherms generate heat by increasing muscle activity, by releasing hormones into their blood streams, or by producing heat in brown fat tissues.

F Panting, sweating, and spreading saliva or urine on their bodies are all options for the evaporative cooling of animals in hot environmental conditions.

Reading 3 "Social Readjustment Scales"

→ Holmes and Rahe (1967) developed the Social Readjustment Rating Scale (SRRS) to measure life change as a form of stress. Ⓐ The scale assigns numerical values to 43 major life events that are supposed to reflect the magnitude of the readjustment required by each change. In responding to the scale, respondents are asked to indicate how often they experienced any of these 43 events during a certain time period (typically, the past year). The person then adds up the numbers associated with each event checked. Ⓑ

→ The SRRS and similar scales have been used in thousands of studies by researchers all over the world. Ⓒ Overall, these studies have shown that people with higher scores on the SRRS tend to be more vulnerable to many kinds of physical illness—and many types of psychological problems as well (Derogatis & Coons, 1993; Gruen, 1993; Scully, Tosi & Banning, 2000). Ⓓ More recently, however, experts have criticized this research, citing problems with the methods used and raising questions about the meaning of the findings (Critelli & Ee, 1996; Monroe & McQuaid, 1994; Wethington, 2000).

First, the assumption that the SRRS measures change exclusively has been shown to be inaccurate. We now have ample evidence that the desirability of events affects adaptational outcomes more than the amount of change that they require (Turner & Wheaton, 1995). Thus, it seems prudent to view the SRRS as a measure of diverse forms of stress, rather than as a measure of change-related stress (McLean & Link, 1994).

→ Second, the SRRS fails to take into account differences among people in their subjective perception of how stressful an event is. For instance, while divorce may deserve a stress value of 73 for *most* people, a particular person's divorce might generate much less stress and merit a value of only 25.

→ Third, many of the events listed on the SRRS and similar scales are highly ambiguous, leading people to be inconsistent as to which events they report experiencing (Monroe & McQuaid, 1994). For instance, what qualifies as "trouble with the boss"? Should you check that because you're sick and tired of your supervisor? What constitutes a "change in living conditions"? Does your purchase of a great new sound system qualify? As you can see, the SRRS includes many "events" that are described inadequately, producing considerable ambiguity about the meaning of one's response. Problems in recalling events over a period of a year also lead to inconsistent responding on stress scales, thus lowering their reliability (Klein & Rubovits, 1987).

Fourth, the SRRS does not sample from the domain of stressful events very thoroughly. Do the 43 events listed on the SRRS exhaust all the major stresses that people typically experience? Studies designed to explore that question have found many significant omissions (Dohrenwend et al., 1993; Wheaton, 1994).

→ Fifth, the correlation between SRRS scores and health outcomes may be inflated because subjects' neuroticism affects both their responses to stress scales and their self-reports of health problems. Neurotic individuals have a tendency to recall more stress than others and to recall more symptoms of illness than others (Watson, David, & Suls, 1999). These tendencies mean that some of the correlation between high stress and high illness may simply reflect the effects of subjects' neuroticism (Critelli & Ee, 1996). The possible contaminating effects of neuroticism obscure the meaning of scores on the SRRS and similar measures of stress.

The Life Experiences Survey

In the light of these problems, a number of researchers have attempted to develop improved versions of the SRRS. For example, the Life Experiences Survey (LES), assembled by Irwin Sarason and colleagues (1978), has become a widely used measure of stress in contemporary research (for examples see Ames et al., 2001; Denisoff & Endler, 2000; Malefo, 2000). The LES revises and builds on the SRRS survey in a variety of ways that correct, at least in part, most of the problems just discussed.

→ Specifically, the LES recognizes that stress involves more than mere change and asks respondents to indicate whether events had a positive or negative impact on them. This strategy permits the computation of positive change, negative change, and total change scores, which helps researchers gain much more insight into which facets of stress are most crucial. The LES also takes into consideration differences among people in their appraisal of stress, by dropping the normative weights and replacing them with personally assigned weightings of the impact of relevant events. Ambiguity in items is decreased by providing more elaborate descriptions of many items to clarify their meaning.

The LES deals with the failure of the SRRS to sample the full domain of stressful events in several ways. First, some significant omissions from the SRRS have been added to the LES. Second, the LES allows the respondent to write in personally important events that are not included on the scale. Third, the LES has an extra section just for students. Sarason et al. (1978) suggest that special, tailored sections of this sort be added for specific populations whenever it is useful.

27. Based on the information in paragraph 1 and paragraph 2, what can be inferred about a person with a score of 30 on the SRRS?

Ⓐ A person with a higher score will experience less stress than this person will.

Ⓑ It is likely that this person has not suffered any major problems in the past year.

Ⓒ The amount of positive change is greater than that of a person with a score of 40.

Ⓓ This person has a greater probability to be ill than a person with a 20 score.

Paragraph 1 and Paragraph 2 are marked with arrows [➔].

28. The word they in the passage refers to

Ⓐ changes
Ⓑ measures
Ⓒ events
Ⓓ outcomes

29. The word diverse in the passage is closest in meaning to

Ⓐ necessary
Ⓑ steady
Ⓒ limited
Ⓓ different

30. In paragraph 4, the author uses divorce as an example to show

Ⓐ how most people respond to high stress situations in their lives

Ⓑ the serious nature of a situation that is listed as a stressful event

Ⓒ the subjective importance of a situation listed on the scale

Ⓓ the numerical value for a stressful event on the SRRS

Paragraph 4 is marked with an arrow [➔].

31. In paragraph 5, how does the author demonstrate that the response events on the SRRS are not consistent?

    Ⓐ By asking questions that could be answered in more than one way
    Ⓑ By giving examples of responses that are confusing
    Ⓒ By comparing several ways to score the stress scales
    Ⓓ By suggesting that people do not respond carefully

    Paragraph 5 is marked with an arrow [➔].

32. According to paragraph 7, why is the SRRS inappropriate for people with neuroses?

    Ⓐ They are ill more often, which affects their scores on the scale.
    Ⓑ Their self-reporting on the scale is affected by their neuroses.
    Ⓒ They tend to suffer more stress than people without neuroses.
    Ⓓ Their response to stress will probably not be recorded on the scale.

    Paragraph 7 is marked with an arrow [➔].

33. The word <u>assembled</u> in the passage is closest in meaning to

    Ⓐ announced
    Ⓑ influenced
    Ⓒ arranged
    Ⓓ distributed

34. The word <u>relevant</u> in the passage is closest in meaning to

    Ⓐ occasional
    Ⓑ modern
    Ⓒ related
    Ⓓ unusual

35. According to paragraph 9, why does the LES ask respondents to classify change as positive or negative?

   Ⓐ To analyze the long-term consequences of change
   Ⓑ To determine which aspects of change are personally significant
   Ⓒ To explain why some people handle stress better than others
   Ⓓ To introduce normative weighting of stress events

   Paragraph 9 is marked with an arrow [→].

36. According to the passage, which of the following is true about the SRRS as compared with the LES?

   Ⓐ The SRRS includes a space to write in personal events that have not been listed.
   Ⓑ The SRRS features a section for specific populations such as students.
   Ⓒ The SRRS assigns numbers to calculate the stress associated with events.
   Ⓓ The SRRS has hints to help people recall events that happened over a year ago.

37. Which of the following statements most accurately reflects the author's opinion of the SRRS?

   Ⓐ There are many problems associated with it.
   Ⓑ It is superior to the LES.
   Ⓒ It should be studied more carefully.
   Ⓓ The scale is most useful for students.

38. Look at the four squares [■] that show where the following sentence could be inserted in the passage.

   This sum is an index of the amount of change-related stress the person has recently experienced.

   Where could the sentence best be added?

   Click on a square [■] to insert the sentence in the passage.

39. **Directions**: Complete the table by matching the phrases on the left with the headings on the right. Select the appropriate answer choices and drag them to the surveys to which they relate. TWO of the answer choices will NOT be used. *This question is worth 4 points.*

To delete an answer choice, click on it. To see the passage, click on **View Text**.

Answer Choices

Ⓐ Limits the events to forty-three major life changes

Ⓑ Calculates subscores for negative and positive changes

Ⓒ Must be taken twice in one year for a reliable score

Ⓓ Incorporates a space to write in additional events

Ⓔ Provides for subjective interpretation of the changes

Ⓕ Is no longer being used by psychologists

Ⓖ Includes sections for specialized populations

Ⓗ Consists of a scale developed in the 1960s

Ⓘ Assigns a standard numerical value to events

SRRS
●
●
●

LES
●
●
●
●

LISTENING SECTION

  Model Test 1, Listening Section

The Listening section tests your ability to understand spoken English that is typical of interactions and academic speech on college campuses. During the test, you will respond to conversations and lectures.

This is the long format for the Listening section. On the long format, you will respond to three conversations and six lectures. After each listening passage, you will answer 5–6 questions about it. Only two conversations and four lectures will be graded. The other conversation and lectures are part of an experimental section for future tests. Because you will not know which conversations and lectures will be graded, you must try to do your best on all of them.

On the official TOEFL® iBT, you will hear each conversation or lecture one time. You may take notes while you listen, but notes are not graded. You may use your notes to answer the questions.

Choose the best answer for multiple-choice questions. Follow the directions on the page or on the screen for computer-assisted questions. Click on **Next** and **OK** to go to the next question. You cannot return to previous questions. You have 20–30 minutes to answer all of the questions. A clock on the screen will show you how much time you have to complete your answers for the section. The clock does not count the time you are listening to the conversations and lectures.

On this Pretest, the audio is marked with an icon of a headphone 🎧 but the audio for the Pretest is not included in this package. You will find the audio for this test in the larger version, *Barron's How to Prepare for the TOEFL® iBT, 12th Edition*. To take the Pretest without the audio, read the scripts. Model Tests 2 and 3, the Progress Tests in this book, include the audio for you to use as you prepare for the TOEFL.

PART I

Listening 1 "Learning Center"

Audio Conversation

Narrator: Listen to a conversation on campus between two students.

Man: Hi. Are you Paula?
Woman: Jim?
Man: Hi. Nice to meet you.
Woman: Glad to meet you.

Q1 Man: So, you need some tutoring in English?

Woman: Yeah. I'm taking English composition, and I'm not doing very well on my essays.
Man: Right. Um, well, first let's see if we can figure out a time to meet . . . that we're both free.
Woman: Okay.
Man: How about Mondays? Maybe in the morning? I don't have any classes until eleven on Mondays.
Woman: That would work, but I was hoping we could, you know, meet more than once a week.

Man:	Oh. Well, Tuesdays are out. I've got classes and, uh, I work at the library part time on Tuesdays and Thursdays. But I could get together on Wednesdays.
Woman:	In the morning?
Man:	Probably nine-thirty would be best. That way we'd have an hour to work before I'd have to get ready for my eleven o'clock.
Woman:	So that would be two hours a week then?
Man:	I could do that.
Woman:	Oh, but, would that be extra? You know, would I need to pay you for the extra session?	Q2
Man:	No. Um, just so you meet me here at the Learning Center, and we both sign in, then I'll get paid. Tutoring is free, to you, I mean. The school pays me. But we both have to show up. If you don't show up and sign in for a session, then I don't get paid. So . . .	Q3
Woman:	Oh, don't worry about that. I really need the help. I won't miss any sessions unless I'm sick or something.
Man:	Okay then. So you want me to help you with your essays?
Woman:	Right. I could bring you some that have, you know, comments on them. I'm getting C's and . . .
Man:	Well, that's not too bad. Once I see some of your writing, we should be able to pull that up to a B.
Woman:	You think so?
Man:	Sure. But I need to explain something. Some of my students in the past . . . they expected me to write their essays for them. But that's not what a tutor is supposed to do. My job is to help you be a better writer.	Q4
Woman:	Oh, I understand that. But you'll read my essays, right?
Man:	Oh yeah. No problem. We'll read them together, and I'll make suggestions.
Woman:	Great. I think part of the problem is I just don't understand the teacher's comments. Maybe you can help me figure them out.
Man:	Sure. Who's the teacher?
Woman:	Simpson.
Man:	No problem. I've tutored a couple of her students, so I know more or less where she's coming from. Okay, then. I guess we'll meet here on Monday.	Q5
Woman:	I'll be here. Nine-thirty you said.
Man:	Just sign in when you get here.

1. What does the woman need?

   Ⓐ A meeting with Professor Simpson
   Ⓑ An English composition class
   Ⓒ An appointment for tutoring
   Ⓓ Information about the Learning Center

2. Why does the woman say this: "Oh, but would that be extra?"

   Ⓐ She is worried that she cannot afford the service.
   Ⓑ She is trying to negotiate the cost of the sessions.
   Ⓒ She is showing particular interest in the man.
   Ⓓ She is expressing surprise about the arrangement.

3. Why is the man concerned about the woman's attendance?

   Ⓐ If she is absent, her grade will be lowered.
   Ⓑ He will not get a paycheck if she is absent.
   Ⓒ She has been sick a lot during the semester.
   Ⓓ Her grades need to be improved.

4. What does the man agree to do?

   Ⓐ He will show the woman how to use the library.
   Ⓑ He will write some compositions for the woman.
   Ⓒ He will talk with the woman's English professor.
   Ⓓ He will show the woman how to improve her writing.

5. What does the man imply about the woman's teacher?

   Ⓐ The professor is very difficult to understand.
   Ⓑ He does not know where she came from.
   Ⓒ Her students seem to like her teaching style.
   Ⓓ He is familiar with her requirements.

Listening 2 "Geology Class"

Audio Lecture

Narrator: Listen to part of a lecture in a geology class.

Professor:

Okay, today we're going to discuss the four major types of drainage patterns. Q6
I trust you've already read the chapter so you'll recall that a drainage pattern Q7
is the arrangement of channels that carry water in an area. And these patterns can be very distinctive since they're determined by the climate, the
topography, and the composition of the rock that underlies the formations.
So, consequently, we can see that a drainage pattern is really a good visual
summary of the characteristics of a particular region, both geologically and
climactically. In other words, when we look at drainage patterns, we can
draw conclusions about the structural formation and relief of the land as well
as the climate.

Now all drainage systems are composed of an interconnected network
of streams, and, when we view them together, they form distinctive patterns.
Although there are at least seven identifiable kinds of drainage patterns, for
our purposes, we're going to limit our study to the four major types. Probably
the most familiar pattern is the dendritic drainage pattern.

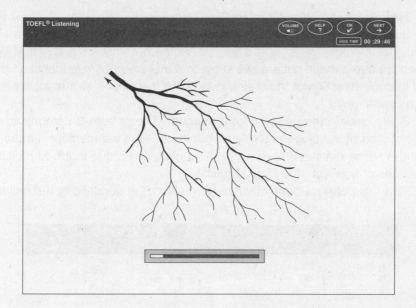

Q8 This is a stream that looks like the branches of a tree. Here's an example of a dendritic pattern. As you can see, it's similar to many systems in nature. In addition to the structure of a tree, it also resembles the human circulation system. This is a very efficient drainage system because the overall length of any one branch is fairly short, and there are many branches, so that allows the water to flow quickly and efficiently from the source or sources.

Okay, let's look at the next example.

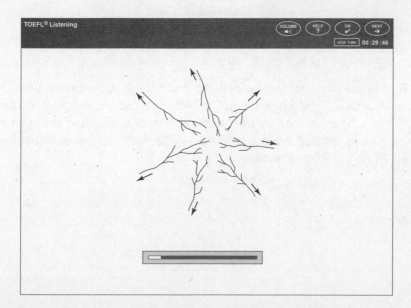

This drainage pattern is referred to as a radial pattern. Notice how the streams flow from a central point. This is usually a high mountain, or a volcano. It kind of looks like the spokes that radiate out from the hub of a wheel. Q9 When we see a radial pattern, we know that the area has experienced uplift and that the direction of the drainage is down the slopes of a relatively isolated central point.

Going back to the dendritic for a moment. The pattern is determined by the direction of the slope of the land, but it, uh, the streams flow in more or less the same direction, and . . . so it's unlike the radial that had multiple directions of flow from the highest point.

Now this pattern is very different from either the dendritic or the radial.

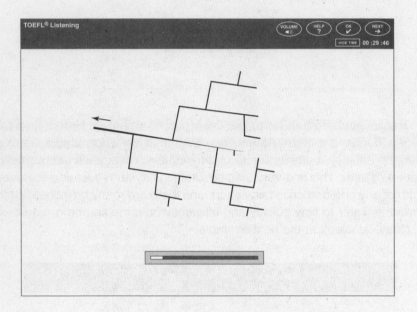

This is called a rectangular pattern, and I think you can see why. Just look at all of those right-angle turns. The rectangle pattern is typical of a landscape that's been formed by fractured joints and faults. And because this broken rock is eroded more easily than unbroken rock, stream beds are carved along the jointed bedrock.

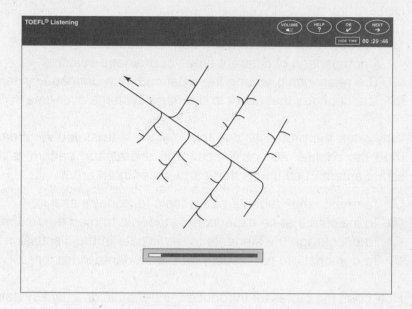

Finally we have the trellis pattern. And here in this example, you can see quite clearly how the tributaries of an almost parallel structure drain into valleys and . . . and form the appearance of a garden trellis. This pattern forms

Q10 in areas where there are alternating bands of variable resistance, and by that I mean that the bands of rock that are very strong and resistant to erosion alternate with bands of rock that are weak and easily eroded. This often happens when a horizontal plain folds and outcroppings appear.

So, as I said, as a whole, these patterns are dictated by the structure and relief of the land. The kinds of rocks on which the streams are developed, the structural pattern of the folds, uh, faults, and . . . uplift will usually determine a drainage system. However, I should also mention that drainage patterns can occasionally appear to be, well, out of sync with the landscape. And this can happen when a stream flows over older structures that have been uncovered by erosion or . . . or when a stream keeps its original drainage system when rocks are uplifted. So when that happens, the pattern appears

Q11 to be contrary to the expected course of the stream. But I'm interested in your understanding the basic drainage systems. So I don't plan to trick you with test questions about exceptional patterns, but I expect you to know that exceptions to the patterns can occur when geological events influence them.

6. What is this lecture mainly about?

  Ⓐ A process for improving drainage systems
  Ⓑ A comparison of different types of drainage systems
  Ⓒ The relationship among the most common drainage systems
  Ⓓ The changes that occur in drainage systems over time

7. Why does the professor say this: 🎧 "I trust you've already read the chapter so you'll recall that a drainage pattern is the arrangement of channels that carry water in an area."

  Ⓐ To remind the students of the topic for today's session
  Ⓑ To indicate that he expects the students to read the textbook
  Ⓒ To encourage the students to participate in the discussion
  Ⓓ To demonstrate his respect for the students in his class

8. How does the professor introduce the dendritic drainage system?

  Ⓐ By demonstrating how this very old system has evolved
  Ⓑ By comparing it to both a tree and the human circulatory system
  Ⓒ By criticizing the efficiency of the branches in the system
  Ⓓ By drawing conclusions about the climate in the area

9. Why does the professor mention the spokes of a wheel?

  Ⓐ To make a point about the stream beds in a trellis pattern
  Ⓑ To contrast the formation with that of a rectangular one
  Ⓒ To explain the structure of a radial drainage system
  Ⓓ To give an example of a dendritic drainage system

10. In the lecture, the professor discusses the trellis drainage pattern. Indicate whether each of the following is typical of this pattern. Click in the correct box for each phrase.

		Yes	No
A	Parallel stream beds flowing beside each other		
B	Stream beds with sharp 90 degree turns		
C	Drainage from the top of a central peak		
D	Hard rock formations on top of soft rock formations		
E	Geological evidence of folding with outcroppings		

11. What does the professor imply when he says this: 🎧 "So I don't plan to trick you with test questions about exceptional patterns."

    Ⓐ The test questions will be very difficult.
    Ⓑ The students should read their textbooks before the test.
    Ⓒ The basic patterns from the notes will be on the test.
    Ⓓ The test will influence the final grade.

Listening 3 "Art Class"

Audio Lecture

Narrator: Listen to part of a lecture in an art class. The professor is discussing drawing.

Professor:

Drawing is a very basic art form. It's appealing because it can be used to make a very quick record of the ideas that an artist may be envisioning, so, a drawing can serve as a visual aid for the artist to remember a certain moment of inspiration and maybe use it for a more detailed work later on. Okay, usually such sketches allow the artist to visualize the proportions and the shapes without much attention to details so these images can be used by painters, architects, sculptors—any artist really. And large renderings, sketches of parts of the whole . . . these can be helpful in the creative process when a . . . a huge image might be more difficult to conceive of in its entirety. Or, a sketch of just one face in a crowd can allow the artist to . . . focus on creating just that part of the image. So, in many artists' studios, countless drawings are strewn about as the final painting or sculpture takes form. And this gives us insight into the creative process, as well the opportunity to see changes from the images at the beginning in the images of the finished work. It's rare, in fact, for an artist to use permanent materials to begin a piece of art. And some painters, for example, even sketch onto the surface of the can-

Q13 vas before applying the pigments. Now, architects are especially prone to sketches because, of course, their buildings are so large that an image in smaller scale is necessary to the imagination and implementation of such
Q14 projects. So, uh, these studies become the basis for future works. And again, this is very interesting as a record of the creative process. Okay so far?

Q12 Okay, drawing has several other functions besides as a temporary reference. For centuries, artists have used drawing as a traditional method of education. By copying the great works, especially of the Old Masters, aspiring artists could learn a lot about proportion, how to capture light and shadow and . . . and so forth. In fact, some artists who later achieve recognition, still continue to use this practice to hone their skills or . . . or simply to pay homage to another artist, as is often the case when a work of art originally created in another medium like a sculpture . . . when it's recreated in the form of a drawing. Many examples of drawings of Michelangelo's sculptures were re-created by well-known artists. One that comes to mind is the *Study of Michelangelo's Bound Slave* by Edgar Degas. The original by Michelangelo was a marble sculpture that was, oh, about seven feet in height, but the small drawing was made in a sketchpad. In any case, the study is also considered a masterpiece, on a small scale, of course.

Q12 So . . . what additional purposes might be served by the medium of drawing? Well, let's remember that photography is a relatively new art form, so prior to the use of photographs to record historical events, a quick drawing by an artist was about the only way to preserve a real-time visual account of an important moment. Although a more permanent visual impression might be rendered later, it would be based on memory and not on the artist's actu-
Q15 al observation. Probably the most often cited example of a sketch that preserved an historical record would be the small drawing of Marie Antoinette as she was taken to the guillotine in a cart through the streets of Paris. Jacques-Louis David sketched this famous drawing on a piece of paper about the size of the palm of his hand. And the artist, the artist reporter, is still important even in modern times, when photography isn't possible, for example, when judges won't permit cameras in the courtroom.

Q17 Okay, to review, we've talked about three functions for drawing—as a visual aid for the artist to complete a future work, as a method of education for aspiring artists or even practiced artists, and as a way to report an event. But the sketchbook has . . . other possibilities. Sometimes a drawing is the final execution of the art. Picasso produced hundreds of drawings in, well, every conceivable medium, but especially in pencil and crayon. I find it very interesting that Picasso did so much of this kind of work . . . drawing, I mean, in his last years. Some critics have argued that he was just laughing at the art world, which was willing to pay outrageous sums for anything with his name on it, and clearly, a drawing can be executed in a short period of time.

But others, other critics, they feel as I do that Picasso was drawing because Q16
it was so basic, and because it was so spontaneous and so much fun. And
also, think about how difficult it really is to produce a quick drawing with a
few lines and, uh, no opportunity to . . . to recreate the original, either by
painting it out or remodeling the clay or changing the building materials,
or . . . or any of the other methods for revision of a finished artistic work that
artists have at their disposal. So, what I'm saying is that drawing when it's
elevated to a finished piece, it must be done with confidence and it must
show a high degree of creativity and mastery of the art form. In a way, it
harkens back to the beginnings of art itself, when some unknown artist must
have stuck a finger in the earth to draw an image or . . . maybe he picked up
a stone and made a drawing on the wall of a cave.

Okay, so, as a first assignment, I want you to make a couple of sketches yourself. I'm not going to grade them. This isn't a studio art class. I just
want you to use a few basic strokes to capture an image. You can do the first
one in pencil, crayon, ink, chalk, or even charcoal . . . whatever you like.
Then, I want you to sketch the same image in a different medium. So, if you
do a face in pencil, I want you to do the same face but in chalk or crayon.
Bring them to class next week and we'll continue our discussion of drawing,
but we'll talk more about the materials artists use to produce drawings, and,
uh, we'll refer to your sketches as examples.

12. What is the lecture mainly about?

    Ⓐ The way that drawing has influenced art
    Ⓑ The relationship between drawing and other art
    Ⓒ The distinct purposes of drawing
    Ⓓ The reason that artists prefer drawing

13. According to the professor, why do architects use sketches?

    Ⓐ Architects are not clear about the final design at the beginning.
    Ⓑ To design large buildings, architects must work in a smaller
       scale.
    Ⓒ Engineers use the architect's sketches to implement the
       details.
    Ⓓ Sketches are used as a record of the stages in development.

14. What does the professor mean when she says this: "Okay, so far?"

Ⓐ She is checking to be sure that the students understand.
Ⓑ She is expressing uncertainty about the information.
Ⓒ She is inviting the students to disagree with her.
Ⓓ She is indicating that she is in a hurry to continue.

15. Why does the professor mention the drawing of Marie Antoinette?

Ⓐ It is an example of a work copied in another medium.
Ⓑ Drawing was typical of the way that artists were educated.
Ⓒ The sketch was a historical account of an important event.
Ⓓ The size of the drawing made it an exceptional work of art.

16. What is the professor's opinion of Picasso?

Ⓐ Picasso was probably playing a joke by offering drawings for sale.
Ⓑ At the end of his career, Picasso may have chosen drawing because it was easy.
Ⓒ Picasso's drawings required the confidence and skill of a master artist.
Ⓓ Cave drawings were the inspiration for many of Picasso's works.

17. According to the lecture, what are the major functions of drawing?

Click on 3 answer choices.

Ⓐ A technique to remember parts of a large work

Ⓑ A method to preserve a historical record

Ⓒ An example of earlier forms of art

Ⓓ An educational approach to train artists

Ⓔ A process for experimenting with media

PART II

Listening 4 "Professor's Office"

Audio Conversation

Narrator:	Listen to a conversation on campus between a student and a professor.
Student:	Thanks for seeing me, Professor Williams.
Professor:	Glad to, Alice. What do you have on your mind?
Student:	Well, I got a little mixed up when I started to go over my notes from the last class, so I had a few questions.
Professor:	Shoot.
Student:	Okay. I understand the three basic sources of personnel for multinational companies. That's fairly self-explanatory.
Professor:	Host country, home country, and third country.
Student:	Right. But then you started talking about staffing patterns that . . . let me see . . . okay . . . you said, "staffing patterns may vary depending on the length of time that the multinational company has been operating," and you gave some examples, but I got confused and now I can't read my notes.

Q18

Q19

Professor:	Okay. Well, one pattern is to rely on home country managers to staff the key positions when the company opens, but gradually moving more host country nationals into upper management as the company grows.
Student:	So, for example, if a French company opened a factory in Canada, then French management would gradually replace themselves with Canadian managers. Is that what you mean?
Professor:	Right. I think I used that very example in class. So do you want to try to explain the second pattern to me?
Student:	Sure. I think it's the one where home country nationals are put in charge of the company if it's located in a developed country, but in a developing country, then home country nationals manage the company sort of indefinitely.
Q20 Professor:	Right again. And an example of that would be . . .
Student:	. . . maybe using German management for a Swiss company in Germany, but, uh, they might send Swiss management to provide leadership for a Swiss company in . . . in . . .
Professor:	How about Zimbabwe?
Student:	This is one of the confusing parts. Zimbabwe has a very old and highly developed culture, so...
Professor:	. . . but it's still defined as a developing country because of the economic base—which is being developed now.
Q21 Student:	Oh, okay. I guess that makes sense. Then the example of the American company with British management . . . when the company is in India . . . that would be a third-country pattern.
Professor:	Yes. In fact, this pattern is fairly prevalent among multinational companies in the United States. Many Scottish or English managers have been hired for top management positions at United States subsidiaries in the former British colonies—India, Jamaica, the West Indies, some parts of Africa . . .
Student:	Okay. So I've got all the examples right now.
Professor:	Anything else?
Student:	Just one thing. There were some typical patterns for certain countries.
Professor:	Like the last example.
Student:	No. This came later in the lecture. Something about Japan and Europe.

Professor:	Oh. Right. I probably said that both <mark>Japanese multinational companies and European companies tend to assign senior-level home country managers to overseas locations for their entire careers, whereas multinational companies in the United States view overseas assignments as temporary,</mark> so they may actually find themselves reporting to a senior-level manager from the host country who has more experience.
Student:	So, for example, a Japanese company in the United States would most probably have senior-level Japanese managers with mid-level managers maybe from the United States. But in Japan, the senior-level Japanese managers at an American company would probably have mid-level American managers reporting to them?
Professor:	Well, generalities are always a little tricky, but for the most part, that would be a typical scenario. Because living as a permanent expatriate is a career move in Japan, but a temporary strategy in the United States.
Student:	Okay. That's interesting.
Professor:	And important for you to know as a business major with an interest in international business. You're still on that track, aren't you?
Student:	I sure am. But, you know, I wasn't thinking in terms of living abroad for my entire career. That really is a huge commitment, and something to ask about going in. Anyway, like you say, most American companies view overseas assignments as temporary. That's more what I have in mind, for myself, I mean.

Q22

18. Why does the woman go to see her professor?

Ⓐ To get notes from a class that she has missed
Ⓑ To clarify some of the information from a lecture
Ⓒ To talk about her career in international business
Ⓓ To ask some questions about a paper she is writing

19. According to the professor, which factor causes staffing patterns to vary?

    Ⓐ The yearly earnings for all of the branch offices
    Ⓑ The number of employees in a multinational company
    Ⓒ The place where a company has its home office
    Ⓓ The number of years that a company has been in business

20. Why does the professor say this: "And an example of that would be . . ."

    Ⓐ To indicate that he is getting impatient
    Ⓑ To encourage the woman to continue
    Ⓒ To show that he does not understand
    Ⓓ To correct the woman's previous comment

21. Which of the following would be an example of a third-country pattern?

    Click on 2 answer choices.

    Ⓐ A Scottish manager in an American company in Africa

    Ⓑ A German manager in a Swiss company in Germany

    Ⓒ A British manager in an American company in India

    Ⓓ A French manager in a French company in Canada

22. According to the professor, how do senior-level Japanese managers view their assignments abroad?

    Ⓐ They consider them to be permanent career opportunities.
    Ⓑ They use them to learn skills that they will use in Japan.
    Ⓒ They understand that the assignment is only temporary.
    Ⓓ They see them as a strategy for their retirement.

Listening 5 "Astronomy Class"

Audio Discussion

Narrator: Listen to part of a discussion in an astronomy class. The professor is talking about the solar system.

Professor:

Okay, let's get started. Um, as you know today I promised to take you on a walk through the solar system, so let's start here with the central object of our solar system—the Sun. As you can see, the Sun is about five inches in diameter and that's about the size of a large grapefruit, which is exactly what I've used to represent it here in our model. So, I'm going to take two steps and that will bring me to the planet closest to the Sun. That would be Mercury. Two more steps to Venus. And one step from Venus to Earth. Let's continue walking three steps from Earth to Mars. And that's as far as I can go here in the classroom, but we can visualize the rest of the journey. Don't bother writing this down. Just stay with me on this. So, to go from Mars to Jupiter, we'd have to walk a little over half the length of a football field, so that would put us about at the library here on campus, and then to get from Jupiter to Saturn, we'd have to walk another 75 yards, so by then we'd be at Harmon Hall. From Saturn to Uranus, we'd have to walk again as far as we'd gone in our journey from the Sun to Saturn, and so we'd probably be at the Student Union. From Uranus to Neptune we'd have to walk the same distance again, which would take us all the way to the graduate dormitory tow-

Q24

ers. From Neptune to Pluto, another 125 yards. So, we'd end up about one third of a mile from this classroom at the entrance to the campus.

Okay. That's interesting, but now I want you to think about the orbits of the planets in those locations. Clearly, the first four planets could orbit fairly comfortably in this room, but to include the others, we'd have to occupy an area of more than six-tenths of a mile, which is all the way from College Avenue to Campus Drive. Remember that for this scale, the Sun is five inches, and most of the planets are smaller than the lead on a sharpened pencil. Okay, with that in mind, I want you to think about space. Sure, there are some moons around a few planets, and a scattering of asteroids and comets, but really, there isn't a lot out there in such a vast area. It's, well, it's pretty empty. And that's what I really want to demonstrate with this exercise.

Now, it would really be even more impressive if you could actually make that walk, and actually you can, if you visit Washington, D.C., where a scale model is set up on the National Mall, starting at the National Air and Space Museum and ending up at the Arts and Industries Museum. I did that a couple of years ago, and it was, well amazing. Even though I knew the distances intellectually, there's nothing like the experience. Has anybody else done that walk?

Student 1:
I have. And you're right. It's an eye-opener. It took me about twenty minutes to go from the Sun to Pluto because I stopped to read the information at each planet, but when I made the return trip, it was about ten minutes.

Professor: Did you take pictures?

Student 1:   I didn't. But, you know, I don't think it would have captured it anyway.

Professor:
225 | I think you're right. What impressed me about doing it was to see what was not there. I mean, how much space was between the bodies in the solar system. And a photograph wouldn't have shown that.

So back to our model. Here's another thought for you. The scale for our model is 1 to 10 billion. Now, let's suppose that we want to go to the nearest star system, the neighbor to our solar system. That would be the Alpha Centauri system, which is a little less than four and a half light years away. Okay. Let's walk it on our model. Here we are on the East Coast of the United States. So if we want to make it all the way to Alpha Centauri, we have to hike all the way to the West Coast, roughly a distance of 2,700 miles. And that's just the closest one. To make a model of the Milky Way Galaxy would require a completely different scale because . . . because the surface of the Earth wouldn't be large enough to accommodate a model at the scale of 1 to 10 billion.

Now, let's stop here for a minute because I just want to be sure that we're all together on the terms *solar system* and *galaxy*. Remember that our solar system is a single star, the Sun, with various bodies orbiting around it— nine planets and their moons, and asteroids, comets, meteors. But the galaxy has a lot of star systems—probably 100 billion of them. Okay? This is important because you can be off by almost 100 billion if you get confused by these terms. Not a good idea.

Okay, then, even if we could figure out a different scale that would let us make a model of the Milky Way Galaxy, even then, it would be challenging to make 100 billion stars, which is what you'd have to do to complete the model. How many would that be exactly? Well, just try to count all the grains of sand on all the beaches on Earth. That would be about 100 billion. But of course, you couldn't even count them in your lifetime, could you? If you'd started counting in 1000 B.C.E. you'd be finishing just about now, with the counting, I mean. But of course, that assumes that you wouldn't sleep or take any breaks.

So, what am I hoping for from this lecture? What do you think I want you to remember?

Student 2:   Well, for one thing, the enormous distances . . .

Student 3:   . . . and the vast emptiness in space.

Professor:
That's good. I hope that you'll also begin to appreciate the fact that the Earth isn't the center of the universe. Our planet, although it's very beautiful and unique, it's still just one planet, orbiting around just one star in just one galaxy.

23. What is the discussion mainly about?

 Ⓐ The discovery of the Alpha Centauri system
 Ⓑ The reason solar systems are confused with galaxies
 Ⓒ The vast expanse of the universe around us
 Ⓓ The model at the National Air and Space Museum

24. Why does the professor say this: 🎧 "Don't bother writing this down. Just stay with me on this."

   Ⓐ The students can read the details in the textbook.
   Ⓑ The professor wants the students to concentrate on listening.
   Ⓒ The facts are probably already familiar to most of the class.
   Ⓓ This lecture is a review of material from a previous session.

25. Why wouldn't a photograph capture a true picture of the solar system walk?

   Ⓐ It would not show the distances between the bodies in space.
   Ⓑ The information on the markers would not be visible in a picture.
   Ⓒ The scale for the model was not large enough to be accurate.
   Ⓓ A photograph would make the exhibit appear much smaller.

26. How does the professor explain the term *solar system*?

   Ⓐ He identifies the key features of a solar system.
   Ⓑ He refers to the glossary in the textbook.
   Ⓒ He gives several examples of solar systems.
   Ⓓ He contrasts a solar system with a galaxy.

27. Why does the professor say this: 🎧 "So what am I hoping for from this lecture? What do you think I want you to remember?"

   Ⓐ He is trying to get the students to pay attention.
   Ⓑ He is correcting something that he said earlier in the lecture.
   Ⓒ He is beginning a summary of the important points.
   Ⓓ He is joking with the students about the lecture.

28. What can be inferred about the professor?

   Ⓐ The professor used to teach in Washington, D.C.
   Ⓑ The professor likes his students to participate in the discussion.
   Ⓒ The professor wants the students to take notes on every detail.
   Ⓓ The professor is not very interested in the subject of the lecture.

Listening 6 "Psychology Class"

Audio Discussion

Narrator: Listen to part of a discussion in a psychology class. The professor is discussing defense mechanisms.

Professor:

Okay, we know from our earlier study of Freud that defense mechanisms | Q29 |
protect us from bringing painful thoughts or feelings to the surface of our
consciousness. We do this because our minds simply can't tolerate these
thoughts. So, defense mechanisms help us to express these painful
thoughts or feelings in another way, while we repress the real problem. The
function of defense mechanisms is to keep from being overwhelmed. Of
course, the avoidance of problems can result in additional emotional issues.
And there's a huge distinction between repression and suppression.
Anybody want to explain the difference?

Student 1:

I'll try it. I think *repression* is an unconscious response to serious events or | Q30 |
images but *suppression* is more conscious and deals with something
unpleasant but not usually, well, terrible experiences.

Professor:

I couldn't have said it better. Now remember that the thoughts or feelings that we're trying to *repress* may include, just to mention a few, anger, depression, competition, uh . . . fear, envy, hate, and so on. For instance, let's suppose that you're very angry with your professor. Not me, of course. I'm referring to another professor. So, you're very angry because he's treated you unfairly in some way that . . . that could cause you to lose your scholarship. Maybe he failed you on an examination that didn't really cover the material that he'd gone over in class, and an F grade in the course is going to be unacceptable to your sponsors. So, this would be very painful, as I'm sure you'd agree. And I'd say it would qualify as a serious event.

So let's take a look at several different types of defense mechanisms that you might employ to repress the feelings of disappointment, rage perhaps, and . . . and even violence that you'd feel toward the professor. Most of them are named so the mechanism is fairly obvious and one of the most common mechanisms is *denial*, which is . . .

Student 2:   If I want to deny something, I'll just say I'm not angry with the professor.

Professor:

Exactly. You may even extend the denial to include the sponsors, and you could tell your friends that they'd never revoke your scholarship. And this mechanism would allow you to deny the problem, even in the face of direct evidence to the contrary. Let's say, a letter from the sponsor indicating that you won't receive a scholarship for the next term. . . . Okay on that one? Okay. How about *rationalization*?

Student 2:   Well, in rationalization, you come up with some reasons *why* the professor might have given an unfair test.

Professor: And how would you do that?

Student 2:   Well, you might defend him. You could say that he gave the test to encourage students to learn information on their own. Is that what you mean?

Professor:

Sure. Because you'd be rationalizing . . . providing a reason that justifies an otherwise mentally intolerable situation. Okay, another example of rationalizing is to excuse the sponsor for refusing to hear your side of the situation. You might say that sponsors are too busy to investigate why students are having problems in their classes. And you might do that while you deny your true feelings that sponsors really should be more open to hearing you out.

Student 3:   So when you deny something, I mean when you use denial, you're refusing to acknowledge a situation, but . . . when you use rationalization, you're excusing the behavior?

Professor:
Excellent summary. So, now let me give you another option. If you use a *reaction formation* as a defense mechanism, you'll proclaim the *opposite* of your feelings. In this case, what would you say about the professor?

Student 4:   I'd say that I like the professor when, in fact, I hate him for destroy . . . depriving me of my opportunity.

Professor:
And you might insist that you have no hard feelings and even go so far as to tell your friends that he's an excellent teacher. You see, a reaction formation turns the expression of your feelings into the opposite reaction, that is, on the surface.

And that brings us to *projection*, which is a defense mechanism that tricks your mind into believing that someone else is guilty of the negative thought or feeling that *you* have.

Student 1:   Can you give us an example of that one?

Professor:
Okay. Feelings of hate for the professor might be expressed by telling classmates about *another* student who hates the professor, or, uh, . . . or even suggesting that the professor has strong feelings of hate for *you* but you really like the professor yourself. So you would project, um, . . . attribute your feelings . . . to someone else. Get it?

Student 1:   So if I hate someone, I'd believe that another person hates him or that he hates me.

Professor: But you wouldn't admit that *you* hate him yourself.

Student 1:   Okay. That's projection.

Professor:

Now *displacement* serves as a defense mechanism when a less threatening person or object is substituted for the person or object that's really the cause of your anxiety. So, instead of confronting the professor about the unfair test, well, you might direct your anger toward the friend who studied for the test with you, and you could blame him for wasting your time on the material that was in the book and notes.

Of course, there are several other defense mechanisms like *fantasy*, which includes daydreaming or watching television maybe to escape the problems at school. Or *regression,* which includes immature behaviors that are no longer appropriate, like, uh, maybe expressing temper in the same way that a preschooler might respond to having a toy snatched away. And your textbook contains a few more that we haven't touched on in class.

Just one more thing, it's good to understand that the notion of unconscious thoughts and the mechanisms that allow us to manage them, that this is a concept that goes in and out of fashion. Many psychologists rejected defense mechanisms altogether during the 70s and 80s, and then in the 90s, cognitive psychologists showed a renewed interest in research in this area. But I must warn you, that although they found similar responses, they tended to give them different names. For instance, *denial* might appear in a more recent study as *positive illusion*, or *scapegoating* might be referred to instead of *displacement*. But when you get right down to it, the same categories of behavior for defense mechanisms still exist in the research even if they're labeled differently. And, uh, in my view, if you compare Freud's traditional defense mechanisms with those that are being presented by more modern researchers, you'll find that Freud is easier to understand and gives us a broader perspective. And, if you understand Freud's categories, well, you'll certainly be able to get a handle on the newer terms. What is exciting about the modern studies is the focus on coping skills and what's being referred to as healthy defenses. So next time, we'll take a look at some of these processes.

29. What is the discussion mainly about?

Ⓐ The difference between suppression and repression
Ⓑ Why Freud's theories of defense mechanisms are correct
Ⓒ Some of the more common types of defense mechanisms
Ⓓ How to solve a student's problem with an unfair professor

30. How does the student explain the term *repression*?

    Ⓐ He contrasts it with suppression.

    Ⓑ He identifies it as a conscious response.

    Ⓒ He gives several examples of it.

    Ⓓ He refers to a study by Freud.

31. Why does the professor say this: "Not me, of course. I'm referring to another professor."

    Ⓐ She is getting the class to pay attention.

    Ⓑ She is making a joke about herself.

    Ⓒ She is asking for a compliment.

    Ⓓ She is criticizing a colleague.

32. Which of the following is an example of *displacement* that was used in the lecture?

    Ⓐ Insisting that the professor dislikes you, when you really dislike him

    Ⓑ Defending the professor even when you are angry about his behavior

    Ⓒ Blaming someone in your study group instead of blaming the professor

    Ⓓ Refusing to acknowledge that a problem exists because of the low grade

33. According to the professor, what happened in the 1990s?

    Ⓐ The concept of defense mechanisms was abandoned.

    Ⓑ New terms were introduced for the same mechanisms.

    Ⓒ Modern researchers improved upon Freud's theory.

    Ⓓ Additional categories were introduced by researchers.

34. How does the professor organize the lecture?

    Ⓐ She has visual aids to explain each point.

    Ⓑ She uses a scenario that students can relate to.

    Ⓒ She provides a handout with an outline.

    Ⓓ She helps students read the textbook.

PART III

Listening 7 "Bookstore"

Audio Conversation

Narrator: Listen to part of a conversation in the bookstore.

Student: Excuse me. I'm looking for someone who can help me with the textbook reservation program.

Manager: Oh, well, I can do that. What do you need?

Student: Okay. Um, my friend told me that I could get used books if I order, I mean, preorder them now.

Manager: That's right. Do you want to do that?

Student: I think so, but I'm not sure how it works.

Manager: Actually, it's fairly straightforward. We have a short form for you to fill out. Do you know what you're going to take next semester?

Student: Yeah, I do.

Manager: And you have the course names and the schedule numbers for all your classes?

Student: Unhuh.

Manager: Okay, then, just put that information down on the form and, uh, make a checkmark in the box if you want recommended books as well as required books. And you said you were interested in used books, right?

Student: Right.

Manager: So mark the box for used books, sign the form and bring it back to me.

Student: Do I have to pay now? Or, do you want a deposit?

Manager: No, you can pay when you pick up the books.

Student: And when can I do that?

Manager: The week before classes begin.

Student: That's good, but, um, what if I change my schedule? I mean, I don't plan to but . . .

Manager: . . . it happens. Don't worry. If you change classes, you can just bring the books back any time two weeks from the first day of class to get a full refund. Of course, you'll need the original cash register receipt and a photo ID and, if it's a new book, you can't have any marks in it. But you said you wanted used books, so it won't matter.   Q36

Student: Yeah, that's the main reason why I want to do this—because I'll have a better chance to get used books.

Manager: If there are used books available and you marked the form, that's what we'll pull for you.

Student: Okay, thanks a lot. I'll just fill this out and bring it back to you later today. I don't have all the numbers with me, the section numbers for the classes.

Manager: Fine. We need those numbers because when different professors are teaching the same class, they don't always order the same books.

Student: Right. So, will you be here this afternoon?

Manager: I probably will, but if I'm not, just give the form to the person in this office. Don't give it to one of the student employees, though. They're usually very good about getting the forms back to the office, but sometimes it gets really busy and . . . you know how it is.   Q37

Student: Sure. Well, I'll bring it back to the office myself.

Manager: That's probably a good idea. And, oh, uh, one more thing. I should tell you that the used books tend to go first, so, if you want to be sure that you get used books . . .   Q38

Student: You know what? I'm going to go right back to the dorm to get those numbers now, while you're still here.   Q39

Manager: Okay. That's good.

35. What does the man need from the bookstore?

Ⓐ A schedule of classes for next term
Ⓑ A form to order books
Ⓒ Specific books for his classes
Ⓓ Information about employment

36. What does the man need if he wants a full refund?

Click on 2 answer choices.

A Identification

B His registration form

C A receipt for the purchase

D Proof of his deposit

37. What does the woman mean when she says this: 🎧 ". . . sometimes it gets really busy and . . . you know how it is."

Ⓐ She is not sure that the student employee will give her the form.
Ⓑ She thinks that he will have to wait for the student employees.
Ⓒ She does not want the man to bother her because she is busy.
Ⓓ She is is not sure that the man understands what to do.

38. What does the woman imply about the used books she sells?

Ⓐ They are purchased before new books.
Ⓑ They do not have marks in them.
Ⓒ She does not recommend buying them.
Ⓓ She would rather sell new books.

39. What does the man need to do now?

Ⓐ Go to the bank to get money for the deposit
Ⓑ Sit down and fill out the form to order books
Ⓒ Take his books back to the dormitory
Ⓓ Locate the schedule numbers for his classes

Listening 8 "Environmental Science Class"

Audio Lecture
Narrator: Listen to part of a lecture in an environmental science class.

Professor:
Hydrogen is the most recent and, I'd say, one of the most promising, in a long list of alternatives to petroleum. Some of the possibilities include batteries, methanol, natural gas, and, well, you name it. But hydrogen fuel cells have a couple of advantages over some of the other options. First of all, they're really quiet, and they don't pollute the atmosphere. Besides that, hydrogen is the most abundant element in the universe, and it can be produced from a number of sources, including ammonia, or . . . or even water. So, it's renewable, and there's an almost unlimited supply.

Okay. Now fuel cells represent a radical departure from the conventional internal combustion engine and even a fairly fundamental change from electric battery power. Like batteries, fuel cells run on electric motors; however, batteries use electricity from an external source and store it for use in the battery while the fuel cells create their own electricity through a chemical process that uses hydrogen and oxygen from the air. Are you with me? Look, by producing energy in a chemical reaction rather than through combustion, a fuel cell can convert, say 40–60 percent of the energy from the hydrogen into electricity. And when this ratio is compared with that of a combustion engine that

Q40

Q4

runs at about half the efficiency of a fuel cell, well, it's obvious that fuel cell technology has the potential to revolutionize the energy industry.

So, fuel cells have the potential to generate power for almost any kind of machinery or equipment that fossil fuels run, but, the most important, um, let's say goal, the goal of fuel cell technology is the introduction of fuel cell powered vehicles. Internationally, the competition is fierce to commercialize fuel cell cars. I guess all of the leading automobile manufacturers worldwide have concept cars that use fuel cells, and some of them can reach speeds of as high as 90 miles per hour. Even more impressive is the per tank storage capacity. Can you believe this? Some of those cars can run for 220 miles between refills. But many of those cars were designed decades ago, so . . . what's the holdup?

Q44 Well, the problem in introducing fuel cell technology is really twofold. In the first place, industries will have to invest millions, maybe even billions of dollars to refine the technology—and here's the real cost—the infrastructure to, uh, support the fueling of the cars. And by infrastructure, I mean basic facilities and services like hydrogen stations to refuel cars and mechanics who know how to repair them. I think you get the picture. And then, consumers will have to accept and use the new products powered by fuel cells. So, we're going to need educational programs to inform the public about the safety and . . . and convenience of fuel cells, if we're going to achieve a successful transition to fuel cell products. But, unfortunately, major funding efforts get interrupted. Here's what I mean. When oil prices are high, then there seems to be more funding and greater interest in basic research and development, and more public awareness of fuel cells, and then the price of oil goes down a little and the funding dries up and people just go back to using their fossil fueled products. And this has been going on for more than thirty years.

Q42 Some government sponsored initiatives have created incentives for fuel cell powered vehicles but probably one of the most successful programs, at least in my opinion, is, uh, the STEP program, which is an acronym for the Sustainable Transportation Energy Program. STEP is a demonstration project sponsored by the government of Western Australia. Now, in this project, gasoline driven buses have been replaced with fuel cell buses on regular transportation routes. I think that British Petroleum is the supplier of the hydrogen fuel, which is produced at an oil refinery in Kwinana, south of Perth. So we need to watch this carefully. Another collaborative research effort is being undertaken by the European Union and the United States. Scientists and engineers are trying to develop a fuel cell that's effectively

Q43 engineered and attractive to the commercial market. Now, under an agreement signed in about 2000, if memory serves, it was 2003, but anyway, the joint projects include the writing of codes and standards, the design of fueling infrastructures, the refinement of fuel cell models, and the demonstration of fuel cell vehicles. In Europe, the private sector will combine efforts with government agencies in the public sector to, uh, to create a long-term plan for the introduction of fuel cells throughout the E.U. And the World Bank is providing funding to promote the development and manufacture of fuel cell buses for public transportation in China, Egypt, Mexico, and India, and we're starting to see some really interesting projects in these areas. So, uh, clearly, fuel cell technology is an international effort.

Okay, at the present time, Japan leads the way in addressing the issues of modifying the infrastructure. Several fueling stations that dispense hydrogen by the cubic meter are already in place, with plans for more. But even when a nationwide system is completed, decisions about how and where to produce the hydrogen and how to transport it will still have to be figured out. Most countries share the view that fleets of vehicles have significant advantages for the introduction of fuel cell powered transportation because, well obviously they can be fueled at a limited number of central locations. And, uh, and other benefits of a fleet are the opportunity to provide training for a maintenance crew and for the drivers. As for consumer education, no one country seems to have made the advances there that . . . that would serve as a model for the rest of us. But perhaps when the demonstration projects have concluded and a few model cars are available to the public, well, more attention will be directed to public information programs. | Q45

40. What is this lecture mainly about?

    Ⓐ An overview of fuel cell technology
    Ⓑ A process for producing fuel cells
    Ⓒ A comparison of fuel cell models
    Ⓓ Some problems in fuel cell distribution

41. What does the professor mean when he says this: 🎧 "Some of the possibilities include batteries, methanol, natural gas, and, well, you name it."

    Ⓐ He wants the students to take notes.
    Ⓑ He would like the students to participate.
    Ⓒ He is impressed with these options.
    Ⓓ He does not plan to talk about the alternatives.

42. Why does the professor mention the STEP program in Australia?

    Ⓐ He has personal experience in this project.
    Ⓑ He is referring to information from a previous discussion.
    Ⓒ He is comparing it to a successful program in Japan.
    Ⓓ He thinks it is a very good example of a project.

43. Why does the professor say this: ". . . if memory serves, it was 2003 . . ."

    Ⓐ To indicate that the date is not important
    Ⓑ To provide a specific date for the contract
    Ⓒ To correct a previous statement about the date
    Ⓓ To show that he is uncertain about the date

44. What are some of the problems associated with fuel cell technology?

    Click on 2 answer choices.

    Ⓐ Noise pollution

    Ⓑ Public acceptance

    Ⓒ Supplies of hydrogen

    Ⓓ Investment in infrastructures

45. What is the professor's attitude toward fuel cells?

    Ⓐ He thinks that the technology is not very efficient.
    Ⓑ He is hopeful about their development in the future.
    Ⓒ He is doubtful that fuel cells will replace fossil fuels.
    Ⓓ He is discouraged because of the delays in production.

Listening 9 "Philosophy Class"

Audio Discussion

Narrator: Listen to part of a discussion in a philosophy class.

Professor:

246 *Humanism* is a philosophical position that places the dignity of the individual
at the center of its movement. A primary principle of humanism—I don't need
247 to spell that for you, do I? Okay, a primary principle of humanism is that
human beings are rational and have an innate predisposition for good.
Although humanism is associated with the beginning of the Reformation, the
humanist philosophy was not new when it became popular in Italy during the
Middle Ages. In fact, according to the ancient Greek philosopher, Protagoras,
mankind was "the measure of all things." And this idea was echoed by
Sophocles when he said, "Many are the wonders of the world, and none so
wonderful as mankind." This is classical humanism. Man as the ideal at the
center of all creation. Even the ancient Greek gods were viewed as resem-
bling man both physically and psychologically. And, in a sense, isn't this per-
sonification of the deity just another way to exalt human beings? But that
aside, it was precisely the rediscovery and translation of classical manuscripts that coincided with the invention of printing presses around the mid-
15th century, which, uh, . . . which provided a catalyst for the humanistic
movement throughout Europe. As the clergy and upper classes participated
in the rediscovery and dissemination of classical literature, humanism
became popular among theologians and scholars, and soon set the stage for
the Renaissance. This one, I'll spell. Does anybody remember the meaning
of the word *renaissance*?

Student 1:   Rebirth, renewal.

Professor:

Right you are. *Renaissance* literally means "rebirth," and it refers to the
return to ancient Greek and Roman art and literature, which, like all things in
the humanistic tradition, they were measured by human standards. Art
returned to the classical principles of harmony and balance. In the field of
architecture, we see both religious and secular buildings styled after ancient
Roman designs, with mathematical proportions and . . . a human scale, a
scale that contrasted with the Medieval Gothic buildings of the previous era.
Public works such as bridges and aqueducts from the Roman occupation
were repaired, restored, or rebuilt. In the sculptures of the period, nude figures were modeled in life-sized images, with true proportions, and it was also
at this point that realism became the standard for painting, with a preference
for naturalistic settings and the placement of figures in . . . realistic proportion to those settings. It was also evident that the portraits tended to be more

personal and authentic. And artists even produced self-portraits at this time. Remember, the figures in the paintings of the previous era tended to be of another world, but Renaissance painters placed recognizable human beings in *this* world. In music, there was an effort to create harmonies that were pleasing to the human ear and melodies that were compatible with the human voice. In addition, music lessons became more widespread as a source of education and enjoyment. Dancing increased in popularity with a concurrent trend toward music that had rhythm and invited movement as a pleasurable activity.

Student 2:   Wasn't that why Latin became so important?

Professor:
Yes. Both Greek and Latin became important as tools for scholarship, and classical Latin became the basis for an international language of the intellectuals throughout Europe. To be true to humanism, and all it represented, it was necessary to be knowledgeable about, and, uh, . . . and faithful to the ancient philosophies as expressed in their writing, and how best to express them than in the original languages? By the way, Latin as a universal language for clerics and the aristocracy, this encouraged the exchange of ideas on a wider scale than ever before, and legitimized in a sense the presumption that mankind was at the center of all things. It also made it possible for individual scholars to make a name for themselves and establish their place in the history of mankind. | Q49

Well, it was at this time that a close association, almost a partnership was forged between art and science. In their efforts to be precise, sculptors and painters studied the human form. In effect, they became anatomists. You may recall the drawing in your textbook, the one by Leonardo da Vinci which demonstrates the geometrical proportions of the human body. And, of course, Alberti, in his many books on architecture, sculpture, and painting . . . he emphasized the study of mathematics as the underlying principle of all the arts. Whereas artists had considered themselves craftsmen in the Middle Ages, the great Renaissance artists viewed themselves as intellectuals, philosophers, if you will, of humanism. They were designing a world for human beings to live in and enjoy. One that was in proportion and in harmony with mankind. So, perhaps you can see why the so-called Renaissance man emerged. | Q48

Student 1:   Okay. But exactly what is the definition of a Renaissance man? I know it means a very talented person, but . . .

Professor:
Good question. Sometimes we use these terms without really defining them.
250 So I would say that a Renaissance man would be talented, as you said, but would also have to demonstrate broad interests . . . in both the arts and the sciences. The quality that was most admired in the Renaissance was the extraordinary, maybe even . . . universality of talents . . . in diverse fields of endeavor. After all, this quality proved that mankind was capable of reason and creation, that humanism was justified in placing man in the center of the world, as the measure of all things in it. With the humanistic philosophy as a justification, scholars would interpret the ancient classics and some of them would argue to a reasonable conclusion a very new and more secular society built on individual, human effort. It was not difficult for the Renaissance man to make the leap of logic from classical humanism to political humanism, which encouraged freedom of thought, and indeed even democracy, within both the church and the state. But that is a topic for another day.

46. What is the main focus of this discussion?

  Ⓐ The Renaissance
  Ⓑ Important scholars
  Ⓒ Humanism
  Ⓓ Political reform

47. Why does the professor say this: 🎧 "I don't need to spell that for you, do I?"

  Ⓐ She thinks that the spelling of the term is not important.
  Ⓑ She assumes that the students know how to spell the term.
  Ⓒ She knows that the term can be found in the textbook.
  Ⓓ She does not want to spend time explaining the term.

48. Why does the professor mention the drawing by Leonardo da Vinci?

  Ⓐ She wants the students to refer to their textbook more often.
  Ⓑ She uses it as an example of the union of art and science.
  Ⓒ She says that it is one of her personal favorites.
  Ⓓ She contrasts his work with that of other artists.

49. According to the professor, what was the effect of using Latin as a universal language of scholarship?

   Ⓐ It facilitated communication among intellectuals in many countries.
   Ⓑ It made Rome the capital of the world during the Renaissance.
   Ⓒ It caused class distinctions to be apparent throughout Europe.
   Ⓓ It created an environment in which new ideas were suppressed.

50. According to the professor, what can be inferred about a Renaissance man?

   Ⓐ He would probably be a master craftsman.
   Ⓑ He would have an aptitude for both art and science.
   Ⓒ He would be interested in classical philosophers.
   Ⓓ He would value logic at the expense of creativity.

51. All of the following characteristics are true of humanism EXCEPT

   Ⓐ Mankind is innately good.
   Ⓑ Scholars must serve society.
   Ⓒ The individual is important.
   Ⓓ Human beings are rational.

STOP   **There is a 10-minute break between the Listening section and the Speaking section.**

SPEAKING SECTION

 Model Test 1, Speaking Section

The Speaking section tests your ability to communicate in English in an academic setting. During the test, you will be presented with six speaking questions. The questions ask for a response to a single question, a conversation, a talk, or a lecture.

On the official TOEFL® iBT, you may take notes as you listen, but notes are not graded. You may use your notes to answer the questions. Some of the questions ask for a response to a reading passage and a talk or a lecture. The reading passages and the questions are written, but most of the directions will be spoken.

Your speaking will be evaluated on both the fluency of the language and the accuracy of the content. You will have 15–20 seconds to prepare and 45–60 seconds to respond to each question. Typically, a good response will require all of the response time but the answer will be complete by the end of the response time.

The time for the Speaking section is about 20 minutes. A clock on the screen will show you how much time you have to prepare your answer and how much time you have to record it.

On this Pretest, the audio is marked with an icon of a headphone but the audio for the Pretest is not included in this package. You will find the audio for this test in the larger version, *Barron's How to Prepare for the TOEFL® iBT, 12th Edition*. To take the Pretest without the audio, read the scripts. Model Tests 2 and 3, the Progress Tests in this book, include the audio for you to use as you prepare for the TOEFL.

Independent Speaking Question 1 "A Marriage Partner"

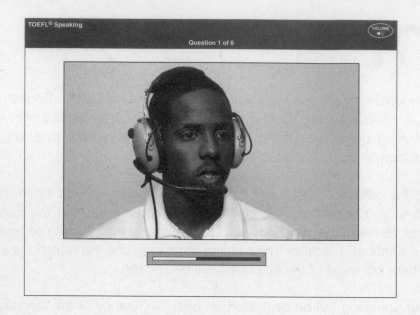

 Read a question about a familiar topic.

Question

Describe an ideal marriage partner. What qualities do you think are most important for a husband or wife? Use specific reasons and details to explain your choices.

Preparation Time: 15 seconds
Recording Time: 45 seconds

Independent Speaking Question 2 "News"

 Read a question that asks your opinion about a familiar topic.

Question
Some people like to watch the news on television. Other people prefer to read the news in a newspaper. Still others use their computers to get the news. How do you prefer to be informed about the news and why? Use specific reasons and examples to support your choice.

Preparation Time: 15 seconds
Recording Time: 45 seconds

Integrated Speaking Question 3 "Meal Plan"

Read a short passage and then read a talk on the same topic.

Reading Time: 45 seconds

<u>Change in Meal Plans</u>
Residence hall students are no longer required to purchase seven-day meal plans. Now two meal plan options will be offered. The traditional seven-day plan will still be available, including three meals every day at a cost of $168 per month. In addition, a five-day plan will be offered, including three meals Monday–Friday at a cost of $120 per month. Students who elect to use the five-day plan may purchase meals on the weekend at three dollars per meal. The food court in the College Union provides several fast-food alternatives. In addition to burgers and pizza, Chinese food, Mexican food, and a salad bar are also available.

TOEFL® Speaking

Question 3 of 6

VOLUME

Now read a conversation between two students who are talking about the plan.

Man:	I don't like to cook, but I don't like to eat in the cafeteria every day either.
Woman:	True. The food does get kind of . . . same old same old.
Man:	My point exactly. And besides, I go home about every other weekend, so paying for my meals when I'm not there doesn't make a lot of sense.
Woman:	Right. So you'll probably sign up for the five-day plan next semester.
Man:	I already did. If I want to eat in the cafeteria some weekend, I can just buy a meal, but I'd probably go out somewhere with my friends if I'm here over the weekend.
Woman:	Well, I don't go home on the weekends as much as you do, but I still eat out a lot on the weekends.
Man:	So the five-day plan might work out better for you, too. I'm really glad to have the option.

Question

The man expresses his opinion of the new meal plan. Report his opinion, and explain the reasons that he gives for having that opinion.

Preparation Time: 30 seconds
Recording Time: 60 seconds

Integrated Speaking Question 4 "Aboriginal People"

Read a short passage and then read part of a lecture on the same topic.

Reading Time: 45 seconds

<u>Aboriginal People</u>

Although the first inhabitants of Australia have been identified by physical characteristics, culture, language, and locale, none of these attributes truly establishes a person as a member of the Aboriginal People. Because the Aboriginal groups settled in various geographical areas and developed customs and lifestyles that reflected the resources available to them, there is great diversity among those groups, including more than 200 linguistic varieties. Probably the most striking comparison is that of the Aboriginal People who inhabit the desert terrain of the Australian Outback with those who live along the coast. Clearly, their societies have developed very different cultures. According to the Department of Education, the best way to establish identity as a member of the Aboriginal People is to be identified and accepted as such by the Aboriginal community.

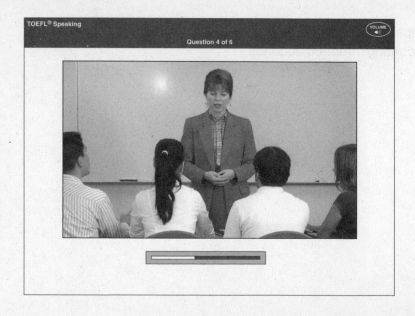

Now read part of a lecture in an anthropology class. The professor is talking about Aboriginal People.

Professor:

According to your textbook, the Aboriginal People are very diverse, and, I would agree with that; however, there are certain beliefs that unite the groups, and in fact, allow them to identify themselves and others as members of the diverse Aboriginal societies. For one thing, unlike the anthropologists who believe that tribes arrived in eastern Australia from Tasmania about 40,000 years ago, the Aboriginal People believe that they have always been in Australia, and that they have sprung from the land. Evidence for this resides in the oral history that has been recorded in stories and passed down for at least fifty generations. This history is referred to as the "Dreaming." The stories teach moral and spiritual values and provide each member of the group with an identity that reflects the landscape where the person's mother first becomes aware of the unborn baby, or to put it in terms of the "Dreaming," where the spirit enters the mother's body. So, I am saying that the way that the Aboriginal People identify themselves and each other, even across groups, is by their membership in the oral history that they share.

Question

Explain how the Aboriginal People are identified. Draw upon information in both the reading and the lecture.

Preparation Time: 30 seconds
Recording Time: 60 seconds

Integrated Speaking Question 5 "Scheduling Conflict"

 Now read a short conversation between a student and his friend.

Friend:	So what time should we pick you up on Friday? Can you be ready by noon or do you need another hour or so?
Student:	I really wanted to spend the weekend with my family, and the ride with you would have made it even more fun, but . . .
Friend:	You mean you aren't going?
Student:	I can't. I'm not doing too well in my economics class, and I have a lecture Friday afternoon. I don't think I should miss it.
Friend:	Well, why don't you borrow the notes from someone? Isn't your roommate in that class?
Student:	Yeah, he is. But I've already asked to borrow his notes once this semester. He didn't seem to mind though.
Friend:	Well, there you are. Unless you want to go to class on Thursday. I'm fairly sure that Dr. Collins teaches the same class Thursday night.

Student: Really? She probably wouldn't mind if I sat in on the Thursday class, but I wonder if she'll give the same lecture. You know, maybe they're one week behind or one week ahead of us.

Friend: I suppose that's possible, but it would be easy enough to find out. You could just tell her that you'd like to attend the Thursday session this week because you need to go out of town. Then you can ride home with us. If there's a problem, you can still borrow your roommate's notes on Sunday when we get back.

Question

Describe the man's problem and the two suggestions that his friend makes about how to handle it. What do you think the man should do, and why?

Preparation Time: 20 seconds
Recording Time: 60 seconds

Integrated Speaking Question 6 "Laboratory Microscope"

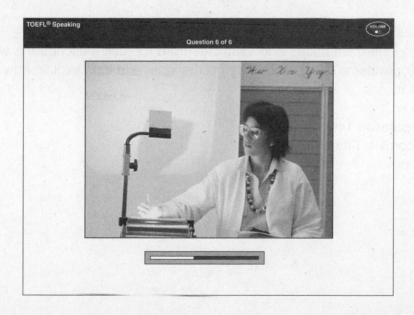

Now read part of a talk in a biology laboratory. The teaching assistant is explaining how to use the microscope.

Teaching Assistant:
All right, now that you all have microscopes at your tables, I want to explain how they work and how to use them. First of all, you should know that they are compound microscopes so they can magnify objects up to 1000 times their size. These microscopes have two systems—an illuminating system and an imaging system. You'll see that the illuminating system has a light source built in, and you can control it by adjusting the lever on the side. Why is this important? Well, the specimen must be pretty thin, or let's say, transparent enough to let light pass through it. So the light source controls the amount of light that passes through the specimen. Okay. The other system provides magnification. Use this lever to switch powers. So, when you switch to a higher power, you see a larger image, and when you switch to a lower power, you see a smaller image. But, I should remind you that the field of view is smaller at a higher power. In other words, at a higher magnification, you see a larger image of a smaller area. Okay. So what about the focus? Well, these microscopes are parfocal, and that means you usually don't have to refocus when you switch to a higher or lower power of magnification. But there are two adjustment knobs—the larger one for coarse adjustment and the smaller one for fine adjustment just in case.

Question
Using the main points and examples from the talk, describe the two major systems of the laboratory microscope, and then explain how to use it.

Preparation Time: 20 seconds
Recording Time: 60 seconds

WRITING SECTION

The Writing section tests your ability to write essays in English similar to those that you would write in college courses.

On the official TOEFL® iBT, you will write two essays. The integrated essay asks for your response to an academic reading passage and a lecture on the same topic. You may take notes as you read and listen, but notes are not graded. You may use your notes to write the essay. The lecture will be spoken, but the directions and the questions will be written. You will have 20 minutes to plan, write, and revise your response. Typically, a good essay for the integrated topic will require that you write 150–225 words.

The independent essay usually asks for your opinion about a familiar topic. You will have 30 minutes to plan, write, and revise your response. Typically, a good essay for the independent topic will require that you write 300–350 words.

A clock on the screen will show you how much time you have to complete each essay.

On this Pretest, the audio is marked with an icon of a headphone 🎧 but the audio for the Pretest is not included in this package. You will find the audio for this test in the larger version, *Barron's How to Prepare for the TOEFL® iBT, 12th Edition*. To take the Pretest without the audio, read the scripts. Model Tests 2 and 3, the Progress Tests in this book, include the audio for you to use as you prepare for the TOEFL.

Integrated Essay "School Organization"

You have 20 minutes to plan, write, and revise your response to a reading passage and a lecture on the same topic. First, read the passage and take notes. Then, read the lecture and take notes. Finally, write your response to the writing question. Typically, a good response will require that you write 150–225 words.

Reading Passage
Time: 3 minutes

Historically, schools in the United States have borrowed the European system of school organization, a system that separates students into grades by chronological age. In general, children begin formal schooling at the age of six in what is referred to as the first grade. For the most part, students progress through twelve grades; however, some students who do not meet minimum requirements for a particular grade may be asked to repeat the year.

Graded schools are divided into primary grades, intermediate grades, and secondary grades. Primary education includes grades 1 through 5 or 6, and may also provide kindergarten as a preparation for first grade. Referred to as elementary school, these grades are usually taught by one teacher in a self-contained classroom. Intermediate grades begin with grade 6 or 7 and offer three years of instruction. At this level, teams of teachers may collaborate to provide subject-based classes similar to those offered in high school. Viewed as a preparation for high school, intermediate education is known as junior high school. At grade 9 or 10, secondary school begins. Classes taught by subject specialists usually last about fifty minutes to allow a student ten minutes to move to the next class before it begins at the top of the hour. At the end of twelve successful grades of instruction, students are eligible for a secondary school diploma, more commonly called a high school diploma.

Model Test 1, Writing Section

 Now read a lecture on the same topic as the passage that you have just read.

Professor:
So what are the problems associated with the graded school system? Well, for one thing, graded schools don't take into account the . . . the differences in academic readiness on the part of individual learners. And by that I mean that some six-year-olds are simply not socially, mentally, or even physically mature enough to begin school, but others are ready in all of those important ways by their fifth or even fourth birthdays. And uh . . . by the time that girls and boys are in their early teens, we can see that there's a significant difference in maturity, in . . . in physical and social maturity but . . . they're still grouped together in intermediate grades in a graded school system.

Okay, besides the obvious differences in individual readiness and maturity, the . . . the whole issue of promotion needs to be reviewed. Grade-level requirements don't really deal with the actual learning that has occurred, uh, in a positive way. Many research studies confirm that repeating an entire year because some of the material is not learned contributes to . . . to boredom, poor self-concept, and . . . and eventually to higher drop-out rates. And since graded schools are using group expectations as measured by perform-ance on standardized tests, this is another way to evaluate the group rather than the individual. So, what happens is that individual differences in how long it takes to learn a concept or . . . or the partial achievement of a grade-level curriculum . . . that is never addressed by the graded school system. Students who need more time to learn have to repeat material that they already know. Students who can learn at a faster rate have to wait for the new material to be presented. So, as you can see, it's not ideal.

Question
Summarize the main points in the lecture, explaining how they cast doubt on the ideas in the reading passage.

Independent Essay "An Important Leader"

Question
Leaders like John F. Kennedy and Martin Luther King have made important contributions to the people of the United States. Name another world leader you think is important. Give specific reasons for your choice

This is the end of Model Test 1.
To check your answers, refer to "Explanatory or Example Answers and Audio Scripts for Model Tests: Model Test 1," Chapter 7, pages 409–436.

3

ACADEMIC SKILLS

TAKING NOTES

Taking notes is writing down information while you are listening or reading. There are three problems that you will confront when you are taking notes.

1. **The professor determines the pace of a lecture**. This means that you have to take notes as quickly as the professor speaks.
2. **The notes must include all the main ideas and major facts**. This means that you have to know how to identify important information when you hear it or read it.
3. **The notes may be used for different reasons**. This means that you have to organize the notes to help you remember, to add to the information from another assignment, or to plan a speech or an essay.

This chapter will help you improve your note taking skills. You will learn how to

- **Separate the major and minor points**
- **Use abbreviations and symbols**

How will these strategies help you on the TOEFL? By learning to take better notes when you hear lectures, you will have the information you need to respond to the listening comprehension questions and to prepare your speaking and writing questions. You will even improve your reading comprehension. Taking excellent notes is one of the most important academic skills for success on the TOEFL and after the TOEFL when you are enrolled in a college or university program.

➤ Separate the major and minor points

In order to use two columns for notes, you must be able to classify the ideas into major and minor points. There are usually three or four major points in a short lecture or reading passage. Each of the major points is supported by examples and details. The examples and details are minor points.

PRACTICAL STRATEGY

When you hear a major point, write it on the left. When you hear a minor point, write it on the right.

PRACTICE ACTIVITY 1

Did you understand? Look at the notes under each topic. The sentences in the notes refer to either the major points or the minor points. Try to organize the notes under the topic by putting the major points in the left column and the minor points in the right column. Your answer is correct if the points are placed correctly on either the left or right. The points do not have to be in exactly the same order. The first one is completed to give you an example. The answers are printed in Chapter 7 on pages 381–383.

EXAMPLE

There are three types of managers in addition to the general manager.

> The line manager is responsible for production.
> For example, a production manager is a line manager.
> A staff manager is in charge of support activities such as human resources.
> Information systems is also overseen by a staff manager.
> A functional manager is the head of a department.

A department chair at a college is a functional manager.
The manager of a sales department at a company is also a functional manager.

3 managers

line manager production	production manager
staff manager support activities	human resources information systems
functional manager head dept	dept chair college sales dept company

1. According to Mead, the self has two sides: the "I" and the "me."

   It is predictable because social conformity is expected.
   This part of the self is less predictable because it is unique.
   This part of the self is formed through socialization by others.
   The "I" represents the individuality of a person.
   For instance, a spontaneous reaction might reveal the "I."
   The "me" represents the expectations and attitudes of others.

2. The mystery of pulsars was resolved in the 1960s.

   We see pulses of light each time the beam sweeps past the Earth.
   The pulsar in the Crab Nebula, for example, currently spins about thirty times per second.
   We also know that pulsars are not perfectly timed because each revolution of a pulsar takes a little longer.
   We know that pulsars are neutron stars, like lighthouses left by supernova explosions. It will probably spin about half as fast two thousand years from now.
   Like a lighthouse, the neutron star revolves.

3. Britain transported convicts to Australia in an effort to solve the problems of overcrowding in prisons.

    There were 11 ships with 750 prisoners aboard.
    Four companies of marines sailed with them as guards.
    They took enough supplies for two years.
    In 1787, the first fleet left for Botany Bay in New South Wales.
    Shortly after arriving in 1788, the colony was moved to Sydney Cove.
    In Sydney, the water supply and soil were better.
    Although Sydney was the new site, for many years it was called Botany Bay.

4. Frederick Carl Frieseke was an American impressionist.

    In Normandy, he began to paint indoor settings.
    In 1905, Frieseke moved to Giverney where he lived until 1920.
    He studied with Whistler in the late 1800s.
    Born in Michigan, he went to Paris in 1897.
    In his later work, he began to use a darker palette.
    From Whistler, he learned the academic style of the salons.
    At Giverney, Frieseke was influenced by Monet.
    Monet was experimenting with the effects of sunlight.
    The style of Monet and his school is known as impressionism.
    By 1920, Frieseke had left Giverney for Normandy.

5. Two types of weathering will break down rock masses into smaller particles.

    Interaction between surface or ground water and chemicals causes chemical weathering.
    With increased precipitation or temperature, chemicals tend to break down faster.
    Mechanical weathering occurs when force and pressure grind rocks down.
    A common example is the wearing away of granite facades on buildings.
    The weathering of feldspar in granite can be caused by a reaction to acids in rain.
    Pressure from freezing and thawing causes rocks to expand and contract.
    When a rock is broken in two by physical forces, it is more vulnerable to weathering.

➤ Use abbreviations and symbols

Use abbreviations for important words and phrases that are repeated. There are two ways to do this. You can use capital letters that will remind you of the word or phrase. For example, in a lecture about Colonial America, you might use C M as an abbreviation for the phrase; in a lecture about the philosophy of John Dewey, you could use D as an abbreviation for the name. Or you can write the beginning of the word or phrase. For Colonial America, you could write Col Am; for John Dewey, J Dew. The abbreviation can be anything that will remind you of the word or phrase when you are reading your notes.

You should also use symbols and abbreviations for small words that are common in the language. The following list includes some of the most commonly used words in English. The abbreviations here are shortened forms for these frequently heard words.

+	and
w	with
w/o	without
=	is, are, means, refers to, like, is called
≠	different, not
#	number
X	times
→	results in, causes, produces, therefore
←	comes from, derives from
ex	example
@	at
1,2,3	first, second, third
<	less, smaller
>	more, larger
btw	between

Practical Strategy

The abbreviations in the list printed above are part of my system for taking notes and some of my students use it, but I encourage you to create your own system because you will probably come up with symbols and abbreviations that will have meaning to you, and you will understand them later when you are reading your notes. There is space for additional words. Be sure to choose something that makes sense to you.

Symbol	Word
	and
	with
	without
	is, are, means, refers to, like, is called
	different, not
	number
	times
	results in, causes, produces, therefore
	comes from, derives from
	example
	at
	first, second, third
	less, smaller
	more, larger
	between

PRACTICE ACTIVITY 2

Did you understand? Now practice taking notes with your system. These are sentences from college lectures. Take notes as quickly as you can. First, read each of the sentences and write your notes here. When you are finished taking notes for all ten sentences, compare your notes with the example notes in Chapter 7 on pages 383–384. Then try to write the original sentences using only your notes. Finally, compare your sentences with the original sentences printed in the answer key or on the next page. An example is shown using my system. Your answer is correct if *you* can read it and if the meaning is the same as the original sentence. The words do not have to be exactly the same.

Activity 2 audio is in the larger version of this book.

EXAMPLE

Friction between moving air and the ocean surface generates undulations of water called *waves*.

Short: Friction btw air + ocean surface → waves
Very short: Fric btw air + Ø surf → waves

Friction between air and the ocean surface causes *waves*.

1. The Ninteenth Amendment to the U.S. Constitution gave women the right to vote, beginning with the elections of 1920.

2. In a suspension bridge, there are two towers with one or more flexible cables attached at each end.

3. A perennial is any plant that continues to grow for more than two years, as for example, trees and shrubs.

4. Famous for innovations in punctuation, typography, and language, Edward Estin Cummings, known to us as e.e. cummings, published his collected poems in 1954.

5. Absolute zero, the temperature at which all substances have zero thermal energy, and thus the lowest possible temperatures, is unattainable in practice.

6. Because Columbus, Ohio, is considered a typical metropolitan area, it is often used for market research to test new products.

7. The cacao bean was cultivated by the Aztecs not only to drink but also as currency in their society.

8. The blue whale is the largest known animal, reaching a length of more than one hundred feet, which is five times its size at birth.

9. Ontario is the heartland of Canada, both geographically, and, I would say, historically as well.

10. Nuclear particles called hadrons, which include the proton and neutron, are made from quarks—very odd particles that have a slight electrical charge but that cannot exist alone in nature.

ADVISOR'S OFFICE

This advice from Dr. Charles Swindell is framed on the wall of my office near my computer so that I can see it every day. I am happy to share it with you.

The longer I live, the more I realize the impact of attitude on life. Attitude to me is more important than facts. It is more important than the past, than education, than money, than circumstances, than failures, than successes, than what other people think or say or do. It is more important than appearance, giftedness, or skill. The remarkable thing is, we have a choice every day regarding the attitude we embrace for that day. We cannot change our past. We cannot change the fact that people may act in a certain way. We cannot change the inevitable. The only thing we can do is play on the one string we have, and that is our attitude. I am convinced that life is 10 percent what happens to me and 90 percent how I react to it. And so it is with you. We are in charge of our attitudes.

Henry Ford said it another way: "If you think you can or you think you can't, you are probably right."

PARAPHRASING

Paraphrasing means using different words to express the same meaning. When you paraphrase, you express an idea that you have heard or read, but you say or write it in your own words. Because you are including all of the information when you paraphrase, the paraphrase is usually about the same length as the original. There are three problems that you will confront when you are paraphrasing.

1. **There is a natural tendency to repeat the same words instead of paraphrasing them.** This means that you need to listen and read for meaning instead of focusing on individual words and grammatical structures.
2. **Reference materials such as a thesaurus may not be used on the TOEFL.** This means that you have to know synonyms for words and phrases.
3. **Sometimes it is not possible to think of a paraphrase.** This means that you must learn how to give credit to sources when you use them in speaking or writing.

This chapter will help you improve your paraphrasing skills. You will learn how to

- **Edit problem paraphrases**
- **Mention the source appropriately**

How will these strategies help you on the TOEFL? By learning to paraphrase well, you will achieve a higher score on all four sections of the TOEFL. There are questions that require you to recognize or produce paraphrases on the Reading, Listening, Writing, and Speaking sections. Paraphrasing is a very important academic skill for success in college or university classes as well. Using someone else's words is called *plagiarizing.* Plagiarizing is a very serious offense and can result in your being expelled from school.

➤ Edit problem paraphrases

Paraphrases begin with sentences. Here are some problems that you can learn to avoid:

- Don't change the meaning
- Don't leave out information
- Don't use too much of the original wording
- Don't copy the original

Original Sentence:

Sometimes students plagiarize material from lectures and reading passages because they don't understand how to make the appropriate changes for an excellent paraphrase.

DON'T CHANGE THE MEANING

This is not an excellent paraphrase because the meaning has been changed from the original:

On occasion, students use paraphrases of excellent lectures and reading passages without understanding the purpose of the changes that they have made in them.

DON'T LEAVE OUT IMPORTANT INFORMATION

This is not an excellent paraphrase because it does not include all of the important information in the original:

On occasion, students use lecture and reading material verbatim.

Don't use too much of the original wording

This is not an excellent paraphrase because it looks and sounds too much like the original:

> On occasion, students plagiarize material from lectures and reading passages because they don't comprehend how to make the necessary changes for an excellent paraphrase.

Don't copy the original

This is not an excellent paraphrase because it is an exact copy of the original.

> Sometimes students plagiarize material from lectures and reading passages because they don't understand how to make the appropriate changes for an excellent paraphrase.

Practice Activity 3

Did you understand? Try to find the problem in each paraphrase and edit it. The first one is completed to give you an example. Example answers are printed in Chapter 7 on pages 384–386.

Example

Original:	Tides are caused by the gravitational pull of both the Sun and the Moon.
Paraphrase:	Tides are produced by the gravitational pull of both the Sun and the Moon.
Problem:	The paraphrase is too much like the original. Only one word was changed.
Edited Paraphrase:	The combined gravitational effects of the Sun and Moon produce tides on Earth.

Why is this better? Because synonyms have been substituted, and an alternative grammatical structure has been used, but the meaning has not changed.

1. Original: Proteins are molecules that regulate the movement of materials across cell walls.

   Paraphrase: Molecules that regulate the movement of materials across cell walls are proteins.

2. Original: The invention of the steam engine played a major role in the Industrial Revolution because it caused the factory system to extend itself to many areas of production apart from the cotton industry.

   Paraphrase: The invention of the steam engine was a primary influence in the Industrial Revolution.

3. Original: Although big companies are trying to maintain a balance between traditional advertising and some of the newer alternatives like blogging, it is often the smaller entrepreneurs who are using bloggers as an efficient way to stack their competition.

   Paraphrase: Big companies are using bloggers to defeat their smaller rivals.

4. Original: Fossils of bones have the appearance of stone, but the holes and pores are actually infused with mineral deposits from the surrounding sediments.

   Paraphrase: Fossils of bones look like stone, but there are mineral deposits from the surrounding sediments in the holes and pores.

5. Original: Pictograms found in many parts of the world about 1500 B.C. constitute the earliest system of writing, although written symbols have been discovered that date from as early as 3500 B.C.

   Paraphrase: Pictograms found in various parts of the world are the earliest evidence of a written system despite the discovery of written symbols.

6. Original: The modern atmosphere is probably the fourth atmosphere in the history of the Earth.

   Paraphrase: The modern atmosphere is probably the fourth atmosphere in the history of the Earth.

7. Original: Whereas alcohol is a depressant, coffee is a stimulant.

   Paraphrase: Alcohol is not like coffee.

8. Original: The Pacific Basin, which includes the continent of Australia and the thousands of islands grouped together as Oceania, covers one third of the surface of the Earth.

   Paraphrase: The Pacific Basin is also called Oceania because it encompasses one third of the Pacific Ocean.

9. Original: In fresco painting, the pigments may be mixed with water and applied to the plaster before it dries so that the lime in the plaster fuses with the pigments on the surface.

   Paraphrase: The lime in wet plaster bonds with the pigments on the surface when the colors are mixed.

10. Original: As Linnaeus originally conceived the biological classification chart, he segregated all living creatures solely according to their degree of physical similarity.

    Paraphrase: Linnaeus originally created the biological classification chart by categorizing all living creatures according to their degree of physical similarity.

➤ Mention the source appropriately

You already know how to introduce a source, but sometimes you need to mention the source more than one time. In that case, there is a pattern that is customarily used to mention the source appropriately.

PRACTICAL STRATEGY

When you cite the source the first time, use the first and last name. The title is optional. When you site the second time, use the last name only. If you cite a third time, use a pronoun, for example, *he* or *she*. After the third citation, you may use the pronoun again if the meaning is clear, or you may repeat the last name for clarity.

In the case of speakers or writers who are not named, the source should still be cited. You may be able to identify and cite the source as a professor, a speaker, an author, a writer, or a student, based on the context in which the information is presented. Use this general description the first time that you cite the source. If it is clear that the person is a man or woman, you can use the correct pronoun when you cite the source a second or third time. After the third citation, you may use the pronoun again if the meaning is clear, or you may repeat the general description for clarity.

PRACTICE ACTIVITY 4

Did you understand? Try to report the information in the notes. Cite the source appropriately. The first report is completed to give you an example. First read the notes, and then check each answer printed in Chapter 7 on pages 386–387.

EXAMPLE

Source: Edwin Hubble (man) astronomer

- demonstrated Andromeda nebula located outside our galaxy
- established the islands universe theory = galaxies exist outside our own
- study resulted in Hubble's constant = standard relationship/ galaxy's distance from Earth and speed recession

Astronomer Edwin Hubble demonstrated that the Andromeda nebula was located outside our galaxy. Hubble established the islands universe theory, which states that galaxies exist outside our own. He published a study that resulted in what is now called Hubble's constant, a standard relationship between a galaxy's distance from Earth and its speed of recession.

Activity 4 audio is in the larger version of this book.

1. Source: Theodore White (man)
   Book—*The Making of the President*

   • 1960 presidential debate—press conference
   • Nixon proceeded—personal debate
   • Kennedy spoke directly to TV viewers
   • estimated Kennedy gained 2 mil votes

2. Source: Paul Cezanne (man)

   • all forms in nature—based on geometric shapes
   • cone, sphere, cylinder primary
   • used outlining to emphasize shapes

3. Source: Marie Curie (woman)

   • won Nobel p physics 1903 w/husband—discovery of radium
   • won Nobel p chemistry 1911—isolation pure radium
   • 1st person 2 Nobel p

4. Source: Erik Erikson (man) psychologist

   • proposed eight stages/personal development
   • psychological crises/each stage shaped sense/self
   • lifelong process

5. Source: Margaret Mead (woman)

   • first fieldwork in Samoa 1925
   • book *Coming of Age in Samoa* best seller—translated many languages
   • still one/most well-known anthropologists
   • people/simple societies provide valuable lessons/industrialized

6. Source: Leonardo da Vinci (man)

- quintessential Renaissance man
- brilliant painter
- interested in mechanics
- work in math clear in perspective

7. Source: Peter Drucker (man) author
- *Management Challenges for the 21st Century*
- five transforming forces
- trends have major implications for long-term strategies of companies

8. Source: Freidrich Mohs (man)

- devised hardness scale/10 minerals
- assigned 10 to diamond—hardest known
- lesser values other min
- scale still useful/relative hardness

9. Source: Maria Montessori (woman)

- proposed educational model
- not transmission knowledge
- free to develop
- success child working independently

10. Source: Jane Goodall (woman)

- collaboration Louis Leaky
- years living w/chimpanzees—Gombe Reserve
- imitated behaviors
- discovered chimp complex social organization
- first document chimp making/using tools
- also identified 20 different sounds/communication

ADVISOR'S OFFICE

Do you talk to yourself? Of course you do. Maybe not aloud, but all of us have mental conversations with ourselves. So the question is *how* do you talk to yourself?

Negative Talk	_Positive Talk_
I can't study all of this.	I am studying every day.
My English is poor.	My English is improving.
I won't get a good score.	I will do my best.
If I fail, I will be so ashamed.	If I need a higher score, I can try again.

How would you talk to good friends to encourage and support them? Be a good friend to yourself. When negative talk comes to mind, substitute positive talk. Encourage yourself to learn from mistakes.

SUMMARIZING

Summarizing is related to paraphrasing because you are using your own words to express an idea that you have heard or read. Remember that when you paraphrase, you are including all of the information, but when you summarize, you are including only the main ideas. A paraphrase is about the same length as the original, but a summary is shorter than the original. There are three problems that you will confront when you are summarizing.

1. **A summary does not include everything in the original.** This means that you should not try to write too much.
2. **Details and examples that support the main points are usually not included in a summary.** This means that you have to be able to discriminate between the main points and the details or examples.
3. **The author's point of view must be maintained.** This means that you cannot express your opinion when you report the information.

This chapter will help you improve your summarizing skills. You will learn how to

- **Use the same organization as the original**
- **Retain the original emphasis**
- **Maintain an objective point of view**

How will these strategies help you on the TOEFL? By learning to summarize, you will be able to answer the questions that are worth the most points on the Reading section. There are also questions that require you to produce summaries on the Writing and Speaking sections. Moreover, research demonstrates that students who understand how to summarize and use this skill when they prepare for tests will be able to remember information better.

➤ Use the same organization as the original

A summary should retain the same organization as the original reading or lecture. For example, if the passage identifies three different types of evergreen trees, then the organization is classification. Your summary should also be organized to classify the three different types of trees. If the passage explains the cause of deforestation in Canada, then the organization of the passage is cause and effect. Your summary should also be organized to demonstrate cause and effect. If the passage explains the life cycle of a pine tree, then the organization is chronological. Your summary should also be organized in chronological order. It is also important NOT to rearrange the order. A good summary begins with the first major point and follows with each major point in the order that it appears in the original.

PRACTICAL STRATEGY

First, determine the organization of the reading or lecture. Then list the major points in the order in which you read or heard them. This list gives you an outline for your summary.

PRACTICE ACTIVITY 5

Did you understand? Put the major points in the order that they should appear in a summary. The answers are printed in Chapter 7 on page 388. Your answers are correct if they are in the same order as the original.

1. Reading

Although stage plays have been set to music since the era of the ancient Greeks when the dramas of Sophocles and Aeschylus were accompanied by lyres and flutes, the usually accepted date for the beginning of opera as we know it is 1600. As part of the celebration of the marriage of King Henry IV of France to the Italian aristocrat Maria de Medici, the Florentine composer Jacopo Peri produced his famous *Euridice*, generally considered to be the first opera. Following his example, a group of Italian musicians, poets, and noblemen called the Camerata revived the style of musical story that had been used in Greek tragedy. Taking most of the plots for their operas from Greek and Roman history and mythology, they began the process of creating an opera by writing a libretto or drama that could be used to establish the framework for the music. They called their compositions *opera in musica* or musical works. It is from this phrase that the word *opera* was borrowed and abbreviated.

For several years, the center of opera was Florence in northern Italy, but gradually, during the baroque period, it spread throughout Italy. By the late 1600s, operas were being written and performed in many places throughout Europe, especially in England, France, and Germany. However, for many years, the Italian opera was considered the ideal, and many non-Italian composers continued to use Italian librettos. The European form de-emphasized the dramatic aspect of the Italian model, however, introducing new orchestral effects and even some ballet.

Furthermore, composers acquiesced to the demands of singers, writing many operas that were little more than a succession of brilliant tricks for the voice, designed to showcase the splendid vocal talent of the singers who had requested them. It was thus that complicated arias, recitatives, and duets evolved. The aria, which is a long solo, may be compared to a song in which the characters express their thoughts and feelings. The recitative, which is also a solo of sorts, is a recitation set to music, the purpose of which is to continue the story line. The duet is a musical piece written for two voices, a musical device that may serve the function of either an aria or a recitative within the opera.

Major Points

ⓐ Three types of musical pieces in opera
ⓑ The first opera in Italy
ⓒ The growth of opera throughout Europe

2. Lecture Script

Read part of a lecture in a biology class. Then put the major points in the same order as the lecture.

 Activity 5 audio is in the larger version of this book.

The protozoans, minute aquatic creatures, each of which consists of a single cell of protoplasm, constitute a classification of the most primitive forms of animal life. The very name protozoan indicates the scientific understanding of the animals. *Proto* means "first" or "primitive" and *zoa* refers to the animal.

They are fantastically diverse, but three major groups may be identified on the basis of their motility. The Mastigophora have one or more long tails that they use to propel themselves forward. The Ciliata, which use the same basic means for locomotion as the Mastigophora, have a larger number of short tails. The Sarcodina, which include amoebae, float or row themselves about on their crusted bodies.

In addition to their form of movement, several other features discriminate among the three groups of protozoans. For example, at least two nuclei per cell have been identified in the Ciliata, usually a large nucleus that regulates growth but decomposes during reproduction, and a smaller one that contains the genetic code necessary to generate the large nucleus.

So all of this seems very straightforward to this point, but now we are going to complicate the picture. Chlorophyll, which is the green substance in plants, is also found in the bodies of some protozoans, enabling them to make at least some of their own food from water and carbon dioxide. Sounds like photosynthesis, doesn't it? But protozoans are animals, right? And plants are the life forms that use photosynthesis. Okay. Well protozoans are not considered plants because, unlike pigmented plants to which some protozoans are otherwise almost identical, they do not live on simple organic compounds. Their cells demonstrate all of the major characteristics of the cells of higher animals, such as eating, breathing, and reproducing.

Now many species of protozoans collect into colonies, physically connected to one another and responding uniformly to outside stimuli. Current research into this phenomenon along with investigations carried out with advanced microscopes may necessitate a redefinition of what constitutes protozoans, even calling into question the basic premise that they have only one cell. Nevertheless, with the current data available, almost 40,000 species of protozoans have been identified. No doubt, as technology improves methods of observation, better models of classification of these simple single cells will be proposed.

Major Points

Ⓐ A method of classification for protozoans—the three types motility

Ⓑ Current research—questions, redefinitions

Ⓒ Similarity to plants—make food from water/CO_2

Ⓓ A definition of protozoans—single cell

Ⓔ Considered animals—eating, breathing, reproducing

➤ Retain the original emphasis

The emphasis should be the same in both the original and the summary. For example, a passage about the three different types of leaves may include all three types, but it may dedicate half of the passage to one type—palmate leaves. In this case, your summary should retain the same emphasis by dedicating half of the summary to palmate leaves.

PRACTICAL STRATEGY

When you read, think in terms of space. How much space does the author devote to each point? When you listen, think in terms of time. How much time does the speaker devote to each point? When you do this, you are determining the emphasis for each point in the original, and you will know how much emphasis to give to these points in your summary.

PRACTICE ACTIVITY 6

Did you understand? Try to identify the emphasis for each part of the original and assign percentages. Then write a summary that retains the original emphasis. The answers and example summaries are printed in Chapter 7 on pages 388–389.

1. Reading

The Federal Reserve System, commonly called the Fed, is an independent agency of the United States government charged with overseeing the national banking system. Since 1913, the Federal Reserve System has served as the central bank for the United States. The Fed's primary function is to control monetary policy by influencing the cost and availability of money and credit through the purchase and sale of government securities. If the Federal Reserve provides too little money, interest rates tend to be high, borrowing is expensive, business activity slows down, unemployment goes up, and the danger of a recession is augmented. On the other hand, if there is too much money, interest rates decline, and borrowing can lead to excess demand, pushing up prices and fueling inflation. In addition to controlling the money supply, the Fed has several other responsibilities. In collaboration with the U.S. Department of the Treasury, the Fed puts new coins and paper currency into circulation by issuing them to banks. It also supervises the activities of member banks abroad and regulates certain aspects of international finance.

The Federal Reserve System consists of twelve district reserve banks and their branch offices along with several committees and councils. All national commercial banks are required by law to be members of the Fed, and all deposit-taking institutions like credit unions are subject to regulation by the Fed regarding the amount of deposited funds that must be held in reserve and that, by definition, therefore, are not available for loans. The most powerful body is the seven-member board of governors in Washington, appointed by the President and confirmed by the Senate. Although it is true that the Federal Reserve does not depend on Congress for budget allocations, and therefore is free from the partisan politics that influence most of the other governmental bodies, it is still responsible for frequent reports to the Congress on the conduct of monetary policies.

In many ways, the Federal Reserve is like a fourth branch of the United States government because it is composed of national policy makers. However, in practice, the Fed does not stray from the financial policies established by the executive branch of the government.

Major Points

- The function and responsibilities of the Fed
- The composition of the Fed
- A comparison of the Fed to a fourth branch of government

2. Lecture Script

Read part of a lecture in a psychology class. Then assign a percentage to each of the major points from the lecture and write a summary using the percentages to determine how much to write on each point.

 Activity 6 audio is in the larger version of this book.

Okay then, let's talk about human memory, which was formerly believed to be rather inefficient as compared with, for example, computers. But we are finding that we probably have a much more sophisticated mechanism than we had originally assumed. Researchers approaching the problem from a variety of points of view have all concluded that there is a great deal more stored in our minds than has been generally supposed. Here's what I mean—Dr. Wilder Penfield, a Canadian neurosurgeon, proved that by stimulating their brains electrically, he could elicit the total recall of complex events in his subjects' lives. Even dreams and other minor events supposedly forgotten for many years suddenly emerged in detail.

The *memory trace* is the term for whatever forms the internal representation of the specific information about an event stored in the memory. So, the trace is probably made by structural changes in the brain, but the problem is that the memory trace isn't really subject to direct observation because it's . . . it's . . . more a theoretical construct that we use to speculate about how information presented at a particular time can cause performance at a later time. So most theories include the strength of the memory trace as a variable in the degree of learning, retention, and retrieval possible for a memory. One theory is that the fantastic capacity for storage in the brain is the result of an almost unlimited combination of interconnections between brain cells, stimulated by patterns of activity. And repeated references to the same information supports recall. Or, to say that another way, improved performance is the result of strengthening the chemical bonds in the memory.

Now here's the interesting part. Psychologists generally divide memory into at least two types—short-term memory and long-term memory, which combine to form what we call *working memory*. Short-term memory contains what we are actively focusing on at any particular time but items are not retained longer than twenty or thirty seconds without verbal rehearsal. We use short-term memory when we look up a telephone number and repeat it to ourselves until we can place the call. In contrast, long-term memory can store facts, concepts, and experiences after we stop thinking about them. All conscious processing of information, as in problem solving, for example, involves both short-term and long-term memory. As we repeat, rehearse, and recycle information, the memory trace is strengthened, allowing that information to move from short-term memory to long-term memory.

Major Points

- The level of sophistication for human memory
- The memory trace
- Working memory

➤ Maintain an objective point of view

An objective point of view is a neutral position. A summary is not an analysis or a commentary. A summary does not invite an opinion.

PRACTICAL STRATEGY

In your summary, you should not agree or disagree with the author's or the speaker's ideas. Don't make judgments. Don't add information. When you report, you should not include *your* opinions or comments. The conclusion should be the author's or the speaker's conclusion, not yours.

PRACTICE ACTIVITY 7

Did you understand? Try to find the opinions in the summary and delete them. Use the original reading to compare the content. The answers are printed in Chapter 7 on pages 389–390.

1. Reading

Charles Ives, who is now acclaimed as the first great American composer of the twentieth century, had to wait many years for the public recognition he deserved. Born to music as the son of a band-master, Ives played drums in his father's community band and organ at the local church. He entered Yale University at twenty to study musical composition with Horatio Parker, but after graduation he chose not to pursue a career in music. He suspected correctly that the public would not accept the music he wrote because Ives did not follow the musical fashion of his times. While his contemporaries wrote lyrical songs, Ives transfigured music and musical form. He quoted, combined, insinuated, and distorted familiar hymns, marches, and battle songs, while experimenting with the effects of polytonality, or the simultaneous use of keys with conflicting rhythms and time. Even when he could convince some musicians to show some interest in his compositions, after assessing them conductors and performers said that they were essentially unplayable.

Ives turned his attention to business. He became a successful insurance executive, building his company into the largest agency in the country in only two decades. Although he occasionally hired musicians to play one of his works privately for him, he usually heard his music only in his imagination. After he recovered from a serious heart attack, he became reconciled to the fact that his ideas, especially the use of dissonance and special effects, were just too different for the musical mainstream to accept. Determined to share his music with the few people who might appreciate it, he published his work privately and distributed it free.

In 1939, when Ives was sixty-five, American pianist John Kirkpatrick played *Concord Sonata* in Town Hall. The reviews were laudatory. One reviewer proclaimed it "the greatest music composed by an American." By 1947, Ives was famous. His *Second Symphony* was presented to the public in a performance by the New York Philharmonic, fifty years after it had been written. The same year, Ives received the Pulitzer Prize. He was seventy-three.

Summary

Charles Ives started his musical career as a member of his father's band and received a degree from Yale University in music, but he became a businessman instead because he was afraid that his music would not be well accepted. His music was very different from the popular songs of his era because he used small phrases from well-known music with unusual rhythms and tones. Fifty years after he wrote his *Second Symphony*, it was performed by the New York Philharmonic, and he was awarded the Pulitzer Prize.

I think that Charles Ives was wrong not to pursue his musical career from the beginning. If he had continued writing music instead of selling insurance, we would have more pieces now.

2. Lecture Script

Read part of a lecture in a geology class. Then delete the opinions from the summary.

 Activity 7 audio is in the larger version of this book.

A geyser is the result of underground water under the combined conditions of high temperatures and increased pressure beneath the surface of the Earth. Now, temperature rises about maybe 1 degree Fahrenheit for every 60 feet under the Earth's surface, and we know that pressure also increases with depth, water that seeps down in cracks and fissures, so when the water, uh, when the water reaches very hot rocks in the Earth's interior, it becomes heated to the temperature of, let's say, 290 degrees.

Okay, then, water under pressure can remain liquid at temperatures above the normal boiling point, but in a geyser, the weight of the water nearer the surface exerts so much pressure on the deeper water that the water at the bottom of the geyser reaches much higher temperatures than the water at the top. And as the deep water becomes hotter, and consequently lighter, it suddenly rises to the surface and shoots out of the ground in the form of steam and hot water. In turn, the explosion agitates all of the water in the geyser reservoir, and what do you think happens then? More explosions. So immediately afterward, the water goes back into the underground reservoir, it starts to heat up again, and the whole process repeats itself.

So, in order to function, then, a geyser must have a source of heat, a reservoir where water can be stored until the temperature rises to an unstable point, an opening through which the hot water and steam can escape, and underground channels for resupplying water after an eruption.

Now, favorable conditions for geysers exist in regions of geologically recent volcanic activity, especially in areas of more than average precipitation. For the most part, geysers are located in three regions of the world—New Zealand, Iceland, and the Yellowstone park area of the United States. I'd say that the most famous geyser in the world is Old Faithful in Yellowstone. It erupts every hour, rising to a height of 125 to 170 feet and expelling more than ten thousand gallons of hot water during each eruption. Old Faithful earned its name, because, un- unlike most geysers, it has never failed to erupt on schedule even once in eighty years of observation.

Summary

In my opinion, geysers are interesting. They happen when under-ground water gets hot and pressure from above causes the water to get hotter and lighter so it goes up to the surface and explodes out. Then, the water runs back into the ground and starts all over again. Geysers have to have heat, a place to store water, an opening where the water can shoot up, and cracks in the ground for the water to go back down into a pool. Geysers are in New Zealand, Iceland, and the United States. Old Faithful in Yellowstone is the most famous geyser, but the best place to see geysers is in New Zealand. I saw the Pohutu Geyser there on my vacation two years ago, and it was awesome.

ADVISOR'S OFFICE

Why are you preparing for the TOEFL? What goal is moti-vating you to study and improve your score? Do you want to attend a university in an English-speaking country? Do you want to try for a scholarship from a sponsor in your country or region? Is the TOEFL required for graduation from your high school? Do you plan to apply for an assist-antship at a graduate school? Do you need the score for a professional license?

Goals can be experienced as mental images. You can close your eyes and imagine everything, just like a movie. See yourself achieving your goal. Watch yourself as you attend school or practice your profession in your ideal environment. See other people congratulating you. Enjoy the success.

Understand that you cannot control reality with visualization. However, it does change your attitude, it helps you to focus, provides motivation, and reduces stress. Positive visualiza-tion is an excellent way to take a short break from studying.

SYNTHESIZING

Synthesizing means to combine two or more sources in order to create something new. It is probably the most complex academic skill because it includes all of the other academic skills that you have studied—taking notes, paraphrasing, and summarizing. In addition, the result of a synthesis should be more than the sum of the parts. There are three problems that you will confront when you are synthesizing.

1. **The relationship between the sources may not be obvious**. This means that you may have to figure out the connection.
2. **One source appears to contain all of the necessary information**. This means that you need to be sure to balance the information so that all of the sources are used.
3. **Synthesis requires a high level of thinking**. This means that you should have a plan in order to create a synthesis.

This chapter will help you improve your synthesizing. You will learn how to

- **Summarize the primary source**
- **Use transition sentences**
- **Include the secondary source**
- **Practice using a procedure**

How will these strategies help you on the TOEFL? By learning to synthesize information from readings and lectures, you will develop ways of thinking that will help you prepare important integrated speaking and writing questions. The ability to synthesize is also required for success in making presentations and writing research papers for college or university classes.

➤ Summarize the primary source

You will often be asked to summarize the main points in the primary source and then relate the secondary source to it. Even if you are not asked to summarize the primary source, you should still begin by using your notes from the primary source.

PRACTICAL STRATEGY

After you have taken notes on both sources, direct your attention to the notes for the primary source. If the directions for your assignment or the question for your test instruct you to summarize the primary source, begin with a summary, using your notes.

PRACTICE ACTIVITY 8

Using the notes from the primary source, write a summary. Do not use the notes from the secondary source in the summary. Compare your summary with the example summary printed in Chapter 7 on pages 390–391.

Reading

Marsupials are a group of mammals that are born alive after a very short gestation period. Since a marsupial appears quite early in its life cycle, it must complete its embryonic development while nursing. In order to survive, the young underdeveloped marsupial must crawl from the exit of the reproductive tract over its mother's body to attach itself to a nipple inside a fold of skin called the *marsupium* but better known as a pouch. During embryonic development, which can be weeks or months, depending on the species, a marsupial nurses and grows inside the pouch. Most marsupials do not form family groups. It is the female marsupial that cares for the offspring. The young marsupial may stay with the mother for more than a year, climbing in and out of the pouch to nurse or sleep.

Although marsupials once ranged throughout North and South America, as well as in Antarctica, only a few species now live outside of New Zealand and Australia where more than 250 species are still found. There is quite a diversity of marsupials within these species, and they have adapted to a number of different habitats; however, some characteristics are universal among them. Auditory and olfactory senses are very important to marsupials because they are nocturnal creatures that depend on their ears and eyes to locate their food at night. Some marsupials prefer plants, although others eat insects or meat. Like other mammals, marsupials are covered with hair. Unlike their placental cousins, however, marsupials have additional bones that project from the pelvis, a support that may strengthen the wall of the abdomen to reinforce the pouch that is their unique adaptation.

Notes for Reading—Primary Source

- marsupials = mammals
- short gestation
    - completes embryonic development nursing
    - reproductive tract → marsupium/pouch w/nipple
- no family groups
    - mother 1 yr +
- once NA, SA, Antarc
    - now few outside NZ + Aust 250 species+
- diversity habitats
- universal characteristics
    - nocturnal
    - smell, hearing important
    - hair
    - additional bones project pelvis, reinforce pouch

Lecture Script

 Activity 8. Read part of a lecture in a biology class.

People call it a bear, but the koala is really a marsupial. So, it is much more like a kangaroo than it is like a bear. Here's what I mean. First, the koala has a gestation period of only about 35 days before it is born. Then a tiny pink, furless creature about 19 millimeters long makes its way from the birth canal into the mother's pouch where it attaches itself to one of two nipples. So it stays in the pouch to complete it's development, and six to seven months later, it pokes its head out and explores a short distance from the mother, jumping back into the pouch until it reaches eight months when it is too big to fit, and for another four months it rides on the mother's back or hangs from her stomach until it finally becomes independent at about one year old. By then, it is about the same size as a Teddy Bear and looks remarkably like one, with a furry coat, rounded ears and a large nose to support its keen senses of smell and hearing. Native to Australia, the koala lives in trees and is a skillful climber. It sleeps in the branches during the day, and at night, it combs the trees for its favorite meal—eucalyptus leaves.

Notes for Lecture—Secondary Source

- koala = marsupial ∅ bear
- gestation 35 d
- pink/no fur
- 19 mm
- birth canal → pouch/1 of 2 nipples
- 6–7 mo develop/explore
- 8 mo too big for pouch
- 4+ mo rides back/stomach
- 1 yr independent
- Teddy Bear = size, fur, round ears/large nose
- keen hearing, smell
- sleeps trees day
- combs eucalyptus leaves night

➤ Use transition sentences

Transition sentences are very useful in a synthesis. They can be used to connect information from the primary source with information from the secondary source. Transition sentences show the specific relationship between the two sources.

PRACTICAL STRATEGY

Learning some patterns for forming transitional sentences can be helpful. The charts below are examples for you to study.

Extension/Agreement

Primary Source	*Secondary Source*
Theory	**Research Study**
A research study on_____	was carried out _____.
	According to _____,

A research study on flow was carried out at Harvard University. According to the study, . . .

Definition	Example

An example of _____   is_____.
                          According to _____,

An example of a familiar opera is "Carmen." According to the lecturer, "Carmen . . . "

Case study	Concept

_____ is a case study of   _____.
                              According to _____,

The Toyota company's campaign in the United States is a case study of advertising products abroad. According to the lecturer, Toyota . . .

Cause	Effect

_____ may have caused   _____.
                           According to _____,

The impact of a large meteor on Earth may have caused the disappearance of dinosaurs. According to the lecturer, the meteor . . .

Solution	Problem

_____ may offer a solution for   _____.
                                    According to _____,

European noise ordinances may offer a solution for the problem of noise pollution in a technological society. According to the lecturer, . . .

Opinion	Opposing Opinion

_____. However, a case may be made for the opposing view. According to_____,

. . . the view that nuclear power plants are dangerous. However, a case may be made for the opposing view. According to the lecturer, . . .

Advantages	Disadvantages

_____. On the other hand, several disadvantages were mentioned _____.

. . . is also an advantage of cooperative learning. On the other hand, several disadvantages were mentioned in the lecture. First, . . .

Idea	Comparison

_____. In comparison, _____. According to_____,

. . . theoretical linguistics. In comparison, applied linguistics answers practical questions. According to the reading, an applied linguist . . .

➤ Include the secondary source

A synthesis is not complete unless information from the secondary source is included.

PRACTICAL STRATEGY

Proofread your synthesis. Look for information from both the primary source and the secondary source.

PRACTICE ACTIVITY 9

Use the information about the primary source and the secondary source to write transition sentences that will connect them. Compare your answers with the example answers printed in Chapter 7 on page 391. Your answers may be slightly different, but you should see the same patterns that you find in the examples.

EXAMPLE

Primary source: Reading
The advantage of observation is the natural setting.
Secondary source: Lecture
The disadvantage of observation is the potential for the researcher to be biased.
Transition sentence to connect advantages with disadvantages.

The advantage of observation is the natural setting. On the other hand, several disadvantages were mentioned in the lecture. First, there is the potential for the researcher to be biased.

1. Primary source: Reading
   A biogeographic realm is a land mass.
   Secondary source: Lecture
   A biome is a major regional ecosystem.
   Transition sentence to connect one concept with another concept in a comparison.

2. Primary source: Reading
   Innovations in industrial production in the 19th century
   Secondary source: Lecture
   Henry Ford's assembly line
   Transition sentence to connect a concept with an example.

3. Primary source: Lecture
   Advantages of stone for sculpture
   Secondary source: Reading
   Disadvantages of stone for sculpture
   Transition sentence to connect the advantages with the disadvantages.

4. Primary source: Reading
    Horticultural societies grow crops using hand tools.
    Secondary source: Lecture
    Agrarian societies cultivate crops with draft animals and plows.
    Transition sentence to connect one concept with another in a contrast.

5. Primary source: Reading
    Changes in the climate of the North American coastline.
    Secondary source: Lecture
    El Nino
    Transition sentence to connect a cause (El Nino) with an effect (changes in climate).

6. Primary source: Reading
    Franchises
    Secondary source: Lecture
    Kentucky Fried Chicken chain
    Transition sentence to connect a business concept with a case study of a restaurant franchise.

7. Primary source: Reading
    Risks for heart problems
    Secondary source: Lecture
    Research on Type A and Type B personalities
    Transition sentence to connect a concept with a research study.

8. Primary source: Lecture
    The United States should convert to metrics.
    Secondary source: Reading
    The United States should retain the English system.
    Transition sentence to connect one opinion with an opposing opinion.

9. Primary source: Reading
    South Africa's natural resources
    Secondary source: Lecture
    Gold minlng
    Transition sentence to connect a concept with an example.

10. Primary source: Reading
    Commuting to work
    Secondary source: Lecture
    Home offices
    Transition sentence to connect a problem (commuting) with a
    solution (home offices).

➤ Practice using a procedure

In order to accomplish a complex task, it helps to have a procedure.
The first step in using a new procedure is putting the steps in order
and learning them.

PRACTICAL STRATEGY

Tell yourself what you are going to do to create a synthesis of two
sources.

Read the passage and take notes.
Listen to the lecture and take notes.
Plan and write a synthesis.

   1. Summarize the primary source.
   2. Create a transition sentence to connect the primary source
      with the secondary source.
   3. Summarize the secondary source while making references to
      the primary source.

PRACTICE ACTIVITY 10

Use the procedure to write a synthesis of a reading and a lecture.
Take as much time as you need to complete the synthesis. Write
150–225 words. Compare your synthesis with the example answer in
Chapter 7 on page 392.

Reading

The *Out of Africa hypothesis*, also called the *replacement hypothesis*, contends that modern humans originated in Africa, probably from a common ancestor. From there, they migrated to other regions, eventually replacing the populations of Neanderthals and other groups of earlier humans that may have survived.

Geneticists who support the *replacement hypothesis* argue that the similarities shared by all of the modern human populations confirm the existence of a common gene pool, and perhaps even one common female ancestor. They point to the fact that many modern human traits have evolved within the past 200,000 years as evidence of the replacement hypothesis. Furthermore, they cite studies of DNA in cell structures called mitochondria, which codes most of the inherited traits from ancestors. Most of these studies demonstrate that the diversity among human populations is very small as compared with other species. They conclude that there was only one small population from which all other populations descended. From their point of view, the evidence supports the theory that modern humans migrated from a relatively small area in Africa almost 150,000 years ago, moving along a route through the Middle East 100,000 years ago, and slowly populating regions throughout the world by displacing the communities of less developed humanlike species that they encountered.

Paleoanthropologists concede that, to date, the oldest fossil remains of modern *Homo sapiens* have been found in Africa, with the next oldest discovered in the Middle East. European fossils are dated at about 50,000 years after the African fossils. Thus, it would appear that the *replacement hypothesis* is substantiated by archaeological evidence.

Lecture Script

Now that you have read the explanation of human migration patterns in the reading, read part of a lecture on a similar topic.

Activity 10

Okay, today I want to talk to you about a hypothesis that explains where humans might have evolved and how they might have migrated around the world. It's an alternative hypothesis to the *replacement hypothesis* that you read about earlier. It's called the *multiregional hypothesis* but I've also heard it referred to as the *continuity hypothesis*. Now, according to the scientists who support this view, modern humans spread throughout Eurasia about a million years ago and regional populations retained some unique anatomical features for hundreds of thousands of years, but they also exchanged some inherited traits with neighboring populations when they mated with them. And we call this exchange of traits *gene flow*.

So through this gene flow, certain characteristics that we consider crucial to modern mankind were inherited, as, for example, an increase in brain size with an accompanying change in the skull. And . . . and this gene flow resulted in the evolution of the early humans whose remains are found throughout Europe and Asia as well as Africa.

Now, scientists who support this theory contend that the populations that migrated were linked by gene flow so that the features that all people have in common spread throughout the world. The relatively slight differences among modern people would have been caused by hundreds of thousands of years of regional evolution. But actually, researchers who support the *continuity hypothesis* tend to focus on the genetic similarities among human populations world-wide, not the differences. We're really amazingly similar as a species. And the fossils of archaic and modern humans in some regions do suggest a continuous evolution in regional traits, like the cheekbone structure, for example, which is further evidence that modern humans may have evolved over a broad area among multiple groups of human ancestors.

Synthesis

Summarize the major points in the reading and explain how the lecturer casts doubt on those points.

ADVISOR'S OFFICE

Perspective means "the way you view experiences." Have you heard the story about the teacup? Two people sit down at a table. There is only enough tea for one cup so they each have half a cup of tea to drink. One person looks at the cup and says, "Oh my, the cup is half empty." The other person looks at the cup and says, "Oh, look, the cup is half full." Which kind of person are you?

At this point in your review, it is easy to become discouraged. However, if you choose the "half full" perspective, you will have more energy to continue your studies. Yes, there is certainly a lot to review. If you understand half of the strategies, you have a choice. You can say, "Oh my, I know only half of this." Instead, you can say, "Oh look, I already know half of this!" You choose.

My advice is *believe in yourself*. Don't look at the long distance you have yet to travel. Celebrate the long distance that you have already traveled. Then you will have the energy and the courage to keep going.

4

REVIEW OF TOEFL® iBT SECTIONS

READING

OVERVIEW OF THE READING SECTION

The Reading section tests your ability to understand reading passages like those in college textbooks. The passages are about 700 words in length.

There are two formats for the Reading section. On the short format, you will respond to three passages. On the long format, you will respond to five passages. After each passage, you will answer 12–14 questions about it. Only three passages will be graded. The other passages are part of an experimental section for future tests. Because you will not know which passages will be graded, you must try to do your best on all of them.

Most questions are worth one point, but the last question in each passage is worth more than one point.

You will have 60 minutes to read all of the passages and answer the questions on the short format and 100 minutes to read all of the passages and answer the questions on the long format. You may take notes while you read, but notes are not graded. You may use your notes to answer the questions. Some passages may include a word or phrase that is underlined in blue. Click on the word or phrase to see a glossary definition or explanation.

Choose the best answer for multiple-choice questions. Follow the directions on the page or on the screen for computer-assisted questions. Click on **Next** to go to the next question. Click on **Back** to return to the previous question. You may return to previous questions for all of the passages in the same reading part, but after you go to the next part, you may not return to passages in a previous part. Be sure that you have answered all of the questions for the passages in each part before you click on **Next** at the end of the passage to move to the next part.

You can click on **Review** to see a chart of the questions you have answered and the questions you have not answered in each part. From this screen, you can return to the question you want to answer in the part that is open.

A clock on the screen will show you how much time you have to complete the Reading section.

REVIEW OF PROBLEMS FOR THE READING SECTION

➤ Prompts

A prompt for the Reading section is usually a passage from an undergraduate college textbook in one of the natural sciences, social sciences, humanities, or arts. The length of the passage is from 650 to 800 words. If there are technical words, they are explained in a glossary after the passage. There are either three or five prompts in the Reading section with twelve to fourteen questions after each prompt. When you are presented with three prompts, all three will be graded. When you are presented with five prompts, only three will be graded, and two will be used for experimental purposes. You should do your best on all five prompts because you will not know which of them will be graded. Problems 1–14 in this review refer to the following prompt:

"Producers, Consumers, and Decomposers"

→ Organisms that are capable of using carbon dioxide as their sole source of carbon are called *autotrophs* (self-feeders), or **producers**. These are the plants. They chemically fix carbon through photosynthesis. Organisms that depend on producers as their carbon source are called *heterotrophs* (feed on others), or **consumers**. Generally, these are animals. From the producers, which manufacture their own food, energy flows through the system along a circuit called the **food chain**, reaching consumers and eventually *decomposers.* Ecosystems generally are structured in a **food web**, a complex network of interconnected food chains, comprising both strong interactions and weak interactions between species in the food web.

Primary consumers feed on producers. Ⓐ Because producers are always plants, the primary consumer is called an **herbivore**, or plant eater. A **carnivore** is a secondary consumer and primarily eats meat. Ⓑ A consumer that feeds on both producers (plants) and consumers (meat) is called an **omnivore**. Ⓒ

Decomposers are the final link in the chain. They renew the entire system by releasing inorganic materials from organic debris. Ⓓ **Decomposers** are bacteria and fungi that digest and recycle the organic debris and waste in the environment. In addition, the *detritus feeders*—worms, mites, termites, centipedes, and others—participate like a small army of workers. Waste products, dead plants and animals, and other organic remains are the principal food source for all these *detritivores.* Inorganic compounds are released in the process and the cycle continues.

→ An example of a complex community is the oceanic food web that includes krill, a primary consumer. *Krill* is a shrimplike crustacean that is a major food for an interrelated group of organisms, including whales, fish, seabirds, seals, and squid in the Antarctic region. All of these organisms participate in numerous other food chains as well, some consuming and some being consumed. _Phytoplankton_ begin this chain by harvesting solar energy in photosynthesis. Phyto-plankton are eaten by _herbivorous zooplankton_ such as krill and other organisms. Krill are eaten by con-sumers at the next <u>trophic level</u>. Because krill are a protein-rich, plentiful food, increasingly factory ships seek them out, such as those from Japan and Russia. The annual krill harvest currently surpasses a million tons, principally as feed for chickens and livestock and as protein for human consumption.

Efficiency in a Food Web

Any assessment of world food resources depends on the level of consumer being targeted. Let us use humans as an example. Many people can be fed if wheat is eaten directly. However, if the grain is first fed to cattle (herbivores) and then we eat the beef, the yield of available food energy is cut by 90% (810 kg of grain is reduced to 82 kg of meat); far fewer people can be fed from the same land area.

In terms of energy, only about 10% of the kilocalo-ries (food calories, not heat calories) in plant matter survive from the primary to the secondary trophic level. When humans consume meat instead of grain, there is a further loss of biomass and added inefficiency. More energy is lost to the environment at each progressive step in the food chain. You can see that an omnivorous diet such as ours is quite expensive in terms of bio-mass and energy.

→ Food web concepts are becoming politicized as world food issues grow more critical. Today, approxi-mately half of the cultivated acreage in the United States and Canada is planted for animal consump-tion—beef and dairy cattle, hogs, chickens, and turkeys. Livestock feed includes approximately 80% of the annual corn and nonexported soybean harvest. In addition, some lands cleared of rain forest in Central and South America were converted to pasture to produce beef for export to restaurants, stores, and fast-food outlets in developed countries. Thus, lifestyle decisions and dietary patterns in North America and Europe are perpetuating inefficient food webs, not to mention the destruction of valuable resources, both here and overseas.

Clearly, some food webs are exceptionally simple, such as eating grains directly, whereas others are more complex. The home gardener's tomatoes may be eaten by a tomato hornworm, which is then plucked off by a passing Robin, which is later eaten by a hawk—and so it goes, in endless cycles.

Glossary
phytoplankton: a plant that lives in the sea and produces its own energy source
trophic level: category measured in steps away from the energy input in an ecosystem

➤ Problems

The problems in this review represent the types of questions that are most frequently tested on the TOEFL. They will appear randomly after a reading passage. Directions will appear with the questions, but if you already recognize the type of problem in the question presented, and you are familiar with the directions, you will save time. The less time you have to spend reading directions, the more time you will have to read the passages and answer the questions. The number of points assigned to each problem is based on the evaluation system for the TOEFL. The frequency level for each problem is based on the average number of thirty-nine questions that are usually included in a Reading section of three prompts.

Average	1–2
High	3–4
Very high	5+

PROBLEM 1: TRUE-FALSE

A *True-False* problem asks you to identify the true statement.
Choose from four sentences.
Points—1
Frequency Level—Average

1. According to paragraph 1, which of the following is true about autotrophs?

● They use a chemical process to produce their own food.
Ⓑ They require plant matter in order to survive.
ⓒ They need producers to provide them with carbon.
Ⓓ They do not interact with other organisms in the food chain.

Paragraph 1 is marked with an arrow [➔].

PROBLEM 2: VOCABULARY

A *Vocabulary* problem asks you to choose a general synonym.
Choose from four words or phrases.
Points—1
Frequency Level—Very high

2. The word <u>sole</u> in the passage is closest in meaning to

Ⓐ major
Ⓑ steady
● only
Ⓓ ideal

PROBLEM 3: TERMS

A *Terms* problem asks you to explain a word that is specific to the reading passage.
Choose from four definitions.
Points—1
Frequency Level—Average

3. Based on the information in paragraph 1, which of the following best explains the term "food web"?

Ⓐ Energy manufactured by producer organisms in the food chain

Ⓑ Another term that defines the food chain

● An interactive system of food chains

Ⓓ Primary and secondary consumers in the food chain

Paragraph 1 is marked with an arrow [➔].

PROBLEM 4: INFERENCE

An *Inference* problem asks you to draw a conclusion based on information in the passage. Choose from four possibilities.
Points—1
Frequency Level— Very High

4. It may be concluded that human beings are omnivores because

Ⓐ people feed on producers for the most part

Ⓑ people are usually tertiary consumers

● people generally eat both producers and consumers

Ⓓ most people are the top carnivores in the food chain

PROBLEM 5: PURPOSE

A *Purpose* problem asks you to understand why the author organizes a passage or explains a concept in a specific way.
Choose from four reasons.
Points—1
Frequency Level—Average

5. Why does the author mention krill in paragraph 4?

Ⓐ To suggest a solution for a problem in the food chain

Ⓑ To provide evidence that contradicts previously stated opinions

Ⓒ To present an explanation for the killing of krill

● To give an example of a complex food web

Paragraph 4 is marked with an arrow [➔].

PROBLEM 6: PARAPHRASE

A *Paraphrase* problem asks you to choose the best restatement.
Choose from four statements.
Points—1
Frequency Level—High

6. Which of the sentences below best expresses the information in the highlighted statement in the passage? The other choices change the meaning or leave out important information.

   Ⓐ Part of the one million tons of krill harvested annually is used for protein in animal feed.

   Ⓑ Both livestock and chickens as well as humans eat krill as a main part of their diets.

   Ⓒ The principal use of krill is for animal feed, although some of the one million tons is eaten by people.

   ● More than one million tons of krill is eaten by both animals and humans every year.

PROBLEM 7: DETAIL

A *Detail* problem asks you to answer a question about a specific point in the passage.
Choose from four possible answers.
Points—1
Frequency Level—Very high

7. According to paragraph 7, how much land is used to grow crops for animal feed?

   Ⓐ 80 percent of the acreage in Europe

   Ⓑ Most of the rain forest in Central America

   ● 50 percent of the farm land in Canada and the United States

   Ⓓ Half of the land in North and South America

   Paragraph 7 is marked with an arrow [→].

PROBLEM 8: CAUSE

A *Cause* problem asks you to explain why something in the passage occurred.
Choose from four reasons.
Points—1
Frequency Level—Average

8. According to paragraph 7, food webs are inefficient because

- ● consumers in developed nations prefer animal protein
- Ⓑ politicians are not paying attention to the issues
- Ⓒ there are not enough acres to grow crops efficiently
- Ⓓ too much of the corn and soybean harvests are exported

Paragraph 7 is marked with an arrow [➜].

PROBLEM 9: REFERENCE

A *Reference* problem asks you to identify a word or phrase in the passage that refers to a pronoun.
Choose from four words or phrases in the passage.
Points—1
Frequency Level—High

9. The word <u>others</u> in the passage refers to

- Ⓐ resources
- ● food webs
- Ⓒ grains
- Ⓓ cycles

PROBLEM 10: OPINION

An *Opinion* problem asks you to recognize the author's point of view.
Choose from four statements.
Points—1
Frequency Level—Average

10. Which of the following statements most accurately reflects the author's opinion about food issues?

    ⓐ Too much grain is being exported to provide food for developed nations.

    ⓑ More forested land needs to be cleared for food production in developing nations.

    ● Food choices in developed nations are very costly in terms of the environment.

    ⓓ More animal protein is needed in the diets of people in developing nations.

PROBLEM 11: INSERT

An *Insert* problem asks you to locate a place in the passage to insert a sentence.
Choose from four options marked with a square.
Points—1
Frequency Level—High

11. Look at the four squares [■] that show where the following sentence could be inserted in the passage.

A tertiary consumer eats primary and secondary consumers and is referred to as the "top carnivore" in the food chain.

Where could the sentence best be added?   B

Click on a square [■] to insert the sentence in the passage.

PROBLEM 12: EXCEPTION

An *Exception* problem asks you to select a statement that includes information NOT in the passage.
Choose from four sentences.
Points—1
Frequency Level—Average

12. According to the passage, all of the following characteristics describe producers EXCEPT

    Ⓐ Producers serve as food for consumers.
    Ⓑ Producers make their own food.
    Ⓒ Producers form the first trophic level.
    ● Producers include bacteria and fungi.

PROBLEM 13: CLASSIFICATION

A *Classification* problem asks you to match phrases with the category to which they refer.
Choose phrases for two or three categories. Two phrases will not be used.

Points—1–4 points for seven choices

Points—1–3 points for five choices

1 point for 4 correct answers
2 points for 5 correct answers
3 points for 6 correct answers
4 points for 7 correct answers

1 point for 3 correct answers
2 points for 4 correct answers
3 points for 5 correct answers

Frequency Level—Average

13. **Directions:** Complete the table by matching the phrases on the left with the headings on the right. Select the appropriate answer choices and drag them to the type of organism to which they relate. TWO of the answer choices will NOT be used. *This question is worth 4 points.*

    To delete an answer choice, click on it. To see the passage, click on **View Text.**

    (Answer choices are on the next page.)

Answer Choices	Producers
Ⓐ Depend upon photosynthesis to survive	• Ⓐ
Ⓑ Has a weak interaction among species	• Ⓗ
Ⓒ Generally consist of animal life forms	**Consumers**
Ⓓ Include both herbivores and carnivores	• Ⓒ
Ⓔ Form the last link in the food chain	• Ⓓ
Ⓕ Eat meat as one of its primary food sources	• Ⓕ
Ⓖ Feed on dead plants and animals	**Decomposers**
Ⓗ Are always some variety of plant life	• Ⓔ
Ⓘ Made exclusively of inorganic materials	• Ⓖ

Problem 14: Summary

A *Summary* problem asks you to complete a summary of the passage. Choose three sentences from six choices. Three sentences will not be used.
Points—1–2
1 point for 2 correct answers
2 points for 3 correct answers
Frequency Level—Average

14. **Directions:** An introduction for a short summary of the passage appears below. Complete the summary by selecting the THREE answer choices that mention the most important points in the passage. Some sentences do not belong in the summary because they express ideas that are not included in the passage or are minor points from the passage. ***This question is worth 2 points.***

The food web is comprised of producers, consumers, and decomposers, which interact in endless cycles.

- Ⓐ
- Ⓑ
- Ⓒ

Answer Choices

A Consumers, primarily animals, feed on producers, plants which manufacture their own food source through photosynthesis.

B Decomposers digest and recycle dead plants and animals, releasing inorganic compounds into the food chain.

C Since more energy is depleted into the environment at each level in the food chain, dietary choices affect the efficiency of food webs.

D Among consumers, human beings are considered omnivores because they eat not only plants but also animals.

E An example of an undersea food web includes phytoplankton, krill, and fish as well as birds, seals, and whales.

F Rain forests are being cut down in order to clear pastureland for cattle that can be exported to countries with fast-food restaurants.

READING STRATEGIES

In addition to the academic skills that you learned in Chapter 3, there are several reading strategies that will help you succeed on the TOEFL and after the TOEFL.

➤ Preview

Research shows that it is easier to understand what you are reading if you begin with a general idea of what the passage is about. Previewing helps you form a general idea of the topic. To preview, first read the title, the headings and subheadings, and any words in bold print or italics. You should do this as quickly as possible. Remember, you are reading not for specific information but for an impression of the topic. Next, read the first sentence of each paragraph and the last sentence of the passage. Again, this should take seconds, not minutes, to complete. This time you are looking for the main idea.

- Look at the title and headings
- Read the first sentence of every paragraph
- Read the last sentence of the passage

➤ Read faster

To read faster, read for meaning. Try to understand sentences or even paragraphs, not individual words. To do this, you should read phrases instead of reading word by word. Practice using the vision that allows you to see on either side of the word you are focusing on with your eyes. This is called *peripheral vision*. When you drive a car, you are looking ahead of you but you are really taking in the traffic situation on both sides. You are using peripheral vision to move forward. This is also important in learning to read faster. Your mind can take in more than one word at the same time. Just think if you stopped your car every time you wanted to know what was going on in the next lane! You would never get to your destination. To read faster, you have to read for ideas. If you don't know the meaning of a word but you understand the sentence, move on. Don't stop to look up the word in your dictionary. Don't stop your car.

- Use peripheral vision
- Read for meaning

➤ Use contexts

Before you can use a context, you must understand what a context is. In English, a *context* is the combination of vocabulary and grammar that surrounds a word. Context can be a sentence or a paragraph or a passage. Context helps you make a general prediction about meaning. If you know the general meaning of a sentence, you also know the general meaning of the words in the sentence. Making predictions from contexts is very important when you are reading a foreign language. In this way, you can read and understand the meaning of a passage without stopping to look up every new word in a dictionary. On an examination like the TOEFL, dictionaries are not permitted in the room. Of course, you have to know some of the words in order to have a context for the words that you don't know. That means that you need to work on learning a basic vocabulary, and then you can make an educated guess about the meaning of new words by using the context.

- Learn basic vocabulary
- Learn new words in context

➤ Make inferences

Sometimes you will find a direct statement of fact in a reading passage. Other times, you will not find a direct statement. Then you will need to use the facts as evidence to make an inference. An *inference* is a logical conclusion based on evidence. It can be about the passage itself or about the author's viewpoint. For example, you may begin reading a passage about the Native Americans who lived on the plains. You continue reading and note that they used buffalo for food. Later, you read that they used buffalo for clothing and shelter. From these facts, you can draw the conclusion that the buffalo was very important in the culture of the plains people. The author did not state this fact directly, but the evidence allows you to make an inference.

- Locate the evidence
- Draw conclusions

➤ Skim and scan

To *scan* is to let your eyes travel quickly over a passage in order to find something specific that you are looking for. By scanning, you can find the place in a reading passage where the answer to a question is found. First, read the question and look for a reference. A reference in the TOEFL will identify a paragraph where the answer to the question is found. For example, you may read, *Paragraph 2 is marked with an arrow [➜]*. You know that you need to scan for the arrow at the beginning of paragraph 2 in the passage. The paraphrased sentences and the vocabulary words on the TOEFL are shaded to help you find them.

If a question does not have a reference like an arrow or shading, then you should find the important content words in the question. *Content words* are usually nouns, verbs, or adjectives. They are called content words because they contain the meaning of a sentence. Now scan the passage for the same content words or synonyms of the words in the questions. Finally, read those specific sentences carefully, and choose the answer that corresponds to the meaning of the sentences you have read.

- Refer to arrows and shading
- Locate the details
- Check for exceptions

➤ Make connections

Reading is like having a conversation with the author. Your mind makes connections with the passage. Sometimes this will happen when you are reading and a word or phrase refers back to a previous point in the passage. On the TOEFL, one question requires you to insert a sentence at the most logical place in a passage. In this case, you are connecting a new sentence with the ideas in the passage. Active readers are always thinking about how the next sentence fits in with what they have already read.

- Find references
- Insert sentences

➤ Summarize

A summary includes only the main idea and the major points in a passage. Although a passage may contain many points, only the most important are included in a summary. In English, many writers tend to use a formula with one main idea and three major points. It is customary to find between two and four major points in a short passage.

When you are reading content material in textbooks or on examinations, pause at the end of a section to summarize. First, re-read the title or the section heading. State the main idea. Then, summarize the major points from that section. You can summarize by speaking or writing. The last question on the TOEFL is often a summary of the entire passage.

- State the main idea
- List the major points

APPLYING THE ACADEMIC SKILLS TO THE TOEFL

➤ Taking Notes

For some people, taking notes while they read the passage is a good strategy. For other people, it is not a good use of their time. They prefer to read once to get a general idea of the passage and then to go back and scan for each question. The way that you use your time is a very personal choice. When you take the model tests in the next chapters, practice by taking notes on some passages and by scanning on other passages. Use the model tests to determine whether you should spend time taking notes on the reading passages.

➤ Paraphrasing

This is the most important academic skill for the Reading section. Many of the questions and answer choices are paraphrases of information from the passage. Your ability to recognize paraphrases will be essential for you to score well on this section.

➤ Summarizing

The last question for every reading passage will require you to summarize the passage either by classifying information or by distinguishing between major points and minor points. Your skill in summarizing will be important because the last question is worth more points than the other questions.

➤ Synthesizing

This important skill is tested in other sections of the TOEFL® iBT.

QUIZ FOR THE READING SECTION

This is a quiz for the Reading section of the TOEFL® iBT. This section tests your ability to understand reading passages like those in college textbooks. During the quiz, you will read one reading passage and respond to 14 questions about it. You will have 25 minutes to read the passage and answer the questions. You may take notes while you read. You may use your notes to answer the questions.

"The Heredity Versus Environment Debate"

During the past century, there has been heated controversy about whether intelligence is determined primarily by heredity or by environment. Ⓐ When IQ tests were undergoing rapid development early in the twentieth century, many psychologists believed that intelligence was determined primarily by heredity. ☐B

→ **Environmentalist view.** By the middle of the twentieth century, numerous studies had counteracted the hereditarian view, and most social scientists took the position that environment is as important as or even more important than heredity in determining intelligence. ☐C Social scientists who stress the **environmentalist view of intelligence** generally emphasize the need for compensatory programs on a continual basis beginning in infancy. Many also criticize the use of IQ tests on the grounds that these tests are culturally biased. ☐D

James Flynn found that "massive" gains have occurred during the twentieth century in the IQ scores of the population in fourteen nations. The major cause of these improvements, according to Flynn's analysis, is not genetic improvement in the population but environmental changes that led to gains in the kinds of skills assessed by IQ tests. Torsten Husen and his colleagues also have concluded, after reviewing large amounts of data, that improvements in economic and social conditions, and particularly in the availability of schooling, can produce substantial gains in average IQ from one generation to the next. In general, educators committed to improving the performance of low-achieving students are encouraged by these studies.

→ **Hereditarian view.** The **hereditarian view of intelligence** underwent a major revival in the 1970s and 1980s, based particularly on the writings of Arthur Jensen, Richard Herrnstein, and a group of researchers who have been conducting the Minnesota Study of Twins. Summarizing previous research as well as their own studies, these researchers concluded that heredity is the major factor in determining intelligence—accounting for up to 80 percent of the variation in IQ scores.

One very controversial study was published by Jensen in the *Harvard Educational Review* in 1969. Pointing out that African-Americans averaged about 15 points below whites on IQ tests, Jensen attributed this gap to a genetic difference between the two races in learning abilities and patterns. Critics countered Jensen's arguments by contending that IQ is affected by a host of environmental factors, such as malnutrition and prenatal care, that are difficult to measure and impossible to separate from hereditary factors. IQ tests are biased, they said, and do not necessarily even measure intelligence. Since his 1969 article, Jensen has continued to cite data that he believes link intelligence primarily to heredity. His critics continue to respond with evidence that environmental factors, and schooling in particular, have a major influence on IQ.

→ **Synthesizers' view.** A number of social scientists have taken a middle, or "synthesizing," position in this controversy. The **synthesizers' view of intelligence** holds that both heredity and environment contribute to differences in measured intelligence. For example, Christopher Jencks, after reviewing a large amount of data, divided the IQ variance into 0.45 due to heredity, 0.35 due to environment, and 0.20 due to interaction between the two ("interaction" meaning that particular abilities thrive or wither in specific environments). Robert Nichols reviewed all these and other data and concluded that the true value for heredity may be anywhere between 0.40 and 0.80 but that the exact value has little importance for policy. In general, Nichols and other synthesizers maintain that heredity determines the fixed limits of a range; within those limits, the interaction between environment and heredity yields the individual's intelligence. In this view, even if we cannot specify exactly how much of a child's intelligence is the result of environmental factors, teachers (and parents) should provide each child with a productive environment in which to realize her or his maximum potential.

Glossary

IQ: intelligence quotient; a numerical value for intelligence

1. According to paragraph 2, which of the following is true about environmentalists?

   Ⓐ They had only a few studies to prove their viewpoint.
   Ⓑ They did not agree with the use of IQ tests to measure intelligence.
   Ⓒ They did not believe that educational programs could raise IQ scores.
   Ⓓ They were already less popular by the mid twentieth century.

   Paragraph 2 is marked with an arrow [➔].

2. Which of the sentences below best expresses the information in the highlighted statement in the passage? The other choices change the meaning or leave out important information.

   Ⓐ Changes in the environment rather than genetic progress caused an increase in IQ scores, according to studies by Flynn.
   Ⓑ Flynn's studies were not conclusive in identifying the skills that resulted in improvements on IQ tests.
   Ⓒ IQ test results in research by Flynn did not improve because of genetics and environment.
   Ⓓ The reason that gains in IQ tests occurred was because of the changes in skills that were tested.

3. The word <u>data</u> in the passage is closest in meaning to

   Ⓐ experts
   Ⓑ advice
   Ⓒ arguments
   Ⓓ information

4. Why does the author mention the Minnesota Study of Twins in paragraph 4?

    Ⓐ To argue that environment is more important than heredity
    Ⓑ To prove the importance of heredity in measuring IQ
    Ⓒ To establish the synthesizer's view of intelligence
    Ⓓ To summarize previous research before designing a new study

Paragraph 4 is marked with an arrow [➜].

5. According to paragraph 4, what can be inferred about the results of the Minnesota Study of Twins?

    Ⓐ Twins brought up in different environments probably had similar IQ scores.
    Ⓑ The environments were more important to IQ than the genetic similarity of twins.
    Ⓒ The study did not support the previous work by Jensen and Herrnstein.
    Ⓓ The IQ scores of twins can vary by as much as 80 percent.

Paragraph 4 is marked with an arrow [➜].

6. According to Jensen's opponents, IQ tests are not reliable because

    Ⓐ heredity is not measured on the current forms of IQ tests
    Ⓑ it is difficult to determine whether a factor is due to heredity or environment
    Ⓒ learning abilities and patterns are different for people of diverse racial heredity
    Ⓓ they only measure intelligence and not many other important factors

7. The word that in the passage refers to

    Ⓐ Jensen's arguments
    Ⓑ IQ tests
    Ⓒ environmental factors
    Ⓓ Jensen's colleagues

8. Based on the information in paragraph 6, which of the following best explains the term <u>synthesizing</u>?

Ⓐ A moderate position between the two extremes
Ⓑ A position for which the evidence is overwhelming
Ⓒ A controversial position that is hotly debated
Ⓓ A modern revision of an outdated position

Paragraph 6 is marked with an arrow [➔].

9. According to a synthesizer's view, how does heredity influence intelligence?

Ⓐ Heredity is very important but not as influential as environment.
Ⓑ Heredity sets limits on intelligence, but environment can overcome them.
Ⓒ A productive environment influences intelligence more than any other factor.
Ⓓ Heredity and environment interact within the limits set at birth.

10. According to the passage, all of the following are true of the hereditarian view EXCEPT

Ⓐ Studies by Jensen and Herrnstein support this point of view.
Ⓑ Many psychologists in the early twentieth century were hereditarians.
Ⓒ Intelligence as measured by IQ tests is a result of genetic predisposition.
Ⓓ Environmental factors are not able to be separated from heredity.

11. Which of the following statements most accurately reflects the author's opinion about IQ tests?

Ⓐ The author believes that IQ tests should be used continuously from infancy.
Ⓑ According to the author, there are too many disadvantages to IQ testing.
Ⓒ The author maintains a neutral point of view about IQ tests in the discussion.
Ⓓ IQ tests should be used in research studies but they should not be used in schools.

12. Look at the four squares [■] that show where the following sentence could be inserted in the passage.

These *hereditarians* thought that IQ tests and similar instruments measured innate differences in people's capacity.

Where could the sentence best be added?

Click on a square [■] to insert the sentence in the passage.

13. Complete the table by matching the phrases on the left with the headings on the right. Select the appropriate answer choices and drag them to the views of intelligence to which they relate. TWO of the answer choices will NOT be used. *This question is worth 4 points.*

To delete an answer choice, click on it. To see the passage, click on **View Text**.

Answer Choices

A Proposed interaction between heredity and environment.

B Attributed lower IQ to malnutrition and lack of health care.

C Suggested an innate range of IQ was influenced by environment.

D Was supported by the Minnesota Twins study in the 1970s.

E Claimed racial composition was a factor in measured IQ.

F Maintained that IQ tests were often biased in favor of the majority culture.

G Cited schooling as a positive consideration in the gains in IQ.

H Stated that social improvements improve performance on IQ tests.

I Advanced this viewpoint when IQ tests were being developed.

Hereditarian
•
•
•

Environmentalist
•
•
•
•

14. **Directions:** An introduction for a short summary of the passage appears below. Complete the summary by selecting the THREE answer choices that mention the most important points in the passage. Some sentences do not belong in the summary because they express ideas that are not included in the passage or are minor points from the passage. ***This question is worth 2 points.***

Historically, psychologists have proposed three viewpoints to explain the influence of heredity and environment on IQ scores.

- •
- •
- •

Answer Choices

Ⓐ Studies by James Flynn verified significant increases in IQ scores among populations in fourteen nations in the last century.

Ⓑ By the 1970s, psychologists reversed their position, citing heredity as the primary determiner of intelligence as measured by IQ tests.

Ⓒ Because IQ tests are unfair to minority cultures, the current view is to disregard previous studies that use them as a basis for measurement.

Ⓓ In the mid 1900s, the popular view was that environment was the more important factor in the development of intelligence.

Ⓔ Before the development of IQ tests, both heredity and environment were thought to influence the relative intelligence of children.

Ⓕ Some modern psychologists have proposed a theory that relies on the interaction between heredity and environment to determine IQ.

STOP **This is the end of the Reading Quiz. To check your answers, refer to the Progress Chart for the Reading Quiz, Chapter 7, page 393.**

STUDY PLAN

What did you learn from taking the quiz? What will you do differently when you take the model tests in the next chapter? Take a few minutes to think, and then write a sentence or two to help you revise your study plan.

EXTRA CREDIT

After you have completed this chapter, you may want to continue a review of reading. Here are some suggestions.

Practice reading on a computer screen. Reading on a computer screen is different from reading on a page. First, there is generally less text visible. Second, you must scroll instead of turning pages. Finally, there may be quite a few icons or other distracting visuals surrounding the passage. To become comfortable with reading on a computer screen, you should take advantage of every opportunity you have to practice. If you have a computer, spend time reading on the screen. Everything you read will help you improve this new skill.

Practice reading the kinds of topics that you will find in the Reading section. The reading passages are similar to the information that you will find in textbooks from general courses taught in colleges and universities during the first two years. If you can borrow English language textbooks, read passages from natural sciences, social sciences, the humanities, and the arts. The kinds of passages in encyclopedias are usually at a reading level slightly below that of textbooks, but they offer an inexpensive way to obtain a lot of reading material for different content areas. If you have access to the Internet, free encyclopedias are available online. An encyclopedia on CD-ROM is another option, which you may be able to use at a local library. If you purchase an encyclopedia on CD-ROM, an edition from a previous year will be cheaper and just as useful for your purposes.

ADVISOR'S OFFICE

If your body is relaxed, your mind can relax more easily. During the TOEFL examination, if you find yourself pursing your lips, frowning, and tightening your shoulders, then use a few seconds to stretch. Clasp your hands and put your arms over your head. Then turn your palms up to the ceiling and look up at your fingers. Pull your arms up as high as you can to stretch your muscles. Be sure not to look at anything but your own hands and the ceiling. That way, you won't be suspected of signaling to a friend. Even a two-second stretch can make a difference. Now, yawn or take a deep breath in and out, and you'll be more relaxed and ready to go on.

LISTENING

OVERVIEW OF THE LISTENING SECTION

The Listening section tests your ability to understand spoken English that is typical of interactions and academic speech on college campuses. During the test, you will respond to conversations and lectures.

There are two formats for the Listening section. On the short format, you will respond to two conversations and four lectures. On the long format, you will respond to three conversations and six lectures. After each listening passage, you will answer 5–6 questions about it. Only two conversations and four lectures will be graded. The other conversation and lectures are part of an experimental section for future tests. Because you will not know which conversations and lectures will be graded, you must try to do your best on all of them.

On the official TOEFL® iBT, you will hear each conversation or lecture one time. You may take notes while you listen, but notes are not graded. You may use your notes to answer the questions.

Choose the best answer for multiple-choice questions. Follow the directions on the page or on the screen for computer-assisted questions. Click on **Next** and **OK** to go to the next question. You cannot return to previous questions. You have 20 minutes to answer all of the questions on the short format and 30 minutes to answer all of the questions on the long format. A clock on the screen will show you how much time you have to complete your answers for the section. The clock does not count the time you are listening to the conversations and lectures.

REVIEW OF PROBLEMS FOR THE LISTENING SECTION

➤ Prompts

A prompt for the Listening section is either a conversation on a college campus or part of a lecture in a college classroom on one of the natural sciences, social sciences, humanities, or arts. Each conversation or lecture is between three and six minutes long. There are either 6 or 9 prompts in the Listening section with 5–6 questions after each prompt. When you are presented with 6 prompts, all 6 will be graded. When you are presented with 9 prompts, only 6 will be graded, and 3 will be used for experimental purposes. You should do your best on all 9 prompts because you will not know which of them will be graded. Problems 15–18 in this review refer to the first prompt. Problems 19–24 refer to the second prompt. The scripts for the prompts in this review chapter have been printed for you to study. On the official TOEFL® iBT, you will not see the prompts, but you will see the questions while you hear them. Model tests 2 and 3 are like the official TOEFL® iBT. You will not see the scripts while you listen to the prompts for the model tests.

CONVERSATION

Problems 15–18, Conversation. Read a conversation on campus between two students.

Man:	Wait up. I need to ask you about something.
Woman:	Oh, hi Jack.
Man:	Hi. Listen, I was just wondering whether you understood what Professor Carson was saying about the review session next Monday?
Woman:	Sure. Why?
Man:	Well, the way I get it, it's optional.
Woman:	Right. He said if we didn't have any questions, we should just use the time to study on our own.
Man:	Okay. That's what I thought. Maybe I'll just skip it then.
Woman:	Well, it's up to you, but the thing is . . . sometimes at a review session, someone else will ask a question, and, you know, the way the professor explains it, it's really helpful, I mean, to figure out what he wants on the test.
Man:	Oh I didn't think about it that way, but it makes sense. So, you're going to go then.
Woman:	Absolutely. Um, I've had a couple of other classes with Carson and the review sessions always helped me get organized for the test.
Man:	Oh.
Woman:	And, if you've missed any of the lectures, he usually has extra handouts from all the classes. So . . .
Man:	Well, I haven't missed any of the sessions.
Woman:	Me neither. But I'm still going to be there. Look, uh, if it's like the other review sessions, the first hour he's going to go over the main points for each class, kind of like an outline of the course. Then from five-thirty to six-thirty, he'll take questions. That's the best part. And the last half hour, he'll stay for individual conferences with people who need extra help. I usually don't stay for that.

Man:	Okay. So we just show up at the regular time and place for class?
Woman:	Or not, if you decide to study on your own.
Man:	Right. But, don't you think he'll notice who's there?
Woman:	He said he wasn't going to take attendance.
Man:	Yeah, but still . . .
Woman:	It's a fairly large class.
Man:	But if he's grading your final and he remembers you were at the review, it might make a difference.
Woman:	Maybe. I think the important thing is just to study really hard and do your best. But, the review sessions help me study. I think they're really good.
Man:	Okay. Thanks. I guess I'll go, too.
Woman:	So I'll see you there.
Man:	Yeah, I think I . . . I'd better go.

➤ Problems

The problems in this review represent the types of questions that are most frequently tested on the TOEFL. The number of points assigned to each problem is based on the evaluation system for the TOEFL. The frequency level for each problem is based on the average number of thirty-four questions that are usually included in a Listening section of six prompts.

Average	1–2
High	3–4
Very high	5+

PROBLEM 15: PURPOSE

A *Purpose* problem asks you to explain why the speakers are having a conversation or why the professor is presenting the material in a lecture. Choose from four reasons.
Points—1
Frequency Level—Average

1. Why does the man want to talk with the woman?

Ⓐ To ask her to help him study for the exam
Ⓑ To get some handouts for a class he has missed
● To clarify his understanding of the review session
Ⓓ To find out her opinion of Professor Carson

Problem 16: Detail

A *Detail* problem asks you to answer a question about a specific point in the conversation or lecture.
Choose from four possible answers.
Points—1
Frequency Level—Very high

2. Why does the woman think that the review session will be helpful?

Ⓐ Because she has some questions that she wants to ask the professor
Ⓑ Because Professor Carson will tell them some of the test questions
● Because it helps to hear the answers to questions that other people ask
Ⓓ Because she needs an individual conference with the professor

Problem 17: Inference

An *Inference* problem asks you to draw a conclusion based on information in the conversation or lecture. Choose from four possible answers.
Points—1
Frequency Level—Very high

3. Why does the man decide to go to the review session?

Ⓐ Because the review session will make up for absences
● Because the woman convinces him that it is a good idea
Ⓒ Because the professor has recommended the session
Ⓓ Because he needs help to organize his class notes

PROBLEM 18: PRAGMATICS

A *Pragmatics* problem asks you to comprehend the function of language on a level deeper than the surface meaning. You may need to understand the purpose or motivation of the speaker, or you may need to interpret the speaker's attitude or doubt about something in the conversation or lecture. Listen to a replay of the sentence or sentences that you must interpret.

Choose from four possible answers.

Points—1

Frequency Level—Very high

4. Listen again to part of the conversation. Then answer the following question.

> Woman: He said he wasn't going to take attendance.
> Man: Yeah, but still . . .
> Woman: It's a fairly large class.

Why does the man say this: "Yeah, but still . . ."?

● He thinks that the professor will notice if a student is absent.
Ⓑ He agrees with the woman about the attendance policy.
Ⓒ He wants to change the subject that they are discussing.
Ⓓ He tries to encourage the woman to explain her opinion.

LECTURE

 Problems 19–24, Lecture. Read part of a lecture in a zoology class.

Professor:
As you know from the textbook, mimicry isn't limited to insects, but it's most common among them, and by mimicry I'm referring to the likeness between two insects that aren't closely related but look very much alike. The insects that engage in mimicry are usually very brightly colored. One of the insects, the one that's characterized by an unpleasant taste, a bad smell, a sting or bite, that insect is called the

model. The mimic looks like the model but doesn't share the characteristic that protects the model from predators. But, of course, the predators associate the color pattern or some other trait with the unpleasant characteristic and leave both insects alone.

Henry Bates was one of the first naturalists who noticed that some butterflies that closely resembled each other were actually unrelated, so mimicry in which one species copies another is called Batesian mimicry. I have some lab specimens of a few common mimics in the cases here in the front of the room, and I want you to have a chance to look at them before the end of the class. There's a day flying moth with brown and white and yellow markings. And this moth is the model because it has a very unpleasant taste and tends to be avoided by moth eaters. But you'll notice that the swallowtail butterfly mounted beside it has very similar coloration, and actually the swallowtail doesn't have the unpleasant taste at all. Another example is the monarch butterfly, which is probably more familiar to you since they pass through this area when they're migrating. But you may not know that they have a very nasty taste because I seriously doubt that any of you have eaten one. But for the predators who *do* eat butterflies, this orange and black pattern on the monarch is a warning signal not to sample it. So, the viceroy butterfly here is a mimic. Same type of coloring but no nasty taste. Nevertheless, the viceroy isn't bothered by predators either, because it's mistaken for the monarch. So how does a predator know that the day flying moth and the monarch aren't good to eat? Well, a bird only has to eat one to start avoiding them all—models and mimics.

A stinging bumblebee is another model insect. The sting is painful and occasionally even fatal for predators. So there are a large number of mimics. For example, there's a beetle that mimics bumblebees by beating its wings to make noise, and the astonishing thing is that it's able to do this at the same rate as the bumblebee so exactly the same buzzing sound is created. I don't have a specimen of that beetle, but I do have a specimen of the hoverfly, which is a mimic of the honeybee, and it makes a similar buzzing sound, too. When you compare the bee with the fly, you'll notice that the honeybee has two sets of wings, and the hoverfly has only one set of wings, but as you can imagine, the noise and the more or less similar body and color will keep most predators from approaching closely enough to count the wings.

Some insects without stingers have body parts that mimic the sharp stinger of wasps or bees. Although the hawk moth is harmless, it has a bundle of hairs that protrudes from the rear of its body. The actual purpose of these hairs is to spread scent, but to predators, the bundle mimics a stinger closely enough to keep them away, especially if the hawk moth is moving in a threatening way as if it were about to sting. There's a hawk moth here in the case, and to me at least, it doesn't look that much like the wasp mounted beside it, but remember when you're looking at a specimen, it's stationary, and in nature the *movement* is also part of the mimicry.

Oh, here's a specimen of an ant, and this is interesting. Another naturalist, Fritz Muller, hypothesized that similarity among a large number of species could help protect *all* of them. Here's what he meant. After a few battles with a stinging or biting ant, especially when the entire colony comes to the aid of the ant being attacked, a predator will learn to avoid ants, even those that don't sting or bite, because they all look alike and the predator associates the bad experience with the group. And by extension, the predator will also avoid insects that mimic ants, like harmless beetles and spiders.

Look at this.

Ant   Spider

I have a drawing of a specimen of a stinging ant beside a specimen of a brownish spider and the front legs of the spider are mounted so they look more like antennae because that's just what the spider does to mimic an ant. That way it appears to have six legs like an ant instead of eight like a spider.

Okay, we have about ten minutes left, and I want you to take this opportunity to look at the specimen cases here in the front of the room. I'll be available for questions if you have them. How about forming two lines on either side of the cases so more of you can see at the same time?

PROBLEM 19: MAIN IDEA

A *Main Idea* problem asks you to identify the topic of the lecture, that is, what the lecture is mainly about.
Choose from four possible answers.
Points—1
Frequency Level—High

  5. What is the lecture mainly about?

  ● An explanation of mimicry among species in the insect world
  Ⓑ A comparison of the features of the viceroy and the monarch butterfly
  Ⓒ A hypothesis to explain why similarity among species protects them all
  Ⓓ A response to questions about the specimens displayed in the cases

PROBLEM 20: ORGANIZATION

An *Organization* problem asks you recognize the rhetorical structure of a lecture or part of a lecture. For example, chronological order, steps in a sequence, cause and effect, comparison.
Choose from four possible answers.
Points—1
Frequency Level—Average

  6. How does the professor organize the lecture?

  ● He shows specimens to demonstrate his points.
  Ⓑ He compares the theories of two naturalists.
  Ⓒ He classifies different types of mimics.
  Ⓓ He puts the ideas in chronological order.

PROBLEM 21: DETAILS

A *Details* problem asks you to answer a question about a specific point in the conversation or lecture.
Choose two or three answers from four to six possibilities.
Points—1
Frequency Level—Average

7. According to the lecture, what are some characteristics of a *model*?

Click on 3 answer choices.

Ⓐ   A pair of wings
■ A foul odor
■ A bad taste
Ⓓ A drab color
■ A painful sting

PROBLEM 22: TECHNIQUE

A *Technique* problem asks you to identify the way that a professor makes a point, for example, by comparing, by providing a definition, by giving an example.
Choose from four possible answers.
Points—1
Frequency Level—Average

8. How does the professor explain Batesian mimicry?

Ⓐ By giving a precise definition
● By providing several examples
Ⓒ By referring to the textbook
Ⓓ By contrasting it with another hypothesis

PROBLEM 23: YES-NO

A *Yes-No* problem asks you to decide whether statements agree or disagree with information in the lecture.
Mark a list of statements in a chart as either *Yes* or *No*.
Points—1–2
Frequency Level—Average

9. In the lecture, the professor explains Fritz Muller's hypothesis. Indicate whether each of the following supports the hypothesis. Click in the correct box for each choice.

		Yes	No
A	Predators avoid species of insects that have harmed them in the past by stinging or biting them.	✔	
B	Predators may be killed when an entire colony of insects joins forces against them.		✔
C	Predators leave harmless insects alone if they are part of a group that includes stinging insects.	✔	
D	Predators will refrain from attacking harmless insects if they look like insects that have stung them before.	✔	
E	Predators protect themselves from harmful insects by stinging or biting them before they are attacked.		✔

PROBLEM 24: CONNECTIONS

A *Connections* problem asks you to relate ideas or information in the lecture.

Match answers with categories, list the order of events or steps in a process, and show relationships on a chart.

Points—1–4

Frequency Level—Average

10. Indicate whether each insect below refers to a model or a mimic. Click in the correct box for each phrase.

Insects	Mimic	Model
A A viceroy butterfly ——————————→		
B A brown spider ——————————→		
C A hawk moth ——————————→		
D A bumblebee ———————————————→		
E A biting ant ———————————————→		

LISTENING STRATEGIES

In addition to the academic skills that you learned in the previous chapter, there are several listening strategies that will help you succeed on the TOEFL and after the TOEFL.

➤ Get organized

Before you begin the Listening section on the official TOEFL, you will have an opportunity to adjust the volume on your headset. Be sure to do it before you dismiss the directions and begin the test. After the test has begun, you may not be able to adjust the volume. When you practice using the model tests in this book, adjust the volume at the beginning. Learn to get it right without touching the volume button again during practice. Then, prepare to listen. The directions tend to be long and boring, especially if you have experience taking model tests and know what to do. Don't get distracted. Be ready to hear the first word in the introduction to the first listening passage.

- Adjust the volume first
- Prepare to listen

➤ Preview

The introductions for the conversations and lecture contain important information that will help you prepare your mind to listen. For example, the narrator may say, "Now get ready to listen to part of a lecture in a history class." When you hear the introduction, you learn two useful facts. First, you know that you will be listening to a lecture. Second, you know that the lecture will be about history. This is helpful because it is a preview for the listening passage.

- Pay attention to the introductions
- Glance at the photo

➤ Use visuals

The photographs and other visuals are there to provide a context for the conversations and lectures. In general, the pictures of people are for orientation to the conversations and lectures, whereas the visuals of objects, art, specimens, maps, charts, and drawings support the meaning of the conversations and lectures. Do *not* focus on the pictures of people. *Do* focus on the other visuals that appear during the conversations and lectures. They could reappear in a question. When you take the model tests, practice selective attention. Look briefly at the pictures of the professor and the students, but be alert to the other visuals. If you become too involved in looking at the people, you may pay less attention to the audio, and you could miss part of the passage.

- Glance at the photos of people
- Focus on content visuals

➤ Read screen text

During the questions for conversations and lectures, watch the screen carefully. You will hear the questions, and you will also see them as text on the screen. If you find that it is to your advantage to close your eyes or look away from the photo during the short conversations, be sure to give your full attention to the screen again while the questions are being asked and the answer choices are presented. By using the model tests, you will be able to develop a rhythm for interacting with the screen that is best for you.

- Read the questions
- Develop a rhythm

➤ Understand campus context

The conversations and lectures take place in a campus context. A glossary at the end of this book contains a listing of campus vocabulary. These words and phrases will help you understand the conversations between campus personnel, professors, and students. Pragmatic understanding will help you understand the function of a sentence. A few examples of function are an apology, an explanation, or a way to get the listener's attention or to change the topic. Pragmatic understanding will also help you interpret the speaker's attitude and the nature of the information—a fact or an opinion. Studying the glossary is an important strategy for the Listening section. Start now.

- Learn campus vocabulary
- Study pragmatic cues for lectures

➤ Concentrate

Sometimes the environment for the TOEFL is not ideal. If the room is small, you may hear a very low hum from another headset or the scratch of pencils on paper when others are taking notes. These sounds can be distracting, especially during the Listening section. The earphones on your headset should suppress most of the noise, but it will be helpful if you have some strategies to help you concentrate. Some students press their earphones more tightly to their ears by holding them with their hands during long listening passages, but this may be clumsy for you when you reach for the mouse to answer questions. Other students train themselves to concentrate in a somewhat distracting environment by taking at least one model test in a small room where other people are studying, such as a library or a study lounge in a dormitory. Remember, you may not be able to control the test environment, but you can control your response to it. By keeping your eyes on the screen and the scratch paper and by remaining calm, you will be able to concentrate better. If the test situation is noisy, don't get angry and start negative talk in your mind. Don't let your emotions interfere with your concentration.

- Focus on the test materials
- Stay calm

APPLYING THE ACADEMIC SKILLS TO THE TOEFL

➤ Taking Notes

Taking notes is probably the most important academic skill for the Listening section. When you take notes, you will organize the information into major points and minor points. You will also record information that you can refer to when you answer questions. Your ability to take notes will be critical for you to score well on this section.

➤ Paraphrasing

Many of the answer choices are paraphrases of information from the passage. Your ability to recognize paraphrases will be helpful as you choose your answers.

➤ Summarizing

The first question in each conversation usually requires you to understand the purpose of the conversation, and the first question in each lecture usually requires you to recognize a summary of the main idea. By mastering the academic skill of summarizing, you will be able to respond correctly to the first question in each prompt. You will also be better prepared to relate ideas and make connections.

➤ Synthesizing

This important skill is tested in other sections of the TOEFL® iBT.

QUIZ FOR THE LISTENING SECTION

This is a quiz for the Listening section of the TOEFL® iBT. This section tests your ability to understand campus conversations and academic lectures. During the quiz, you read one conversation and one lecture. On the official TOEFL you will hear each conversation or lecture one time and respond to questions about them. You may take notes while you listen. You may use your notes to answer the questions.

CONVERSATION

Questions 1–4, Conversation. Read a conversation on campus between a professor and a student.

Student:	Hi Professor Taylor.
Professor:	Hi Jack.
Q1 Student:	I was hoping that I could talk with you for a few minutes. It's about the test.
Professor:	Oh, okay.
Student:	Well, I've never taken an open-book test, and I just don't know what to expect. Does that mean I can use my book during the test . . . as a reference?
Professor:	Exactly. And you can use your notes and the handouts, too.
Student:	Really?
Q2 Professor:	Yes, but Jack, since you've never taken an open-book test, I should warn you. It isn't as easy as it seems.
Student:	Because?
Professor:	Because you don't have enough time to look up every answer and still finish the test.
Student:	Oh.
Professor:	That's the mistake that most students make. You see, the purpose of an open-book test is to allow you to look up a detail or make a citation. But the students who are looking up every answer spend too much time on the first few questions, and then they have to leave some of the questions at the end blank.
Student:	So it's important to pace yourself.

Professor: It is. The test is one hour long and there are twenty questions so you have to be working on question ten in half an hour.

Student: Right. That's clear enough. So, how do I prepare for an open-book test?

Professor: Well, the first thing to do is to organize your notes into subject categories, so you can refer easily to topics that might appear in the test questions. And then study your book, just like you would for any other test. Well, some people mark passages in the book with flags to make it easier to locate certain facts, but other than that, just prepare for a test like you usually do. `Q3`

Student: Right . . . Uh, Professor Taylor, could I ask you . . . um . . . why are you making this test open-book? I mean, we have to study for it like always, so . . . . I hope you don't mind that I asked. I'm just curious.

Professor: I don't mind at all. Jack, I think an open-book test provides an opportunity for real learning. Too many of my students used to memorize small facts for a test and then forget all about the broad concepts. I want you to study the concepts so you will leave my class with a general perspective that you won't forget. `Q4`

Student: Wow. I can relate to that.

Professor: Most people can. But, the way I see it, this is a psychology class, not a memory class.

Student: Well, thanks for taking the time to explain everything, Dr. Taylor.

Professor: You're welcome, Jack. See you next week then.

Student: Okay. Have a nice weekend.

Professor: You, too.

1. Why does the man go to see his professor?

    (A) To borrow a reference book that he needs
    (B) To ask a question about the material
    (C) To get advice about studying for a test
    (D) To pick up some handouts from the class

2. Why does the student say this: "Because?"

   Ⓐ To challenge the professor's idea
   Ⓑ To encourage the professor to explain
   Ⓒ To try to change the subject
   Ⓓ To interrupt the professor respectfully

3. How should Jack prepare for the test?

   Ⓐ He should memorize the material in the book.
   Ⓑ He should study the questions before the test.
   Ⓒ He should organize his notes by topic.
   Ⓓ He should not change his usual study plan.

4. Why does the professor give open-book tests?

   Ⓐ Because she believes it helps students with memorization
   Ⓑ Because her tests contain a large number of small facts
   Ⓒ Because her students are more successful with the course
   Ⓓ Because she thinks it provides a better learning experience

LECTURE

Questions 5–14, Lecture. Read part of a lecture in an economics class. The professor is talking about supply-side economics.

Q5 The fundamental concept in supply-side economics is that tax cuts will spur economic growth because these tax cuts will allow entrepreneurs to invest their tax savings, thereby creating more jobs and profits, which ultimately allow the entrepreneur and the additional employees to pay more taxes, even though the rates are lower. Let's go through that again, step by step. Q13 First, taxes are lowered. Then business owners use their tax savings to hire more workers. This increases profits so the business owner pays more taxes at a lower rate, and in addition, the newly hired workers all pay taxes as well. So there's more income flowing into the government through taxes.

Q6   Historically in the United States, several presidents have championed tax cuts to get the economy moving. Although this top-down economic theory is more popular among Republicans who have traditionally been aligned

with business interests, in 1960, John Fitzgerald Kennedy, a Democratic | Q7 |
president, also used tax cuts to improve economic conditions. He probably
wouldn't qualify as a true supply-sider, but he *did* understand and capitalize
on the basic concept. But it's perhaps Ronald Reagan who is most closely
associated with supply-side economics. So much so that his policies in the
1980s were referred to as Reaganomics. During his term of office, Reagan
cut taxes, but actually, the huge increases in spending, especially for the military budget, caused supply-siders to debate with their conservative cousins.

You see, *conservative* and *supply-side* are not the same thing.
Traditional conservative economists insist that tax cuts should be accompanied by fiscal responsibility, that is, spending cuts by government. But supply-side economists aren't concerned with spending. They rely on tax cuts to
do the job. Period. Back to the supply-side policies under Reagan, well, the
supply-siders believed that the economic growth resulting from tax cuts
would be so great and the total increase in taxes so high that the United
States economy would grow beyond its deficit spending. When this didn't
happen, some economists distanced themselves from the label *supply-side*
while advocating tax cuts with greater attention to spending.

Even Milton Friedman, Nobel laureate and an influential member of the
Chicago School of Economics—even Friedman is now pointing out that the
problem is how to hold down government spending, which accounts for
about half of the national income. But he still looks to tax cuts as a solution.

So, a more recent problem for supply-siders, in addition to the fiscal
responsibility issue, is that corporate business tends to move their investment and jobs overseas, which critics say eventually will lead to high unem-
ployment in the United States. But Friedman insists that by moving jobs | Q8 |
abroad, incomes and dollars are created that sooner or later will be used to
purchase goods that are made in the United States and produce jobs in the
United States. It's supply-side economics with a global perspective.

In fact, conservatives and supply-siders alike argue that progress in the
American economy has been made from technological changes and
increased productivity—producing different goods or more goods with fewer
workers. Dr. Barry Asmus cites the example of the millions of tons of copper
wire that had to be produced for us to communicate by telephone across
country. Now, a few satellites will do the job. Clearly, the people who were
employed in the copper wire industry suffered unemployment when the
change in technology occurred. Or, another example, in the case of manu- | Q1 |
facturing, thirty years ago, a General Electric plant required 3000 workers to
produce one dishwasher every minute. Now, the same plant needs 300 | Q1 |
people to produce one dishwasher every six seconds. So, you might focus
on the fact that many workers will be without jobs making dishwashers, but
what do you suppose supply-siders would say? Think this through. They

would counter with the argument that the dishwasher will be cheaper as a result of the increased productivity, so more people can buy dishwashers and still have some money left. Again Asmus reasons that if the consumers spend money on more goods, they create jobs because workers are needed to produce the goods they buy. If they invest their money, they also create more jobs by supporting the economy.

So some people do lose jobs because of technology, productivity, and the shift of manufacturing overseas, and only 70 percent find better-paying jobs when they transition to another job. Yes, that's true, and it's a personally painful transition for those involved. But the argument by supply-siders and many conservatives as well is that this is temporary unemployment and the important word here is *temporary*. So the temporary unemployment occurs in the process of shifting people not just from one job to another but from one segment of the economy to another. To use an analogy, it would be like the shift from farming to manufacturing that's occurred worldwide as better methods allowed fewer farmers to produce food and resulted in the movement of farmers from the country to the cities where they became employed in manufacturing. And now there's a shift from manufacturing to technology, which, if supply-siders and conservative economists are to be believed, will result in an even higher standard of living in the United States and globally. But, of course, the success of the United States within the global economy will largely depend on a favorable balance of trade—how much we can produce in this country in the new segments of the economy and how much we can sell abroad.

5. What is the lecture mainly about?

Ⓐ Changes in economic systems
Ⓑ Tax incentives for business
Ⓒ Supply-side economics
Ⓓ A favorable balance of trade

6. How does the professor organize the lecture?

Ⓐ By contrasting several economic systems
Ⓑ By taking a historical perspective
Ⓒ By arguing against Friedman and Asmus
Ⓓ By pointing out the benefits of Reaganomics

7. According to the lecturer, what did Kennedy and Reagan have in common?

Ⓐ They were both honored as Nobel laureates in economics.
Ⓑ They cut taxes to spur the economy during their administrations.
Ⓒ They identified themselves with supply-side economics.
Ⓓ They both taught at the Chicago School of Economics.

8. What would Milton Freidman most likely say about moving a manufacturing plant from the United States to a site abroad?

Ⓐ He would oppose it because it would cause people to lose their jobs.
Ⓑ He would consider it an opportunity for business to cut costs.
Ⓒ He would view it as a natural process in the shift to technology.
Ⓓ He would be concerned about the decrease in productivity.

9. According to Barry Asmus, what are two key ways that consumers contribute to the creation of new jobs?

Click on 2 answer choices.

Ⓐ By investing their tax savings

Ⓑ By purchasing cheaper goods

Ⓒ By moving on to better paying jobs

Ⓓ By spending more money

10. How does the professor explain the shift from manufacturing to technology?

Ⓐ He points to the global economy as the explanation for it.
Ⓑ He disagrees with most economists about the long-term effects.
Ⓒ He compares it with the change from agriculture to manufacturing.
Ⓓ He believes that it is too soon to draw any conclusions about it.

11. Why does the professor mention the General Electric plant?

    Ⓐ Because the plant is a good example of increased productivity
    Ⓑ Because unemployment resulted from company decisions
    Ⓒ Because the company was able to retrain their employees
    Ⓓ Because the plant was down-sized and many jobs were lost

12. Why does the professor say this: 🎧 "Think this through."

    Ⓐ He would like the students to answer the question.
    Ⓑ He is joking with the students about the supply-siders.
    Ⓒ He wants the students to follow his logical answer.
    Ⓓ He is impatient because the students aren't paying attention.

13. In the lecture, the professor explains supply-side economics. Indicate whether each of the following strategies supports the theory. Click in the correct box for each choice.

		Yes	No
A	Reduce tax rates		
B	Cut government spending		
C	Increase productivity		
D	Tolerate temporary unemployment		
E	Discourage consumer spending		

14. Put the following events in the correct order.

    Ⓐ Businesses hire more employees with the tax savings.
    Ⓑ The government works to affect a reduction in taxes.
    Ⓒ The businesses and their employees pay more taxes.
    Ⓓ Profits increase because of the growth in businesses.

STOP **This is the end of the Listening Quiz. To check your answers, refer to the Progress Chart for the Listening Quiz, Chapter 7, page 397.**

STUDY PLAN

What did you learn from taking the quiz? What will you do differently when you take the model tests in the next chapters? Take a few minutes to think, and then write a sentence or two to help you revise your study plan.

EXTRA CREDIT

After you have completed this chapter, you may want to continue a review of listening. Here are some suggestions.

Listen to an international news broadcast in English. Be sure to select a television or radio program that includes reporters from various English-speaking countries, especially Canada, the United States, Australia, and Great Britain. The Listening section of the TOEFL now includes voices that represent a variety of English accents. The purpose of this activity is to understand diverse speech. Don't take notes. Just listen and try to understand as much as you can.

Watch educational television programs. The Learning Channel, Discovery, PBS, BBC, and others provide narrated programming with visuals on subjects that simulate lecture topics on the TOEFL. Take notes while you watch the program. During commercial breaks, mute the program and try to summarize the major points that you have heard, using your notes.

Attend lectures in English. Local colleges and clubs often have free lectures in English. Choose to attend lectures that simulate college classrooms. In addition, several web sites offer lectures and talks. Select topics from natural science, social science, humanities, and the arts.

www.npr.org; click on *archives*

www.c-span.org; click on *booknotes*

ADVISOR'S OFFICE

There is usually a ten-minute break after the Listening section. What you do during the break is important. If you start to talk in your language with friends who are nervous or negative, you will go back into the Speaking section nervous and negative. Choose a friend who is willing to speak English with you during the break. Use the time to encourage each other with positive talk. If you speak English, you will continue thinking in English, and you will make a smooth transition into the next section of the TOEFL. If you are also thinking positively, you will be ready to do your best.

SPEAKING

OVERVIEW OF THE SPEAKING SECTION

The Speaking section tests your ability to communicate in English in an academic setting. During the test, you will be presented with six speaking questions. The questions ask for a response to a single question, a conversation, a talk, or a lecture.

You may take notes as you listen, but notes are not graded. You may use your notes to answer the questions. Some of the questions ask for a response to a reading passage and a talk or a lecture. The reading passages and the questions are written, but most of the directions will be spoken.

Your speaking will be evaluated on both the fluency of the language and the accuracy of the content. You will have 15–20 seconds to prepare and 45–60 seconds to respond to each question. Typically, a good response will require all of the response time, but the answer will be complete by the end of the response time. You will have about 20 minutes to complete the Speaking section.

A clock on the screen will show you how much time you have to prepare your answer and how much time you have to record it.

REVIEW OF PROBLEMS FOR THE SPEAKING SECTION

➤ Prompts

A prompt for the Speaking section is either spoken or written. For example, a prompt might be a question, a conversation, part of a lecture, a written announcement, or part of a textbook passage. Each question has a slightly different prompt. There are six sets of prompts in the Speaking section with 1 question after each set. Problems 1–6 in this review refer to the kinds of prompts that are typical on the TOEFL® iBT. The scripts for the spoken prompts have been printed for you to study while you listen to them. On the official TOEFL, you will not see the spoken prompts. You will see the written announcements and textbook passages, and you will also see the questions while you hear them. Model tests 1 and 2 are like the official TOEFL® iBT. You will not see the scripts while you listen to the prompts for the model tests.

➤ Problems

The problems in this review represent the types of questions that are most frequently tested on the TOEFL. The task for each problem is explained. Each problem appears as one of the 6 questions included in the Speaking section.

PROBLEM 25: EXPERIENCES

In this question, you will be asked to speak about a personal experience. This may be a place, a person, a possession, a situation, or an occasion. After you hear the question, you will make a choice from your experience and then explain why you made that choice.

You will have 15 seconds to prepare and 45 seconds to speak.

Task

- Describe your experience
- Explain the reasons for your choice

Problem 25, Example Question

Where would you like to study in the United States?

Example Notes—Answer and Reasons

Washington, D.C.

- Family in the area—advice, help
- International city—food, stores
- Tours—sites, trains to other cities
- Universities—excellent, accepted at 1

Problem 25, Example Answer

I'd like to study at a university in Washington, D.C., because I have family in the area, and . . . and it would be nice to have them close by so I could visit them on holidays and in case I need advice or help. I've been to Washington several times, and I like it there. It's an international city with restaurants and stores where I can buy food and other things from my country while, uh, while I'm living abroad. And Washington is an exciting place. I've gone on several tours, but I still have many places on my list of sites to see. Also, um, there are trains to New York and Florida so I could take advantage of my free time to see other cities. Um, as for the universities, there are several, uh, several excellent schools in Washington and . . . and I'd probably be accepted at one of them.

Checklist 1

✔ The talk answers the topic question.
✔ The point of view or position is clear.
✔ The talk is direct and well-organized.
✔ The sentences are logically connected.
✔ Details and examples support the main idea.
✔ The speaker expresses complete thoughts.
✔ The meaning is easy to comprehend.
✔ A wide range of vocabulary is used.
✔ There are only minor errors in grammar.
✔ The talk is within a range of 125–150 words.

PROBLEM 26: PREFERENCES

In this question, you will be asked to speak about a personal preference. This may be a situation, an activity, or an event. After you hear
the question, you will make a choice between two options presented
and then explain why you made that choice.

You will have 15 seconds to prepare and 45 seconds to speak.

Task

- Choose between two options
- Explain the reasons for your preference

 Problem 26, Example Question

*Some students live in dormitories on campus. Other students live in
apartments off campus. Which living situation do you think is better
and why?*

Example Notes—Choice and Reasons

Dormitories

- More interaction—practice English, study
- Less responsibility—meals, laundry, cleaning
- Better location—library, recreation, classroom buildings

Problem 26, Example Answer

A lot of my friends live off campus, but I think that living in a dormitory is a better situation, uh, especially for the first year at a new college. Dormitories are structured to provide opportunities for interaction and for making friends. As a foreign student, it would be an advantage to be in a dormitory to practice English with other residents and to find study groups in the dormitory. And dorm students have, uh, less responsibility for meals, laundry, and . . . and, uh, cleaning because there are meal plans and services available, uh, as part of the fees. Besides, there's only one check to write so, uh, the book, uh, the bookkeeping . . . it's minimal. And the dormitory offers an ideal location near the library and, um, all the recreational facilities, and . . . and the classroom buildings.

Checklist 2

✔ The talk answers the topic question.
✔ The point of view or position is clear.
✔ The talk is direct and well-organized.
✔ The sentences are logically connected.
✔ Details and examples support the main idea.
✔ The speaker expresses complete thoughts.
✔ The meaning is easy to comprehend.
✔ A wide range of vocabulary is used.
✔ There are only minor errors in grammar.
✔ The talk is within a range of 125–150 words.

PROBLEM 27: REPORTS

In this question, you will be asked to read a short passage and listen to a speaker on the same topic. The topic usually involves a campus situation and the speaker's opinion about it. After you hear the question, you will be asked to report the speaker's opinion and relate it to the reading passage.

You will have 45 seconds to read the passage. After you have listened to the talk, you will have 30 seconds to prepare and 60 seconds to speak.

Task

- Summarize a situation and an opinion about it
- Explain the reason or the background
- Connect listening and reading passages

Reading
45 seconds

Announcement concerning a proposal for a branch campus

The university is soliciting state and local funding to build a branch campus on the west side of the city where the I-19 expressway crosses the 201 loop. This location should provide convenient educational opportunities for students who live closer to the new campus as well as for those students who may choose to live on the west side once the campus is established. The city plan for the next ten years indicates that there will be major growth near the proposed site, including housing and a shopping area. By building a branch campus, some of the crowding on the main campus may be resolved.

 Problem 27, Talk

I understand that a branch campus on the city's west side would be convenient for students who live near the proposed site, and it might attract more local students, but I oppose the plan because it will redirect funds from the main campus where several classroom buildings need repair. Hanover Hall for one. And, uh, a lot of the equipment in the chemistry and physics labs should be replaced. In my lab classes, we don't do some of the experiments because, uh, because we don't have enough equipment. And we need more teachers on the main campus. I'd like to see the branch campus funding allocated for teachers' salaries in order to decrease the student-teacher ratios. Most of the freshman classes are huge, and there's very little interaction with professors. Um, a branch campus would be a good addition, but not until some of the problems on the main campus have been taken care of.

Example Notes—Situation and Opinion

Plans to open a branch campus

- convenient for students near
- might attract more students
- relieve crowding on main campus

But will redirect funds from main campus

- buildings need repair
- equipment should be replaced
- more teachers—smaller classes

 Problem 27, Example Question

The man expresses his opinion of the proposal in the announcement. Report his opinion and explain the reasons he gives for having that opinion.

 Problem 27, Example Answer

The man concedes that the branch campus might be advantageous for students living close to the new location, but he's concerned that the funding for a branch campus will affect funding on main campus for . . . for important capital improvements such as classroom buildings that are, uh, in need of repair. Um, and equipment in the science labs is getting old, so it needs to be replaced. And he also points out that more teachers are needed for the main campus in order to reduce student-teacher ratios, which . . . which would improve the quality of the teaching and the, uh, amount of interaction in classes.

So the man feels that more attention should be given to the main campus and funding should be directed to improve the main campus before a branch campus is considered.

Checklist 3

✔ The talk summarizes the situation and opinion.
✔ The point of view or position is clear.
✔ The talk is direct and well-organized.
✔ The sentences are logically connected.
✔ Details and examples support the opinion.
✔ The speaker expresses complete thoughts.
✔ The meaning is easy to comprehend.
✔ A wide range of vocabulary is used.
✔ Errors in grammar are minor.
✔ The talk is within a range of 125–150 words.

PROBLEM 28: EXAMPLES

In this question, you will be asked to listen to a speaker and read a short passage on the same topic. The topic usually involves a general concept and a specific example of it. Sometimes the speaker provides a contradictory point of view. After you hear the question, you will be asked to explain the example and relate it to the concept or contrast the opposing views.

You will have 45 seconds to read the passage. After you have listened to the talk, you will have 30 seconds to prepare and 60 seconds to speak.

Task

- Explain how an example supports a concept OR
  Contrast one view with another view
- Connect listening and reading passages

Reading
45 seconds

The telegraphic nature of early sentences in child language is a result of the omission of grammatical words such as the article *the* and auxiliary verbs *is* and *are* as well as word endings such as *-ing*, *-ed*, or *-s*. By the end of the third year, these grammatical forms begin to appear in the speech of most children. It is evident that a great deal of grammatical knowledge is required before these structures can be used correctly, and errors are commonly observed. The correction of grammatical errors is a feature of the speech of preschoolers four and five years old. The study of the errors in child language is interesting because it demonstrates when and how grammar is acquired.

 Problem 28, Lecture

English uses a system of about a dozen word endings to express grammatical meaning—the *–ing* for present time, *-s* for possession and plurality, and, uh, the *cd* for the past, to mention only a few. But, um, how and when do children learn them? Well, in a classic study by Berko in the 1950s, investigators . . . they elicited a series of forms that required the target endings. For example, a picture was shown of a bird, and . . . and the investigator identified it by saying, "This is a Wug." Then the children were shown two similar birds, to, uh, . . . to elicit the sentence, "There are two___." And if the children completed the sentence by saying "Wugs," well, then it was inferred that they had learned the *–s* ending. Okay. Essential to that study was the use of nonsense words like "Wug," since the manipulation of the endings could have been supported by words that the children had . . . had already heard. In any case, charts were developed to demonstrate the, uh, the gradual natural of grammatical acquisition. And the performance by children from eighteen months to four years confirmed the basic theory of child language that the, uh, . . . the gradual reduction of grammatical errors . . . that these are evidence of language acquisition.

Example Notes—Concept and Example

Word endings—grammatical relationships

- *-ed* past
- *-s* plural

Wug experiment—Berko

- Nonsense words—not influenced by familiar
- Manipulated endings
- Data about development

Problem 28, Example Question

Describe the Wug experiment and explain why the results supported the basic theory of child language acquisition.

Problem 28, Example Answer

In English, there are several important word endings that express grammatical relationships, for example, the *-ed* ending signals that the speaker's talking about the past and the *-s* ending means "more than one," uh, when it's used at the end of a noun. So, when children learn English, they, um, they make errors in these endings, but they gradually refine their use until they master them. In the Wug experiment, Berko created nonsense words to get children to use endings . . . so . . . so the researchers could, uh, follow their development. It was important not to use *real* words because the children might have been influenced by a word they'd heard before. So this experiment provided data about the time it takes and the age when endings are learned. It supported the basic theory of child language that, um, sorting out grammatical errors is a feature of the speech of . . . of four-year-olds . . . and a stage in language acquisition.

Checklist 4

✔ The talk relates an example to a concept.
✔ Inaccuracies in the content are minor.
✔ The talk is direct and well-organized.
✔ The sentences are logically connected.
✔ Details and examples support the opinion.
✔ The speaker expresses complete thoughts.
✔ The meaning is easy to comprehend.
✔ A wide range of vocabulary is used.
✔ The speaker paraphrases in his/her own words.
✔ The speaker credits the lecturer with wording.
✔ Errors in grammar are minor.
✔ The talk is within a range of 125–150 words.

PROBLEM 29: PROBLEMS

In this question, you will be asked to listen to a conversation and explain a problem as well as the solutions that are proposed.

After you have listened to the conversation, you will have 20 seconds to prepare and 60 seconds to speak.

Task

- Describe a problem and several recommendations
- Express an opinion about the better solution OR
  Propose an alternative solution

 Problem 29, Conversation

Student 1: Did your scholarship check come yet?
Student 2: Yeah, it came last week. Didn't yours?
Student 1: No. That's the problem. And everything's due at the same time—tuition, my dorm fee, and let's not forget about books. I need about four hundred dollars just for books.
Student 2: Well, do you have any money left from last semester, in your checking account, I mean?

Student 1:	Some, but not nearly enough. The check probably won't be here until the end of the month and I won't get paid at work for two more weeks . . . I don't know what I'm going to do.
Student 2:	How about your credit card? Could you use that?
Student 1:	Maybe, but I'm afraid I'll get the credit card bill before I get the scholarship check; then I'll be in worse trouble because of, you know, the interest rate for the credit card on top of everything else.
Student 2:	I see your point. Still, the check might come before the credit card bill. You might have to gamble, unless . . .
Student 1:	I'm listening.
Student 2:	Well, unless you take out a student loan. A short-term loan. They have them set up at the Student Credit Union. Isn't that where you have your checking account?
Student 1:	Umhum.
Student 2:	So you could take out a short-term loan and pay it off on the day that you get your check. It wouldn't cost that much for interest because it would probably be only a few weeks. That's what I'd do.

Example Notes—Problem and Possible Solutions, Opinion, and Reasons

Problem—not enough money

- Scholarship check late
- Books, tuition, dorm due

Solutions

- Use credit card
- Take out student loan

Opinion—support student loan

- Paid same day
- $ not much

Problem 29, Example Question

Describe the woman's budgeting problem and the two suggestions that the man makes. What do you think the woman should do and why?

Problem 29, Example Answer

The woman doesn't have enough money for her expenses. Um, she has to pay tuition and her dorm fee is due at the same time. Besides that, she needs to buy books. So the problem is everything has to be paid now, and she won't get her scholarship check until the end of the month, and she won't get her paycheck for two weeks. Um, the man suggests that she use her credit card because she won't have to pay it off until the end of the month, but the problem is . . . the . . . the interest would be substantial if the scholarship check is delayed. The other idea—to take out a student loan—that seems better because the loan could be paid off on the day the check arrives instead of a fixed date, and it wouldn't cost much to get a short-term loan at the Student Credit Union. So . . . I support applying for a student loan.

Checklist 5

✔ The talk summarizes the problem and recommendations.
✔ The speaker's point of view or position is clear.
✔ The talk is direct and well-organized.
✔ The sentences are logically connected.
✔ Details and examples support the opinion.
✔ The speaker expresses complete thoughts.
✔ The meaning is easy to comprehend.
✔ A wide range of vocabulary is used.
✔ Errors in grammar are minor.
✔ The talk is within a range of 125–150 words.

PROBLEM 30: SUMMARIES

In this question, you will be asked to listen to part of an academic lecture and to give a summary of it.

After you have listened to the lecture, you will have 20 seconds to prepare and 60 seconds to speak.

Task

- Comprehend part of an academic lecture
- Summarize the main points

 Problem 30, Lecture

Two types of irrigation methods that are used worldwide are mentioned in your textbook. Flood irrigation—that's been a method in use since ancient times—and we still use it today where water's cheap. Basically, canals connect a water supply like a river or a reservoir to the fields where ditches are constructed with valves, uh, valves that allow farmers to siphon water from the canal, sending it down through the ditches. So that way the field can be totally flooded, or smaller, narrow ditches along the rows can be filled with water to irrigate the crop. But, this method does have quite a few disadvantages. Like I said, it's contingent upon cheap water because it isn't very efficient and the flooding isn't easy to control, I mean, the rows closer to the canal usually receive much more water, and of course, if the field isn't flat, then the water won't be evenly distributed. Not to mention the cost of building canals and ditches and maintaining the system. So let's consider the alternative—the sprinkler system. In this method of irrigation, it's easier to control the water and more efficient since the water's directed only on the plants. But, in hot climates, some of the water can evaporate in the air. Still, the main problem with sprinklers is the expense for installation and maintenance because there's a very complicated pipe system and that usually involves a lot more repair and even replacement of parts, and of course, we have to factor in the labor costs in feasibility studies for sprinklers.

Example Notes—Main Points

Flood

- Not efficient
- Difficult to control—flat fields
- Initial expense to build canals, ditches
- Requires maintenance

Sprinkler

- Complicated pipe system
- Expensive to install, maintain, repair, replace
- Labor cost

 Problem 30, Example Question

Using examples from the lecture, describe two general types of irrigation systems. Then explain the disadvantages of each type.

 Problem 30, Example Answer

Two methods of irrigation were discussed in the lecture. First, flood irrigation. It involves the release of water into canals and drainage ditches that flow into the fields. The disadvantages of the flood method, um, well, it isn't very efficient since more water is used in flooding than the crops actually, uh, need, and also it isn't easy to control. Another problem is the initial expense for the construction of the canals and the connecting ditches as well as . . . as maintenance. And besides that, if the fields aren't flat, the water doesn't—I mean, it isn't distributed evenly. The second method is sprinkler irrigation, which uses less water and provides better control, but there is some evaporation, and the pipe system's complicated and can be expensive to install and maintain. So . . . there's usually a lot more labor cost because the equipment must be repaired and replaced more often that a canal system.

Checklist 6

✔ The talk summarizes a short lecture.
✔ Inaccuracies in the content are minor.
✔ The talk is direct and well-organized.
✔ The sentences are logically connected.
✔ Details and examples support the opinion.
✔ The speaker expresses complete thoughts.
✔ The meaning is easy to comprehend.
✔ A wide range of vocabulary is used.
✔ The speaker paraphrases in his/her own words.
✔ The speaker credits the lecturer with wording.
✔ Errors in grammar are minor.
✔ The talk is within a range of 125–150 words.

SPEAKING STRATEGIES

In addition to the academic skills that you learned in the previous chapter, there are several speaking strategies that will help you succeed on the TOEFL and after the TOEFL.

➤ Anticipate the first question

You will probably be asked to talk about familiar topics at the beginning of the Speaking section. If you think about some of these topics, you will know how to answer when you hear the questions. A few seconds to prepare does not give you enough time to organize your thoughts unless you have the advantage of prior preparation.

You may be asked to choose a favorite person, place, activity, or item to talk about. To prepare for this question, spend a few minutes thinking about your personal favorites.

- Prepare some answers
- Read them aloud

EXAMPLE

My favorite pastime is

_____*traveling*_____ .

1. My favorite teacher is

_____ .

2. My favorite city is

_____ .

3. My favorite class is

_____ .

4. My favorite book is

_____ .

5. My favorite movie is

_____ .

6. My favorite sport is

_____ .

7. My favorite vacation place is

_____ .

8. My favorite holiday is

_____ .

9. My favorite music is

_____ .

10. My favorite person is

_____ .

➤ Support your answers

The directions in speaking questions usually ask you to give examples or reasons to support your answers. Develop the habit of adding the word *because* after your opinions, and provide at least two reasons to support your position. You will become a better thinker and a better speaker. For example, "My favorite pastime is traveling *because* I like to meet people and I enjoy learning about different places." "My favorite city is San Diego *because* the climate is beautiful year round and there are many interesting sights in or near the city."

- Use the word *because*
- Give two or three examples or reasons

➤ Understand the task

You must listen to the question to understand how to organize your answer. If you are being asked to state an opinion, you should state your opinion and argue only one side of the issue. If you are being asked to argue both sides of the issue and take a stand, then the task is very different. In that case, you will have to make a case for both sides before you state your opinion.

- Read the question carefully
- Respond to the topic

➤ Pronounce to communicate

Everyone has an accent in English. People from Australia have an Australian accent. People from the United States have an American accent. People from Britain have a British accent. See what I mean? The important point is that your accent is okay as long as the listener can understand you. It is good to try to improve your pronunciation, but communication is more important for the TOEFL and for your academic and professional life.

- Accept your accent
- Improve communication

➤ Sound confident

If you speak in a very low voice, hesitating and apologizing, the listener makes some negative assumptions. This person is not confident. This person probably doesn't know the answer. Try to speak up and sound assertive without being aggressive. It helps to start with a smile on your face.

- Speak up
- Be assertive

➤ Read 135 words per minute

Yes, this is a speaking strategy. To succeed on the Speaking section, you will be asked to read short passages of about 100 words each, and you will have about 45 seconds in which to complete the reading. This reading speed is not impossibly fast, but you will have to avoid re-reading phrases in order to finish within the time limit. When you take the quiz at the end of this section, you will hear a cue to start reading, and a question at the end of 45 seconds. This will help you time yourself. You probably already read 135 words per minute. If not, work on reading faster, using the reading strategies at the beginning of this chapter.

- Time yourself
- Increase speed to 135

➤ Adapt notes

The system for taking notes that you learned in Chapter 3 can be made more effective by adapting it for each question. Use the task and the question to anticipate an outline for your notes. Refer to the example notes for Problems 25–30 on pages 199–211 for models of adapted notes.

- Use a system for taking notes
- Adapt the format for each question

➤ Pace yourself

There is no time for a long introduction. You have one minute or less to make your point. Start immediately with a direct statement. For example, "The lecturer compares bacteria and viruses." Include the most important points. When you practice speaking, using the model tests in this book, you will hear a prompt to start and a beep to end your speech. On the TOEFL, you must stop when the beep sounds. Always time yourself when you are practicing for the Speaking section. If you are not using the audio timing, then set a kitchen timer for the number of seconds that corresponds to the type of test problem that you are practicing—45 or 60—and then begin speaking. When the bell rings, stop speaking. Did you complete your thought or did you have more to say? Learn to pace yourself. Soon you will develop a sense of timing for the questions and you will know how much you can say in a short answer.

- Start with a direct statement
- Make a few major points
- Set a timer

➤ Prepare key phrases

Some key phrases are useful for each of the problems in the Speaking section.

Question 1: Experiences

My favorite _____ is _____ because _____ .

Question 2: Preferences

Although some people _____ , I prefer _____ because _____ .

Although there are many good reasons why _____, I favor _____ because _____ .

Although a good argument can be made for _____ , my preference is _____ because _____ .

Question 3: Reports

The speaker supports _____ because _____ .

The speaker opposes _____ because _____ .

Question 4: Examples

According to the (reading, lecture) _____ .

_____ is an example of _____ .

Question 5: Problems

The problem is that _____ .

According to _____ , one solution is to _____ .

Another possibility is to _____ .

I think that the best solution is to _____ because _____ .

It seems to me that _____ is the best solution because _____ .

Question 6: Summaries

Definition: According to the lecturer, a _____ is _____ .

Description: According to the lecturer, a _____ has (three) characteristics.

Classification: (Two) types of _____ were discussed in the lecture.

Chronology:	The lecturer explained the sequence of events for _____ .
Comparison:	The lecturer compared _____ with _____ .
Contrast:	The lecturer contrasted _____ with _____ .
Cause and Effect:	The lecturer explains why _____ .
Problem and Solution:	The lecturer presents several solutions for the problem of _____ .

- Study the key phrases
- Practice using them

➤ Use verbal pauses

If you get to a point where you don't know what to say, it is better to use some verbal pauses to think instead of stopping and thinking in silence. Silence on the tape is going to lose points for you. You can say, *Okay, Now, Um, And,* or *Uh.* All of these verbal pauses are very common in the speech of native speakers. Of course, if you use these too often, you will also lose points because they will distract the listener and you won't have enough time to answer the question completely.

- Learn verbal pauses
- Use them when necessary

➤ Correct yourself

How can you correct yourself while you are speaking? First, recognize the difference between mistakes and slips. Most of the time, you *don't know* that you have made a mistake, but you *do know* when you make a slip. Even native speakers make mistakes and slips in grammar. In a very long sentence, we can forget whether the subject was singular or plural, and we can make a mistake. But sometimes we hear our mistake, and we correct slips by backing up and starting over. Some commonly used phrases to correct a previous grammatical slip are *I mean* or *that is*. For example, "The worker bees that take care of the young is called, I mean are called, nurses." These phrases can be used to correct content, too. For example, "Drones are female bees, I mean, male bees." A good rule is to always correct slips in content and correct slips in grammar and word choice if you can do it quickly and move along without interrupting the flow of your speech.

- Correct slips
- Use common phrases

➤ Speak to the criteria for evaluation

There are checklists for each question on the Speaking section. Use these checklists to evaluate your speaking. If you do not know how to use the checklist, get some extra help. For other options to evaluate your speaking, see pages 226–227.

- Keep the checklists in mind
- Take advantage of other options

➤ Stay positive

It is natural to be a little anxious about speaking in a second language, but it is important not to become negative and frightened. Negative thoughts can interfere with your concentration, and you may not hear the questions correctly. Take some deep breaths before each question and say this in your mind: "I am a good speaker. I am ready to speak." If you begin to have negative thoughts during the test, take another deep breath and think "confidence" as you breathe in. Focus on listening to the questions. Focus on taking notes.

- Take deep breaths
- Use positive self-talk

APPLYING THE ACADEMIC SKILLS TO THE TOEFL

➤ Taking notes

Taking notes is an important academic skill for the Speaking section because you will use them to organize your talk and you will refer to them while you are speaking. When you take notes, it will help you to adapt to the type of question presented. Use the example notes in this chapter to help you. Your ability to take notes will support your success on every question in the Speaking section.

➤ Paraphrasing

Many of the answer choices are paraphrases of information from the passage. Your ability to recognize paraphrases will be helpful as you choose your answers.

➤ Summarizing

You will be speaking a minute or less in response to each question. You must be brief, but you must also include all of your major points. In other words, you must summarize. The first two questions in the Speaking section require you to talk about familiar topics. In these questions, you can summarize your experiences. The last two questions require you to summarize the information in a conversation and a lecture. Your ability to summarize will be crucial for you to score well on this section.

➤ Synthesizing

This important skill is tested in two questions on the Speaking section. Question 3 requires you to synthesize the information in a talk and in a short reading. Question 4 requires you to synthesize the information in a reading passage and in a lecture. You will receive points not only for speaking well but also for including accurate content. The ability to integrate reading and listening by synthesizing information will be necessary for you to achieve a high score on the Speaking section.

QUIZ FOR THE SPEAKING SECTION

This is a quiz for the Speaking section of the TOEFL® iBT. This section tests your ability to communicate in English in an academic context. During the quiz, you will respond to six speaking questions. You may take notes. You may use your notes to answer the questions. The reading passages and the questions are printed in the book for this quiz, but most of the directions will be spoken on the official TOEFL® iBT. The entire script for the quiz and example answers is printed in Chapter 7 on pages 398–406.

 Quiz for the Speaking Section

QUESTION 1

If you were asked to choose one movie that has influenced your thinking, which one would you choose? Why? What was especially impressive about the movie? Use specific reasons and details to explain your choice.

Preparation Time: 15 seconds
Recording Time: 45 seconds

QUESTION 2

Some people think that teachers should be evaluated by the performance of their students on standardized tests at the end of the term. Other people maintain that teachers should be judged by their own performance in the classroom, and not by the scores that their students achieve on tests. Which approach do you think is better and why? Use specific reasons and examples to support your opinion.

Preparation Time: 15 seconds
Recording Time: 45 seconds

QUESTION 3

Reading Time: 45 seconds

Policy for Tuition

In order to qualify for instate tuition, a student must have lived within this state for a period of not less than one year. Furthermore, the instate address must be the permanent residence of the student. College campus addresses may not be used as permanent residences. The student's driver's license and any vehicles must be registered in the state, and the previous year's state tax form must have been submitted to this state. Voter registration and a high school diploma may also be used as evidence of instate status. Spouses and children of military personnel qualify for instate tuition without residence requirements.

Student:

Well, I agree with most of the policy, but what I don't understand is why I have to use my parents' address as my permanent address. This is my third year in a dorm on campus, and I've gone to school every summer, so I've lived in this state for three consecutive years. I don't pay state taxes because I don't earn enough as a full-time student to, uh, to pay taxes, but I don't receive support from my parents either. I have a small grant and a student loan that I'm responsible for, and . . . and I plan to live and work in this state after I graduate, so, um, I think students like me should be eligible for a waiver.

The student expresses his opinion of the policy for instate tuition. Report his opinion and explain the reasons that he gives for having that opinion.

Preparation Time: 30 seconds
Recording Time: 60 seconds

QUESTION 4

Reading Time: 45 seconds

Communication with Primates

Early experiments to teach primates to communicate with their voices failed because of the differences in their vocal organs, not their intellectual capacity. Dramatic progress was observed when researchers began to communicate by using American Sign Language. Some chimpanzees were able to learn several hundred signs that they put together to express a number of relationships similar to the initial language acqusition of children. In addition, success was achieved by using plastic symbols on a magnetic board, each of which represented a word. For example, a small blue triangle represented an apple. Chimpanzees were able to respond correctly to basic sequences and even to form some higher-level concepts by using the representative system.

Professor:

Let me tell you about an experiment that didn't turn out quite like the researcher had expected. Dr. Sue Savage-Rumbaugh had been trying to train a chimpanzee to use a keyboard adapted with symbols. But no luck. What is interesting about the experiment is that the chimpanzee's adopted son Kanzi, also a bonobo Chimpanzee, well, Kanzi had been observing the lessons and had acquired a rather impressive vocabulary. After that, Kanzi was not given structured training, but he was taught language while walking through the forest or in other informal settings with his trainers. By six years of age, Kanzi had acquired a vocabulary of more than 200 words and was able to form sentences by combining words with gestures or with other words. So, the question is this: should we proceed by trying to teach language to primates in a classroom environment, or should we simply live with them and interact informally like we do with beginning learners of language in our own species? I tend to side with those who elect to support language acquisition in natural settings.

Explain the importance of the Kanzi experiment in the context of research on primate communication.

Preparation Time: 30 seconds
Recording Time: 60 seconds

QUESTION 5

Friend:	Did you decide to take Johnson's class?
Student:	Yeah. I'm going to work it out somehow. Yesterday I walked from the chemistry lab to Hamilton Hall—that's where Johnson's class is.
Friend:	And?
Student:	And it took me twenty minutes.
Friend:	Uh-oh. You only have fifteen minutes between classes, so that means you'll be five minutes late. Listen, why don't you buy a bike? I'm sure you could cut at least five minutes off your time if you took the bike trail.
Student:	I thought about that. But then I'd have to get a license, and I'd have to find somewhere to store it at night. I thought it might be a hassle.
Friend:	Oh, it's not so bad. I have a bike. The license is only ten dollars, and I just park my bike on the deck outside my apartment when the weather's good. And the weather should be okay for most of spring semester.
Student:	That's true.
Friend:	Well, your other option is to talk with Dr. Johnson. Maybe he'll give you permission to be five minutes late to his class because of the distance from your lab. Actually, I've had several classes with him, and he seems very approachable. Anyway, it's an alternative to the bike, if you don't want to do that.

Describe the woman's problem and the two suggestions that her friend makes about how to handle it. What do you think the woman should do, and why?

Preparation Time: 20 seconds
Recording Time: 60 seconds

QUESTION 6

Professor:
Of course, stars are too hot to support life, but the light from a star warms orbiting planets or moons, supplying the energy needed for life to develop. Besides energy, a liquid, let's say, a chemical solvent of some kind, is also

necessary. On Earth, the solvent in which life developed was water, but others such as ammonia, hydrogen fluoride, or methane might also be appropriate. So, in order for the solvent to remain in liquid form, the planet or moon must lie within a certain range of distances from the star. Why is this so? Well, think about it. If the planet is too close to the star, the solvent will change into a gas, boiling and evaporating. If it is too far from the star, the solvent will freeze, transforming into a solid. For our sun and life as we know it, the habitable zone appears to lie between the orbits of Venus and Mars. Within this range, water remains liquid. And until recently, this area was indeed the accepted scientific definition of the habitable zone for our solar system. But now scientists have postulated that the habitable zone may be larger than originally supposed. They speculate that the strong gravitational pull caused by larger planets may produce enough energy to heat the cores of orbiting moons. So that means that these moons may support life. There may be habitable zones far beyond Venus!

Using the main points and examples from the lecture, describe the habitable zone, and then explain how the definition has been expanded by modern scientists.

Preparation Time: 20 seconds
Recording Time: 60 seconds

STOP   **This is the end of the Speaking Quiz. To check your answers, refer to the Progress Chart for the Speaking Quiz, Chapter 7, page 404.**

STUDY PLAN

What did you learn from taking the quiz? What will you do differently when you take the model tests in the next chapters? Take a few minutes to think and then write a sentence or two to help you revise your study plan.

EXTRA CREDIT

After you have completed this chapter, you may want to continue a review of speaking. Here are some suggestions.

Listen to good models of speaking in similar situations. Research is clearly on the side of those who advocate listening as a method to improve speaking. This means that one of the best ways to learn to speak well is to listen to good speakers. It is also important to simulate the kind of speaking situation that you will be required to complete. On the TOEFL, you have six questions and six situations. If you ask similar questions to excellent speakers and listen carefully to their responses, you will learn a great deal. That is why this book contains recorded examples of the answers that excellent speakers might provide for the questions in this review chapter and in the Speaking section of each model test. For extra credit and improvement, ask teachers or English-speaking friends to record their answers to the Speaking questions in this book. Don't give them the questions in advance. Use the same presentation and timing that you are using for the model tests. Then listen to their answers.

Practice using the telephone to speak. Call a friend to practice some of the speaking questions by phone. Speak directly into the phone. Ask your friend to confirm that you are speaking at a good volume to be heard clearly and that you sound confident, but not arrogant. If your friend is a native speaker, you can ask some of the Speaking questions and listen to the responses. Some telephones have a recording option. With your friend's permission, you can record the call.

OPTIONS FOR EVALUATION

It is difficult to evaluate your own speaking. If you are taking an English class, ask your teacher to use the checklists in this chapter to evaluate your speaking. You need to know how you are progressing in relationship to the criteria on the checklists because that is how you will be evaluated on the TOEFL® iBT.

If you do not have good options to have your speaking evaluated without a fee, there is a fee-based option that will provide professional evaluations. See page 527 for details.

ADVISOR'S OFFICE

When you face a challenge, "fake it until you can make it." This means that you should act as though everything were working out well, even when you have doubts. Put a smile on your face, even if it isn't real, and eventually it will be a real smile. Stand up straight with your head high and walk with purpose. You will start to actually feel more confident. If you are acting like a successful person, it may feel strange at first. But the more you practice your role as a successful person, the more comfortable you will be. Soon, when you reach your goals and you are truly successful, you will have practiced the role, and you will be the person you have been playing.

WRITING

OVERVIEW OF THE WRITING SECTION

The Writing section tests your ability to write essays in English similar to those that you would write in college courses.

During the test, you will write two essays. The integrated essay asks for your response to an academic reading passage and a lecture on the same topic. You may take notes as you read and listen, but notes are not graded. You may use your notes to write the essay. The lecture will be spoken, but the directions and the questions will be written. You will have 20 minutes to plan, write, and revise your response. Typically, a good essay for the integrated topic will require that you write 150–225 words.

The independent essay usually asks for your opinion about a familiar topic. You will have 30 minutes to plan, write, and revise your response. Typically, a good essay for the independent topic will require that you write 300–350 words.

A clock on the screen will show you how much time you have to complete each essay.

REVIEW OF PROBLEMS FOR THE WRITING SECTION

➤ Prompts

A prompt for the Writing section is either a question that refers to both a spoken and written text for the integrated essay or a written question for the independent essay. Problems 31–34 in this review refer to the kind of prompts that are typical on the TOEFL. On the official TOEFL® iBT, you will be asked to respond to one integrated question and one independent question. The scripts for the spoken prompts have been printed for you to study while you listen to them. On the official TOEFL® iBT, you will not see the spoken prompt. You will see the written question and textbook passage.

➤ Problems

The problems in this review represent the types of questions that are most frequently tested on the TOEFL. The task for each problem is explained. Each problem appears as one of the two questions included in the Writing section.

PROBLEM 31: SYNTHESIS OF OPPOSING IDEAS

In this integrated essay question, you will be asked to read a short passage from a textbook and then listen to part of a short lecture about the same topic. The ideas in the textbook and the lecture will not agree. After you read the question, you write an essay that includes information from both the reading and the lecture.

You will have 20 minutes to plan, write, and revise your essay. Typically, a good response will require that you write 150–225 words.

Task

- Read a short passage and take notes
- Listen to a short lecture and take notes
- Answer a question using information from *both* the reading and the lecture

Reading Passage
Time: 3 minutes

In his classic book *The Interpretation of Dreams*, published in 1900, Sigmund Freud identified wish fulfillment as the origin of many dreams. For example, a student who is concerned about taking an important exam may dream about the exam, or, more likely, some type of symbol for the exam will appear in a dream. Since thoughts must be translated into concrete images, dreams are expressed in pictures rather than in words. Freud advanced the notion of dream symbols, that is, images with deep symbolic meaning. In the case of the exam, it might be expressed as an obstacle or a hurdle in a race. In Freud's view, dreams have much in common with daydreams. There is a wish that is forbidden or repressed in some way, and forces that oppose it. In the case of dreams while sleeping, they offer a compromise, that is, a way for the wish to be expressed safely.

According to Freud, dreams can be viewed as a way to reveal the unconscious. To that end, there are two levels to every dream, including the manifest content, which is obvious and direct, and the latent content, which is symbolic. To return to the example of the student's dream, the manifest content would be the hurdle in the race, but the latent content would be the exam that is in the dreamer's subconscious. Because some wishes and desires are too disturbing or too socially inappropriate to surface from the unconscious to the conscious mind, the symbols that are employed may make the wish difficult to expose. The student may actually want to cheat in order to succeed on the exam, but in a dream, borrowing a friend's book may be a more acceptable way to express that desire. In a sense, the dream serves to protect the mind from a conflict in the unconscious.

Reading Passage Notes
Freud 1900 Interp. Dreams

- wish fulfillment ← d

Ex

- student d exam or symbol
- d = pictures Ø words
- symbols images
- exam = obstacle in race

D = daydreams

- wish repressed
- d safe express
- d reveal unconscious

2 levels = manifest content = obvious, direct/obstacle race
latent content = symbolic/exam

- wishes disturbing or inapprop
- symbols protect from conflict

Problem 31, Lecture. Now read a lecture on the same topic as the passage you have just read.

As you will recall from the reading in your textbook, Freud's psychodynamic theory is premised on the assumption that dreams arise from a troubled subconscious mind, and so they have deep meaning. But there are other points of view that you should be familiar with. Allan Hobson and Robert McCarley propose a very different theory of dreams. They turn to biochemical research and physiology for answers. Using data from their study of sleep activity in cats, and by the way, they used cats because cats have brain waves and muscle movements during sleep that are very similar to those of humans. In any case, Hobson and McCarley determined that the kind of sleep associated with dreams is controlled from the brain stem and, furthermore, that there are chemicals in the stem that regulate the firing of certain neurons. So they posit that during dream sleep, brain cells that control movement and balance are activated, but the messages do not transfer to the body and, consequently, no movement is initiated. Still, the brain is trying to interpret the messages, so dreams occur.

But how does this explain what we dream about? I mean the content. Well, let's take the example of a common dream. Let's say, you are trying to escape from something. The brain receives a message to run, but the legs don't respond. According to the activation-synthesis theory, the dream that results will probably include something about being chased and running away. In other words, you will play out the physical movement in a dream. But, according to the proponents of the activation-synthesis theory, there isn't any hidden meaning in your dream. Your unfulfilled desires have nothing to do with it. For the neurophysiologists, a dream is just a chemical response to brain cells.

Lecture Notes
Hobsin + MacKarly

- biochemical research + physiology
- sleep activity cats/brain waves, muscle movements = humans
- dreams ←
- chemicals → firing neurons   brain cells → movement
- Ø transfer body = no movement/interpret message dream

Ex

- escape dream
- brain message – run   Ø legs → chase + run
- activation synthesis theory
- no hidden meaning or unfulfilled desires
- chem. response to brain cells

Essay Question

Summarize the main points in the lecture, contrasting them with the ideas in the reading passage.

Integrated Essay

In research with cats, Hobsin and MacKarly concluded that dreams are the result of chemicals in the brain that cause neurons to fire. Although the brain is signaling the body to move, the message does not reach the muscles. Instead, it is interpreted in a dream. The example the lecturer cited was a dream in which a person wants to escape. The brain signals the legs to run, but instead, the dreamer sees images of himself being chased. According to the theory, dreams are simply a chemical response to neurological activity.

This new model, called activation synthesis theory, contrasts sharply with the earlier theory that Freud put forward in his classic book *The Interpretation of Dreams*, in which he explained dreaming as symbolic images that reveal repressed desires and unfulfilled wishes. Furthermore, Freud interpreted dreams on two levels. The first, manifest content, was the literal or direct interpretation, whereas the second, latent content, exposed the symbolic nature of the image. For example, a student who is worried about an exam may dream about an obstacle in a race, creating the manifest content of the obstacle on a race track because of the underlying latent content associated with the exam.

For Hobsin and MacKarly, no unfulfilled wishes are relevant in the student's dream. The chemistry of the brain and not the psyche causes the vision of the race track and all other images in dreams.

Checklist for Integrated Essay

✔ The essay answers the topic question.
✔ Inaccuracies in the content are minor.
✔ The essay is direct and well-organized.
✔ The sentences are logically connected.
✔ Details and examples support the main idea.
✔ The writer expresses complete thoughts.
✔ The meaning is easy to comprehend.
✔ A wide range of vocabulary is used.
✔ The writer paraphrases in his/her own words.

✔ The writer credits the author with wording.
✔ Errors in grammar and idioms are minor.
✔ The academic topic essay is within a range of 150–225 words.

Evaluator's Comments
The essay answers the topic question and the content is accurate. The writer credits the researchers and paraphrases ideas. It is a well-organized essay with logically connected sentences. The meaning is clear.

PROBLEM 32: SYNTHESIS OF SUPPORTING IDEAS

In this integrated essay question, you will be asked to read a short passage from a textbook and then listen to part of a short lecture about the same topic. The ideas in the textbook and the lecture will agree. After you read the question, you write an essay that includes information from both the reading and the lecture.

You will have 20 minutes to plan, write, and revise your essay. Typically, a good response will require that you write 150–225 words.

Task

- Read a short passage and take notes
- Listen to a short lecture and take notes
- Answer a question using information from *both* the reading and the lecture

Reading Passage
Time: 3 minutes

According to the nebular hypothesis, between 4 and 5 million years ago, a large cloud of dust and gas collected around the region in which the current solar system is positioned. Although similar clouds of dust and gas referred to as nebulae are relatively common and may be found throughout the galaxy, in this cloud as much as 99 percent of the material consisted of hydrogen and helium, and all other naturally occurring elements were also included in small proportions.

Gravity initiated a collapse in the cloud, which in turn caused it to spin rapidly. This spinning resulted in a disk shape with a rounded middle and flat edges. Random regions exerted a stronger gravitational pull and solid elements began to connect and, ultimately, to break apart into small objects called planetesimals ranging in size from a few feet to a few miles. As these planetesimals collided and captured each other, distinct masses concentrated in areas approximately where the planets are now found.

At the same time that the planets were forming, the Sun began to transform itself into a star. The star, which had retained almost 99 percent of the nebula's original mass, radiated light and heat. The planets nearest the center, which we call the terrestrial planets, were formed from materials that did not disintegrate at higher temperatures, whereas the planets farther away, called the Jovian planets, contained virtually the same mix of helium, hydrogen, and trace elements as the original nebula and were able to condense at much lower temperatures. Asteroids and comets were also swirling around the system, including matter that was not collected by collision with a planet or the gravitational pull of a planet. The fact that the orbits of all the planets lie near the same plane is further evidence of the solar system's rapid rotation when the nebular cloud began to flatten out.

Reading Passage Notes
Nebular Hypothesis

- 4–5 m yrs ago
- cloud dust + gas → solar system
- 99% hydrogen + helium w/all elements
- gravity collapse → spin/disk rounded mid + flat edges
- random regions = strong gravity → connect + break apart planetisimals
- planetisimals collided + captured → planets
- Sun 99% nebula's mass → light + heat

- planets near = terrestrial/not disintegrate higher temp
    far = Jovian/same mix hydrogen + helium etc as
        cloud/condense lower temp
- asteroids + comets swirl
- orbits near same plane = evidence rapid rotation

Problem 32, Lecture. Now read a lecture on the same topic as the passage you have just read.

Newer high-speed computers have allowed us to perform experiments by modeling events that would be very difficult to duplicate under natural conditions. And we have been able to do some interesting research with models of the collapse of an interstellar cloud under the influence of its own gravitational pull. The modeling has led to a general consensus that stars form in that way—a process of collapse, I mean. So, although the experiments are not definitive, they lead us to the logical conclusion that when a star is born, it will probably have a circumstellar nebula with conditions that are very favorable to the formation of planets. In effect, we have been able to watch the conditions that existed at the beginning of the formation of the solar system, and observe how the planets were formed. And that's pretty amazing. Furthermore, the modeling suggests that the planetary formation seems to be a natural consequence of the process that initiates the formation of a star. So, this suggests that planetary systems are the rule, rather than the exception. And that means that an organized search for other planetary systems should yield some rather interesting results. We may find that the nebular hypothesis is valid not only for our solar system but also for other systems in the universe. Besides that, when we do the math, we have to assume that at least some of the stars would produce solar systems with planets that could support life.

Lecture Notes
Computer model

- research collapse interstellar cloud influence gravity
- stars form = process collapse
- star born probably nebula = conditions form planets

- natural result process initiates formation star
- planetary systems rule, not exception
- N H other systems universe
- math → some stars →   solar systems → support life

Essay Question

Summarize the nebular hypothesis that is described in the reading and then explain how the lecture supports the hypothesis.

Integrated Essay

The nebular hypothesis posits that between four and five million years ago a cloud of dust and gas containing all of the elements in the solar system collapsed under the force of gravity, an event which caused the cloud to spin and flatten into a disk. Then, a stronger gravitational pull caused bodies to merge and pull apart, forming planetesimals that eventually shaped the planets that exist today. The planets near the Sun, which we call the terrestrial planets, tolerated higher temperatures, but the planets farther away had a composition more similar to the original cloud and condensed when exposed to the lower temperature. The fact that the planets orbit close to the same plane is evidence for the hypothesis. Furthermore, new technologies have allowed us to test the hypothesis with a computer model, which replicates the original conditions. According to scientists, the formation of planets is a natural result of the process that occurs in the formation of a star. Moreover, the nebular hypothesis suggests that there are other solar systems in the universe, some of which could support life.

Checklist for Integrated Essay

✔ The essay answers the topic question.
✔ Inaccuracies in the content are minor.
✔ The essay is direct and well-organized.
✔ The sentences are logically connected.
✔ Details and examples support the main idea.
✔ The writer expresses complete thoughts.
✔ The meaning is easy to comprehend.
✔ A wide range of vocabulary is used.
✔ The writer paraphrases in his/her own words.
✔ The writer credits the author with wording.

✔ Errors in grammar and idioms are minor.
✔ The essay is within a range of 150–225 words.

Evaluator's Comments
The writer has responded to both parts of the question, using transition words to connect the sentences logically. The content is accurate and easy to understand. Excellent vocabulary selection and variety of grammatical structures support the well-paraphrased essay.

PROBLEM 33: OPINION

In this independent essay question, you will be asked to write an essay about a familiar topic. This may be a place, a person, a possession, a situation, or an occasion. After you read the question, you will state your opinion and then explain why you have that opinion.

You will have 30 minutes to plan, write, and revise your essay. Typically, a good response will require that you write a minimum of 300 words.

Task

- State your opinion
- Explain the reasons for your opinion

Question
Some students apply for admission only to their first-choice school, while others apply to several schools. Which plan do you agree with, and why? Be sure to include details and examples to support your opinion.

Example Notes
Several schools

- application Ø guarantee admission
  competitive standards
  no space
  w/o school 1 semester
  $ but saves time

- learn about options
  communications
  discover advantages
  assistantships
  negative experience
- I plan 3 schools
  1 choice happy
  options open

Independent Essay

Although I understand students who desire to concentrate all of their energy on applications to their first-choice schools, I support making application to several different schools. There are two reasons why I feel this is important. First, application does not guarantee admission, even for a very highly qualified applicant. The school that a student prefers may have very competitive standards for acceptance. In spite excellent academic credentials, high scores on admissions tests such as the SAT and the TOEFL, and exceptional supporting documents, some qualified applicants may be turned away because not enough space to accommodate them. If students apply to their first-choice schools, and they are not accepted for reasons that could not be anticipated, they may find themselves in the position of being without a school for at least a semester while they scramble to apply to the schools they had considered as second or third choices. It is expensive to apply to a large number of schools because of the application fees, but making application to three schools can save time, which is also a valuable commodity.

Another reason to apply to several schools is the opportunity to learn more about each the educational options during the application process. While materials are being submitted and communication is occurring between the student and the school officials, advantages at the second- or third-choice school may be discovered as a result of the information exchanged. Scholarships, grants, and other opportunities may be extended when the committee is reviewing the application at one of the schools. For example, an unpublicized research assistantship may be available because of the prior work experience that an applicant has included on the application form. Conversely, the experience that the student has in applying to the first-choice school may be so negative that another school will be more attractive than the first-choice institution.

When I am ready to study at a university, I plan to apply to three schools—two with very competitive standards, and one with moderate standards. If I am admitted at my first-choice school, I will be happy, but I will leave my options open during the application process just in case I discover some advantages at one of the other schools.

Checklist for Independent Essay

✔ The essay answers the topic question.
✔ The point of view or position is clear.
✔ The essay is direct and well-organized.
✔ The sentences are logically connected.
✔ Details and examples support the main idea.
✔ The writer expresses complete thoughts.
✔ The meaning is easy to comprehend.
✔ A wide range of vocabulary is used.
✔ Various types of sentences are included.
✔ Errors in grammar and idioms are minor.
✔ The essay is within a range of 300–350 words.

Evaluator's Comments

The writing sample is well-organized. It addresses the question and does not digress from the topic. There is a logical progression of ideas, and the writer uses good transitions. Opinions are supported by examples. The writer demonstrates excellent language proficiency, as evidenced by a variety of grammatical structures and acceptable vocabulary. The reader can understand this opinion without re-reading. There are only a few grammatical errors that appear to have occurred because of time constraints. They have been corrected below:

Line 7	in spite of
Line 10	because there is not enough space
Line 19	each of the educational options

PROBLEM 34: ARGUMENT

In this independent essay question, you will be asked to argue both sides of an issue and then take a stand for one side.

You will have 30 minutes to plan, write, and revise your essay. Typically, a good response will require that you write a minimum of 300 words.

Task

- Argue one side—advantages and disadvantages
- Argue the other side—advantages and disadvantages
- Take a stand for one of the arguments
- Explain the reasons for your preference

Question

Some students like to take distance-learning courses by computer. Other students prefer to study in traditional classroom settings with a teacher. Consider the advantages of both options, and make an argument for the way that students should organize their schedules.

Example Notes

Advantages distance

- attend class at your convenience
- complete assignments at own pace
- repeat lectures

Advantages traditional

- structured environment
- more personal relationship
- immediate response to questions
- study groups + friendships

Independent Essay

Both distance-learning courses and traditional classes provide important but different experiences for college students. On the one hand, there are many advantages to distance-learning courses. One of the most important benefits is the opportunity to attend class on your convenience. This is very important for students who hold full-time jobs since they can choose to take their classes on a schedule that allows them to continue working. Another advantage is the chance to complete assignments at your own pace. For students who can work more quick than their classmates, it is possible to earn more credits during the semester. A huge advantage to international students is the option of listen to lectures more than once.

On the other hand, there are advantages to attending a traditional class. The structured environment is beneficial, especially for students who are not as highly motivating. In addition, it is more likely that you will develop a personal relationship with the teacher, an advantage not only for the course but also after the course when you need a recommendation. By seeing you and talking with you face-to-face, the teacher will remember you better. It is also easier to get an immediate response to questions because you only have to raise your hand instead sending e-mail and waiting for an answer. Last, the opportunity for study groups and friendships is different and more personal when you sit in the same room.

Given all the advantages of both types of courses, I think that students would be wise to register for distance-learning courses and traditional classroom courses during their college experiences. By participating in distance-learning courses, they can work independently in classes that may be more difficult for them, repeating the lectures on computer at convenient times. By attending traditional classes, they can get to know the teachers personally and will have good references when they need them. They will also make friends in the class. By sharing information with other students, they can organize their schedules for the following semester, chosing the best classes and including both distance-learning and traditional courses.

Checklist for Independent Essay

✔ The essay answers the topic question.
✔ The point of view or position is clear.
✔ The essay is direct and well-organized.
✔ The sentences are logically connected.
✔ Details and examples support the main idea.

✔ The writer expresses complete thoughts.

✔ The meaning is easy to comprehend.

✔ A wide range of vocabulary is used.

✔ Various types of sentences are included.

✔ Errors in grammar and idioms are minor.

✔ The general topic essay is within a range of 300–350 words.

Evaluator's Comments

The writing sample is well-organized with a good topic sentence and good support statements. It addresses both sides of the question and does not digress from the topic. There is a logical progression of ideas and excellent language proficiency, as evidenced by a variety of grammatical structures and appropriate vocabulary. Transition words and phrases support the reader's comprehension of the arguments without re-reading. There are only a few grammatical errors that have been corrected below:

Lines 4–5	at your convenience
Line 9	more quickly
Line 11	the option of listening
Line 14	motivated
Line 20	instead of
Line 32	choosing

WRITING STRATEGIES

In addition to the academic skills that you learned in the previous chapter, there are several writing strategies that will help you succeed on the TOEFL and after the TOEFL. Some of the strategies are more appropriate for the integrated essay and others are more useful for the independent essay.

Integrated Essay

The integrated question asks for a synthesis of the content in a lecture and a reading passage. It is usually the first essay question.

➤ Report

When you are writing about content, it is important not to offer your opinions. To do this, you must distinguish between content and opinion. Content may include both facts and the ideas of the author or lecturer. Opinion is what *you* think. Your job in an integrated essay is to report the facts and ideas without making judgments and without expressing your opinions.

- State the facts and ideas
- Avoid expressing your opinions

➤ Identify sources

In the question for the integrated essay, you will be directed to the primary source. For example, the question may ask you to summarize content *from the reading* or to summarize the main points *in the lecture*. This is a cue to begin with a summary from the primary source identified in the question—either the reading or the lecture. Then, you will be asked to support or contrast the information in the primary source with the information in the secondary source. Go to the other source after you have completed your summary. Be sure to include information from both sources, but begin with the primary source.

- Begin with the primary source
- Include both sources

➤ Make connections

Supporting Transitions	Opposing Transitions
When the secondary source agrees with the primary source, use supporting transitions.	*When the secondary source* does not *agree with the primary source, use opposing transitions.*
Moreover, Furthermore, In addition,	In contrast, On the other hand,

- Establish the relationship between sources
- Choose appropriate transitions

➤ Include a variety of structures

Essays with a variety of sentence structures are more interesting, and they receive higher scores. Complex sentence structures, achieved by combining simple sentences, also improve scores.

- Vary sentence structures
- Combine sentences

➤ Edit your writing

If you use all of your time to write, you won't have enough time to edit your writing. Students who take the time to read what they have written will find some of their own mistakes and can correct them before submitting the final essays. Be sure to edit both the independent essay and the integrated essay. To edit most effectively, use the grading checklist that raters will use to evaluate your writing.

- Re-read your essay
- Edit with the checklist

Independent Essay

The independent question on the TOEFL asks for your opinion. It is usually the second essay question.

➤ Respond to the topic

It is very important to read the question carefully and analyze the topic. If you write on a topic other than the one that you have been assigned, your essay will not be scored.

- Analyze the topic
- Write on the assigned topic

➤ Be direct

When you are asked for your *opinion*, it is appropriate to begin with a direct statement. The following phrases and clauses introduce an opinion:

Introduction	Opinion
Introductory phrase,	**Direct statement = Subject + Verb**
In my opinion,	school uniforms are a good idea.
In my view,	
From my point of view,	
From my perspective,	
Introductory Clause	**Direct statement = Subject + Verb**
I agree that	school uniforms are a good idea.
I disagree that	
I think that	
I believe that	
I support the idea that	
I am convinced that	
It is clear to me that	

- Begin with an introductory phrase or clause
- Make a direct statement of opinion

➤ Concede the opposing view

Sometimes you will be offered two choices. When stating a *preference*, it is polite to concede that the opposing view has merit. The following words and phrases express concession: *although, even though, despite,* and *in spite of.* For example:

Concession	Opinion
Concession clause	**Direct statement = Subject + Verb**
Although there are many advantages to living in the city,	I prefer life in a small town.
Even though technology can damage the environment,	I think it causes more good than harm.
Despite the differences among cultures,	I believe that peace is possible.
In spite of the benefits of studying in a group,	I prefer to study alone.

- Begin with a concession clause
- Make a direct statement of opinion

➤ Use an outline sentence

Some books call the second sentence in an essay the *topic sentence,* the *controlling sentence,* the *thesis statement,* or the *organizing sentence.* The purpose of this sentence is to outline the essay for the reader. Here are some examples of outline sentences.

First sentence:
Although there are many advantages to living in the city, I prefer life in a small town.
Outline sentence:
Three personal experiences convince me that small towns provide a better life style.

First sentence:
Despite the differences among cultures, I believe that peace is possible.
Outline sentence:
History provides several encouraging examples.

First sentence:
In spite of the benefits of studying in a group, I prefer to study alone.
Outline sentence:
There are three reasons why I have this preference.

- Outline the essay for the reader
- Write an outline sentence

➤ Think in English

How do English-speaking writers think? According to research by Robert Kaplan, they organize their thoughts in a linear pattern. This means that they think in a straight line. Details and examples must relate to the main points. Digressions are not included.

For essays that require an opinion, the organization would look like this:

Opinion

↓

In my view, school uniforms are a good idea.

Outline Sentence

↓

Three reasons convince me that wearing uniforms will improve the educational experience of students.

Reason 1

↓

In the first place, uniforms are not as expensive as brand name clothing.

Example/Detail

For example, a new school uniform costs about $30, but designer jeans and a name-brand shirt cost five times that amount. An expensive book would be a better investment.

Reason 2

↓

Second, it is easier to get ready for school.

Example/Detail

When there are five choices, it requires time and thought to decide what to wear. Uniforms simplify the problem of choosing a shirt to complement a certain pair of pants and, furthermore, selecting socks and shoes to go with them. All of these decisions take time and divert attention from preparing for classes.

Reason 3   Finally, students who wear uniforms identify
                      themselves with their school.

   ↓

Example/Detail   Wearing the school colors establishes that
                      each student is part of the group.

Conclusion   In conclusion, I think schools that require uni-
                      forms send a positive message to their stu-
                      dents. They communicate that it is more impor-
                      tant to be the best student than it is to have the
                      best clothing.

- Think in a straight line
- Connect each idea with the next

➤ Write a strong conclusion

In TOEFL essays, it is not appropriate to apologize for not having written enough, for not having enough time, or for not using good English
skills. An apology will cause you to lose points. In addition, a good
conclusion does not add new information. It does not introduce a new
idea. A strong conclusion is more like a summary of the ideas in one
last sentence.

- Summarize the main idea
- Avoid apologies and new topics

APPLYING THE ACADEMIC SKILLS TO THE TOEFL

➤ Taking Notes

Taking notes is an important academic skill for the Writing section
because you will use them to organize your essay. Because you will
not be graded on the notes, you should not worry about making them
perfect. It is more important for them to be useful to you.

➤ Paraphrasing

In the integrated essay, you must be careful not to use the exact words from the reading or the lecture. Plagiarizing will result in a failing score on the essay. You must use the skills that you learned to paraphrase in your essay.

➤ Summarizing

As you will remember, summarizing is one of the steps in synthesizing. You will often be asked to summarize the primary source before you relate it to the secondary source.

➤ Synthesizing

Part 1 of the Writing section is the integrated essay. It is a synthesis of information from a reading passage and a lecture. Synthesizing is the most important academic skill for the integrated essay.

QUIZ FOR THE WRITING SECTION

This is a quiz for the Writing section of the TOEFL® iBT. This section tests your ability to write essays in English. During the quiz, you will respond to two writing questions. You may take notes as you read academic information. You may use your notes to write the essays. Once you begin, you have 20 minutes to write the first essay and 30 minutes to write the second essay.

QUESTION 1

Reading Passage
Time: 3 minutes

A win-win negotiation is concluded when both parties gain something of value in exchange for making concessions. Although the balance of power may change during the negotiation process, negotiators on both sides must remain open to options that will ultimately allow for a fair exchange. To achieve a resolution that benefits both parties, everyone involved must be willing to listen carefully to each other's concerns. To arrive at a conclusion that is good for everyone, negotiators must reveal what they value and what they don't value. Good negotiators look for something that their side does not value but to which the other side assigns a high value. By offering it, they lose nothing, but the other side gains something, thereby feeling more disposed to concede something that the other side perceives as valuable. In addition to listening for ways to help the other side, everyone has to be aware of the limitations that both sides may bring to the table. There are some options that cannot be explored because they are not possible for one of the parties. For example, a price that does not allow a profit margin for the company that manufactures it is not a point of negotiation, unless the other side can offer a way to increase profits or productivity. If that isn't possible, then perhaps a service that saves the buyer money might be a way to balance the firm pricing structure of the goods.

A win-win negotiation allows both parties to feel that they made a good deal, but another positive outcome is the way that the people involved feel about each other. In traditional bargaining, people on opposite sides of a negotiation tend to view each other as adversaries, a relationship that is often difficult to change after the negotiation has ended and the collaboration is supposed to begin. In a win-win setting, the parties approach the negotiation as colleagues who want to support each other's success. When the deal has been made and the collaboration begins, the people involved are already committed to working together for their mutual benefit.

Question 1, Lecture. Now read a lecture on the same topic as the passage you have just read.

Professor:
Let me tell you about a case study that is often used as an example of how a win-win situation can be negotiated by both parties. Tony was a computer software designer who had come up with a great idea for a computer game, but his problem was that he couldn't afford to quit his job while he worked on the game because he had to make a living for his family. He thought it would probably take him about a year to actually complete the programming for the game if he worked in his spare time. Okay. Well, he put together a proposal, and took it to a multinational company that had launched several successful

computer games. But the problem was that the company made him a very low offer—just a thousand dollars a month for twelve months. And although that would have paid his bills during the time that he would have been working on the program, he knew that the game had a huge potential for return on the company's investment. So he felt like he would be taking all the risk without having the opportunity to share in the reward. But when the company refused to give him any additional upfront money, then, instead of getting angry, Tony went back with a counteroffer. He agreed to accept the $12,000 as an advance on the profits that he expected the game to generate. And he suggested that they share the future revenues in a ratio of 40:60—40 percent for Tony and 60 percent for the company. The company was interested, but explained to Tony that they would be investing over a million dollars in order to produce and market the game and would need a larger share in order to proceed. So they agreed on a 30:70 split. And, as it happened, the game was a big success, the company made a huge profit and Tony was able to quit his regular job and start his own game design company. So— everybody won. They were both able to minimize their risk and increase their profits.

Question
Summarize the points made in the reading passage, and then explain how the case study from the lecture supports the reading.

Writing Time: 20 minutes
Typical Response: 150–225 words

Question 2
Some people like to communicate by e-mail and voice mail. Other people like to communicate by telephone or face-to-face. Which type of communication do you prefer, and why? Be sure to include details and examples to support your opinion.

Writing Time: 30 minutes
Typical Response: 300–350 words

This is the end of the Writing Quiz. To check your answers, refer to the Progress Chart for the Writing Quiz, Chapter 7, page 407.

STUDY PLAN

What did you learn from taking the quiz? What will you do differently when you take the model tests in the next chapters? Take a few minutes to think and then write a sentence or two to help you revise your study plan.

EXTRA CREDIT

After you have completed this chapter, you may want to continue a review of writing. Here are some suggestions.

Become familiar with the independent writing topics. Topics previously used for independent questions on the CBT TOEFL Writing section are listed in the TOEFL® iBT *Information Bulletin* available free from Educational Testing Service. They are also listed on the web site at *www.ets.org*. Read through the questions, and think about how you would respond to each of the topics. Since most of them require you to state an opinion, it is helpful to form a general opinion on each topic.

Read good examples of expository writing. Research confirms that reading is important to the development of writing. This means that one of the best ways to learn to write well is to read good models of writing. By being exposed to good writing, you will acquire good techniques. That is why this book contains examples of the answers that excellent writers might create in response to the questions in this review chapter and in the Writing section of each model test. It is important to read these example answers carefully. Remember that you will be asked to produce expository, not literary essays. For this reason, you should read opinion essays instead of short stories. It is also a good idea to read summaries of content material. Many popular college textbooks in English provide summaries at the end of the chapters. In general, these summaries are good models for you to read.

OPTIONS FOR EVALUATION

It is difficult to evaluate your own writing. If you are taking an English class, ask your teacher to use the checklists in this chapter to evaluate your writing. You need to know how you are progressing in relationship to the criteria on the checklists because that is how you will be evaluated on the TOEFL.

If you do not have good options to have your writing evaluated without a fee, there are fee-based options that will provide professional evaluations. See page 527 for details.

ADVISOR'S OFFICE

Keep your eyes on the destination, not on the road. There are short roads and long roads to the same destination, but the important point is to arrive where you want to be. Of course, there are several reasons why you prefer to achieve a successful score on the TOEFL the first time that you attempt it. It is costly to take the test again, and you are eager to begin your academic studies or professional life. Nevertheless, a goal is seldom destroyed by a delay, so don't destroy your positive attitude, either. If you take the time to prepare, you will probably be able to take the short road, but if you have not studied English very long, you may need more practice. Please don't compare yourself to anyone else. They are on their road, and you are on yours. Just keep going. You will get there.

5
MODEL TEST 2: PROGRESS TEST

READING SECTION

The Reading section tests your ability to understand reading passages like those in college textbooks. The passages are about 700 words in length.

This is the long format for the Reading section. On the long format, you will respond to five passages. After each passage, you will answer 12–14 questions about it. Only three passages will be graded. The other passages are part of an experimental section for future tests. Because you will not know which passages will be graded, you must try to do your best on all of them.

Most questions are worth 1 point, but the last question in each passage is worth more than 1 point.

You will have 100 minutes to read all of the passages and answer the questions. You may take notes while you read, but notes are not graded. You may use your notes to answer the questions. Some passages may include a word or phrase that is underlined in blue on the Official TOEFL® iBT. Click on the word or phrase to see a glossary definition or explanation.

Choose the best answer for multiple-choice questions. On the official TOEFL® iBT, follow the directions on the page or on the screen for computer-assisted questions. Click on **Next** to go to the next question. Click on **Back** to return to the previous question. You may return to previous questions for all of the passages in the same reading part, but after you go to the next part, you will not be able to return to passages in a previous part. Be sure that you have answered all of the questions for the passages in each part before you click on **Next** at the end of the passage to move to the next part.

You can click on **Review** to see a chart of the questions you have answered and the questions you have not answered in each part. From this screen, you can return to the question you want to answer in the part that is open.

A clock on the screen will show you how much time you have to complete the Reading section.

PART I

Reading 1 "Resources and Industrialism in Canada"

→ While the much-anticipated expansion of the western frontier was unfolding in accordance with the design of the National Policy, a new northern frontier was opening up to enhance the prospects of Canadian industrial development. ᴀ Long the preserve of the fur trade, the Canadian Shield and the western Cordilleras became a treasury of minerals, timber and hydroelectric power in the late 19th and early 20th centuries. As early as 1883, CPR [Canadian Pacific Railway] construction crews blasting through the rugged terrain of northern Ontario discovered copper and nickel deposits in the vicinity of Sudbury. ʙ As refining processes, uses, and markets for the metal developed, Sudbury became the world's largest nickel producer. The building of the Temiskaming and Northern Ontario Railway led to the discovery of rich silver deposits around Cobalt north of Lake Nipissing in 1903 and touched off a mining boom that spread northward to Kirkland Lake and the Porcupine district. C Although the economic importance of these mining operations was enduring, they did not capture the public imagination to the same extent as the Klondike gold rush of the late 1890s. D

→ Fortune-seekers from all parts of the world flocked to the Klondike and Yukon River valleys to pan for gold starting in 1896. At the height of the gold rush in 1898, the previously unsettled subarctic frontier had a population of about 30,000, more than half of which was concentrated in the newly established town of Dawson. In the same year, the federal government created the Yukon Territory, administered by an appointed commissioner, in an effort to ward off the prospect of annexation to Alaska. Even if the economic significance of the Klondike strike was somewhat exaggerated and short-lived, the tales of sudden riches, heroic and tragic exploits, and the rowdiness and lawlessness of the mining frontier were immortalized through popular fiction and folklore, notably the poetic verses of Robert W. Service.

→ Perhaps less romantic than the mining booms, the exploitation of forest and water resources was just as vital to national development. The Douglas fir, spruce, and cedar stands of British Columbia along with the white pine forests of Ontario satisfied construction demands on the treeless prairies as well as in the growing cities and towns of central Canada and the United States. British Columbia's forests also supplied lumber to Asia. In addition, the softwood forest wealth of the Cordilleras and the Shield was a valuable source of pulpwood for the development of the pulp and paper industry, which made Canada one of the world's leading exporters of newsprint. Furthermore, the fast flowing rivers of the Shield and Cordilleras could readily be harnessed as sources of hydroelectric power, replacing coal in the booming factories of central Canada as well as in the evolving mining and pulp and paper industries. The age of electricity under public ownership and control was ushered in by the creation of the Ontario Hydro-Electric Power Commission (now Ontario Hydro) in 1906 to distribute and eventually to produce this vital source of energy.

→ Western settlement and the opening of the northern resource frontier stimulated industrial expansion, particularly in central Canada. As the National Policy had intended, a growing agricultural population in the West increased the demand for eastern manufactured goods, thereby giving rise to agricultural implements works, iron and steel foundries, machine shops, railway yards, textile mills, boot and shoe factories, and numerous smaller manufacturing enterprises that supplied consumer goods. By keeping out lower-priced foreign manufactured goods, the high tariff policies of the federal government received much credit for protecting existing industries and encouraging the creation of new enterprises. To climb the tariff wall, large American industrial firms opened branches in Canada, and the governments of Ontario and Quebec aggressively urged them on by offering bonuses, subsidies, and guarantees to locate new plants within their borders. Canadian industrial enterprises became increasingly attractive to foreign investors, especially from the United States and Great Britain. Much of the over $600 million of American capital that flowed into Canada from 1900 to 1913 was earmarked for mining and the pulp and paper industry, while British investors contributed near $1.8 billion, mostly in railway building, business development, and the construction of urban infrastructure. As a result, the gross value of Canadian manufactured products quadrupled from 1891 to 1916.

1. Why does the author mention the railroads in paragraph 1?

   Ⓐ Because miners were traveling to camps in the West
   Ⓑ Because mineral deposits were discovered when the railroads were built
   Ⓒ Because the western frontier was being settled by families
   Ⓓ Because traders used the railroads to transport their goods

   Paragraph 1 is marked with an arrow [➜].

2. In paragraph 1, the author identifies Sudbury as

   Ⓐ an important stop on the new railroad line
   Ⓑ a large market for the metals produced in Ontario
   Ⓒ a major industrial center for the production of nickel
   Ⓓ a mining town in the Klondike region

   Paragraph 1 is marked with an arrow [➜].

3. The word enhance in the passage is closest in meaning to

   Ⓐ disrupt
   Ⓑ restore
   Ⓒ identify
   Ⓓ improve

4. According to paragraph 2, why was the Yukon Territory created?

   Ⓐ To encourage people to settle the region
   Ⓑ To prevent Alaska from acquiring it
   Ⓒ To establish law and order in the area
   Ⓓ To legalize the mining claims

   Paragraph 2 is marked with an arrow [➜].

5. The word previously in the passage is closest in meaning to

   Ⓐ frequently
   Ⓑ suddenly
   Ⓒ routinely
   Ⓓ formerly

6. How did the poetry by Robert Service contribute to the development of Canada?

   Ⓐ It made the Klondike gold rush famous.
   Ⓑ It encouraged families to settle in the Klondike.
   Ⓒ It captured the beauty of the western Klondike.
   Ⓓ It prevented the Klondike's annexation to Alaska.

7. According to paragraph 3, the forest industry supported the development of Canada in all of the following ways EXCEPT

   Ⓐ by supplying wood for the construction of homes and buildings
   Ⓑ by clearing the land for expanded agricultural uses
   Ⓒ by producing the power for the hydroelectric plants
   Ⓓ by exporting wood and newsprint to foreign markets

Paragraph 3 is marked with an arrow [➔].

8. The word <u>Furthermore</u> in the passage is closest in meaning to

   Ⓐ Although
   Ⓑ Because
   Ⓒ Therefore
   Ⓓ Moreover

9. Which of the sentences below best expresses the information in the highlighted statement in the passage? The other choices change the meaning or leave out important information.

   Ⓐ New businesses and industries were created by the federal government to keep the prices of manufactured goods low.
   Ⓑ The lower price of manufacturing attracted many foreign businesses and new industries to the area.
   Ⓒ Federal taxes on cheaper imported goods were responsible for protecting domestic industries and supporting new businesses.
   Ⓓ The federal tax laws made it difficult for manufacturers to sell their goods to foreign markets.

10. The word <u>them</u> in the passage refers to

     Ⓐ governments
     Ⓑ plants
     Ⓒ firms
     Ⓓ policies

11. According to paragraph 4, British and American businesses opened affiliates in Canada because

     Ⓐ the Canadian government offered incentives
     Ⓑ the raw materials were available in Canada
     Ⓒ the consumers in Canada were eager to buy their goods
     Ⓓ the infrastructure was attractive to investors

Paragraph 4 is marked with an arrow [→].

12. Look at the four squares [■] that show where the following sentence could be inserted in the passage.

Railway construction through the Kootenay region of southeastern British Columbia also led to significant discoveries of gold, silver, copper, lead, and zinc.

Where could the sentence best be added?

Click on a square [■] to insert the sentence in the passage.

13. **Directions:** An introduction for a short summary of the passage appears below. Complete the summary by selecting the THREE answer choices that mention the most important points in the passage. Some sentences do not belong in the summary because they express ideas that are not included in the passage or are minor points from the passage. *This question is worth 2 points.*

The northern frontier provided many natural resources that contributed to the industrial expansion of Canada.

-
-
-

Answer Choices

Ⓐ The Yukon Territory was created in 1898 during the gold rush in the Klondike and Yukon River valleys.

Ⓑ The frontier was documented in the popular press, which published tales of heroes and gold strikes.

Ⓒ Significant discoveries of mineral deposits encouraged prospectors and settlers to move into the territories.

Ⓓ Wheat and other agricultural crops were planted after the forests were cleared, creating the central plains.

Ⓔ Powered by hydroelectricity, lumber and paper mills exploited the forests for both domestic and foreign markets.

Ⓕ Incentives encouraged American and British investors to help expand manufacturing plants in Canada.

PART II

Reading 2 "Looking at Theatre History"

→ One of the primary ways of approaching the Greek theatre is through archeology, the systematic study of material remains such as architecture, inscriptions, sculpture, vase painting, and other forms of decorative art. Ⓐ Serious on-site excavations began in Greece around 1870, but W. Dörpfeld did not begin the first extensive study of the Theatre of Dionysus until 1886. Ⓑ Since that time, more than 167 other Greek theatres have been identified and many of them have been excavated. Ⓒ Nevertheless, they still do not permit us to describe the precise appearance of the *skene* (illustrations printed in books are conjectural reconstructions), since many pieces are irrevocably lost because the buildings in later periods became sources of stone for other projects and what remains is usually broken and scattered. Ⓓ That most of the buildings were remodeled many times has created great problems for those seeking to date both the parts and the successive versions. Despite these drawbacks, archeology provides the most concrete evidence we have about the theatre structures of ancient Greece. But, if they have told us much, archeologists have not completed their work, and many sites have scarcely been touched.

→ Perhaps the most controversial use of archeological evidence in theatre history is vase paintings, thousands of which have survived from ancient Greece. (Most of those used by theatre scholars are reproduced in Margarete Bieber's *The History of the Greek and Roman Theatre*.) Depicting scenes from mythology and daily life, the vases are the most graphic pictorial evidence we have. But they are also easy to misinterpret. Some scholars have considered any vase that depicts a subject treated in a surviving drama or any scene showing masks, flute players, or ceremonials to be valid evidence of theatrical practice. This is a highly questionable assumption, since the Greeks made widespread use of masks, dances, and music outside the theatre and since the myths on which dramatists drew were known to everyone, including vase painters, who might well depict the same subjects as dramatists without being indebted to them. Those vases showing scenes unquestionably theatrical are few in number.

→ Written evidence about ancient Greek theatre is often treated as less reliable than archeological evidence because most written accounts are separated so far in time from the events they describe and because they provide no information about their own sources. Of the written evidence, the surviving plays are usually treated as the most reliable. But the oldest surviving manuscripts of Greek plays date from around the tenth century, C.E., some 1500 years after they were first performed. Since printing did not exist during this time span, copies of plays had to be made by hand, and therefore the possibility of textual errors creeping in was magnified. Nevertheless, the scripts offer us our readiest access to the cultural and theatrical conditions out of which they came. But these scripts, like other kinds of evidence, are subject to varying interpretations. Certainly performances embodied a male perspective, for example, since the plays were written, selected, staged, and acted by men. Yet the existing plays feature numerous choruses of women and many feature strong female characters. Because these characters often seem victims of their own powerlessness and appear to be governed, especially in the comedies, by sexual desire, some critics have seen these plays as rationalizations by the male-dominated culture for keeping women segregated and cloistered. Other critics, however, have seen in these same plays an attempt by male authors to force their male audiences to examine and call into question this segregation and cloistering of Athenian women.

→ By far the majority of written references to Greek theatre date from several hundred years after the events they report. The writers seldom mention their sources of evidence, and thus we do not know what credence to give them. In the absence of material nearer in time to the events, however, historians have used the accounts and have been grateful to have them. Overall, historical treatment of the Greek theatre is something like assembling a jigsaw puzzle from which many pieces are missing: historians arrange what they have and imagine (with the aid of the remaining evidence and logic) what has been lost. As a result, though the broad outlines of Greek theatre history are reasonably clear, many of the details remain open to doubt.

Glossary

skene: a stage building where actors store their masks and change their costumes

14. According to paragraph 1, why is it impossible to identify the time period for theatres in Greece?

- Ⓐ There are too few sites that have been excavated and very little data collected about them.
- Ⓑ The archeologists from earlier periods were not careful, and many artifacts were broken.
- Ⓒ It is confusing because stones from early sites were used to build later structures.
- Ⓓ Because it is very difficult to date the concrete that was used in construction during early periods.

Paragraph 1 is marked with an arrow [→].

15. What can be inferred from paragraph 1 about the *skene* in theatre history?

    Ⓐ Drawings in books are the only accurate visual records.
    Ⓑ Not enough evidence is available to make a precise model.
    Ⓒ Archaeologists have excavated a large number of them.
    Ⓓ It was not identified or studied until the early 1800s.

    Paragraph 1 is marked with an arrow [➔].

16. The word <u>primary</u> in the passage is closest in meaning to

    Ⓐ reliable
    Ⓑ important
    Ⓒ unusual
    Ⓓ accepted

17. The word <u>precise</u> in the passage is closest in meaning to

    Ⓐ attractive
    Ⓑ simple
    Ⓒ difficult
    Ⓓ exact

18. In paragraph 2, the author explains that all vases with paintings of masks or musicians may not be evidence of theatrical subjects by

    Ⓐ arguing that the subjects could have been used by artists without reference to a drama
    Ⓑ identifying some of the vases as reproductions that were painted years after the originals
    Ⓒ casting doubt on the qualifications of the scholars who produced the vases as evidence
    Ⓓ pointing out that there are very few vases that have survived from the time of early dramas

    Paragraph 2 is marked with an arrow [➔].

19. The word <u>controversial</u> in the passage is closest in meaning to

    Ⓐ accepted
    Ⓑ debated
    Ⓒ limited
    Ⓓ complicated

20. In paragraph 3, the author states that female characters in Greek theatre

    Ⓐ had no featured parts in plays
    Ⓑ were mostly ignored by critics
    Ⓒ did not participate in the chorus
    Ⓓ frequently played the part of victims

    Paragraph 3 is marked with an arrow [➜].

21. According to paragraph 3, scripts of plays may not be accurate because

    Ⓐ the sources cited are not well known
    Ⓑ copies by hand may contain many errors
    Ⓒ they are written in very old language
    Ⓓ the printing is difficult to read

    Paragraph 3 is marked with an arrow [➜].

22. The word <u>them</u> in the passage refers to

    Ⓐ events
    Ⓑ sources
    Ⓒ writers
    Ⓓ references

23. Why does the author mention a jigsaw puzzle in paragraph 4?

Ⓐ To demonstrate the difficulty in drawing conclusions from partial evidence

Ⓑ To compare the written references for plays to the paintings on vases

Ⓒ To justify using accounts and records that historians have located

Ⓓ To introduce the topic for the next reading passage in the textbook

Paragraph 4 is marked with an arrow [➜].

24. Which of the following statements most accurately reflects the author's opinion about vase paintings?

Ⓐ Evidence from written documents is older than evidence from vase paintings.

Ⓑ The sources for vase paintings are clear because of the images on them.

Ⓒ The details in vase paintings are not obvious because of their age.

Ⓓ There is disagreement among scholars regarding vase paintings.

25. Look at the four squares [■] that show where the following sentence could be inserted in the passage.

These excavations have revealed much that was previously unknown, especially about the dimensions and layout of theatres.

Where could the sentence best be added?

Click on a square [■] to insert the sentence in the passage.

26. **Directions:** An introduction for a short summary of the passage appears below. Complete the summary by selecting the THREE answer choices that mention the most important points in the passage. Some sentences do not belong in the summary because they express ideas that are not included in the passage or are minor points from the passage. *This question is worth 2 points.*

Greek theatre has been studied by a variety of methods.

-
-
-

Answer Choices

Ⓐ Because the Greeks enjoyed dancing and music for entertainment outside of the theatre, many scenes on vases are ambiguous.

Ⓑ Historical accounts assembled many years after the actual theatrical works were presented give us a broad perspective of the earlier theatre.

Ⓒ Although considered less reliable, written records, including scripts, provide insights into the cultural aspects of theatre.

Ⓓ Archaeological excavations have uncovered buildings and artifacts, many of which were vases with theatrical scenes painted on them.

Ⓔ For the most part, men wrote the plays for Greek theatre, but choruses and even strong roles were played by women.

Ⓕ Computer simulations can recreate the image of a building that is crumbling as long as the dimensions and layout are known.

Reading 3 "Geothermal Energy"

→ Geothermal energy is natural heat from the interior of the Earth that is converted to heat buildings and generate electricity. The idea of harnessing Earth's internal heat is not new. As early as 1904, geothermal power was used in Italy. Today, Earth's natural internal heat is being used to generate electricity in 21 countries, including Russia, Japan, New Zealand, Iceland, Mexico, Ethiopia, Guatemala, El Salvador, the Philippines, and the United States. Total worldwide production is approaching 9,000 MW (equivalent to nine large modern coal-burning or nuclear power plants)—double the amount in 1980. Some 40 million people today receive their electricity from geothermal energy at a cost competitive with that of other energy sources. In El Salvador, geothermal energy is supplying 30% of the total electric energy used. However, at the global level, geothermal energy supplies less than 0.15% of the total energy supply.

→ Geothermal energy may be considered a nonrenewable energy source when rates of extraction are greater than rates of natural replenishment. However, geothermal energy has its origin in the natural heat production within Earth, and only a small fraction of the vast total resource base is being utilized today. Although most geothermal energy production involves the tapping of high heat sources, people are also using the low-temperature geothermal energy of groundwater in some applications.

Geothermal Systems

→ Ⓐ The average heat flow from the interior of the Earth is very low, about 0.06 W/m^2. Ⓑ This amount is trivial compared with the 177 W/m^2 from solar heat at the surface in the United States. However, in some areas, heat flow is sufficiently high to be useful for producing energy. For the most part, areas of high heat flow are associated with plate tectonic boundaries.

Oceanic ridge systems (divergent plate boundaries) and areas where mountains are being uplifted and volcanic island arcs are forming (convergent plate boundaries) are areas where this natural heat flow is anomalously high. C

On the basis of geological criteria, several types of hot geothermal systems (with temperatures greater than about 80°C, or 176°F) have been defined, and the resource base is larger than that of fossil fuels and nuclear energy combined. A common system for energy development is hydrothermal convection, characterized by the circulation of steam and/or hot water that transfers heat from depths to the surface. D

Geothermal Energy and the Environment
→ The environmental impact of geothermal energy may not be as extensive as that of other sources of energy, but it can be considerable. When geothermal energy is developed at a particular site, environmental problems include on-site noise, emissions of gas, and disturbance of the land at drilling sites, disposal sites, roads and pipelines, and power plants. Development of geothermal energy does not require large-scale transportation of raw materials or refining of chemicals, as development of fossil fuels does. Furthermore, geothermal energy does not produce the atmospheric pollutants associated with burning fossil fuels or the radioactive waste associated with nuclear energy. However, geothermal development often does produce considerable thermal pollution from hot wastewaters, which may be saline or highly corrosive, producing disposal and treatment problems.

→ Geothermal power is not very popular in some locations among some people. For instance, geothermal energy has been produced for years on the island of Hawaii, where active volcanic processes provide abundant near-surface heat. There is controversy, however, over further exploration and development. Native Hawaiians and others have argued that the exploration and development of geothermal energy degrade the tropical forest as developers construct roads, build facilities, and drill wells. In addition, religious and cultural issues in Hawaii relate to the use of geothermal energy. For example, some people are offended by using the "breath and water of Pele" (the volcano goddess) to make electricity. This issue points out the importance of being sensitive to the values and cultures of people where development is planned.

Future of Geothermal Energy

At present, geothermal energy supplies only a small fraction of the electrical energy produced in the United States. However, if developed, known geothermal resources in the United States could produce about 20,000 MW which is about 10% of the electricity needed for the western states. Geohydrothermal resources not yet discovered could conservatively provide four times that amount (approximately 10% of total U.S. electric capacity), about equivalent to the electricity produced from water power today.

27. In paragraph 1, the author introduces the concept of geothermal energy by

Ⓐ explaining the history of this energy source worldwide
Ⓑ arguing that this energy source has been tried unsuccessfully
Ⓒ comparing the production with that of other energy sources
Ⓓ describing the alternatives for generating electric power

Paragraph 1 is marked with an arrow [➔].

28. What is true about geothermal energy production worldwide?

Ⓐ Because it is a new idea, very few countries are developing geothermal energy sources.

Ⓑ Only countries in the Southern Hemisphere are using geothermal energy on a large scale.

Ⓒ Until the cost of geothermal energy becomes competitive, it will not be used globally.

Ⓓ Geothermal energy is already being used in a number of nations, but it is not yet a major source of power.

29. The word approaching in the passage is closest in meaning to

Ⓐ hardly

Ⓑ mostly

Ⓒ nearly

Ⓓ briefly

30. The word that in the passage refers to

Ⓐ electricity

Ⓑ cost

Ⓒ energy

Ⓓ people

31. In paragraph 2, the author states that geothermal energy is considered a nonrenewable resource because

Ⓐ the production of geothermal energy is a natural process

Ⓑ geothermal energy comes from the Earth

Ⓒ we are not using very much geothermal energy now

Ⓓ we could use more geothermal energy than is naturally replaced

Paragraph 2 is marked with an arrow [➔].

32. Which of the sentences below best expresses the information in the highlighted statement in the passage? The other choices change the meaning or leave out important information.

   Ⓐ High heat is the source of most of the geothermal energy but low heat groundwater is also used sometimes.
   Ⓑ Even though low temperatures are possible, high heat is the best resource for energy production for groundwater.
   Ⓒ Both high heat and low heat sources are used for the production of geothermal energy from groundwater.
   Ⓓ Most high heat sources for geothermal energy are tapped from applications that involve low heat in groundwater.

33. According to paragraph 3, the heat flow necessary for the production of geothermal energy

   Ⓐ is like solar heat on the Earth's surface
   Ⓑ happens near tectonic plate boundaries
   Ⓒ must always be artificially increased
   Ⓓ may be impractical because of its location

   Paragraph 3 is marked with an arrow [➔].

34. The word considerable in the passage is closest in meaning to

   Ⓐ large
   Ⓑ dangerous
   Ⓒ steady
   Ⓓ unexpected

35. In paragraph 5, the author mentions the atmospheric pollution and waste products for fossil fuel and nuclear power

   Ⓐ to introduce the discussion of pollution caused by geothermal energy development and production
   Ⓑ to contrast pollution caused by fossil fuels and nuclear power with pollution caused by geothermal energy
   Ⓒ to argue that geothermal production does not cause pollution like other sources of energy do
   Ⓓ to discourage the use of raw materials and chemicals in the production of energy because of pollution

   Paragraph 5 is marked with an arrow [➔].

36. According to paragraph 6, the production of geothermal energy in Hawaii is controversial for all of the following reasons EXCEPT

   Ⓐ The volcanoes in Hawaii could be disrupted by the rapid release of geothermal energy.

   Ⓑ The rainforest might be damaged during the construction of the geothermal energy plant.

   Ⓒ The native people are concerned that geothermal energy is disrespectful to their cultural traditions.

   Ⓓ Some Hawaiians oppose using geothermal energy because of their religious beliefs.

Paragraph 6 is marked with an arrow [➔].

37. What is the author's opinion of geothermal energy?

   Ⓐ Geothermal energy has some disadvantages, but it is probably going to be used in the future.

   Ⓑ Geothermal energy is a source that should be explored further before large-scale production begins.

   Ⓒ Geothermal energy offers an opportunity to supply a significant amount of power in the future.

   Ⓓ Geothermal energy should replace water power in the production of electricity for the United States.

38. Look at the four squares [■] that show where the following sentence could be inserted in the passage.

One such region is located in the western United States, where recent tectonic and volcanic activity has occurred.

Where could the sentence best be added?

Click on a square [■] to insert the sentence in the passage.

39. **Directions**: Complete the table by matching the phrases on the left with the headings on the right. Select the appropriate answer choices and drag them to Fossil Fuels or Geothermal Energy. TWO of the answer choices will NOT be used. *This question is worth 4 points.*

To delete an answer choice, click on it. To see the passage, click on **View Text**.

Answer Choices

Ⓐ Radioactive waste materials must be buried.

Ⓑ Only a small amount of electricity is currently generated.

Ⓒ Transportation of raw materials is usually very costly.

Ⓓ Cultural beliefs question the use of this natural resource.

Ⓔ Gas emissions and disposal sites are problematic.

Ⓕ Water treatment problems occur as a result.

Ⓖ It is a renewable resource for power.

Ⓗ Refinement of chemicals is necessary.

Ⓘ Air pollution is a by-product of the process.

Fossil Fuels

-
-
-

Geothermal Energy

-
-
-
-

PART III

Reading 4 "Migration from Asia"

The Asian migration hypothesis is today supported by most of the scientific evidence. The first "hard" data linking American Indians with Asians appeared in the 1980s with the finding that Indians and northeast Asians share a common and distinctive pattern in the arrangement of the teeth. But perhaps the most compelling support for the hypothesis comes from genetic research. Studies comparing the DNA variation of populations around the world consistently demonstrate the close genetic relationship of the two populations, and recently geneticists studying a virus sequestered in the kidneys of all humans found that the strain of virus carried by Navajos and Japanese is nearly identical, while that carried by Europeans and Africans is quite different.

→ The migration could have begun over a land bridge connecting the continents. During the last Ice Age 70,000 to 10,000 years ago, huge glaciers locked up massive volumes of water and sea levels were as much as 300 feet lower than today. Asia and North America were joined by a huge subcontinent of ice-free, treeless grassland, 750 miles wide. Geologists have named this area Beringia, from the Bering Straits. Summers there were warm, winters were cold, dry and almost snow-free. This was a perfect environment for large mammals—mammoth and mastodon, bison, horse, reindeer, camel, and saiga (a goatlike antelope). Small bands of Stone Age hunter-gatherers were attracted by these animal populations, which provided them not only with food but with hides for clothing and shelter, dung for fuel, and bones for tools and weapons. Accompanied by a husky-like species of dog, hunting bands gradually moved as far east as the Yukon River basin of northern Canada, where field excavations have uncovered the fossilized jawbones of several dogs and bone tools estimated to be about 27,000 years old.

→ Other evidence suggests that the migration from Asia began about 30,000 years ago—around the same time that Japan and Scandinavia were being settled. This evidence is based on blood type. The vast majority of modern Native Americans have type O blood and a few have type A, but almost none have type B. Because modern Asian populations include all three blood types, however, the migrations must have begun before the evolution of type B, which geneticists believe occurred about 30,000 years ago.

By 25,000 years ago human communities were established in western Beringia, which is present-day Alaska. Ⓐ But access to the south was blocked by a huge glacial sheet covering much of what is today Canada. How did the hunters get over those 2,000 miles of deep ice? The argument is that the climate began to warm with the passing of the Ice Age, and about 13,000 B.C.E. glacial melting created an ice-free corridor along the eastern front range of the Rocky Mountains. Ⓑ Soon hunters of big game had reached the Great Plains.

→ In the past several years, however, new archaeological finds along the Pacific coast of North and South America have thrown this theory into question. Ⓒ The most spectacular find, at Monte Verde in southern Chile, produced striking evidence of tool making, house building, rock painting, and human footprints conservatively dated at 12,500 years ago, long before the highway had been cleared of ice. Ⓓ Many archaeologists now believe that migrants moved south in boats along a coastal route rather than overland. These people were probably gatherers and fishers rather than hunters of big game.

➔ There were two later migrations into North America. About 5000 B.C.E. the Athapascan or Na-Dene people began to settle the forests in the northwestern area of the continent. Eventually Athapascan speakers, the ancestors of the Navajos and Apaches, migrated across the Great Plains to the Southwest. The final migration began about 3000 B.C.E. after Beringia had been submerged, when a maritime hunting people crossed the Bering Straits in small boats. The Inuits (also known as the Eskimos) colonized the polar coasts of the Arctic, the Yupiks the coast of southwestern Alaska, and the Aleuts the Aleutian Islands.

While scientists debate the timing and mapping of these migrations, many Indian people hold to oral traditions that include a long journey from a distant place of origin to a new homeland.

40. The word <u>distinctive</u> in the passage is closest in meaning to

   Ⓐ new
   Ⓑ simple
   Ⓒ different
   Ⓓ particular

41. According to paragraph 2, why did Stone Age tribes begin to migrate into Beringia?

   Ⓐ To intermarry with tribes living there
   Ⓑ To trade with tribes that made tools
   Ⓒ To hunt for animals in the area
   Ⓓ To capture domesticated dogs

   Paragraph 2 is marked with an arrow [➔].

42. The phrase <u>Accompanied by</u> in the passage is closest in meaning to

   Ⓐ Found with
   Ⓑ Joined by
   Ⓒ Threatened by
   Ⓓ Detoured with

43. The word <u>which</u> in the passage refers to

   Ⓐ migrations
   Ⓑ evolution
   Ⓒ geneticists
   Ⓓ populations

44. Why does the author mention blood types in paragraph 3?

   Ⓐ Blood types offered proof that the migration had come from Scandinavia.
   Ⓑ The presence of type B in Native Americans was evidence of the migration.
   Ⓒ The blood typing was similar to data from both Japan and Scandinavia.
   Ⓓ Comparisons of blood types in Asia and North America established the date of migration.

   Paragraph 3 is marked with an arrow [➔].

45. How did groups migrate into the Great Plains?

   Ⓐ By walking on a corridor covered with ice
   Ⓑ By using the path that big game had made
   Ⓒ By detouring around a huge ice sheet
   Ⓓ By following a mountain trail

46. Why does the author mention the settlement at Monte Verde, Chile, in paragraph 5?

Ⓐ The remains of boats suggest that people may have lived there.

Ⓑ Artifacts suggest that humans reached this area before the ice melted on land.

Ⓒ Bones and footprints from large animals confirm that the people were hunters.

Ⓓ The houses and tools excavated prove that the early humans were intelligent.

Paragraph 5 is marked with an arrow [➡].

47. The word Eventually in the passage is closest in meaning to

Ⓐ In the end

Ⓑ Nevertheless

Ⓒ Without doubt

Ⓓ In this way

48. Which of the sentences below best expresses the information in the highlighted statement in the passage? The other choices change the meaning or leave out important information.

Ⓐ Beringia was under water when the last people crossed the straits in boats about 3000 B.C.E.

Ⓑ Beringia sank after the last people had crossed the straits in their boats about 3000 B.C.E.

Ⓒ About 3000 B.C.E., the final migration of people in small boats across Beringia had ended.

Ⓓ About 3000 B.C.E., Beringia was flooded, preventing the last people from migrating in small boats.

49. According to paragraph 6, all of the following are true about the later migrations EXCEPT

    Ⓐ The Athapascans traveled into the Southwest United States.
    Ⓑ The Eskimos established homes in the Arctic polar region.
    Ⓒ The Aleuts migrated in small boats to settle coastal islands.
    Ⓓ The Yupiks established settlements on the Great Plains.

    Paragraph 6 is marked with an arrow [➔].

50. Which of the following statements most accurately reflects the author's opinion about the settlement of the North American continent?

    Ⓐ The oral traditions do not support the migration theory.
    Ⓑ The anthropological evidence for migration should be reexamined.
    Ⓒ Migration theories are probably not valid explanations for the physical evidence.
    Ⓓ Genetic markers are the best evidence of a migration from Asia.

51. Look at the four squares [■] that show where the following sentence could be inserted in the passage.

    Newly excavated early human sites in Washington State, California, and Peru have been radiocarbon dated to be 11,000 to 12,000 years old.

    Where could the sentence best be added?

    Click on a square [■] to insert the sentence in the passage.

52. **Directions:** An introduction for a short summary of the passage appears below. Complete the summary by selecting the THREE answer choices that mention the most important points in the passage. Some sentences do not belong in the summary because they express ideas that are not included in the passage or are minor points from the passage. *This question is worth 2 points.*

There is considerable evidence supporting a theory of multiple migrations from Asia to the Americas.

-
-
-

Answer Choices

A Ancient stories of migrations from a faraway place are common in the cultures of many Native American nations.

B The people who inhabited Monte Verde in southern Chile were a highly evolved culture as evidenced by their tools and homes.

C Genetic similarities between Native American peoples and Asians include the arrangement of teeth, viruses, and blood types.

D Hunters followed the herds of big game from Beringia south along the Rocky Mountains into what is now called the Great Plains.

E Excavations at archaeological sites provide artifacts that can be used to date the various migrations that occurred by land and sea.

F The climate began to get warmer and warmer, melting the glacial ice about 13,000 B.C.E.

Reading 5 "Physical and Chemical Properties and Changes"

→ Sugar, water, and aluminum are different substances. Each substance has specific properties that do not depend on the *quantity* of the substance. Properties that can be used to identify or characterize a substance—and distinguish that substance from other substances—are called **characteristic properties**. They are subdivided into two categories: physical properties and chemical properties.

The characteristic physical properties of a substance are those that identify the substance without causing a change in the composition of the substance. They do not depend on the quantity of substance. $\boxed{A}$ Color, odor, density, melting point, boiling point, hardness, metallic luster or shininess, ductility, malleability, and viscosity are all characteristic physical properties. For example, aluminum is a metal that is both ductile and malleable. $\boxed{B}$ Another example of a physical property is water. Whether a small pan of water is raised to its boiling point or a very large kettle of water is raised to its boiling point, the temperature at which the water boils is the same value, 100 degrees C or 212 degrees F. $\boxed{C}$ Similarly, the freezing point of water is 0 degrees C or 32 degrees F. These values are independent of quantity. $\boxed{D}$

Characteristic properties that relate to changes in the composition of a substance or to how it reacts with other substances are called chemical properties. The following questions pertain to the chemical properties of a substance.

1. Does it burn in air?
2. Does it decompose (break up into smaller substances) when heated?
3. What happens when it is placed in an acid?
4. What other chemicals will it react with, and what substances are obtained from the reaction?

Characteristic physical and chemical properties—also called **intensive properties**—are used to identify a substance. In addition to the characteristic physical properties already mentioned, some intensive physical properties include the tendency to dissolve in water, electrical conductivity, and density, which is the ratio of mass to volume.

Additional intensive chemical properties include the tendency of a substance to react with another substance, to tarnish, to corrode, to explode, or to act as a poison or carcinogen (cancer-causing agent).

Extensive properties of substances are those that depend on the quantity of the sample, including measurements of mass, volume, and length. Whereas intensive properties help identify or characterize a particular kind of matter, extensive properties relate to the amount present.

If a lump of candle wax is cut or broken into smaller pieces, or if it is melted (a change of state), the sample remaining is still candle wax. When cooled, the molten wax returns to a solid. In these examples, only a physical change has taken place; that is, the composition of the substance was not affected.

→ When a candle is burned, there are both physical and chemical changes. After the candle is lighted, the solid wax near the burning wick melts. This is a physical change; the composition of the wax does not change as it goes from solid to liquid. Some of the wax is drawn into the burning wick where a chemical change occurs. Here, wax in the candle flame reacts chemically with oxygen in the air to form carbon dioxide gas and water vapor. In any chemical change, one or more substances are used up while one or more new substances are formed. The new substances produced have their own unique physical and chemical properties.

The apparent disappearance of something, like the candle wax, however, is not necessarily a sign that we are observing a chemical change. For example, when water evaporates from a glass and disappears, it has changed from a liquid to a gas (called water vapor), but in both forms it is water. This is a phase change (liquid to gas), which is a physical change. When attempting to determine whether a change is physical or chemical, one should ask the critical question: Has the fundamental composition of the substance changed? In a chemical change (a reaction), it has, but in a physical change, it has not.

Glossary
ductility: can be drawn into wire
malleability: can be shaped
viscosity: thick, resistant to flow

53. According to paragraph 1, what do physical properties and chemical properties have in common?

Ⓐ They are both used to create most of the substances.
Ⓑ They include basic substances like sugar and water.
Ⓒ They are classified as characteristic properties of substances.
Ⓓ They change in proportion to the amount of the substance.

Paragraph 1 is marked with an arrow [➔].

54. The word <u>pertain</u> in the passage is closest in meaning to

Ⓐ compare
Ⓑ relate
Ⓒ explain
Ⓓ change

55. The word <u>which</u> in the passage refers to

Ⓐ properties
Ⓑ tendency
Ⓒ density
Ⓓ ratio

56. According to the passage, a *carcinogen*

Ⓐ explodes under pressure
Ⓑ conducts electricity
Ⓒ causes cancer
Ⓓ tarnishes in air

57. Which of the sentences below best expresses the information in the highlighted statement in the passage? The other choices change the meaning or leave out important information.

Ⓐ Properties that are classified as intensive identify the type of substance and the extent of it present in the surrounding matter.
Ⓑ The quantity of a substance influences its extensive properties, but the characteristics of the substance define the intensive properties.
Ⓒ Where the intensive and extensive properties are found in substances is important in identifying their characteristics.
Ⓓ Both intensive and extensive properties tend to have quantitative rather than qualitative characteristics present.

58. In paragraph 8, the author contrasts the concepts of physical and chemical changes by

Ⓐ listing several types for each concept
Ⓑ providing clear definitions for them
Ⓒ identifying the common characteristics
Ⓓ using a wax candle as an example

Paragraph 8 is marked with an arrow [➔].

59. The word <u>unique</u> in the passage is closest in meaning to

    Ⓐ distinctive
    Ⓑ idealized
    Ⓒ primary
    Ⓓ significant

60. What can be inferred about phase changes?

    Ⓐ They are always chemical changes.
    Ⓑ They are sometimes physical changes.
    Ⓒ They are dependent on extensive properties.
    Ⓓ They usually produce new substances.

61. The word <u>critical</u> in the passage is closest in meaning to

    Ⓐ last
    Ⓑ important
    Ⓒ difficult
    Ⓓ simple

62. According to the passage, the classification of characteristic properties as "physical" or "chemical" is determined by

    Ⓐ whether there has been a change in the structure of the substance
    Ⓑ what happens when the quantity of the substance is increased
    Ⓒ their classification as either extensive or intensive samples
    Ⓓ the disappearance of a substance from one form to another

63. All of the following are mentioned as characteristic physical properties EXCEPT

    Ⓐ dissolving in water
    Ⓑ carrying an electrical charge
    Ⓒ resisting continuous flow
    Ⓓ decomposing when heated

64. Look at the four squares [■] that show where the following sentence could be inserted in the passage.

It can be made into wire or thin, flexible sheets.

Where could the sentence best be added?

Click on a square [■] to insert the sentence in the passage.

65. **Directions:** Complete the table by matching the phrases on the left with the headings on the right. Select the appropriate answer choices and drag them to the characteristic properties to which they refer. TWO of the answer choices will NOT be used. *This question is worth 4 points.*

To delete an answer choice, click on it. To see the passage, click on **View Text**.

Properties	Physical Properties
A Color of the substance	●
B Reaction in an acid	●
C Decomposition in heat	●
D Temperature at which it boils	**Chemical Properties**
E The tendency to shine	●
F The inclination to tarnish	●
G The shape of the substance	●
H Toxic if swallowed or inhaled	●
I The relative amount in nature	

LISTENING SECTION

 Model Test 2, Listening Section, CD 1, Track 1

The Listening section tests your ability to understand spoken English that is typical of interactions and academic speech on college campuses. During the test, you will respond to conversations and lectures.

This is the short format for the Listening section. On the short format, you will respond to two conversations and four lectures. After each listening passage, you will answer 5–6 questions about it.

You will hear each conversation or lecture one time. You may take notes while you listen, but notes are not graded. You may use your notes to answer the questions.

Choose the best answer for multiple-choice questions. On the official TOEFL® iBT, follow the directions on the page or on the screen for computer-assisted questions. Click on **Next** and **OK** to go to the next question. You cannot return to previous questions. You have 20–30 minutes to answer all of the questions. A clock on the screen will show you how much time you have to complete your answers for the section. The clock does not count the time you are listening to the conversations and lectures.

PART I

Listening 1 "Professor's Office"

1. Why does the man go to see his professor?

   (A) To prepare for the next midterm
   (B) To clarify a question from the midterm
   (C) To find out his grade on the midterm
   (D) To complain about his grade on the midterm

2. Why does the man say this:

   (A) He is giving something to the professor.
   (B) He is trying to justify his position.
   (C) He is apologizing because he does not understand.
   (D) He is signaling that he will explain his problem.

3. What did the man do wrong?

   Ⓐ He did not finish the test within the time limit.
   Ⓑ He did not study enough before the test.
   Ⓒ He did not answer one question completely.
   Ⓓ He did not understand a major concept.

4. According to the student, what is *divergent evolution*?

   Ⓐ A population that evolves differently does not have a common ancestor.
   Ⓑ A similar environment can affect the evolution of different species.
   Ⓒ A similar group that is separated may develop different characteristics.
   Ⓓ The climate of an area will allow scientists to predict the life forms.

5. What will Jerry probably do on the next test?

   Ⓐ He will look for questions with several parts.
   Ⓑ He will read the entire test before he begins.
   Ⓒ He will ask for more time to finish.
   Ⓓ He will write an outline for each essay.

Listening 2 "Art History Class"

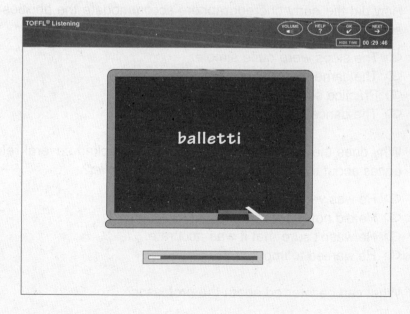

6. What is the discussion mainly about?

Ⓐ Catherine de Medici's entertainments
Ⓑ The figures for court dancing
Ⓒ The development of the ballet
Ⓓ The relationship between dance and meals

7. Why does the professor say this:

Ⓐ To end his explanation and begin the lecture
Ⓑ To apologize to the students about their tests
Ⓒ To comment about the students' grades
Ⓓ To regain the attention of the class

8. According to the professor, what does the term *balletti* mean?

Ⓐ A dramatic story
Ⓑ A parade of horses
Ⓒ A dance done in figures
Ⓓ An outdoor entertainment

9. How did the early choreographers accommodate the abilities of amateur performers?

Ⓐ The steps were quite simple.
Ⓑ The same performance was repeated.
Ⓒ Practice sessions were lengthy.
Ⓓ The dance was seen from a distance.

10. Why does the professor mention that he checked several references about the length of *Queen Louise's Ballet*?

Ⓐ He was very interested in the ballet.
Ⓑ He did not know much about it.
Ⓒ He wasn't sure that it was accurate.
Ⓓ He wanted to impress the class.

11. What can be inferred about the professor?

Ⓐ He is not very polite to his class.
Ⓑ He encourages the students to participate.
Ⓒ He is not very interested in the topic.
Ⓓ He is probably a good dancer.

Listening 3 "Linguistics Class"

12. What is the discussion mainly about?

    Ⓐ The history of the English language
    Ⓑ Different types of grammar
    Ⓒ A linguistic perspective for Latin
    Ⓓ Standard language in schools

13. How does the professor make his point about *native intuition*?

    Ⓐ He explains how to perform an easy experiment.
    Ⓑ He tells the class about his personal experience.
    Ⓒ He provides several examples of sentences.
    Ⓓ He contrasts it with non-native intuition.

14. What are two key problems for descriptive grammar?

    Click on 2 answer choices.

    Ⓐ The information is very complicated and subject to change.

    Ⓑ The formal language must be enforced in all situations.

    Ⓒ The language can be organized correctly in more than one way.

    Ⓓ The description takes time because linguists must agree.

15. Why does the student say this:

    Ⓐ She is disagreeing with the professor.
    Ⓑ She is confirming that she has understood.
    Ⓒ She is trying to impress the other students.
    Ⓓ She is adding information to the lecture.

16. According to the professor, why were Latin rules used for English grammar?

    Ⓐ Latin was a written language with rules that did not change.
    Ⓑ The Romans had conquered England and enforced using Latin.
    Ⓒ English and Latin had many vocabulary words in common.
    Ⓓ English was taking the place of Latin among educated Europeans.

17. Why does the professor discuss the rule to avoid ending a sentence with a preposition?

    Ⓐ It is a good example of the way that descriptive grammar is used.

    Ⓑ It shows the students how to use formal grammar in their speech.

    Ⓒ It is a way to introduce a humorous story into the lecture.

    Ⓓ It demonstrates the problem in using Latin rules for English.

PART II

Listening 4 "College Campus"

18. What is the purpose of this conversation?

   Ⓐ The woman is encouraging the man to be more serious about his studies.
   Ⓑ The woman is looking for alternatives to living in dormitory housing.
   Ⓒ The man is convincing the woman to join the International Student Association.
   Ⓓ The man is trying to find out why the woman didn't go to the talent show.

19. What does the man imply about the house where he is living?

   Ⓐ He prefers the house to the dorm.
   Ⓑ He is living at the house to save money.
   Ⓒ He does not like doing chores at the house.
   Ⓓ He thinks that the house is very crowded.

20. How does the man feel about the International Student Association?

   Ⓐ He is sorry that only women can join the club.
   Ⓑ He enjoys meeting people with different backgrounds.
   Ⓒ He wishes that they would have more activities.
   Ⓓ He will probably join the organization.

21. What does the woman mean when she says this:

   Ⓐ She is trying to persuade the man.
   Ⓑ She is not sure that she understood.
   Ⓒ She is expressing doubt about the time.
   Ⓓ She is changing her mind about going.

22. What does the woman agree to do?

   Ⓐ Join the club
   Ⓑ Eat at a restaurant
   Ⓒ Go to a meeting
   Ⓓ Study with the man

Listening 5 "Zoology Class"

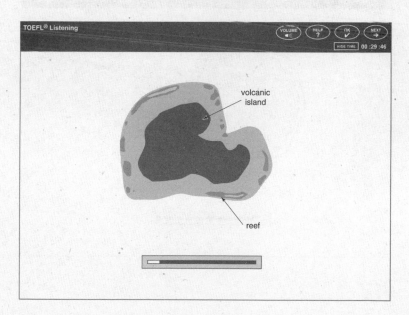

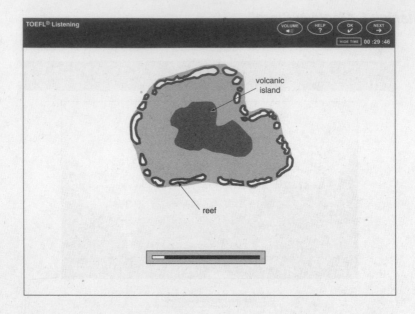

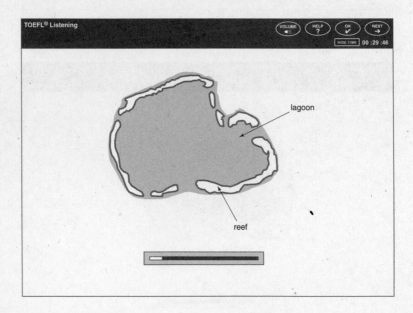

23. According to the professor, how do coral reefs grow?

    Ⓐ They become very large by eating other species.
    Ⓑ They connect coralite shells to build structures.
    Ⓒ They fill with ocean water to expand their size.
    Ⓓ They collect debris from ocean life in their habitat. ✓

24. Why are so many egg bundles released during mass spawning?

    Ⓐ Some of the egg bundles will not be fertilized.
    Ⓑ Half of the egg bundles will not float. ✓
    Ⓒ A number of the egg bundles will be eaten.
    Ⓓ Most of the egg bundles will break open.

25. According to the professor, what is *budding*?

    Ⓐ The division of a polyp in half to reproduce itself.
    Ⓑ The growth of limestone between the shells of polyps.
    Ⓒ The diversity that occurs within a coral reef.
    Ⓓ The increase in size of a polyp as it matures. ✓

26. What is the relationship between zooxanthella and coral polyps?

    Click on 2 answer choices.

    Ⓐ The coral and the zooxanthella compete for the same food.

    Ⓑ The zooxanthella uses the coral for a shelter from enemies.

    Ⓒ The coral eats food produced by the zooxanthella.

    Ⓓ The same predators attack both coral and zooxanthella.

27. Which of the following reefs is probably an atoll?

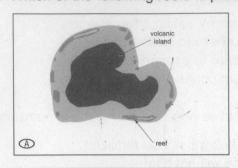

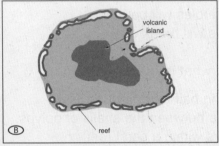

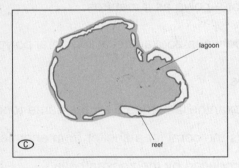

28. In the lecture, the professor explains coral reefs. Indicate whether each of the following is a true statement about coral reefs. Click in the correct box for each phrase.

		Yes	No
A	In general, the organism is quite simple.		
B	The structure of a reef can be very large.		
C	The living coral grows on top of dead shells.		
D	Mass spawning is not very effective.		

Listening 6 "Business Class"

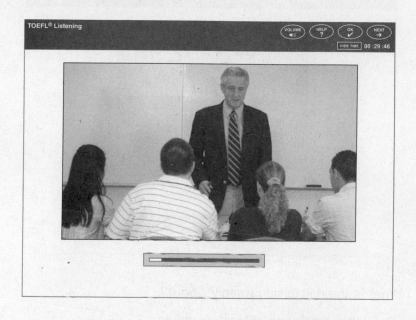

29. What is the discussion mainly about?

    Ⓐ Global marketing of food products
    Ⓑ International business in Europe
    Ⓒ Surprises in food preferences abroad
    Ⓓ Packaging food for exportation

30. How does the professor organize the lecture?

    Ⓐ He compares domestic and foreign products.
    Ⓑ He relates the textbook to his professional experience.
    Ⓒ He refers to case studies from the textbook.
    Ⓓ He presents information from most to least important.

31. Why does the student say this:

    Ⓐ She is asking the professor a question about his previous point.
    Ⓑ She is offering a possible answer to the professor's question.
    Ⓒ She is changing the subject of the class discussion.
    Ⓓ She is checking her comprehension of the professor's opinion.

32. What technique does the professor use to encourage student discussion?

    Ⓐ He gives students positive reinforcement by praising their efforts.

    Ⓑ He asks the students to talk among themselves in small groups.

    Ⓒ He assigns a different part of the textbook to each student.

    Ⓓ He calls on each student by name to contribute to the discussion.

33. What did Ted Levitt mean by "the pluralization of consumption"?

    Ⓐ More people would begin to travel.

    Ⓑ More multinational corporations would produce brands.

    Ⓒ More consumers will have the means to afford goods.

    Ⓓ More people will want the same products.

34. What does the professor say about television and movie companies?

    Ⓐ He indicates that some companies hire foreign marketing experts.

    Ⓑ He criticizes the way that they advertise their programs and films.

    Ⓒ He notes that they are one of the most widely distributed exports.

    Ⓓ He points out that they are paid to display brand-name products.

STOP

Please turn off the audio.
There is a 10-minute break between the
Listening section and the Speaking section.

SPEAKING SECTION

 Model Test 2, Speaking Section, CD 1, Track 2

The Speaking section tests your ability to communicate in English in an academic setting. During the test, you will be presented with six speaking questions. The questions ask for a response to a single question, a conversation, a talk, or a lecture.

You may take notes as you listen, but notes are not graded. You may use your notes to answer the questions. Some of the questions ask for a response to a reading passage and a talk or a lecture. The reading passages and the questions are written, but most of the directions will be spoken.

Your speaking will be evaluated on both the fluency of the language and the accuracy of the content. You will have 15–20 seconds to prepare and 45–60 seconds to respond to each question. Typically, a good response will require all of the response time, but the answer will be complete by the end of the response time.

The time for the Speaking section is about 20 minutes. A clock on the screen will show you how much time you have to prepare your answer and how much time you have to record it.

Independent Speaking Question 1 "A Birthday"

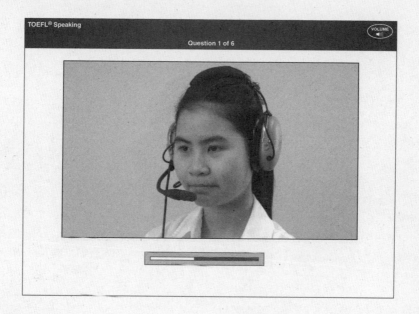

 Listen for a question about a familiar topic.

Question

Explain how birthdays are celebrated in your country. Use specific examples and details in your explanation.

Preparation Time: 15 seconds
Recording Time: 45 seconds

Independent Speaking Question 2 "Course Requirements"

 Listen for a question that asks your opinion about a familiar topic.

Question

Some students would rather write a paper than take a test. Other students would rather take a test instead of writing a paper. Which option do you prefer and why? Use specific reasons and examples to support your opinion.

Preparation Time: 15 seconds
Recording Time: 45 seconds

Integrated Speaking Question 3 "Health Insurance"

Read a short passage and listen to a talk on the same topic.

Reading Time: 45 seconds

<u>Health Insurance</u>
All students may purchase health insurance at the time of registration by marking the insurance box on the course request form. Those students who choose not to use the health insurance option may still use the services of the Student Health Center, but their accounts must be settled at the time of each visit, and the alternative health insurance carrier must be billed directly by the students for reimbursement. International students are required to purchase student health insurance from the university and will be charged automatically at registration. Alternative health insurance carriers may not be substituted. No exceptions will be made.

Now listen to the foreign student advisor. He is explaining the policy and expressing his opinion about it.

Question

The foreign student advisor expresses his opinion of the policy for health insurance. Report his opinion and explain the reasons that he gives for having that opinion.

Preparation Time: 30 seconds
Recording Time: 60 seconds

Integrated Speaking Question 4 "Antarctica"

Read a short passage and then listen to part of a lecture on the same topic.

Reading Time: 45 seconds

Antarctica
Antarctica and the ocean that surrounds it constitute 40 percent of the planet, but in spite of its vast area, it has remained a frontier with no permanent towns or transportation networks. Between 1895 and 1914, explorers planted their flags, claiming various sectors and the raw materials in them for their countries. Nevertheless, the remote location and the harsh environment have encouraged a spirit of cooperation among nations who maintain claims. Furthermore, because Antarctica plays a crucial role in the global environmental system, the exploitation of resources could have unpredictable consequences for the entire world. The Antarctic Treaty, signed in 1961 and expanded in 1991, ensures scientific collaboration, protects the environment, and prohibits military activities.

  Now listen to part of a lecture in a geography class. The professor is talking about Antarctica.

Question
Explain why many countries have staked claims in Antarctica, and why national interests have not been pursued.

Preparation Time: 30 seconds
Recording Time: 60 seconds

Integrated Speaking Question 5 "Extra Money"

 Now listen to a short conversation between a student and her friend.

Question

Describe the woman's problem and the two suggestions that her friend makes about how to handle it. What do you think the woman should do, and why?

Preparation Time: 20 seconds
Recording Time: 60 seconds

Integrated Speaking Question 6 "Research References"

Now listen to part of a lecture in a sociology class. The professor is discussing the criteria for using older research references.

Question

Using the main points and examples from the lecture, describe the two criteria for using an older research reference presented by the professor.

Preparation Time: 20 seconds
Recording Time: 60 seconds

WRITING SECTION

The Writing section tests your ability to write essays in English similar to those that you would write in college courses.

During the test, you will write two essays. The integrated essay asks for your response to an academic reading passage and a lecture on the same topic. You may take notes as you read and listen, but notes are not graded. You may use your notes to write the essay. The lecture will be spoken, but the directions and the questions will be written. You will have 20 minutes to plan, write, and revise your response. Typically, a good essay for the integrated topic will require that you write 150–225 words.

The independent essay usually asks for your opinion about a familiar topic. You will have 30 minutes to plan, write, and revise your response. Typically, a good essay for the independent topic will require that you write 300–350 words.

A clock on the screen will show you how much time you have to complete each essay.

Integrated Essay "The Turing Test"

You have 20 minutes to plan, write, and revise your response to a reading passage and a lecture on the same topic. First, read the passage and take notes. Then, listen to the lecture and take notes. Finally, write your response to the writing question. Typically, a good response will require that you write 150–225 words.

Reading Passage
Time: 3 minutes

Do computers think? It isn't a new question. In fact, Alan Turing, a British mathematician, proposed an experiment to answer the question in 1950, and the test, known as the Turing Test, is still used today. In the experiment, a group of people are asked to interact with something in another room through a computer terminal. They don't know whether it is another person or a computer that they are interacting with. They can ask any questions that they want. They can type their questions onto a computer screen, or they can ask their questions by speaking into a microphone. In response, they see the answers on a computer screen or they hear them played back by a voice synthesizer. At the end of the test, the people have to decide whether they have been talking to a person or to a computer. If they judge the computer to be a person, or if they can't determine the difference, then the machine has passed the Turing Test.

Since 1950, a number of contests have been organized in which machines are challenged to the Turing Test. In 1990, Hugh Loebner sponsored a prize to be awarded by the Cambridge Center for Behavioral Studies—a gold medal and a cash award of $100,000 to the designer of the computer that could pass the Turing Test; however, so far, no computer has passed the test.

Model Test 2, Writing Section, CD 1, Track 3

Now listen to a lecture on the same topic as the passage that you have just read.

Question

Summarize the main points in the reading passage, and then explain how the lecture casts doubt on the ideas in the reading.

Independent Essay "Family Pets"

Question

Read and think about the following statement:

Pets should be treated like family members.

Do you agree or disagree with this statement? Give reasons to support your opinion.

| This is the end of Model Test 2. To check your answers, refer to "Explanatory or Example Answers and Audio Scripts for Model Tests: Model Test 2," Chapter 7, pages 437–478. |

6

MODEL TEST 3: PROGRESS TEST

READING SECTION

The Reading section tests your ability to understand reading passages like those in college textbooks. The passages are about 700 words in length.

This is the long format for the Reading section. On the long format, you will respond to five passages. After each passage, you will answer 12–14 questions about it. Only three passages will be graded. The other passages are part of an exerimental section for future tests. Because you will not know which passages will be graded, you must try to do your best on all of them.

Most questions are worth 1 point, but the last question in each passage is worth more than 1 point.

You will have 100 minutes to read all of the passages and answer the questions. You may take notes while you read, but notes are not graded. You may use your notes to answer the questions. Some passages may include a word or phrase that is underlined in blue. Click on the word or phrase to see a glossary definition or explanation.

Choose the best answer for multiple-choice questions. On the official TOEFL® iBT, follow the directions on the page or on the screen for computer-assisted questions. Click on **Next** to go to the next question. Click on **Back** to return to the previous question. You may return to previous questions for all of the passages in the same reading part, but after you go to the next part, you will not be able to return to passages in a previous part. Be sure that you have answered all of the questions for the passages in each part before you click on **Next** at the end of the passage to move to the next part.

You can click on **Review** to see a chart of the questions you have answered and the questions you have not answered in each part. From this screen, you can return to the question you want to answer in the part that is open.

A clock on the screen will show you how much time you have to complete the Reading section.

PART I

Reading 1 "Exotic and Endangered Species"

→ When you hear someone bubbling enthusiastically about an **exotic species**, you can safely bet the speaker isn't an ecologist. This is a name for a resident of an established community that was deliberately or accidentally moved from its home range and became established elsewhere. Unlike most imports, which can't take hold outside their home range, an exotic species permanently insinuates itself into a new community.

Sometimes the additions are harmless and even have beneficial effects. More often, they make native species **endangered species**, which by definition are extremely vulnerable to extinction. Of all species on the rare or endangered lists or that recently became extinct, *close to 70 percent owe their precarious existence or*

demise to displacement by exotic species. Two examples are included here to illustrate the problem.

During the 1800s, British settlers in Australia just
couldn't bond with the koalas and kangaroos, so they
started to import familiar animals from their homeland.
In 1859, in what would be the start of a wholesale dis-
aster, a northern Australian landowner imported and
then released two dozen wild European rabbits
(Oryctolagus cuniculus). Good food and good sport
hunting—that was the idea. An ideal rabbit habitat with
no natural predators was the reality.

Six years later, the landowner had killed 20,000
rabbits and was besieged by 20,000 more. The rabbits
displaced livestock, even kangaroos. Now Australia
has 200 to 300 million hippityhopping through the
southern half of the country. They overgraze perennial
grasses in good times and strip bark from shrubs and
trees during droughts. You know where they've been;
they transform grasslands and shrublands into eroded
deserts. They have been shot and poisoned. Their
warrens have been plowed under, fumigated, and
dynamited. Even when all-out assaults reduced their
population size by 70 percent, the rapidly reproducing
imports made a comeback in less than a year. Did the
construction of a 2,000-mile-long fence protect western Australia? No. Rabbits made it to the other side
before workers finished the fence.

→ In 1951, government workers introduced a myxoma virus by way of mildly infected South American rabbits, its normal hosts. This virus causes *myxomatosis.*
The disease has mild effects on South American rabbits that coevolved with the virus but nearly always had
lethal effects on *O. cuniculus.* Biting insects, mainly
mosquitoes and fleas, quickly transmit the virus from
host to host. Having no coevolved defenses against
the novel virus, the European rabbits died in droves.

But, as you might expect, natural selection has since favored rapid growth of populations of *O. cuniculus* resistant to the virus.

→ In 1991, on an uninhabited island in Spencer Gulf, Australian researchers released a population of rabbits that they had injected with a calcivirus. The rabbits died quickly and relatively painlessly from blood clots in their lungs, hearts, and kidneys. In 1995, the test virus escaped from the island, possibly on insect vectors. It has been killing 80 to 95 percent of the adult rabbits in Australian regions. At this writing, researchers are now questioning whether the calcivirus should be used on a widespread scale, whether it can jump boundaries and infect animals other than rabbits (such as humans), and what the long-term consequences will be.

A vine called kudzu *(Pueraria lobata)* was deliberately imported from Japan to the United States, where it faces no serious threats from herbivores, pathogens, or competitor plants. In temperate parts of Asia, it is a well-behaved legume with a well-developed root system. It *seemed* like a good idea to use it to control erosion on hills and highway embankments in the southeastern United States. Ⓐ With nothing to stop it, though, kudzu's shoots grew a third of a meter per day. Vines now blanket streambanks, trees, telephone poles, houses, and almost everything else in their path. Attempts to dig up or burn kudzu are futile. Grazing goats and herbicides help, but goats eat other plants, too, and herbicides contaminate water supplies. Ⓑ Kudzu could reach the Great Lakes by the year 2040.

→ On the bright side, a Japanese firm is constructing a kudzu farm and processing plant in Alabama. The idea is to export the starch to Asia, where the demand currently exceeds the supply. Ⓒ Also, kudzu may eventually help reduce logging operations. ☐D☐ At the Georgia Institute of Technology, researchers report that kudzu might become an alternative source for paper.

1. Based on the information in paragraph 1, which of the following best explains the term "exotic species"?

   Ⓐ Animals or plants on the rare species list
   Ⓑ A permanent resident in an established community
   Ⓒ A species that has been moved to a different community
   Ⓓ An import that fails to thrive outside of its home range

   Paragraph 1 is marked with an arrow [➔].

2. The word <u>itself</u> in the passage refers to

   Ⓐ most imports
   Ⓑ new community
   Ⓒ home range
   Ⓓ exotic species

3. The word <u>bond</u> in the passage is closest in meaning to

   Ⓐ move
   Ⓑ connect
   Ⓒ live
   Ⓓ fight

4. According to the author, why did the plan to introduce rabbits in Australia fail?

   Ⓐ The rabbits were infected with a contagious virus.
   Ⓑ Most Australians did not like the rabbits.
   Ⓒ No natural predators controlled the rabbit population.
   Ⓓ Hunters killed the rabbits for sport and for food.

5. All of the following methods were used to control the rabbit population in Australia EXCEPT

   Ⓐ They were poisoned.
   Ⓑ Their habitats were buried.
   Ⓒ They were moved to deserts.
   Ⓓ They were surrounded by fences.

6. Why does the author mention mosquitoes and fleas in paragraph 5?

   Ⓐ Because they are the origin of the myxoma virus
   Ⓑ Because they carry the myxoma virus to other animals
   Ⓒ Because they die when they are infected by myxoma
   Ⓓ Because they have an immunity to the myxoma virus

Paragraph 5 is marked with an arrow [➔].

7. According to paragraph 6, the Spencer Gulf experiment was dangerous because

   Ⓐ insect populations were exposed to a virus
   Ⓑ rabbits on the island died from a virus
   Ⓒ the virus may be a threat to humans
   Ⓓ some animals are immune to the virus

Paragraph 6 is marked with an arrow [➔].

8. The word <u>consequences</u> in the passage is closest in meaning to

   Ⓐ stages
   Ⓑ advantages
   Ⓒ results
   Ⓓ increases

9. Why does the author give details about the kudzu farm and processing plant in paragraph 8?

   Ⓐ To explain why kudzu was imported from abroad
   Ⓑ To argue that the decision to plant kudzu was a good one
   Ⓒ To give a reason for kudzu to be planted in Asia
   Ⓓ To offer partial solutions to the kudzu problem

   Paragraph 8 is marked with an arrow [➔].

10. The word <u>exceeds</u> in the passage is closest in meaning to

    Ⓐ surpasses
    Ⓑ destroys
    Ⓒ estimates
    Ⓓ causes

11. Which of the following statements most accurately reflects the author's opinion about exotic species?

    Ⓐ Exotic species should be protected by ecologists.
    Ⓑ Importing an exotic species can solve many problems.
    Ⓒ Ecologists should make the decision to import an exotic species.
    Ⓓ Exotic species are often disruptive to the ecology.

12. Look at the four squares [■] that show where the following sentence could be inserted in the passage.

    Asians use a starch extract from kudzu in drinks, herbal medicines, and candy.

    Where could the sentence best be added?

    Click on a square [■] to insert the sentence in the passage.

13. **Directions:** An introduction for a short summary of the passage appears below. Complete the summary by selecting the THREE answer choices that mention the most important points in the passage. Some sentences do not belong in the summary because they express ideas that are not included in the passage or are minor points from the passage. *This question is worth 2 points.*

Exotic species often require containment because they displace other species when they become established in a new environment.

- ●

- ●

- ●

Answer Choices

A Rabbits were able to cross a fence 2,000 miles long that was constructed to keep them out of western Australia.

B Methods to control exotic species include fences, viruses, burning, herbicides, natural predators, and harvesting.

C Rabbits that were introduced in Australia and kudzu which was introduced in the United States, are examples of species that caused problems.

D Researchers may be able to develop material from the kudzu vine that will be an alternative to wood pulp paper.

E The problem is that exotic species make native species vulnerable to extinction.

F A virus that is deadly to rabbits may have serious effects for other animals.

PART II

Reading 2 "Paleolithic Art"

→ The several millennia following 30,000 B.C. saw a powerful outburst of artistic creativity. The artworks produced range from simple shell necklaces to human and animal forms in ivory, clay, and stone to monumental paintings, engravings, and relief sculptures covering the huge wall surfaces of caves. From the moment in 1879 that cave paintings were discovered at Altamira, scholars have wondered why the hunter-artists of the Old Stone Age decided to cover the walls of dark caverns with animal images. Various answers have been given, including that they were mere decoration, but this theory cannot explain the narrow range of subjects or the inaccessibility of many of the paintings. In fact, the remoteness and difficulty of access of many of the cave paintings and the fact they appear to have been used for centuries are precisely what have led many scholars to suggest that the prehistoric hunters attributed magical properties to the images they painted. According to this argument, by confining animals to the surfaces of their cave walls, the artists believed they were bringing the beasts under their control. Some have even hypothesized that rituals or dances were performed in front of the images and that these rites served to improve the hunters' luck. Still others have stated that the painted animals may have served as teaching tools to instruct new hunters about the character of the various species they would encounter or even to serve as targets for spears!

By contrast, some scholars have argued that the magical purpose of the paintings was not to facilitate the *destruction* of bison and other species. Instead, they believe prehistoric painters created animal images to assure the *survival* of the herds. Paleolithic peoples depended on for their food supply and for their clothing. [A] A central problem for both the hunting-magic and food-creation theories is that the animals that seem to have been diet staples of Old Stone Age peoples are not those most frequently portrayed. [B]

Other scholars have sought to reconstruct an elaborate mythology based on the cave paintings, suggesting that Paleolithic humans believed they had animal ancestors. Still others have equated certain species with men and others with women and also found sexual symbolism in the abstract signs that sometimes accompany the images. [C] Almost all of these theories have been discredited over time, and art historians must admit that no one knows the intent of these paintings. [D] In fact, a single explanation for all Paleolithic murals, even paintings similar in subject, style, and *composition* (how the motifs are arranged on the surface), is unlikely to apply universally. For now, the paintings remain an enigma.

→ That the paintings did have meaning to the Paleolithic peoples who made and observed them cannot, however, be doubted. In fact, signs consisting of checks, dots, squares, or other arrangements of lines often accompany the pictures of animals. Several observers have seen a primitive writing form in these representations of nonliving things, but the signs, too, may have had some other significance. Some look like traps and arrows and, according to the hunting-magic theory, may have been drawn to insure success in capturing or killing animals with these devices. At Pech-Merle in France, the "spotted horses" painted on the cave wall may not have spots. Some scholars have argued that the "spots," which appear both within and without the horses' outlines, are painted rocks thrown at the animals.

→ Representations of human hands also are common. Those around the Pech-Merle horses, and the majority of painted hands at other sites, are "negative," that is, the artist placed one hand against the wall and then painted or blew pigment around it. Occasionally, the artist dipped a hand in paint and then pressed it against the wall, leaving a "positive" imprint. These handprints, too, must have had a purpose. Some scholars have considered them "signatures" of cult or community members or, less likely, of individual artists.

14. According to paragraph 1, the cave art was difficult to find because the artists

Ⓐ were probably trying to keep their work a secret from their tribe

Ⓑ could have begun their painting while they were confined in the caves

Ⓒ may have chosen a location deep in the caves to hold ceremonies

Ⓓ had to practice before they made images that more people could see

Paragraph 1 is marked with an arrow [→].

15. According to paragraph 1, Paleolithic people may have used cave art for all of the following purposes EXCEPT

Ⓐ People may have danced in front of the images.

Ⓑ Hunters could have used the figures for target practice.

Ⓒ Shamans might have performed magical rituals in the caves.

Ⓓ Animals may have been kept in the caves near the drawings.

Paragraph 1 is marked with an arrow [→].

16. The word <u>access</u> in the passage is closest in meaning to

Ⓐ admission

Ⓑ meaning

Ⓒ site

Ⓓ research

17. The word <u>facilitate</u> in the passage is closest in meaning to

     Ⓐ specify
     Ⓑ permit
     Ⓒ assist
     Ⓓ discover

18. The word <u>those</u> in the passage refers to

     Ⓐ peoples
     Ⓑ staples
     Ⓒ animals
     Ⓓ theories

19. The word <u>discredited</u> in the passage is closest in meaning to

     Ⓐ not attentive
     Ⓑ not believed
     Ⓒ not hopeful
     Ⓓ not organized

20. Which of the sentences below best expresses the information in the highlighted statement in the passage? The other choices change the meaning or leave out important information.

     Ⓐ It is true that the paintings were meaningful to the Paleolithic peoples.
     Ⓑ Doubtless, the Paleolithic peoples were the ones who made the paintings.
     Ⓒ There is no doubt about the meaning of the Paleolithic paintings.
     Ⓓ Paintings that had meaning for the Paleolithic peoples are doubtful.

21. How have some scholars interpreted the arrangement of lines into geometric shapes near the animal paintings?

     Ⓐ They are probably more pictures of animals.
     Ⓑ They may be an early writing system.
     Ⓒ It is possible that they have no significance.
     Ⓓ Probably most of the lines are scratches from age.

22. According to paragraph 4, why do scholars believe that the spots on the horses may represent a hunting scene?

    Ⓐ Other cave paintings near this one include hunting scenes.
    Ⓑ The spots are made of rocks that were attached to the wall.
    Ⓒ The spots are painted outside the horses' forms as well as inside them.
    Ⓓ The primitive writing is interpreted as an accounting of a hunt.

    Paragraph 4 is marked with an arrow [➔].

23. According to paragraph 5, why did artists leave a positive imprint of their hands on cave paintings?

    Ⓐ It represents human beings in the cave paintings.
    Ⓑ It could have been a way for them to sign their work.
    Ⓒ It was a hunter's handprint among the herd of animals.
    Ⓓ It might have been a pleasing image without much meaning.

    Paragraph 5 is marked with an arrow [➔].

24. Which of the following statements most accurately reflects the author's opinion about the purpose of cave paintings?

    Ⓐ The cave paintings were part of a hunting ritual.
    Ⓑ Artists were honoring their animal ancestors in cave paintings.
    Ⓒ The exact purpose of cave paintings is not known.
    Ⓓ Decoration was probably the main reason for painting in caves.

25. Look at the four squares [■] that show where the following sentence could be inserted in the passage.

    At Altamira, for example, faunal remains show that red deer, not bison, were eaten.

    Where could the sentence best be added?

    Click on a square [■] to insert the sentence in the passage.

26. **Directions:** An introduction for a short summary of the passage appears below. Complete the summary by selecting the THREE answer choices that mention the most important points in the passage. Some sentences do not belong in the summary because they express ideas that are not included in the passage or are minor points from the passage. *This question is worth 2 points.*

The purpose of the art discovered on cave walls is a topic of discussion among scholars.

-
-
-

Answer Choices

[A] Some of the lines and the geometrical figures beside the drawings could be a very early form of a writing system.

[B] It is possible that the paintings were created as part of a magical ritual either to guarantee a good hunt or an abundance of animals.

[C] At Altamira, excavations indicate that the protein diet of the inhabitants was probably deer rather than bison.

[D] Perhaps the artists were paying homage to their animal ancestors by recreating their mythology in the pictures.

[E] The art may be more recent than first assumed when the caves were originally discovered in the late 1800s.

[F] There are a number of human handprints arranged around the Pech-Merle horses that could have been pressed there by the artists.

Reading 3 "Group Decision Making"

Advantages of Group Decision Making

→ Committees, task forces, and ad hoc groups are frequently assigned to identify and recommend decision
alternatives or, in some cases, to actually make important decisions. In essence, a group is a tool that can
focus the experience and expertise of several people on
a particular problem or situation. Thus, a group offers
the advantage of greater total knowledge. Groups accumulate more information, knowledge, and facts than
individuals and often consider more alternatives. Each
person in the group is able to draw on his or her unique
education, experience, insights, and other resources
and contribute those to the group. The varied backgrounds, training levels, and expertise of group members also help overcome tunnel vision by enabling the
group to view the problem in more than one way.

→ Participation in group decision making usually leads
to higher member satisfaction. People tend to accept a
decision more readily and to be better satisfied with it
when they have participated in making that decision. In
addition, people will better understand and be more
committed to a decision in which they have had a say
than to a decision made for them. As a result, such a
decision is more likely to be implemented successfully.

Disadvantages of Group Decision Making

→ While groups have many potential benefits, we all
know that they can also be frustrating. A One obvious
disadvantage of group decision making is the time
required to make a decision. B The time needed for
group discussion and the associated compromising and
selecting of a decision alternative can be considerable.
C Time costs money, so a waste of time becomes a
disadvantage if a decision made by a group could
have been made just as effectively by an individual
working alone. D Consequently, group decisions
should be avoided when speed and efficiency are the
primary considerations.

A second disadvantage is that the group discussion may be dominated by an individual or subgroup. Effectiveness can be reduced if one individual, such as the group leader, dominates the discussion by talking too much or being closed to other points of view. Some group leaders try to control the group and provide the major input. Such dominance can stifle other group members' willingness to participate and could cause decision alternatives to be ignored or overlooked. All group members need to be encouraged and permitted to contribute.

→ Another disadvantage of group decision making is that members may be less concerned with the group's goals than with their own personal goals. They may become so sidetracked in trying to win an argument that they forget about group performance. On the other hand, a group may try too hard to compromise and consequently may not make optimal decisions. Sometimes this stems from the desire to maintain friendships and avoid disagreements. Often groups exert tremendous social pressure on individuals to conform to established or expected patterns of behavior. Especially when they are dealing with important and controversial issues, interacting groups may be prone to a phenomenon called groupthink.

→ Groupthink is an agreement-at-any-cost mentality that results in ineffective group decision making. It occurs when groups are highly cohesive, have highly directive leaders, are insulated so they have no clear ways to get objective information, and—because they lack outside information—have little hope that a better solution might be found than the one proposed by the leader or other influential group members. These conditions foster the illusion that the group is invulnerable, right, and more moral than outsiders. They also encourage the development of self-appointed "mind guards" who bring pressure on dissenters. In such situations, decisions—often important decisions—are made without consideration of alternative frames or alternative options. It is difficult to imagine conditions more conducive to poor decision making and wrong decisions.

Recent research indicates that groupthink may also result when group members have preconceived ideas about how a problem should be solved. Under these conditions, the team may not examine a full range of decision alternatives, or it may discount or avoid information that threatens its preconceived choice.

27. In paragraph 1, the author states that groups frequently

   Ⓐ generate more options than individuals
   Ⓑ agree on the way that the problem should be approached
   Ⓒ make recommendations instead of decisions
   Ⓓ are chosen to participate because of their experience

   Paragraph 1 is marked with an arrow [➜].

28. According to paragraph 2, why do group decisions tend to be more successful?

   Ⓐ When more people are involved, there are more ideas from which to choose.
   Ⓑ People are more accepting of decisions when they have been involved in them.
   Ⓒ Implementing ideas is easier with a large number of people to help.
   Ⓓ People like to be participants in decisions that are successful.

   Paragraph 2 is marked with an arrow [➜].

29. The word <u>considerable</u> in the passage is closest in meaning to

   Ⓐ valuable
   Ⓑ significant
   Ⓒ predictable
   Ⓓ unusual

30. The word <u>Consequently</u> in the passage is closest in meaning to

    Ⓐ About now
    Ⓑ Without doubt
    Ⓒ Before long
    Ⓓ As a result

31. According to paragraph 3, group discussion can be problematic because

    Ⓐ individual decisions are always more effective
    Ⓑ it takes more time for a group to arrive at a decision
    Ⓒ it costs more to pay all of the group members
    Ⓓ interaction among group members can be a problem

    Paragraph 3 is marked with an arrow [➜].

32. What can be inferred about a group leader?

    Ⓐ A good leader will provide goals for the group to consider and vote on.
    Ⓑ The purpose of the leader is to facilitate the participation of all of the members.
    Ⓒ A group leader should be the dominant member of the group.
    Ⓓ Expectations for group behavior must be presented by the group leader.

33. The word <u>controversial</u> in the passage is closest in meaning to

    Ⓐ accepted
    Ⓑ debatable
    Ⓒ recent
    Ⓓ complicated

34. The phrase <u>the one</u> in the passage refers to

    Ⓐ solution
    Ⓑ information
    Ⓒ hope
    Ⓓ leader

35. According to paragraph 5, how does the author explain compromise in a group?

    Ⓐ The group may try to make a better decision by compromising.
    Ⓑ A compromise may be the best way to encourage groupthink.
    Ⓒ Compromising may allow the group members to remain friends.
    Ⓓ To compromise can help one member to reach a personal goal.

    Paragraph 5 is marked with an arrow [➔].

36. What does the term "mind guards" refer to?

    Ⓐ People who conform to the group opinion without thinking
    Ⓑ Group members who try to force others to agree with the group
    Ⓒ Members of the group who are the most ethical and influential
    Ⓓ Those people who disagree without offering an alternative view

37. According to paragraph 6, why are alternative solutions often rejected in groupthink?

    Ⓐ Dissenters exert pressure on the group.
    Ⓑ Group leaders are not very creative.
    Ⓒ Information is not made available.
    Ⓓ The group is usually right.

    Paragraph 6 is marked with an arrow [➔].

38. Look at the four squares [■] that show where the following sentence could be inserted in the passage.

    In fact, the traditional group is prone to a variety of difficulties.

    Where could the sentence best be added?

    Click on a square [■] to insert the sentence in the passage.

39. **Directions**: Complete the table by matching the phrases on the left with the headings on the right. Select the appropriate answer choices and drag them to the advantages or disadvantages of group decision making. TWO of the answer choices will NOT be used. *This question is worth 4 points.*

To delete an answer choice, click on it. To see the passage, click on **View Text**.

Answer Choices

    Ⓐ Sometimes a strong leader will dominate the group.

    Ⓑ Sometimes personal objectives dictate the outcome.

    Ⓒ Most of the time people are happier with the decision.

    Ⓓ It is usually possible to gather more data.

    Ⓔ It will probably take much longer to arrive at a decision.

    Ⓕ The group may tend to make decisions based on friendship.

    Ⓖ Discussion is required before a decision is made.

    Ⓗ Implementation is often much easier after the decision.

    Ⓘ A group member may disagree with the majority opinion.

Advantages

-
-
-

Disadvantages

-
-
-
-

PART III

Reading 4 "Four Stages of Planetary Development"

Planetary Development

➔ In our study of the planet Earth, we will find a four-stage history of planetary development. The moon and all the terrestrial planets have passed through these stages, although differences in the way the planets were altered by these stages have produced dramatically different worlds. The moon, for example, is much like Earth, but its evolution has been dramatically altered by its smaller size. As we explore the solar system, we will discover not entirely new processes but rather familiar effects working in slightly different ways.

The Four Stages

The first stage of planetary evolution is *differentiation*, the separation of material according to density. Earth now has a dense core and a lower-density crust, and that structure must have originated very early.

Differentiation would have occurred easily if Earth were molten when it was young. Two sources of heat could have heated Earth. First, heat of formation would be created by in-falling material. A <u>meteorite</u> hitting Earth at high velocity converts most of its energy of motion into heat, and the in-falling of a large number of meteorites could release tremendous heat. If Earth formed rapidly, this heat would have accumulated much more rapidly than it could leak away, and Earth may have been molten when it formed. A second source of heat requires more time to develop. The decay of radioactive elements trapped in the Earth releases heat gradually; but, as soon as Earth formed, that heat would have begun to accumulate and could have helped melt Earth to facilitate differentiation. Most of Earth's radioactive elements are now concentrated in the crust, where they continue to warm and soften the rock layers.

Earth formed by material falling together, but meteorites could have left no trace until a crust solidified. Once Earth had a hard surface, the meteorites could form craters. This second stage in planetary evolution, *cratering*, was violent. The heavy bombardment was intense because the solar nebula was filled with rocky and icy debris, and the young Earth was battered by meteorites that pulverized the newly forming crust. The largest meteorites blasted out crater basins hundreds of kilometers in diameter. As the solar nebula cleared, the amount of debris decreased, and the level of cratering fell to its present low level. Although meteorites still occasionally strike Earth and dig craters, cratering is no longer the dominant influence on Earth's geology. As we compare other worlds with Earth, we will discover traces of this intense period of cratering, the heavy bombardment, on every old surface in the solar system.

→ The third stage, *flooding*, no doubt began while cratering was still intense. The fracturing of the crust and the heating caused by radioactive decay allowed molten rock just below the crust to well up through fissures and flood the deeper basins. We will discuss such flooded basins on other worlds, such as the moon, but all traces of this early lava flooding have been destroyed by later geological activity in Earth's crust. On Earth, flooding continued as the atmosphere cooled and water fell as rain, filling the deepest basins to produce the first oceans. Ⓐ Notice that on Earth flooding involves both lava and water, a circumstance that we will not find on most worlds. Ⓑ

The fourth stage, *slow surface evolution*, has continued for the last 3.5 billion years or more. C Earth's surface is constantly changing as sections of crust slide over each other, push up mountains, and shift continents. D Almost all traces of the first billion years of Earth's geology have been destroyed by the active crust and erosion.

Earth as a Planet

All terrestrial planets pass through these four stages, so in that respect, Earth is a good basic reference planet for comparative <u>planetology</u>. Some planets have emphasized one stage over another, and some planets have failed to progress fully through the four stages. Nevertheless, Earth is a good standard of comparison. Every major process on any rocky world in our solar system is represented in some form on Earth.

On the other hand, Earth is peculiar in two ways. First, it has large amounts of liquid water on its surface. Fully 75 percent of its surface is covered by this liquid and no other planet in our solar system is known to have such extensive liquid water on its surface. Furthermore, some of the matter on the surface of this world is alive, and a small part of that living matter is aware. We do not know how the presence of living matter has affected the evolution of Earth, but this process seems to be totally missing from other worlds in our solar system.

Glossary

meteorite: a mass that falls to the surface of a planet from space

planetology: the study of planets

40. Why does the author mention the moon in paragraph 1?

    Ⓐ To explain the stages in planetary development for the Earth
    Ⓑ To contrast the evolution of the moon with that of the Earth
    Ⓒ To demonstrate that the moon passed through different stages
    Ⓓ To give an example of exploration in the solar system

    Paragraph 1 is marked with an arrow [➜].

41. The word <u>its</u> in the passage refers to

    Ⓐ meteorite
    Ⓑ Earth
    Ⓒ velocity
    Ⓓ motion

42. Which of the sentences below best expresses the information in the highlighted statement in the passage? The other choices change the meaning or leave out important information.

    Ⓐ The Earth was probably liquid because the heat collected faster than it dissipated if the formation took place quickly.
    Ⓑ Because of the rapid formation of the Earth, the crust took a long time to cool before it became a solid.
    Ⓒ The liquid core of the Earth was created when the planet first formed because the heat was so high and there was little cooling.
    Ⓓ The cooling caused the Earth to form much more quickly as it met with the intense heat of the new planet.

43. The word <u>pulverized</u> in the passage is closest in meaning to

    Ⓐ melted into liquid
    Ⓑ broken into small parts
    Ⓒ frozen very hard
    Ⓓ washed very clean

44. What can be inferred about radioactive matter?

   Ⓐ It is revealed by later activity.
   Ⓑ It generates intense heat.
   Ⓒ It is an important stage.
   Ⓓ It fractures the planet's crust.

45. The word <u>dominant</u> in the passage is closest in meaning to

   Ⓐ most limited
   Ⓑ most likely
   Ⓒ most rapid
   Ⓓ most important

46. According to paragraph 5, how were the oceans formed?

   Ⓐ Ice gouged out depressions in the Earth.
   Ⓑ Rain filled the craters made by meteorites.
   Ⓒ Earthquakes shifted the continents.
   Ⓓ Molten rock and lava flooded the basins.

   Paragraph 5 is marked with an arrow [➜].

47. What is the author's opinion of life on other planets?

   Ⓐ She does not know whether life is present on other planets.
   Ⓑ She is certain that no life exists on any planet except Earth.
   Ⓒ She does not express an opinion about life on other planets.
   Ⓓ She thinks that there is probably life on other planets.

48. According to the passage, which stage occurs after cratering?

   Ⓐ Flooding
   Ⓑ Slow surface evolution
   Ⓒ Differentiation
   Ⓓ Erosion

49. All of the following are reasons why the Earth is a good model of planetary development for purposes of comparison with other planets EXCEPT

   Ⓐ The Earth has gone through all four stages of planetary evolution.
   Ⓑ Life on Earth has affected the evolution in a number of important ways.
   Ⓒ All of the fundamental processes on terrestrial planets have occurred on Earth.
   Ⓓ There is evidence of extensive cratering both on Earth and on all other planets.

50. Look at the four squares [■] that show where the following sentence could be inserted in the passage.

   Also, moving air and water erode the surface and wear away geological features.

   Where could the sentence best be added?

   Click on a square [■] to insert the sentence in the passage.

51. The word <u>peculiar</u> in the passage is closest in meaning to

   Ⓐ different
   Ⓑ better
   Ⓒ interesting
   Ⓓ new

52. **Directions:** An introduction for a short summary of the passage appears below. Complete the summary by selecting the THREE answer choices that mention the most important points in the passage. Some sentences do not belong in the summary because they express ideas that are not included in the passage or are minor points from the passage. *This question is worth 2 points.*

There are four stages of development for the terrestrial planets.

-

-

-

Answer Choices

A All rocky planets go through different stages in their evolution because of variations in composition.

B In spite of several unique features, the Earth is a good example of how a planet proceeds through the stages.

C Fewer meteorites fall to Earth now than in the earlier stages of the planet's evolutionary history.

D About three quarters of the surface of the Earth is submerged by the water in its oceans.

E Differentiation and cratering are early stages that are influenced by in-falling meteorites.

F Flooding includes both lava and water, while slow surface evolution causes shifting in the crust.

Reading 5 "Speech and Writing"

It is a widely held misconception that writing is more perfect than speech. To many people, writing somehow seems more correct and more stable, whereas speech can be careless, corrupted, and susceptible to change. Some people even go so far as to identify language with writing and to regard speech as a secondary form of language used imperfectly to approximate the ideals of the written language.

→ One of the basic assumptions of modern linguistics, however, is that speech is primary and writing is secondary. The most immediate manifestation of language is speech and not writing. Writing is simply the representation of speech in another physical medium. Spoken language encodes thought into a physically transmittable form, while writing, in turn, encodes spoken language into a physically preservable form. Writing is a two-stage process. All units of writing, whether letters or characters, are based on units of speech, i.e., words, sounds, or syllables. When linguists study language, they take the spoken language as their best source of data and their object of description (except in instances of languages like Latin for which there are no longer any speakers).

There are several reasons for maintaining that speech is primary and writing is secondary. Ⓐ First, writing is a later historical development than spoken language. Ⓑ Current archeological evidence indicates that writing was first utilized in Sumer, that is, modern-day Iraq, about 6,000 years ago. Ⓒ As far as physical and cultural anthropologists can tell, spoken language has probably been used by humans for hundreds of thousands of years. Ⓓ

→ Second, writing does not exist everywhere that spoken language exists. This seems hard to imagine in our highly literate society, but the fact is that there are still many communities in the world where a written form of language is not used, and even in those cultures using a writing system, there are individuals who fail to learn the written form of their language. In fact, the majority of the Earth's inhabitants are illiterate, though quite capable of spoken communication. However, no society uses only a written language with no spoken form.

Third, writing must be taught, whereas spoken language is acquired automatically. All children, except children with serious learning disabilities, naturally learn to speak the language of the community in which they are brought up. They acquire the basics of their native language before they enter school, and even if they never attend school, they become fully competent speakers. Writing systems vary in complexity, but regardless of their level of sophistication, they must all be taught.

Finally, neurolinguistic evidence (studies of the brain in action during language use) demonstrates that the processing and production of written language is overlaid on the spoken language centers in the brain. Spoken language involves several distinct areas of the brain; writing uses these areas and others as well.

→ So what gives rise to the misconception that writing is more perfect than speech? There are several reasons. For one thing, the product of writing is usually more aptly worded and better organized, containing fewer errors, hesitations, and incomplete sentences than are found in speech. This perfection of writing can be explained by the fact that writing is the result of deliberation, correction, and revision, while speech is the spontaneous and simultaneous formulation of ideas; writing is therefore less subject to the constraint of time than speech is. In addition, writing is ultimately associated with education and educated speech. Since the speech of the educated is more often than not set up as the "standard language," writing is associated indirectly with the varieties of language that people tend to view as "correct." However, the association of writing with the standard variety is not a necessary one, as evidenced by the attempts of writers to transcribe faithfully the speech of their characters. Mark Twain's *Huckleberry Finn* and John Steinbeck's *Of Mice and Men* contain examples of this. Furthermore, because spoken language is physically no more than sound waves through the air, it is transient, but writing tends to last, because of its physical medium (characters on some surface), and can be preserved for a very long time. Spelling does not seem to vary from individual to individual or from place to place as easily as pronunciation does. Thus, writing has the appearance of being more stable. Spelling does vary, however, as exemplified by the differences between the American ways of spelling *gray* and words with the suffixes *–ize* and *–ization* as compared with the British spelling of *grey* and *–ise* and *–isation*. Writing could also change if it were made to follow the changes of speech. The fact that people at various times try to carry out spelling reforms amply illustrates this possibility.

53. The word <u>approximate</u> in the passage is closest in meaning to

    Ⓐ make better than
    Ⓑ come close to
    Ⓒ take out of
    Ⓓ get on with

54. According to paragraph 2, what can be inferred about linguistic research?

    Ⓐ Linguists do not usually study Latin.
    Ⓑ Research on writing is much easier.
    Ⓒ Studies always require several sources.
    Ⓓ Researchers prefer speech samples.

Paragraph 2 is marked with an arrow [➔].

55. According to paragraph 4, what is true about literacy?

    Ⓐ Only a minority of the world's population can read and write.
    Ⓑ Literate populations are more capable than other groups.
    Ⓒ The modern world has a very highly literate population.
    Ⓓ Many people fail to become literate because it is difficult.

    Paragraph 4 is marked with an arrow [➔].

56. Which of the sentences below best expresses the information in the highlighted statement in the passage? The other choices change the meaning or leave out important information.

    Ⓐ Writing that has a very complex system must be learned.
    Ⓑ All writing has to be taught because the systems are variable.
    Ⓒ In spite of complex features in writing systems, people can learn them.
    Ⓓ Both simple and complex writing systems require direct instruction.

57. The word <u>deliberation</u> in the passage is closest in meaning to

    Ⓐ work
    Ⓑ thought
    Ⓒ time
    Ⓓ intelligence

58. Why does the author mention Mark Twain and John Steinbeck in paragraph 7?

    Ⓐ To demonstrate that speech cannot be transcribed
    Ⓑ To provide examples of two good writing styles
    Ⓒ To prove that a nonstandard variety can be written
    Ⓓ To contrast varieties of speech for their characters

    Paragraph 7 is marked with an arrow [➔].

59. The word <u>transient</u> in the passage is closest in meaning to

   Ⓐ unimportant
   Ⓑ temporary
   Ⓒ interesting
   Ⓓ clear

60. According to paragraph 7, what is true about spelling?

   Ⓐ Spelling does not change from one geographical region to another.
   Ⓑ British and American spellings are more similar than pronunciation.
   Ⓒ Pronunciation in English is not related to spelling changes.
   Ⓓ Changes in spelling are occasionally initiated because of speech.

   Paragraph 7 is marked with an arrow [→].

61. The phrase <u>this possibility</u> in the passage refers to

   Ⓐ writing could also change
   Ⓑ the changes of speech
   Ⓒ people try to carry out
   Ⓓ spelling reforms illustrate

62. Which of the following statements most closely represents the author's opinion?

   Ⓐ Speech and writing have historical similarities.
   Ⓑ Standard speech is the best model for writing.
   Ⓒ Writing is not more perfect than speech.
   Ⓓ Writing should not change like speech does.

63. How does the author organize the passage?

   Ⓐ Cause and effect
   Ⓑ Chronological narrative
   Ⓒ Persuasive argument
   Ⓓ Contrastive analysis

64. Look at the four squares [■] that show where the following sentence could be inserted in the passage.

The Sumerians probably devised written characters for the purpose of maintaining inventories of livestock and merchandise.

Where could the sentence best be added?

Click on a square [■] to insert the sentence in the passage.

65. **Directions**: Complete the table by matching the phrases on the left with the headings on the right. Select the appropriate answer choices and drag them to the type of language to which they relate. TWO of the answer choices will NOT be used. *This question is worth 4 points.*

To delete an answer choice, click on it. To see the passage, click on **View Text**.

Answer Choices

Ⓐ Not observable in brain activity

Ⓑ A primary form of language

Ⓒ Direct representation of thought

Ⓓ A two-stage process

Ⓔ An earlier development

Ⓕ Associated with education

Ⓖ Contains fewer errors

Ⓗ No regional variations

Ⓘ Acquired naturally

Speech
●
●
●
●

Writing
●
●
●

LISTENING SECTION

 Model Test 3, Listening Section, CD 2, Track 1

The Listening section tests your ability to understand spoken English that is typical of interactions and academic speech on college campuses. During the test, you will respond to conversations and lectures.

This is the short format for the Listening section. On the short format, you will respond to two conversations and four lectures. After each listening passage, you will answer 5–6 questions about it.

You will hear each conversation or lecture one time. You may take notes while you listen, but notes are not graded. You may use your notes to answer the questions.

Choose the best answer for multiple-choice questions. Follow the directions on the page or on the screen for computer-assisted questions. Click on **Next** and **OK** to go to the next question. You cannot return to previous questions. You have 25–30 minutes to answer all of the questions. A clock on the screen will show you how much time you have to complete your answers for the section. The clock does not count the time you are listening to the conversations and lectures.

PART I

Listening 1 "Professor's Office"

1. Why does the man go to see his professor?

    Ⓐ To borrow some books for his project
    Ⓑ To hand in the first book report
    Ⓒ To ask about the professor's requirements
    Ⓓ To talk about literary movements

2. How is the second part of the reading list different from the first part?

    Ⓐ More minority authors are represented.
    Ⓑ All of the writers are from North America.
    Ⓒ It includes books from the Post Modern Period.
    Ⓓ In addition to novels, some plays are on the list.

3. What does the man mean when he says this:

    Ⓐ He does not understand the term.
    Ⓑ He is interested in the idea.
    Ⓒ He is not sure how to pronounce it.
    Ⓓ He thinks that the word is humorous.

4. What will the man probably do before the next meeting?

    Ⓐ Write a synopsis of each book on the list
    Ⓑ Make a list of books that he wants to read
    Ⓒ Finish the art project on his computer
    Ⓓ Prepare to talk with the professor

5. What can be inferred about the professor?

    Ⓐ She does not have regular office hours.
    Ⓑ She is willing to help her students.
    Ⓒ She is not very flexible with assignments.
    Ⓓ She teaches British literature.

Listening 2 "Environmental Science Class"

6. What aspect of wind power is the lecture mainly about?

    Ⓐ Electrical power in California
    Ⓑ Alternative energy sources
    Ⓒ Problems associated with turbines
    Ⓓ Wind as a renewable energy option

7. Which two regions of the United States have the greatest potential for supplying wind power?

    Click on 2 answer choices.

    Ⓐ The Eastern Seaboard

    Ⓑ The Midwestern Plains

    Ⓒ The Desert Southwest

    Ⓓ The Pacific Northwest

8. Why does the professor say this:

    Ⓐ He is disagreeing with the figures.
    Ⓑ He is expressing surprise at the statistics.
    Ⓒ He is correcting a previous statement.
    Ⓓ He is trying to maintain the students' interest.

9. In the lecture, the professor identifies several problems associated with wind power. Indicate whether each of the following is one of the problems mentioned. Click in the correct box for each phrase.

	Yes	No
A Poor television reception		
B Noisy turbines		
C Expensive operating costs		
D Remote areas		
E Dangerous blades for birds		

10. How did the Tellus Institute solve the problem of intermittent wind?

    Ⓐ By building twice as many wind farms in problem areas
    Ⓑ By moving wind farms into areas of steady winds
    Ⓒ By using more wind turbines on each wind farm
    Ⓓ By separating one wind farm into two locations

11. What is the professor's opinion about the future of wind power?

    Ⓐ He thinks that wind power will require more research before it becomes practical.
    Ⓑ He supports the use of wind power only as a secondary source of energy.
    Ⓒ He feels that most of the world's energy problems will be solved by wind power.
    Ⓓ He believes that there are too many problems associated with wind power.

Listening 3 "Philosophy Class"

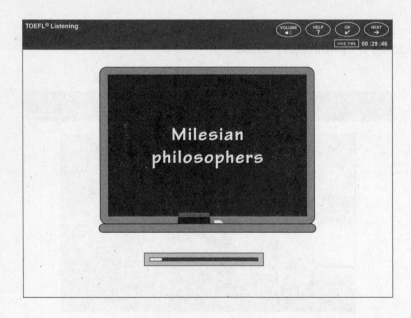

12. What is the discussion mainly about?

    Ⓐ The laws of motion
    Ⓑ The origin of water
    Ⓒ The nature of the universe
    Ⓓ The spirit of the world

13. Why does the student mention evolutionary theory?

    Ⓐ He is digressing from the main topic.
    Ⓑ He is trying to embarrass the professor.
    Ⓒ He is expressing doubt about Greek philosophy.
    Ⓓ He is comparing evolution to Anaximander's theory.

14. Why does the professor say this:

    Ⓐ She is not happy with the student's response.
    Ⓑ She is introducing an alternative view.
    Ⓒ She is going to expand on the comment.
    Ⓓ She is ending the discussion.

15. What view did the three Milesian philosophers share?

    Ⓐ They all believed that the mythology had a basis in fact.
    Ⓑ They introduced a scientific approach to explaining nature.
    Ⓒ They thought that water was the original element.
    Ⓓ They all agreed with the teachings of Socrates.

16. What can be inferred about the early Greek philosophers?

    Ⓐ They were exploring the physical sciences.
    Ⓑ They recorded many of the Greek myths.
    Ⓒ They were primarily interested in religion.
    Ⓓ They had contact with other European scholars.

17. What does the professor mean when she says this:

    Ⓐ She is expressing strong agreement.
    Ⓑ She is introducing doubt.
    Ⓒ She is maintaining a neutral position.
    Ⓓ She is asking the students to agree.

PART II

Listening 4 "Professor's Office"

18. Why does the woman want to talk with her professor?

Ⓐ She wants to make an appointment outside of office hours.
Ⓑ She needs to get him to approve the topic for her research.
Ⓒ She has some questions about the report she is writing.
Ⓓ She would like a recommendation for a job in the lab.

19. What advice does the professor give the woman?

Ⓐ Have some friends read the research
Ⓑ Refer to the explanation in the textbook
Ⓒ Ask a chemistry major to help her
Ⓓ Include more references in the report

20. What does the professor offer to do?

    Ⓐ Read a draft of the report before she submits it
    Ⓑ Help her find some better references
    Ⓒ Show her how to complete the experiment
    Ⓓ Give her a job in the laboratory

21. Why does the professor say this:

    Ⓐ He realizes that she won't have time to revise the report.
    Ⓑ He is concerned that she will not complete the research.
    Ⓒ He recalls that he will not be available to help her.
    Ⓓ He wants her to get an extension to finish the project.

22. What is the professor's opinion of the woman?

    Ⓐ He assumes that she is too busy to work.
    Ⓑ He is very impressed with her attitude.
    Ⓒ He thinks that she is not a serious student.
    Ⓓ He wants her to change her major to chemistry.

Listening 5 "Biology Class"

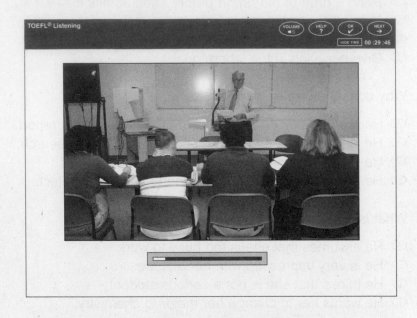

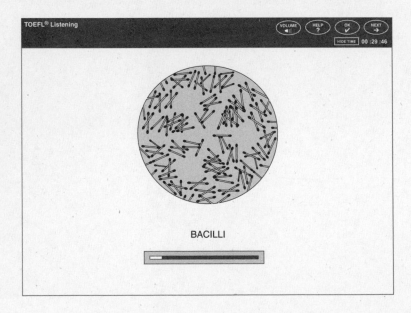

BACILLI

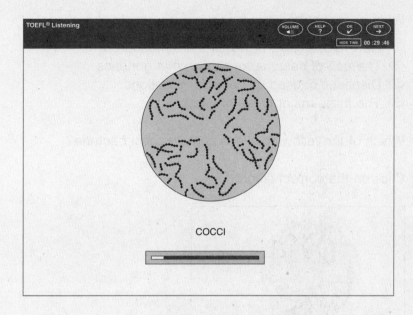

COCCI

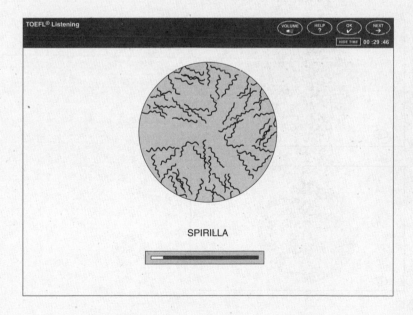

SPIRILLA

23. What aspect of bacteria is this lecture mainly about?

    Ⓐ How microscopic organisms are measured
    Ⓑ The use of bacteria for research in genetics
    Ⓒ Diseases caused by bacterial infections
    Ⓓ The three major types of bacteria

24. Which of the following slides contain cocci bacteria?

Click on the correct diagram.

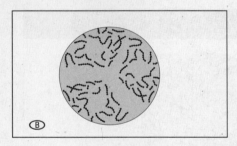

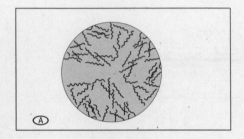

25. Which two characteristics are common in bacteria?

    Click on 2 answer choices.

    Ⓐ They have one cell.

    Ⓑ They are harmful to humans.

    Ⓒ They reproduce quickly.

    Ⓓ They die when exposed to air.

26. Why are bacteria being used in the research study at the university?

    Ⓐ Bacteria have unusual cell formations.
    Ⓑ Bacteria live harmlessly on the skin.
    Ⓒ Bacteria are similar to other life forms.
    Ⓓ Bacteria cause many diseases in humans.

27. How does the professor help the students to remember the types of bacteria?

    Ⓐ He shows them many examples of slides.
    Ⓑ He tells them to look at specimens in the lab.
    Ⓒ He uses the first letter to represent the shape.
    Ⓓ He explains the various DNA structures.

28. Why does the professor say this:

    Ⓐ He is showing the students some slides.
    Ⓑ He does not want the students to ask questions.
    Ⓒ He wants the students to pay attention.
    Ⓓ He thinks that the information is very clear.

Listening 6 "History Class"

29. What is the lecture mainly about?

Ⓐ Provisions of the Homestead Act
Ⓑ How to construct a log cabin
Ⓒ Frontier homes in the West
Ⓓ Early construction materials

30. How does the professor organize his lecture?

Ⓐ He makes a persuasive argument in favor of sod homes.
Ⓑ He narrates stories about life on the Western frontier.
Ⓒ He explains the process for becoming a homesteader.
Ⓓ He contrasts several types of homes in the West.

31. What does the professor imply about construction materials for early homes?

Ⓐ Settlers used the materials from the natural environment.
Ⓑ Not many of the materials from that era have survived.
Ⓒ Most of the supplies had to be shipped in by railroad.
Ⓓ Wagons and tents were used in constructing homes.

32. What is the evidence for the inexpensive price of a sod home?

Ⓐ Short stories and novels
Ⓑ Letters written to relatives
Ⓒ Newspaper advertisements
Ⓓ Personal records and accounts

33. Why does the professor say this:

Ⓐ To criticize the sod house
Ⓑ To demonstrate uncertainty
Ⓒ To draw a conclusion
Ⓓ To uphold an opinion

34. In the lecture, the professor identifies attributes for different frontier homes. Indicate whether each attribute refers to a sod house or a log cabin. Click in the correct box for each phrase.

		Sod House	Log Cabin
A	A mud roof		
B	A rock foundation		
C	Chinked walls		
D	Notching techniques		
E	Thick brick insulation		

Please turn off the audio.
There is a 10-minute break between the
Listening section and the Speaking section.

SPEAKING SECTION

 Model Test 3, Speaking Section, CD 2, Track 2

The Speaking section tests your ability to communicate in English in an academic setting. During the test, you will be presented with six speaking questions. The questions ask for a response to a single question, a conversation, a talk, or a lecture.

You may take notes as you listen, but notes are not graded. You may use your notes to answer the questions. Some of the questions ask for a response to a reading passage and a talk or a lecture. The reading passages and the questions are written, but most of the directions will be spoken.

Your speaking will be evaluated on both the fluency of the language and the accuracy of the content. You will have 15–20 seconds to prepare and 45–60 seconds to respond to each question. Typically, a good response will require all of the response time but the answer will be complete by the end of the response time.

The time for the Speaking section is about 20 minutes. A clock on the screen will show you how much time you have to prepare your answer and how much time you have to record it.

Independent Speaking Question 1 "A Good Son or Daughter"

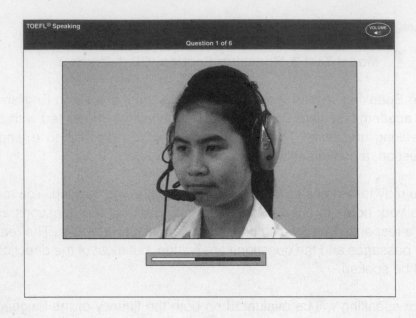

 Listen for a question about a familiar topic.

Question

In your opinion, what are the characteristics of a good son or daughter in a family? Use specific examples and details to explain your answer.

Preparation Time: 15 seconds
Recording Time: 45 seconds

Independent Speaking Question 2 "Job Opportunities"

 Listen for a question that asks your opinion about a familiar topic.

Question
Some people are attracted to jobs that include a great deal of travel. Other people prefer jobs that allow them to return to their homes every evening. Which type of job opportunity would you prefer and why? Use specific reasons and examples to support your opinion.

Preparation Time: 15 seconds
Recording Time: 45 seconds

Integrated Speaking Question 3 "Excused Absence"

Read a short passage and listen to a talk on the same topic.

Reading Time: 45 seconds

Policy for Excused Absence

You may request an excused absence once per semester without explanation. Just e-mail me and specify the date that you will be absent from class. If you plan to be absent on the day of a test or an exam, however, you must provide an explanation and make arrangements for a makeup test or exam. Please see me in my office for an excused absence from a test or exam. If you must be absent for more than one session, your grade may be affected. Your grade may be lowered one letter for each additional absence after the excused absence.

Now listen to a student who is talking with friends about the policy.

Question
The student expresses his opinion of the professor's policy for excused absences. Report his opinion and explain the reasons that he gives for having that opinion.

Preparation Time: 30 seconds
Recording Time: 60 seconds

Integrated Speaking Question 4 "Insects"

Read a short passage and then listen to part of a lecture on the same topic.

Reading Time: 45 seconds

Insects
An insect belongs to the class of invertebrates called arthropods. Regardless of size, all adult insects have a similar body structure, which includes a head, a thorax, and an abdomen. The head contains not only the brain and mouth but also the sensory organs, usually a pair of eyes and a pair of antennae. The thorax is the central part of the insect's body where the wings and legs are attached, allowing the insect to move in the air and on feeding surfaces. Typically, insects have three pairs of legs and two pairs of wings. The third part of the insect's body structure consists of an abdomen where food is processed and also where the reproductive organs are found.

 Now listen to part of a lecture in a biology class. The professor is talking about insects.

Question
Describe the structure of an insect and explain why a spider is not strictly considered an insect.

Preparation Time: 30 seconds
Recording Time: 60 seconds

Integrated Speaking Question 5 "Meeting People"

 Now listen to a short conversation between a student and his friend.

Question
Describe the man's problem, and the two suggestions that his friend makes about how to handle it. What do you think the man should do, and why?

Preparation Time: 20 seconds
Recording Time: 60 seconds

Integrated Speaking Question 6 "Skinner Box"

 Now listen to part of a lecture in a psychology class. The professor is discussing the Skinner Box.

Question

Using the main points and examples from the lecture, describe the Skinner Box, and then explain how the device is used in psychology experiments.

Preparation Time: 20 seconds
Recording Time: 60 seconds

WRITING SECTION

The Writing section tests your ability to write essays in English similar to those that you would write in college courses.

During the test, you will write two essays. The integrated essay asks for your response to an academic reading passage and a lecture on the same topic. You may take notes as you read and listen, but notes are not graded. You may use your notes to write the essay. The lecture will be spoken, but the directions and the questions will be written. You will have 20 minutes to plan, write, and revise your response. Typically, a good essay for the integrated topic will require that you write 150–225 words.

The independent essay usually asks for your opinion about a familiar topic. You will have 30 minutes to plan, write, and revise your response. Typically, a good essay for the independent topic will require that you write 300–350 words.

A clock on the screen will show you how much time you have to complete each essay.

Integrated Essay "Primordial Soup"

You have 20 minutes to plan, write, and revise your response to a reading passage and a lecture on the same topic. First, read the passage and take notes. Then, listen to the lecture and take notes. Finally, write your response to the writing question. Typically, a good response will require that you write 150–225 words.

Reading Passage
Time: 3 minutes

The origin of life was highly speculative until a graduate student at the University of Chicago, Stanley Miller designed and conducted an empirical research project under the guidance of his graduate advisor, Harold Urey. In this classic experiment, the researchers tried to simulate the chemical evolution process that generated life. Miller and Urey took a five-liter flask half filled with water and connected it with glass tubing to another flask into which they inserted tungsten electrodes. They then mixed methane, hydrogen, and ammonia into the water in the lower flask and heated it to induce evaporation, while at the same time subjecting it to continuous electrical charges that jumped across the space between the electrodes in the upper flask. The atmosphere was cooled again so that the water could condense and trickle back into the first flask in a continuous cycle. In this way, they sought to recreate the conditions in the early atmosphere of Earth, which they speculated was probably subjected to powerful electrical storms. In about an hour, the water turned orange. At the end of the first week, they observed that almost 15 percent of the carbon was converted into organic compounds. After several weeks, the liquid in the flask clouded and then gradually turned a dark brown. When they analyzed it, Miller and Urey found that it contained a large number of amino acids, which form one of the basic structures of living organisms. They then hypothesized that the amino acids that they had created in the laboratory might be typical of the chemical mixture of the early oceans on Earth, and further, that additional amino acids could have been added to the mixture in the early oceans by carbon enriched meteorites or comets.

When the scientific results were popularized, the mixture became known as "primordial soup." However, much was still unknown about the process that caused the first cell to develop within the soup. The molecules produced were relatively simple organic molecules, not a complete living biochemical system. Nevertheless, the experiment established that natural processes could produce the building blocks of life without requiring life to synthesize them in the first place. The experiment served as inspiration for a large number of further investigations.

Model Test 3, Writing Section, CD 2, Track 3

Now listen to a lecture on the same topic as the passage that you have just read.

Question

Summarize the main points in the reading passage, explaining how the lecture casts doubt on the ideas.

Independent Essay "Learning a Foreign Language"

Question

Many people have learned a foreign language in their own country; others have learned a foreign language in the country in which it is spoken. Which is better? Give the advantages of each and support your viewpoint.

 This is the end of Model Test 3.
To check your answers, refer to "Explanatory or Example Answers and Audio Scripts for Model Tests: Model Test 3," Chapter 7, pages 479–520.

7

ANSWERS AND AUDIO SCRIPTS FOR ACTIVITIES, QUIZZES, AND MODEL TESTS

ANSWERS FOR PRACTICE ACTIVITIES IN CHAPTER 3

PRACTICE ACTIVITY 1

1. According to Mead, the self has two sides: the "I" and the "me."

The "I" represents the individuality of a person.	For instance, a spontaneous reaction might reveal the "I." This part of the self is less predictable because it is unique.
The "me" represents the expectations and attitudes of others.	This part of the self is formed through socialization by others. It is predictable because social conformity is expected.

2. The mystery of pulsars was resolved in the 1960s.

We know that pulsars are neutron stars, like lighthouses left by supernova explosions.	Like a lighthouse, the neutron star revolves. We see pulses of light each time the beam sweeps past the Earth.
We also know that pulsars are not perfectly timed because each revolution of a pulsar takes a little longer.	The pulsar in the Crab Nebula, for example, currently spins about thirty times per second. It will probably spin about half as fast two thousand years from now.

3. Britain transported convicts to Australia in an effort to solve the problems of overcrowding in prisons.

In 1787, the first fleet left for Botany Bay in New South Wales.	There were 11 ships with 750 prisoners aboard. Four companies of marines sailed with them as guards. They took enough supplies for two years.
Shortly after arriving in 1788, the colony was moved to Sydney Cove.	In Sydney, the water supply and soil were better. Although Sydney was the new site, for many years it was called Botany Bay.

4. Frederick Carl Frieseke was an American impressionist.

Born in Michigan, he went to Paris in 1897.	He studied with Whistler in the late 1800s. From Whistler, he learned the academic style of the salons.
In 1905, Frieseke moved to Giverney where he lived until 1920.	At Giverney, Frieseke was influenced by Monet. Monet was experimenting with the effects of sunlight. The style of Monet and his school is known as impressionism.
By 1920, Frieseke had left Giverney for Normandy.	In Normandy, he began to paint indoor settings. In his later work, he began to use a darker palette.

5. Two types of weathering will break down rock masses into smaller particles.

Interaction between surface or ground water and chemicals causes chemical weathering.	With increased precipitation or temperature, chemicals tend to break down faster. The weathering of feldspar in granite can be caused by a reaction to acids in rain. A common example is the wearing away of granite facades on buildings.
Mechanical weathering occurs when force and pressure grind rocks down.	Pressure from freezing and thawing causes rocks to expand and contract. When a rock is broken in two by physical forces, it is more vulnerable to weathering.

PRACTICE ACTIVITY 2

These are sentences from college lectures. Compare your notes with the example notes here.

1. The Nineteenth Amendment to the U.S. Constitution gave women the right to vote, beginning with the elections of 1920.
   19 → women vote/1920
2. In a suspension bridge, there are two towers with one or more flexible cables firmly attached at each end.
   suspension = 2 towers w/flex cables @ ends
3. A perennial is any plant that continues to grow for more than two years, as for example, trees and shrubs.
   perennial = plant 2+ yrs ex. trees, shrubs
4. Famous for innovations in punctuation, typography, and language, Edward Estlin Cummings, known to us as e.e. cummings, published his collected poems in 1954.
   ee. cummings → innovations punctuation, typo, language 1954 poems
5. Absolute zero, the temperature at which all substances have zero thermal energy, and thus the lowest possible temperatures, is unattainable in practice.
   absolute zero = temp. all substances 0 thermal energy → lowest temps
6. Because Columbus, Ohio, is considered a typical metropolitan area, it is often used for market research to test new products.
   Columbus, O = typical metro → market research new products

7. The cacao bean was cultivated by the Aztecs not only to drink but also as currency in their society.

cocao bean ← Aztecs = currency

8. The blue whale is the largest known animal, reaching a length of more than one hundred feet, which is five times its size at birth.

blue whale = largest animal 100′ = 5× birth size

9. Ontario is the heartland of Canada, both geographically, and, I would say, historically as well.

Ontario = heartland Canada geograph + hist

10. Nuclear particles called hadrons, which include the proton and neutron, are made from quarks—very odd particles that have a slight electrical charge but that cannot exist alone in nature.

nuclear particles = hadrons = proton + neutron ← quarks = particles slight electric charge ∅ nature

PRACTICE ACTIVITY 3

1. Problem: The paraphrase is too much like the original. Only the subject and complement have been reversed in this alternative grammatical structure.

Edited
Paraphrase: Molecules that function as regulators in the transmission of substances across cell walls are known as proteins.

Why is this better? Because synonyms have been substituted for all the nontechnical vocabulary and the subject and complement are reversed in an alternative grammatical structure.

2. Problem: The paraphrase is not complete. Information about the factory system and the cotton industry are not included.

Edited
Paraphrase: The factory system spread across a large number of enterprises in addition to cotton manufacturing as a result of the introduction of steam engines.

Why is this better? Because the relationship between cause and effect has been retained using different vocabulary and grammar.

3. Problem: The paraphrase is not correct. The meaning has been changed.

Edited
Paraphrase: Small enterprises are frequently using bloggers to compete effectively with large businesses that are still

employing more conventional marketing strategies as well as some of the more recent options.

Why is this better? Because the meaning of the original sentence has been retained.

4. Problem: The paraphrase is too much like the original. Too many words and phrases are the same, and the grammatical structure is too similar.

Edited
Paraphrase: Although fossilized bones may look like stone, minerals from sedimentary material fill the spaces.

Why is this better? Because synonyms have been substituted for all the nontechnical vocabulary, and the subject and complement are reversed in an alternative grammatical structure.

5. Problem: The paraphrase is incomplete. The dates are important here.

Edited
Paraphrase: About 3500 B.C., two thousand years after written symbols were introduced in 1500 B.C., the first pictographic writing system appeared simultaneously in various regions of the known world.

Why is this better? Because the chronology is not clear without a time frame. The date solves this problem.

6. Problem: This is not a paraphrase. It is copied directly from the original.

Edited
Paraphrase: In all likelihood, the Earth's current atmosphere was preceded by three earlier atmospheres.

Why is this better? Because copying directly from a source is the worst kind of plagiarism. Even when you are in a hurry, be sure that you are not copying.

7. Problem: This is not a paraphrase. It is too general.
Edited
Paraphrase: Alcohol depresses the central nervous system, but coffee increases neural transmission.

Why is this better? Because details are necessary for a paraphrase to be specific. A general statement does not include enough information.

8. Problem: This paraphrase changes the meaning of the original statement.

   Edited
   Paraphrase: Australia and the islands of Oceania comprise the Pacific Basin, an area that encompasses about 33 percent of the Earth's surface.

Why is this better? Because this paraphrase retains the original meaning. The area is one third of the surface of the Earth, not one third of the Pacific Ocean.

9. Problem: The paraphrase is incomplete. It does not identify the process as fresco painting.

   Edited
   Paraphrase: The lime in wet plaster bonds with the colors on the surface when the paints are mixed for frescos.

Why is this better? Because the process described in the paraphrase is identified as fresco painting.

10. Problem: The paraphrase is too much like the original. Too many words and phrases are repeated.

   Edited
   Paraphrase: The Linnaean chart used to classify all biological species was initially created to categorize each specimen in conformity with its resemblance to other organisms.

Why is this better? Because the edited paraphrase retains the meaning of the original, but the words and phrases are different, and the grammatical structure is changed.

PRACTICE ACTIVITY 4

1. In his book, *The Making of the President,* Theodore White noted that the 1960 presidential debate was more like a press conference. According to White, Nixon proceeded as though he were engaged in a personal debate. In contrast, Kennedy spoke directly to the TV viewers. He estimated that Kennedy gained two million votes as a result.

2. <u>Paul Cezanne</u> believed that all forms in nature were based on geometric shapes. <u>Cezanne</u> identified the cone, sphere, and cylinder as the primary forms. <u>He</u> used outlining to emphasize these shapes.

3. Along with her husband, <u>Marie Curie</u> won the Nobel prize for physics in 1903 for the discovery of radium. <u>Curie</u> then received the Nobel prize for chemistry in 1911 for the isolation of pure radium. <u>She</u> was the first person to be awarded two Nobel prizes.

4. Psychologist <u>Erik Erikson</u> proposed eight stages of personal development. <u>Erikson</u> claimed that psychological crises at each stage shaped the sense of self. <u>He</u> believed that development was a lifelong process.

5. <u>Margaret Mead</u> did her first fieldwork in Samoa in 1925. <u>Mead's</u> book, *Coming of Age in Samoa*, was a best seller that was translated into many languages. <u>She</u> is still one of the most well-known anthropologists in the world. <u>Mead</u> believed that people in simple societies could provide valuable lessons for the industrialized world.

6. <u>Leonardo da Vinci</u> was the quintessential Renaissance man. A brilliant painter, <u>da Vinci</u> was perhaps best remembered for his art. But <u>he</u> was also interested in mechanics, and his understanding of mathematics is clear in his use of perspective.

7. Author <u>Peter Drucker</u> wrote *Management Challenges for the 21st Century*. In this book, <u>Drucker</u> proposed five transforming forces. <u>He</u> predicted that these trends will have major implications for the long-term strategies of companies.

8. <u>Freidrich Mohs</u> devised a scale of hardness for ten minerals. By assigning 10 to diamond, the hardest known mineral, <u>Mohs</u> was able to attribute relative values to all the other minerals. <u>His</u> scale is still useful in the study of minerals today.

9. <u>Maria Montessori</u> proposed an educational model that has become known as the Montessori method. <u>Montessori</u> insisted that education should not be merely the transmission of knowledge but the freedom to develop as a person. <u>She</u> felt her greatest success was achieved when a child began working independently.

10. In collaboration with Louis Leaky, <u>Jane Goodall</u> spent years living with chimpanzees on the Gombe Reserve. <u>Goodall</u> imitated their behaviors and discovered that chimpanzees lived within a complex social organization. <u>She</u> was the first to document chimpanzees making and using tools, and she also identified twenty different sounds that were part of a communication system.

PRACTICE ACTIVITY 5

1. Reading

1. **B**   The first opera in Italy
2. **C**   The growth of opera throughout Europe
3. **A**   Three types of musical pieces in opera

2. Lecture

Read part of a lecture in a biology class. Then put the major points in the same order as the lecture.

1. **D**   A definition of protozoans—single cell
2. **A**   A method of classification for protozoans—the three types motility
3. **C**   Similarity to plants—make food from water + CO_2
4. **E**   Considered animals—eating, breathing, reproducing
5. **B**   Current research—questions, redefinitions

PRACTICE ACTIVITY 6

1. Reading

50%   The function and responsibilities of the Fed
40%   The composition of the Fed
10%   A comparison of the Fed to a fourth branch of government

Although the summary below is actually closer to 50%, 30%, 20%, it still maintains a reasonably accurate emphasis.

Summary

The function of the Federal Reserve System is to regulate money and credit by buying and selling government securities, thereby influencing periods of recession and inflation. Moreover, the Fed cooperates with the Department of the Treasury to issue new coins and paper notes to banks and participates in international financial policies through member banks overseas.

The Fed includes twelve district reserve banks and branches, all national commercial banks and credit unions, as well as several committees and councils, including the powerful board of governors appointed by the President.

Because of its powerful membership, the Fed has been compared to a fourth branch of government, but the President's policies are usually implemented.

2. Lecture

Read part of a lecture in a psychology class. Then assign a percentage to each of the following points from the lecture and write a summary using the percentages to determine how much to write on each point.

25%	The level of sophistication for human memory
40%	The memory trace
35%	Working memory

Although the summary below is actually closer to 25%, 35%, 40%, it still maintains a reasonably accurate emphasis.

Summary

Human memory is more highly developed than previously thought. Penfield's experiments prove that detailed memories can be recalled when the brain is stimulated electrically. Using the memory trace, a theoretical model, we can conjecture how facts are retrieved and used at a later time. Current thinking assumes that chemical bonds can be improved by repeated exposure to the same information. The concept of working memory includes both short-term memory, which includes recall for twenty or thirty seconds, and long-term memory, which stores facts and experiences more permanently. Information is transferred from short-term to long-term memory when the memory trace is reinforced.

PRACTICE ACTIVITY 7

1. Reading

Summary

Charles Ives started his musical career as a member of his father's band and received a degree from Yale University in music, but he became a businessman instead because he was afraid that his music would not be well accepted. His music was very different from the popular songs of his era because he used small phrases from well-known music with unusual rhythms and tones. Fifty years after he wrote his *Second Symphony*, it was performed by the New York Philharmonic, and he was awarded the Pulitzer Prize. I think that Charles Ives was wrong not to pursue his musical career from the beginning. If he had continued writing music instead of selling insurance, we would have more pieces now.

2. Lecture

Read part of a lecture in a geology class. Then delete the opinions from the summary.

Summary

In my opinion, geysers are interesting. They happen when underground water gets hot and pressure from above causes the water to get hotter and lighter so it goes up to the surface and explodes out. Then, the water runs back into the ground and starts all over again. Geysers have to have heat, a place to store water, an opening where the water can shoot up, and cracks in the ground for the water to go back down into a pool. Geysers are in New Zealand, Iceland, and the United States. Old Faithful in Yellowstone is the most famous geyser, but the best place to see geysers is in New Zealand. I saw the Pohutu Geyser there on my vacation two years ago, and it was awesome.

PRACTICE ACTIVITY 8

Summary

Marsupials are mammals that are distinguished by the way that they complete their embryonic development. Marsupials emerge after a short gestation and find their way from the birth canal to the mother's pouch, where they attach themselves to one of the nipples to nurse until they are fully developed. Marsupials are not prone to family groupings, but the young stay with the mother for a year or longer.

Although marsupials were once abundant on several continents, today there are few outside of New Zealand and Australia where more than 250 species may still be found. Some of the characteristics that they share are a keen sense of smell and hearing, which are important to their nocturnal nature, and additional pelvic bones that support the pouch.

PRACTICE ACTIVITY 9

1. Transition sentence to connect one concept with another concept in a comparison. <u>In comparison</u>, a biome is a major regional ecosystem. According to the lecturer, . . .
2. Transition sentence to connect a concept with an example. <u>An example</u> of an innovation in industrial production in the 19th century <u>is</u> Henry Ford's assembly line. According to the lecturer, . . .
3. Transition sentence to connect the advantages with the disadvantages. <u>On the other hand</u>, stone has several disadvantages. According to the reading, . . .
4. Transition sentence to connect one concept with another in a contrast. <u>In contrast</u>, agrarian societies cultivate crops with draft animals and plows. According to the lecturer, . . .
5. Transition sentence to connect a cause (El Nino) with an effect (changes in climate). El Nino <u>may have caused</u> the changes in the climate of the North American coastline. According to the lecturer, . . .
6. Transition sentence to connect a business concept with a case study of a restaurant franchise. The Kentucky Fried Chicken chain <u>is a case study of</u> franchises. According to the lecturer, . . .
7. Transition sentence to connect a concept with a research study. <u>A research study on</u> risks for heart problems <u>was carried out with</u> Type A and Type B personalities. According to the study, . . .
8. Transition sentence to connect one opinion with an opposing opinion. The case that the United States should convert to metrics is strong. <u>However, a case may be made for the opposing view that</u> the United States should retain the English system. According to the reading, . . .
9. Transition sentence to connect a concept with an example. <u>An example of</u> South Africa's natural resources <u>is</u> gold. According to the lecturer, gold mining . . .
10. Transition sentence to connect a problem (commuting) with a solution (home offices). Home offices <u>may offer a solution for</u> the problems associated with commuting to work. According to the lecture, . . .

PRACTICE ACTIVITY 10

Now that you have read the explanation of human migration patterns in the reading, read part of a lecture on a similar topic.

Synthesis

Summarize the major points in the reading and explain how the lecturer casts doubt on those points.

According to the replacement hypothesis, also called the Out of Africa hypothesis, modern humans evolved from a common ancestor in Africa. As they migrated to Asia and Europe, and finally spread throughout the world, they replaced the less evolved populations that they encountered. Proof for this hypothesis comes from both genetic and paleontological research. The large number of genetic traits that human populations have in common are confirmed by DNA investigations in mitochondria structures. In addition, the oldest fossils identified as modern human remains have been discovered in Africa.

Nevertheless, the lecturer casts doubt on the replacement theory, offering the continuity hypothesis as an alternative. Also known as the multiregional hypothesis, the continuity hypothesis proposes that advanced human populations migrated and mated with less advanced regional populations, introducing new traits into these populations. Because the regional populations were not replaced, they retained some of their unique characteristics. The exchange of traits, referred to as gene flow, accounts for the genetic similarity of modern human beings. The retention of regional genetic material explains why some traits, such as cheekbone structure, are limited to discrete populations, and casts doubt on the replacement hypothesis. The fact that modern human remains are found in widespread sites also supports the alternative hypothesis that the lecturer presents.

ANSWERS FOR QUIZZES IN CHAPTER 4

READING

➤ Progress Chart for the Reading Quiz

The chart below will help you evaluate your progress and determine what you need to read again. First, use the Correct Answer column to grade the quiz. Next, check the Problem Types to locate which ones you answered incorrectly. Review the Referral Pages that correspond to the Reading Problem for each question that you missed. Finally, review the Academic Skills in Chapter 3.

Quiz Question	Problem Types	Correct Answer	Academic Skill	Referral Pages
1	True-False	B	Paraphrasing	Problem 1, page 154
2	Paraphrase	A	Paraphrasing	Problem 6, page 156
3	Vocabulary	D	Paraphrasing	Problem 2, page 154
4	Purpose	B	Paraphrasing	Problem 5, page 155
5	Inference	A		Problem 4, page 155
6	Cause	B	Paraphrasing	Problem 8, page 157
7	Reference	C		Problem 9, page 157
8	Terms	A	Paraphrasing	Problem 3, page 154
9	Detail	D	Paraphrasing	Problem 7, page 156
10	Exception	D	Taking Notes	Problem 12, pages 158–159
11	Opinion	C		Problem 10, pages 157–158
12	Insert	B		Problem 11, page 158
13	Classification: Hereditarian Environmentalist	D E I B F G H	Summarizing	Problem 13, pages 159–160
14	Summary	D B F	Summarizing	Problem 14, pages 160–161

LISTENING

➤ Script for the Listening Quiz

This is a quiz for the Listening section of the TOEFL® iBT. This section tests your ability to understand campus conversations and academic lectures. During the quiz, you will read one conversation and one lecture. On the official TOEFL, you will hear each conversation or lecture one time and respond to twelve questions about them. You may take notes. You may use your notes to answer the questions. To check your answers, refer to the question number in the margin on pages 189–190 and 191–193 beside the shaded area in the scripts to which that question refers.

CONVERSATION

 Questions 1–4, Conversation. Read a conversation on campus between a professor and a student.

Audio	1. Why does the man go to see his professor?
Answer	**C** To get advice about studying for the test
Audio	2. Listen again to part of the conversation. Then answer the following question.
Replay	"Yes, but Jack, since you've never taken an open-book test, I should warn you. It isn't as easy as it seems." "Because?" "Because you don't have enough time to look up every answer and still finish the test."
Audio	Why does the student say this:
Replay	"Because?"
Answer	**B** To encourage the professor to explain. When it is asked in a neutral tone, this one-word question invites further explanation.
Audio	3. How should Jack prepare for the test?
Answer	**C** He should organize his notes by topic.
Audio	4. Why does the professor give open-book tests?
Answer	**D** Because she thinks it provides a better learning experience.

LECTURE

 Questions 5–14, Lecture. Read part of a lecture in an economics class. The professor is talking about supply-side economics.

Audio   5. What is the lecture mainly about?
Answer   C Supply-side economics

Audio   6. How does the professor organize the lecture?
Answer   B By taking an historical perspective

Audio   7. According to the lecturer, what did Kennedy and Reagan have in common?
Answer   B They cut taxes to spur the economy during their administrations.

Audio   8. What would Milton Freidman most likely say about moving a manufacturing plant from the United States to a site abroad?
Answer   C He would view it as a natural process in the shift to technology.

Audio   9. According to Barry Asmus, what are two key ways that consumers contribute to the creation of new jobs?
Answer   A By investing their tax savings
               D By spending more money

Audio   10. How does the professor explain the shift from manufacturing to technology?
Answer   C He compares it with the change from agriculture to manufacturing.

Audio   11. Why does the professor mention the General Electric plant?
Answer   A Because the plant is a good example of increased productivity

Audio   12. Listen again to part of the lecture. Then answer the following question.
Replay   "Now, the same plant needs 300 people to produce one dishwasher every six seconds. So, you might focus on the fact that many workers will be without jobs making dishwashers, but what do you suppose supply-siders would say? Think this through."

Audio   Why does the professor say this:
Replay   "Think this through."
Answer   C He wants the students to follow his logical answer.

Audio   13. In the lecture, the professor explains supply-side econom-
                   ics. Indicate whether each of the following strategies sup-
                   ports the theory.
Answer

	Yes	No
A Reduce tax rates	✔	
B Cut government spending		✔
C Increase productivity	✔	
D Tolerate temporary unemployment	✔	
E Discourage consumer spending		✔

Audio   14. Put the following events in the correct order.
Answer   B The government works to affect a reduction in taxes.
                 A Businesses hire more employees with the tax savings.
                 D Profits increase because of the growth in businesses.
                 C The businesses and their employees pay more taxes.

➤ Progress Chart for the Listening Quiz

The chart below will help you evaluate your progress and determine what you need to read again. First use the Correct Answer column to grade the quiz. Next, check the Problem Types to locate which ones you answered incorrectly and review the Referral Pages that correspond to the Listening Problem for each question that you missed. Finally, review the Academic Skills in Chapter 3.

Quiz Question	Problem Types	Correct Answer	Academic Skill	Referral Pages
1	Purpose	C	Taking Notes Summarizing	Problem 15, pages 177–178
2	Pragmatics	B		Problem 18, page 179
3	Inference	C		Problem 17, page 178
4	Detail	D	Taking Notes Paraphrasing	Problem 16, page 178
5	Main Idea	C	Summarizing	Problem 19, page 182
6	Organization	B	Taking Notes	Problem 20, page 182
7	Detail	B	Taking Notes Paraphrasing	Problem 16, page 178
8	Inference	C		Problem 17, pages 177–178
9	Details	A D	Taking Notes Paraphrasing	Problem 21, pages 182–183
10	Technique	C		Problem 22, page 183
11	Inference	A		Problem 17, pages 177–178
12	Pragmatics	C		Problem 18, page 179
13	Yes-No	A C D Yes B E No	Taking Notes Paraphrasing	Problem 23, pages 183–184
14	Connections	B A D C	Summarizing	Problem 24, pages 184–185

SPEAKING

➤ Script for the Speaking Quiz

This is a quiz for the Speaking section of the TOEFL® iBT. This section tests your ability to communicate in English in an academic context. During the quiz, you will respond to six speaking questions. You may take notes as you listen. You may use your notes to answer the questions. The reading passages and the questions are printed in the book, but most of the directions will be spoken on the official TOEFL® iBT.

 Speaking Quiz

Narrator 2: Number 1. Listen for a question about a familiar topic. After you hear the question, you have 15 seconds to prepare and 45 seconds to record your answer.

Narrator 1: If you were asked to choose one movie that has influenced your thinking, which one would you choose? Why? What was especially impressive about the movie? Use specific reasons and details to explain your choice.

Narrator 2: Please prepare your answer after the beep.

Beep

[Preparation time: 15 seconds]

Narrator 2: Please begin speaking after the beep.

Beep

[Recording time: 45 seconds]

Beep

Narrator 2: Number 2. Listen for a question that asks your opinion about a familiar topic. After you hear the question, you have 15 seconds to prepare and 45 seconds to record your answer.

Narrator 1: Some people think that teachers should be evaluated by the performance of their students on standardized tests at the end of the term. Other people maintain that teachers should be judged by their own performance in the classroom, and not by the scores that their students achieve on tests. Which approach do you think is better and why? Use specific reasons and examples to support your opinion.

Narrator 2: Please prepare your answer after the beep.

Beep

[Preparation time: 15 seconds]

Narrator 2: Please begin speaking after the beep.

Beep

[Recording time: 45 seconds]

Beep

Narrator 2: Number 3. Read a short passage and listen to a talk on the same topic. Then listen for a question about them. After you hear the question, you have 30 seconds to prepare and 60 seconds to record your answer.

Narrator 1: A meeting is planned to explain the residence requirements for instate tuition. Read the policy in the college catalogue on page 222. You have 45 seconds to complete it. Please begin reading now.

[Reading time: 45 seconds]

Narrator 1: Now listen to a student who is speaking at the meeting. He is expressing his opinion about the policy.

Student:
Well, I agree with most of the policy, but what I don't understand is why I have to use my parents' address as my permanent address. This is my third year in a dorm on campus, and I've gone to school every summer, so I've lived in this state for three consecutive years. I don't pay state taxes because I don't earn enough as a full-time student to, uh, to pay taxes, but I don't receive support from my parents either. I have a small grant and a student loan that I'm

responsible for, and . . . and I plan to live and work in this state after I graduate, so, um, I think students like me should be eligible for a waiver.

Narrator 1: The student expresses his opinion of the policy for instate tuition. Report his opinion and explain the reasons that he gives for having that opinion.

Narrator 2: Please prepare your answer after the beep.

Beep

[Preparation time: 30 seconds]

Narrator 2: Please begin speaking after the beep.

Beep

[Recording time: 60 seconds]

Beep

Narrator 2: Number 4. Read a short passage and listen to a lecture on the same topic. Then listen for a question about them. After you hear the question, you have 30 seconds to prepare and 60 seconds to record your answer.

Narrator 1: Now read the passage about communication with primates printed on page 223. You have 45 seconds to complete it. Please begin reading now.

[Reading time: 45 seconds]

Narrator 1: Now listen to part of a lecture in a zoology class. The professor is talking about a primate experiment.

Professor:
Let me tell you about an experiment that didn't turn out quite like the researcher had expected. Dr. Sue Savage-Rumbaugh had been trying to train a chimpanzee to use a keyboard adapted with symbols. But no luck. What is interesting about the experiment is that the chimpanzee's adopted son Kanzi, also a bonobo Chimpanzee, well, Kanzi had been observing the lessons and had acquired a rather impressive vocabulary. After that, Kanzi was not given structured training, but he was taught language while walking

through the forest or in other informal settings with his trainers. By six years of age, Kanzi had acquired a vocabulary of more than 200 words and was able to form sentences by combining words with gestures or with other words. So, the question is this: should we proceed by trying to teach language to primates in a classroom environment, or should we simply live with them and interact informally like we do with beginning learners of language in our own species? I tend to side with those who elect to support language acquisition in natural settings.

Narrator 1: Explain the importance of the Kanzi experiment in the context of research in primate communication.

Narrator 2: Please prepare your answer after the beep.

Beep

[Preparation time: 30 seconds]

Narrator 2: Please begin speaking after the beep.

Beep

[Recording time: 60 seconds]

Beep

Narrator 2: Number 5. Listen to a short conversation. Then listen for a question about it. After you hear the question, you have 20 seconds to prepare and 60 seconds to record your answer.

Narrator 1: Now listen to a conversation between a student and her friend.

Friend:	Did you decide to take Johnson's class?
Student:	Yeah. I'm going to work it out somehow. Yesterday I walked from the chemistry lab to Hamilton Hall—that's where Johnson's class is.
Friend:	And?
Student:	And it took me twenty minutes.
Friend:	Uh-oh. You only have fifteen minutes between classes, so that means you'll be five minutes late. Listen, why don't you buy a bike? I'm sure you could cut at least five minutes off your time if you took the bike trail.

Student: I thought about that. But then I'd have to get a license, and I'd have to find somewhere to store it at night. I thought it might be a hassle.

Friend: Oh, it's not so bad. I have a bike. The license is only ten dollars, and I just park my bike on the deck outside my apartment when the weather's good. And the weather should be okay for most of spring semester.

Student: That's true.

Friend: Well, your other option is to talk with Dr. Johnson. Maybe he'll give you permission to be five minutes late to his class because of the distance from your lab. Actually, I've had several classes with him, and he seems very approachable. Anyway, it's an alternative to the bike, if you don't want to do that.

Narrator 1: Describe the woman's problem, and the two suggestions that her friend makes about how to handle it. What do you think the woman should do, and why?

Narrator 2: Please prepare your answer after the beep.

Beep

[Preparation time: 20 seconds]

Narrator 2: Please begin speaking after the beep.

Beep

[Recording time: 60 seconds]

Beep

Narrator 2: Number 6. Listen to part of a lecture. Then listen for a question about it. After you hear the question, you have 20 seconds to prepare, and 60 seconds to record your answer.

Narrator 1: Now listen to part of a lecture in an astronomy class. The professor is discussing the habitable zone.

Professor:
Of course, stars are too hot to support life, but the light from a star warms orbiting planets or moons, supplying the energy needed for life to develop. Besides energy, a liquid, let's say, a chemical solvent of some kind, is also necessary. On Earth, the solvent in which life developed was water, but others such as ammonia, hydrogen fluoride, or methane might also be appropriate. So, in order for the solvent to remain in liquid form, the planet or moon must lie within a certain range of distances from the star. Why is this so? Well, think about it. If the planet is too close to the star, the solvent will change into a gas, boiling and evaporating. If it is too far from the star, the solvent will freeze, transforming into a solid. For our sun and life as we know it, the habitable zone appears to lie between the orbits of Venus and Mars. Within this range, water remains liquid. And until recently, this area was indeed the accepted scientific definition of the habitable zone for our solar system. But now scientists have postulated that the habitable zone may be larger than originally supposed. They speculate that the strong gravitational pull caused by larger planets may produce enough energy to heat the cores of orbiting moons. So that means that these moons may support life. There may be habitable zones far beyond Venus!

Narrator 1: Using the main points and examples from the lecture, describe the habitable zone, and then explain how the definition has been expanded by modern scientists.

Narrator 2: Please prepare your answer after the beep.

Beep

[Preparation time: 20 seconds]

Narrator 2: Please begin speaking after the beep.

Beep

[Recording time: 60 seconds]

Beep

Progress Chart for the Speaking Quiz

The chart below will help you evaluate your progress and determine what you need to practice again. First, compare your answers on the quiz with the Example Answers. Use the Checklists in the Review to evaluate specific features of your speech. Next, check the Problem Types to locate which ones were most difficult for you. Review the Referral Pages that correspond to the Speaking Problem for each question that you missed. Finally, review the Academic Skills in Chapter 3.

Quiz Question	Problem Types	Correct Answer	Academic Skill	Referral Pages
1	Experiences	1	Summarizing Taking Notes	Problem 25, pages 198–200
2	Preferences	2	Summarizing Taking Notes	Problem 26, pages 200–201
3	Reports	3	Synthesizing Taking Notes	Problem 27, pages 201–204
4	Examples	4	Synthesizing Taking Notes	Problem 28, pages 204–207
5	Problems	5	Summarizing Taking Notes	Problem 29, pages 207–209
6	Summaries	6	Summarizing Taking Notes	Problem 30, pages 210–212

QUESTION 1: EXAMPLE ANSWER

The movie that has influenced my thinking the most is *Fantasia* because it's my first memory of classical music and ballet. One reason the movie was so impressive is, um, I was at a very impressionable age when I saw it—five years old. Besides that, it was made using the latest technology. In the 1950s, it was amazing to see detailed animation and . . . and hear high quality sound. But what really influenced me was the music and the dance scenes. I especially remember Mickey Mouse dancing with the brooms and I'm sure I took ballet lessons because of it. The coordination of the storm scene with the music from *The Hall of the Mountain King* still impresses me when I see it today and, thanks to Walt Disney, classical music is still my favorite music.

QUESTION 2: EXAMPLE ANSWER

I think it's good to evaluate teachers by their student's performace on standardized tests because when teachers and students are judged by the same criteria, they'll work efficiently toward the same goals. Now some teachers argue that tests aren't important but still, students need good scores for admission to universities so the tests are important to them. If teachers were evaluated on the same basis, then they would pay more attention to the criteria on tests to design their lessons so both students and teachers would benefit. Another reason to use this evaluation is to compare teachers from different schools on a standardized scale. And this system would be more fair, too, because the possibility of a teacher getting a high evaluation because of friendship with the supervisor is also eliminated.

QUESTION 3: EXAMPLE ANSWER

The student said that he mostly agreed with the policy for instate tuition but he disagreed with a couple of requirements. For one thing, you can't use a campus address as a permanent address, but he's a dorm student, and he explained that he's lived in the dorm for three years because he's gone to school every summer without returning to his parent's home to live so the dorm really is his permanent address right now. He doesn't think he should have to use his parent's out-of-state address. Besides that, he hasn't been subsidized by his parents. In the policy, the most recent taxes must be filed in the state of residence but, uh, he didn't make enough money to pay taxes. He didn't mention in which state he had his voter's registration or car registration and driver's licenses, but he said that he plans to continue living and working in the state after graduation, and he thought that he should be eligible for a waiver of the out-of-state fees.

QUESTION 4: EXAMPLE ANSWER

The experiment with Kanzi is important because it supports the theory that language should be acquired in natural settings instead of in a formal classroom. Previous research to teach primates to communicate included direct instruction in American Sign Language and, uh, also plastic shapes that could be arranged on a magnetic board. Earlier research . . . I think it was with Kanzi's mother . . . it replicated this formal approach. But when Kanzi learned vocabulary by observing the lessons, the direction of the experiment changed. In informal settings with trainers, Kanzi acquired a vocabulary of about 200 words, and began to create sentences with words and gestures to . . . to communicate with human, uh, companions. Children of our own species learn by informal interaction with adults. The Kanzi experiment suggests that this may be a better way to teach language to primates.

QUESTION 5: EXAMPLE ANSWER

The problem is that the woman has only fifteen minutes between classes but it takes twenty minutes to walk from the chemistry lab to Hamilton Hall where Professor Johnson's class is held. So she would like to take the class with Johnson but she would be late. Um, her friend suggests that she buy a bike but her concern is that she would need a license and would have to store the bike somewhere at night. The other, uh, recommendation is . . . is to ask Dr. Johnson for permission to enter the class five minutes late. So . . . I think the woman should talk with the professor first. Her friend says he's approachable and he might give her permission to be late for class. The first five minutes in a class is usually just business anyway—taking attendance and handing back papers—so she wouldn't miss much. And, if he refuses, then she can always resort to the other alternative. She can buy a bike and a license, and she can find a place to store it.

QUESTION 6: EXAMPLE ANSWER

The habitable zone is an area in which life can develop. There are several requirements, including an energy source and a chemical solvent that retains its liquid form. Okay, that means that the moon or the planet where life may develop has to be close enough to the energy source—probably a star—close enough that the solvent will remain a liquid. Outside the habitable zone, it would freeze or boil, depending on whether it was far way or too close to the star. In the case of Earth, the Sun supplied the energy and water was the chemical solvent. So, for life to evolve in ways similar to our own, the habitable zone would have to fall between Venus and Mars. But, modern scientists are questioning whether the forces of gravity on larger planets might not generate enough energy to heat up the cores of the moons that orbit them. Now, if that's the case, then there could be habitable zones at a great distance from Venus, which was the previously determined limit for a habitable zone in our solar system.

WRITING

➤ Script for the Writing Quiz

This is a quiz for the Writing section of the TOEFL® iBT. This section tests your ability to write essays in English. During the quiz, you will respond to two writing questions. You may take notes as you read the academic information. You may use your notes to write the essays. Once you begin, you have 20 minutes to write the first essay and 30 minutes to write the second essay.

 Question 1

Now read a lecture on the same topic as the passage you have just read.

➤ Progress Chart for the Writing Quiz

The chart below will help you to evaluate your progress and determine what you need to practice again. First, compare your answers on the quiz with the Example Essays. Use the Checklists in the Review to evaluate specific features of your writing. Next, check the Problem Types to locate which was most difficult for you. Read the Referral Pages that correspond to the Writing Problem for the question that you found most difficult. Finally, review the Academic Skills in Chapter 3.

Quiz Question	Problem Types	Checklists	Academic Skill	Referral Pages
1	Integrated	Content	Paraphrasing Summarizing Synthesizing	Problems 31, 32, pages 228–237
2	Independent	Opinion		Problems 33, 34, pages 237–242

QUESTION 1: EXAMPLE ESSAY

A win-win negotiation is a successful compromise in which both sides improve their situation through mutual cooperation. The key is for one party to offer the other party something that they will perceive as valuable but which does not harm the party conceding it. This, in turn, provides an incentive for the other side to make a similar offer. In this way, both sides will win. Unlike traditional negotiations in which the negotiators have an adversarial relationship, in a win-win negotiation, they view each other as collaborators who are working toward a mutual goal. After the terms have been agreed upon, it is much more likely that the relationship will continue to develop with a view to cooperating with each other to insure the continuing success of both parties.

One case study of a win-win negotiation is often cited as an example. Tony had an idea for a computer game but was unable to develop it because of constraints on his time and limitations in funding. In the negotiations with a large company to produce the game, Tony and the company made several offers and counteroffers in order to arrive at a mutually beneficial agreement. Although Tony could have become angry about the original offer of $12,000, he made a counteroffer. He agreed to accept their offer if they would concede an additional share of the future revenues. When the company reviewed his counteroffer, they conceded that he should receive a share and offered slightly less than Tony had proposed. Because they continued to negotiate toward a win-win situation, both parties were able to decrease their risk and increase their revenues, sharing in the success of the game. The company was very pleased with their return on investment, and Tony was able to launch his own game design company. In short, both parties won.

QUESTION 2: EXAMPLE ESSAY

Although it can be argued that voice mail and e-mail are more efficient, and in many ways, more convenient, I still prefer to communicate in person, or if that is not possible, by telephone. In my experience, face-to-face interactions are best for a number of reasons. In the first place, when you hear the speaker's tone of voice, you are better able to judge the attitude and emotions that can be easily hidden in a written reply. In addition, the exchange is more immediate. Even instant messaging isn't as fast as a verbal interaction in person or by phone. E-mail seems efficient; however, sometimes multiple messages over several days are required to clarify the information that a short phone call would have taken care of in one communication. We have all tried to return a voice mail only to hear a recording on the original caller's voice mail. Clearly, no real communication is possible in a situation that allows only one person to talk. Moreover, the body language and the expression on the speaker's face often communicate more than the words themselves. Research indicates that more than 80 percent of a message is nonverbal. The way that a speaker stands or sits can indicate interest or disagreement. The eye contact and the movement of the eyebrows and the mouth can actually communicate the opposite of the words that the speaker is saying. Finally, no technology has succeeded in duplicating a firm handshake to close a deal, a hug to encourage a friend, or a kiss goodbye. Until e-mail and voice mail can provide the subtle communication, the immediate interaction, and the emotional satisfaction of a face-to-face conversation, complete with facial expressions and gestures, I will prefer to talk instead of to type.

EXPLANATORY OR EXAMPLE ANSWERS AND AUDIO SCRIPTS FOR MODEL TESTS

MODEL TEST 1: PRETEST

➤ Reading

READING 1 "BEOWULF"

1. **C** "...*Beowulf* was written by an anonymous [author unknown] Englishman in Old English." Choice A is not correct because it is one of four surviving manuscripts. Choice B is not correct because it was written in old English about Germanic characters. Choice D is not correct because scholars do not know if it is the sole surviving epic from about A.D. 1000.

2. **B** "Although *Beowulf* was written by an anonymous Englishman in Old English, the tale takes place in that part of Scandinavia from which [that part of Scandinavia] Germanic tribes emigrated to England."

3. **A** "Iron was accessible everywhere in Scandinavia, usually in the form of 'bog iron' found in the layers of peat in peat bogs." Choice B is not correct because the author had already stated that the best swords had iron or iron-edged blades. Choice C is not correct because the Celts taught the Northmen how to use the materials, but they did not provide the bog iron. Choice D is not correct because the bog iron does not relate to the date, although 500 B.C. is mentioned as the time when the Northmen learned how to forge iron.

4. **A** *Society in Anglo-Saxon England* paraphrases "Anglo-Saxon society." . . . *both advanced* paraphrases "neither primitive," and *cultured* paraphrases "nor uncultured." Two negatives [*nor* and *–un*] produce an affirmative meaning.

5. **B** In this passage, *rare* is a synonym for "unique." Context comes from the reference to the "sole surviving epic" in the beginning of the same sentence.

6. **B** ". . . the original manuscript was probably lost during the ninth century . . ., in which the Danes destroyed the Anglo-Saxon monasteries and their great libraries." Choice A is true but it is not the reason that scholars believe the original manuscript was lost. Choice C is

not correct because the Danes were invaders, not poets. Choice D is not correct because the location of the discovery is not mentioned, although the author may have been a monk.

7. **D**   "Although the *Beowulf* manuscript was written in about A.D. 1000, it was not discovered until the seventeenth century." Choice A is not correct because the first century was the date the manuscript was written, not discovered. Choice B is not correct because the ninth century was the date when the original manuscript may have been lost. Choice C is not correct because some scholars think that the manuscript was written in the eleventh century.

8. **A**   Because the word "apparently" means "appearing to be so," the author is expressing doubt about the information that follows, ". . . [the *Beowulf* poet] was a Christian." Choice B is not correct because the word "obviously" would be used. Choice C is not correct because the phrases "for example" or "for instance" would signal an example. Choice D is not correct because evidence would not be presented as "appearing to be so."

9. **A**   ". . . Beowulf is a very appealing hero . . . Like Hercules." Choice B is not correct because a fight with a dragon is mentioned in reference to Beowulf but not to Hercules. Choice C is not correct because the Danish hero's welcome is the only reference to a speech, and it was jealous, not inspiring. Choice D is not correct because the time period for the life of Hercules is not mentioned.

10. **B**   In this passage, *demonstrates* is a synonym for "exhibits."

11. **C**   In this passage, *refuse* is a synonym for "reject." Context comes from the contrast with "accept" in the previous sentence.

12. **B**   Addition is a transitional device that connects the insert sentence with the previous sentence. *Moreover* signals that additional, related information will follow. ". . . they [scholars] disagree" refers to "Scholars do not know" in the previous sentence.

13. **E, D, F**   summarize the passage. Choice A is true, but it is a minor point that establishes the time period for the poem and refers to major point D. Choice B is true, but it is a detail that refers to major point E and explains why there may be only one manuscript. Choice C is not clear from the information in the passage.

READING 2 "THERMOREGULATION"

14. **A**   "The most basic mechanism [for maintenance of warm body temperature] is the high metabolic rate." Choices B, C, and D are all ways to maintain body temperature, but they are not the most fundamental adaptation.

15. **D** "In some mammals, certain hormones can cause mitochondria to increase their metabolic activity and produce heat instead of ATP. This **nonshivering thermogenesis (NST). . . .**" Choice A is not correct because thermogenesis is the activity that generates heat, not the heat loss. Choice B is not correct because brown fat is one example of a more generalized process. Choice C is not correct because thermogenesis is a response to the environment to maintain the health of the animal, not a process that maintains the environment.

16. **B** A passive grammatical structure in the passage is paraphrased by an active grammatical structure in the answer choice.

17. **D** In this passage, *smallest* is a synonym for "minimal."

18. **B** "For example, heat loss from a human is reduced when arms and legs cool." Choice A is not correct because goose bumps, not heat loss in the extremities, is a vestige of our evolution. Choice C is not correct because no direct comparisons of these processes are made in the paragraph. Choice D is not correct because the types of insulation are mentioned before the concept of vasodilatation and vasoconstriction are introduced.

19. **D** In this passage, *control* is a synonym for "regulate." Context comes from the reference to "temperature differences" at the end of the same sentence.

20. **B** "The loss of heat to water occurs 50 to 100 times more rapidly than heat loss to air." Choice A is not correct because hair loses insulating power when wet, but the evolution of marine animals is not mentioned. Choice C is not correct because dry hair insulates better than wet hair. Choice D is not correct because there are land animals that are of similar size.

21. **D** ". . . marine mammals maintain body core temperatures of about 36–38°C with metabolic rates about the same as those [metabolic rates] of land mammals of similar size."

22. **A** ". . . capable of astonishing feats of thermoregulation. For example, small birds called chickadees . . . hold body temperature nearly constant." Choice B is not correct because the food supply supports thermoregulation, which is the main point of the example. Choice C is not correct because chickadees are capable of astonishing feats of thermoregulation. Choice D is not correct because the reason for heat production in animals is explained before the example of the chickadee.

23. **D** Choice A is mentioned in paragraph 6, sentence 7. Choice B is mentioned in paragraph 6, sentence 8. Choice C is mentioned in paragraph 6, sentences 3 and 4.

24. **B** In this passage, *improve* is a synonym for "enhance." Context comes from the reference to "promote" in the previous sentence.

25. **A** Reference is a transitional device that connects the insert sentence with the previous sentence. ". . . a layer of fur or feathers" and "how much still air the layer [of fur or feathers] traps" in the insert sentence refers to ". . . fur or feathers" and "a thicker layer of air" in the previous sentence.

26. **E, C, F** summarize the passage. Choice A is a minor point that supports major point C. Choice B is true but it is not mentioned in the passage. Choice D is a minor point that supports major point F.

READING 3 "SOCIAL READJUSTMENT SCALES"

27. **D** "Overall, these studies have shown that people with higher scores on the SRRS tend to be more vulnerable to many kinds of physical illness." Choice A is not correct because a person with a higher score will experience more, not less, stress. Choice B is not correct because the numerical values for major problems are not identified, and a score of 30 does not have meaning unless it is compared with a higher or lower score. Choice C is not correct because the effects of positive or negative change are not mentioned in the first two paragraphs.

28. **C** ". . . the desirability of events affects adaptational outcomes more than the amount of change that they [events] require."

29. **D** In this passage, *different* is a synonym for "diverse."

30. **C** ". . . divorce may deserve a stress value of 73 for *most* people, a particular person's divorce might generate much less stress and merit a value of only 25." Choice A is not correct because a particular person is compared with most people. Choice B is not correct because the serious nature of divorce is not mentioned. Choice D is not correct because the numerical value of 73 for most people is questioned.

31. **A** ". . . what qualifies as 'trouble with the boss'? Should you check that because you're sick and tired of your supervisor? What constitutes a 'change in living conditions'? Does your purchase of a great new sound system qualify?" Choice B is not correct because the author does not offer examples of responses to the questions posed. Choice C is not correct because options for scores are not provided in paragraph 5. Choice D is not correct because the author suggests that people do not respond consistently but whether they respond carefully is not mentioned.

32. **B** ". . . subjects' neuroticism affects both their responses to stress scales and their self-reports of health problems." Choice A is not correct because they recall more symptoms, but they are not ill

more often. Choice C is not correct because they recall more stress, but they do not necessarily suffer more actual stress. Choice D is not correct because the effects of neuroticism obscures the meaning of the scores that are recorded.

33. **C** In this passage, *arranged* is a synonym for "assembled."

34. **C** In this passage, *related* is a synonym for "relevant."

35. **B** ". . . dropping the normative weights and replacing them with personally assigned weightings." Choice A is not correct because long-term consequences are not included in positive, negative, and total change scores. Choice C is not correct because the differences in people reflect their appraisal of stress, not how they handle stress. Choice D is not correct because normative weighting is replaced by personally assigned weightings.

36. **C** In paragraph 1, the authors state that the SRRS ". . . assigns numerical values." Choices A and B are not correct because they are mentioned in paragraph 10 in reference to the LES, not the SRRS. Choice D is not correct because recalling events from one year ago is a problem on the SRRS.

37. **A** "The LES deals with the failure of the SRRS to sample the full domain of stressful events." Choice B is not correct because the author explains several ways that the LES deals with the failure of the SRRS. Choice C is not correct because it has been used in thousands of studies by researchers all over the world. Choice D is not correct because the LES, not the SRRS, has a special section for students.

38. **B** Reference is a transitional device that connects the insert sentence with the previous sentence. "This sum" in the insert sentence refers to the phrase "adds up the numbers" in the previous sentence.

39. SRRS: **A, H, I**   LES: **B, D, E**   Not used: **C, F, G**

➤ Listening

  Model Test 1, Listening Section

LISTENING 1 "LEARNING CENTER"

Audio   1.   What does the woman need?
Answer **C**   An appointment for tutoring

Audio   2.   Listen again to part of the conversation and then answer the following question.

Replay   "Oh, but, would that be extra? You know, would I need to pay you for the extra session?"

Audio   Why does the woman say this:

Replay   "Oh, but would that be extra?"

Answer   A   Her tone indicates that she is worried.

Audio   3.   Why is the man concerned about the woman's attendance?

Answer   B   He will not get a paycheck if she is absent.

Audio   4.   What does the man agree to do?

Answer   D   He will show the woman how to improve her writing.

Audio   5.   What does the man imply about the woman's teacher?

Answer   D   ". . . know . . . where she's coming from" means "to understand her."

LISTENING 2 "GEOLOGY CLASS"

Audio   6.   What is this lecture mainly about?

Answer   B   A comparison of different types of drainage systems

Audio   7.   Listen again to part of the lecture and then answer the following question.

Replay   "Okay, today we're going to discuss the four major types of drainage patterns. I trust you've already read the chapter so you'll recall that a drainage pattern is the arrangement of channels that carry water in an area."

Audio   Why does the professor say this:

Replay   "I trust you've already read the chapter so you'll recall that a drainage pattern is the arrangement of channels that carry water in an area."

Answer   B   "I trust you" means "I expect you to."

Audio   8.   How does the professor introduce the dendritic drainage system?

Answer   B   By comparing it to both a tree and the human circulatory system

Audio   9.   Why does the professor mention the spokes of a wheel?
Answer   **C**   To explain the structure of a radial drainage system

Audio   10.   In the lecture, the professor discusses the trellis drainage pattern. Indicate whether each of the following is typical of this pattern. Click in the correct box for each phrase.

Answer   **A, D, E:** YES   **B** refers to the rectangular pattern, and **C** refers to the dendritic.

Audio   11.   What does the professor imply when he says this:
Replay   "So I don't plan to trick you with test questions about exceptional patterns."
Answer   **C**   The basic patterns from the notes will be on the test. Professors who "trick" students ask questions that have not been discussed in class.

LISTENING 3 "ART CLASS"

Audio   12.   What is the lecture mainly about?
Answer   **C**   The distinct purposes of drawing

Audio   13.   According to the professor, why do architects use sketches?
Answer   **B**   To design large buildings, architects must work in a smaller scale.

Audio   14.   Listen again to part of the lecture and then answer the following question.
Replay   "So, uh, these studies become the basis for future works. And again, this is very interesting as a record of the creative process. Okay so far?"
Audio   What does the professor mean when she says this:
Replay   "Okay so far?"
Answer   **A**   Professors sometimes pause for a comprehension check by asking if everything is okay. This gives students an opportunity to answer questions.

Audio   15.   Why does the professor mention the drawing of Marie Antoinette?
Answer   **C**   The sketch was an historical account of an important event.

Audio   16.   What is the professor's opinion of Picasso?

Answer   C   Picasso's drawings required the confidence and skill of a master artist.

Audio   17.   According to the lecture, what are the major functions of drawing?

Answer   A   A technique to remember parts of a large work

B   A method to preserve an historical record

D   An educational approach to train artists

LISTENING 4 "PROFESSOR'S OFFICE"

Audio   18.   Why does the woman go to see her professor?

Answer   B   To clarify some of the information from a lecture

Audio   19.   According to the professor, which factor causes staffing patterns to vary?

Answer   D   The number of years that a company has been in business

Audio   20.   Listen again to part of the conversation and then answer the following question.

Replay   "I think it's the one where home country nationals are put in charge of the company if it's located in a developed country, but in a developing country, then home country nationals manage the company sort of indefinitely."

"Right again. And an example of that would be . . . "

Audio   Why does the professor say this:

Replay   "And an example of that would be . . . "

Answer   B   Sometimes professors begin a statement and pause to allow the student to continue.

Audio   21.   Which of the following would be an example of a third-country pattern?

Answer   A   A Scottish manager in an American company in Africa

C   A British manager in an American company in India

Audio   22.   According to the professor, how do senior-level Japanese managers view their assignments abroad?

Answer   A   They consider them to be permanent career opportunities.

LISTENING 5 "ASTRONOMY CLASS"

Audio   23.   What is the discussion mainly about?
Answer   **C**   The vast expanse of the universe around us.

Audio   24.   Listen again to part of the lecture and then answer the following question.
Replay   "And that's as far as I can go here in the classroom, but we can visualize the rest of the journey. Don't bother writing this down. Just stay with me on this."
Audio   Why does the professor say this:
Replay   "Don't bother writing this down. Just stay with me on this."
Answer   **B**   Sometimes a professor will tell students to stop taking notes, which usually means that the information is not a main point or, in this case, the professor wants the students to concentrate on listening.

Audio   25.   Why wouldn't a photograph capture a true picture of the solar system walk?
Answer   **A**   It would not show the distances between the bodies in space.

Audio   26.   How does the professor explain the term *solar system*?
Answer   **D**   He contrasts a solar system with a galaxy.

Audio   27.   Listen again to part of the lecture and then answer the following question.
Replay   "So, what am I hoping for from this lecture? What do you think I want you to remember?"
"Well, for one thing, the enormous distances . . . "
". . . and the vast emptiness in space."
"That's good. I hope that you'll also begin to appreciate the fact that the Earth isn't the center of the universe."
Audio   Why does the professor say this:
Replay   "So, what am I hoping for from this lecture? What do you think I want you to remember?"
Answer   **C**   When professors ask their students to think about what they might want them to remember, this usually signals the beginning of a summary of the important points.

Audio   28.   What can be inferred about the professor?
Answer   **B**   The professor likes his students to participate in the discussion.

LISTENING 6 *"PSYCHOLOGY CLASS"*

Audio 29. What is the discussion mainly about?
Answer C Some of the more common types of defense mechanisms

Audio 30. How does the student explain the term *repression*?
Answer A He contrasts it with suppression.

Audio 31. Listen again to part of the discussion and then answer the following question.
Replay "For instance, let's suppose that you're very angry with your professor. Not me, of course. I'm referring to another professor. So, you're very angry because he's treated you unfairly in some way that . . . that could cause you to lose your scholarship."
Audio Why does the professor say this:
Replay "Not me, of course. I'm referring to another professor."
Answer B The professor's tone is not serious. She is joking.

Audio 32. Which of the following is an example of *displacement* that was used in the lecture?
Answer C Blaming someone in your study group instead of blaming the professor

Audio 33. According to the professor, what happened in the 1990s?
Answer B New terms were introduced for the same mechanisms.

Audio 34. How does the professor organize the lecture?
Answer B She uses a scenario that students can relate to. She talks about the way that a student might respond to a professor by using defense mechanisms.

LISTENING 7 *"BOOKSTORE"*

Audio 35. What does the man need from the bookstore?
Answer B A form to order books

Audio 36. What does the man need if he wants a full refund?
Answer A Identification
         C A receipt for the purchase

Audio	37.	Listen again to part of the conversation and then answer the following question.
Replay		"Don't give it to one of the student employees, though. They're usually very good about getting the forms back to the office, but sometimes it gets really busy and . . . you know how it is."
Audio		What does the woman mean when she says this:
Replay		". . . sometimes it gets really busy and . . . you know how it is."
Answer	A	She is not sure that the student employee will give her the form. The phrase "you know how it is" implies that the man will be able to make a logical conclusion. If the student employees are very busy, they might forget to take the forms to the office.
Audio	38.	What does the woman imply about the used books she sells?
Answer	A	They are purchased before new books.
Audio	39:	What does the man need to do now?
Answer	D	Locate the schedule numbers for his classes. They are in his room at the dorm.

LISTENING 8 "ENVIRONMENTAL SCIENCE CLASS"

Audio	40.	What is this lecture mainly about?
Answer	A	An overview of fuel cell technology. The professor discusses the process for producing energy, the efficiency of the cells, the problems, and some model programs.
Audio	41.	Listen again to part of the lecture and then answer the following question.
Replay		"Hydrogen is the most recent and, I'd say, one of the most promising, in a long list of alternatives to petroleum. Some of the possibilities include batteries, methanol, natural gas, and, well, you name it."
Audio		What does the professor mean when he says this:
Replay		"Some of the possibilities include batteries, methanol, natural gas, and, well, you name it."
Answer	D	He does not plan to talk about the alternatives. The comment "you name it" implies that there are a large number of alternatives and that he is not interested in them.

Audio   42.   Why does the professor mention the STEP program in Australia?

Answer   D   He thinks it is a very good example of a project.

Audio   43.   Listen again to part of the conversation and then answer the following question.

Replay   "Now, under an agreement signed in about 2000, if memory serves, it was 2003, but anyway, the joint projects include the writing of codes and standards, the design of fueling infrastructures, the refinement of fuel cell models, and the demonstration of fuel cell vehicles."

Audio   Why does the professor say this:

Replay   " . . . if memory serves, it was 2003 . . . "

Answer   D   To show that he is uncertain about the date

Audio   44.   What are some of the problems associated with fuel cell technology?

Answer   B   Public acceptance

D   Investment in infrastructures

Audio   45.   What is the professor's attitude toward fuel cells?

Answer   B   He is hopeful about their development in the future. He would like more attention to be directed to public information programs, which would solve one of the major problems for fuel cell technology.

LISTENING 9 "PHILOSOPHY CLASS"

Audio   46.   What is the main focus of this discussion?

Answer   C   The other topics are mentioned in the discussion as they relate to the main focus: Humanism.

Audio   47.   Listen again to part of the discussion and then answer the following question.

Replay   "A primary principle of humanism—I don't need to spell that for you, do I? Okay, a primary principle of humanism is that human beings are rational and have an innate predisposition for good."

Audio   Why does the professor say this:

Replay   "I don't need to spell that for you, do I?"

Answer   B   Her tone indicates that she assumes that the students know how to spell the term. Later, she spells a more difficult term.

Audio   48.   Why does the professor mention the drawing by Leonardo da Vinci?

Answer   B   She uses it as an example of the union of art and science.

Audio   49.   According to the professor, what was the effect of using Latin as a universal language of scholarship?

Answer   A   It facilitated communication among intellectuals in many countries.

Audio   50.   According to the professor, what can be inferred about a Renaissance man?

Answer   B   He would have an aptitude for both art and science.

Audio   51.   All of the following characteristics are true of humanism EXCEPT

Answer   B   Scholars must serve society.

➤ Speaking

Model Test 1, Speaking Section

INDEPENDENT SPEAKING QUESTION 1 "MARRIAGE PARTNER"

Narrator 2: Number 1. Listen for a question about a familiar topic. After you hear the question, you have 15 seconds to prepare and 45 seconds to record your answer.

Narrator 1: Describe an ideal marriage partner. What qualities do you think are most important for a husband or wife? Use specific reasons and details to explain your choices.

Narrator 2: Please prepare your answer after the beep.

Beep

[Preparation time: 15 seconds]

Narrator 2: Please begin speaking after the beep.

Beep

[Recording time: 45 seconds]

Beep

INDEPENDENT SPEAKING QUESTION 2 "NEWS"

Narrator 2: Number 2. Listen for a question that asks your opinion about a familiar topic. After you hear the question, you have 15 seconds to prepare and 45 seconds to record your answer.

Narrator 1: Some people like to watch the news on television. Other people prefer to read the news in a newspaper. Still others use their computers to get the news. How do you prefer to be informed about the news and why? Use specific reasons and examples to support your choice.

Narrator 2: Please prepare your answer after the beep.

Beep

[Preparation time: 15 seconds]

Narrator 2: Please begin speaking after the beep.

Beep

[Recording time: 45 seconds]

Beep

INTEGRATED SPEAKING QUESTION 3 "MEAL PLAN"

Narrator 2: Number 3. Read a short passage and listen to a talk on the same topic. Then listen for a question about them. After you hear the question, you have 30 seconds to prepare and 60 seconds to record your answer.

Narrator 1: A new meal plan is being offered by the college. Read the plan in the college newspaper printed on page 98. You have 45 seconds to complete it. Please begin reading now.

[Reading time: 45 seconds]

Narrator 1: Now listen to two students who are talking about the plan.

Man:	I don't like to cook, but I don't like to eat in the cafeteria every day either.
Woman:	True. The food does get kind of . . . same old same old.
Man:	My point exactly. And besides, I go home about every other weekend, so paying for my meals when I'm not there doesn't make a lot of sense.

Woman:	Right. So you'll probably sign up for the five-day plan next semester.
Man:	I already did. If I want to eat in the cafeteria some weekend, I can just buy a meal, but I'd probably go out somewhere with my friends if I'm here over the weekend.
Woman:	Well, I don't go home on the weekends as much as you do, but I still eat out a lot on the weekends.
Man:	So the five-day plan might work out better for you, too. I'm really glad to have the option.

Narrator 1: The man expresses his opinion of the new meal plan. Report his opinion, and explain the reasons that he gives for having that opinion.

Narrator 2: Please prepare your answer after the beep.

Beep

[Preparation time: 30 seconds]

Narrator 2: Please begin speaking after the beep.

Beep

[Recording time: 60 seconds]

Beep

 Model Test 1, Speaking Section

INTEGRATED SPEAKING QUESTION 4 "ABORIGINAL PEOPLE"

Narrator 2: Number 4. Read a short passage and listen to a lecture on the same topic. Then listen for a question about them. After you hear the question, you have 30 seconds to prepare and 60 seconds to record your answer.

Narrator 1: Now read the passage about Aboriginal People printed on page 100. You have 45 seconds to complete it. Please begin reading now.

[Reading time: 45 seconds]

Narrator 1: Now listen to part of a lecture in an anthropology class. The professor is talking about Aboriginal People.

Professor:
According to your textbook, the Aboriginal People are very diverse, and, I would agree with that; however, there are certain beliefs that unite the groups, and in fact, allow them to identify themselves and others as members of the diverse Aboriginal societies. For one thing, unlike the anthropologists who believe that tribes arrived in eastern Australia from Tasmania about 40,000 years ago, the Aboriginal People believe that they have always been in Australia, and that they have sprung from the land. Evidence for this resides in the oral history that has been recorded in stories and passed down for at least fifty generations. This history is referred to as the "Dreaming." The stories teach moral and spiritual values and provide each member of the group with an identity that reflects the landscape where the person's mother first becomes aware of the unborn baby, or to put it in terms of the "Dreaming," where the spirit enters the mother's body. So, I am saying that the way that the Aboriginal People identify themselves and each other, even across groups, is by their membership in the oral history that they share.

Narrator 1: Explain how the Aboriginal People are identified. Draw upon information in both the reading and the lecture.

Narrator 2: Please prepare your answer after the beep.

Beep

[Preparation time: 30 seconds]

Narrator 2: Please begin speaking after the beep.

Beep

[Recording time: 60 seconds]

Beep

INTEGRATED SPEAKING QUESTION 5 "SCHEDULING CONFLICT"

Narrator 2: Number 5. Listen to a short conversation. Then listen for a question about it. After you hear the question, you have 20 seconds to prepare and 60 seconds to record your answer.

Narrator 1: Now listen to a conversation between a student and his friend.

Friend: So what time should we pick you up on Friday? Can you be ready by noon or do you need another hour or so?

Student:	I really wanted to spend the weekend with my family, and the ride with you would have made it even more fun, but . . .
Friend:	You mean you aren't going?
Student:	I can't. I'm not doing too well in my economics class, and I have a lecture Friday afternoon. I don't think I should miss it.
Friend:	Well, why don't you borrow the notes from someone? Isn't your roommate in that class?
Student:	Yeah, he is. But I've already asked to borrow his notes once this semester. He didn't seem to mind though.
Friend:	Well, there you are. Unless you want to go to class on Thursday. I'm fairly sure that Dr. Collins teaches the same class Thursday night.
Student:	Really? She probably wouldn't mind if I sat in on the Thursday class, but I wonder if she'll give the same lecture. You know, maybe they're one week behind or one week ahead of us.
Friend:	I suppose that's possible, but it would be easy enough to find out. You could just tell her that you'd like to attend the Thursday session this week because you need to go out of town. Then you can ride home with us. If there's a problem, you can still borrow your roommate's notes on Sunday when we get back.

Narrator 1: Describe the man's problem and the two suggestions that his friend makes about how to handle it. What do you think the man should do, and why?

Narrator 2: Please prepare your answer after the beep.

Beep

[Preparation time: 20 seconds]

Narrator 2: Please begin speaking after the beep.

Beep

[Recording time: 60 seconds]

Beep

INTEGRATED SPEAKING QUESTION 6 "LABORATORY MICROSCOPE"

Narrator 2: Number 6. Listen to part of a talk. Then listen for a question about it. After you hear the question, you have 20 seconds to prepare and 60 seconds to record your answer.

Narrator 1: Now listen to part of a talk in a biology laboratory. The teaching assistant is explaining how to use the microscope.

Teaching Assistant:
All right, now that you all have microscopes at your tables, I want to explain how they work and how to use them. First of all, you should know that they are compound microscopes so they can magnify objects up to 1000 times their size. These microscopes have two systems—an illuminating system and an imaging system. You'll see that the illuminating system has a light source built in, and you can control it by adjusting the lever on the side. Why is this important? Well, the specimen must be pretty thin, or let's say, transparent enough to let light pass through it. So the light source controls the amount of light that passes through the specimen. Okay. The other system provides magnification. Use this lever to switch powers. So, when you switch to a higher power, you see a larger image, and when you switch to a lower power, you see a smaller image. But, I should remind you that the field of view is smaller at a higher power. In other words, at a higher magnification, you see a larger image of a smaller area. Okay. So what about the focus? Well, these microscopes are parfocal, and that means you usually don't have to refocus when you switch to a higher or lower power of magnification. But there are two adjustment knobs—the larger one for coarse adjustment and the smaller one for fine adjustment just in case.

Narrator 1: Using the main points and examples from the talk, describe the two major systems of the laboratory microscope, and then explain how to use it.

Narrator 2: Please prepare your answer after the beep.

Beep

[Preparation time: 20 seconds]

Narrator 2: Please begin speaking after the beep.

Beep

[Recording time: 60 seconds]

Beep

➤ Writing

INTEGRATED ESSAY "SCHOOL ORGANIZATION"

First, read the passage on page 106 and take notes.

 Model Test 1, Writing Section

Narrator: Now listen to a lecture on the same topic as the passage that you have just read.

Professor:
So what are the problems associated with the graded school system? Well, for one thing, graded schools don't take into account the . . . the differences in academic readiness on the part of individual learners. And by that I mean that some six-year-olds are simply not socially, mentally, or even physically mature enough to begin school, but others are ready in all of those important ways by their fifth or even fourth birthdays. And uh . . . by the time that girls and boys are in their early teens, we can see that there's a significant difference in maturity, in . . . in physical and social maturity but . . . they're still grouped together in intermediate grades in a graded school system.

Okay, besides the obvious differences in individual readiness and maturity, the . . . the whole issue of promotion needs to be reviewed. Grade-level requirements don't really deal with the actual learning that has occurred, uh, in a positive way. Many research studies confirm that repeating an entire year because some of the material is not learned contributes to . . . to boredom, poor self-concept, and . . . and eventually to higher drop-out rates. And since graded schools are using group expectations as measured by performance on standardized tests, this is another way to evaluate the group rather than the individual. So, what happens is that individual differences in how long it takes to learn a concept or . . . or the partial achievement of a grade-level curriculum . . . that is never addressed by the graded school system. Students who need more time to learn have to repeat material that they already know. Students who can learn at a faster rate have to wait for the new material to be presented. So, as you can see, it's not ideal.

➤ Example Answers and Checklists for Speaking and Writing

 Model Test 1, Example Answers

EXAMPLE ANSWER FOR INDEPENDENT SPEAKING QUESTION 1 "MARRIAGE PARTNER"

In my view, three characteristics are essential for a marriage partner. Compatibility is very important because spending the rest of your life with someone is a huge commitment, and without compatibility in values and interests, and goals, it could be a struggle rather than a partnership. Um, I also think that a good marriage partner should fit into your family. Without acceptance and affection for you as a couple, you could risk the relationships you have with family members. And attraction is another factor. Since fidelity is part of the marriage contract, the expression of love will be limited to your partner, so it should be a person you're attracted to.

Checklist 1

✔ The talk answers the topic question.
✔ The point of view or position is clear.
✔ The talk is direct and well-organized.
✔ The sentences are logically connected.
✔ Details and examples support the main idea.
✔ The speaker expresses complete thoughts.
✔ The meaning is easy to comprehend.
✔ A wide range of vocabulary is used.
✔ There are only minor errors in grammar.
✔ The talk is within a range of 125–150 words.

EXAMPLE ANSWER FOR INDEPENDENT SPEAKING QUESTION 2 "NEWS"

Although newspapers contain some information that's limited to local interests and I like to turn to those pages, for the most part, I prefer to get my news on TV and on my computer. The problem with printed news is it takes so long to produce it that the stories could have changed or more important news could have happened minutes after the newspaper is delivered. So, I scan the local stories in the paper when I get home from work, then I watch the international news on TV at night for the most current information, and the following morning, I click on one of the web sites that offer the most recent updates of the lead stories. That way, I'm taking advantage of the best aspects of all the news media, and I stay current locally and internationally.

Checklist 2

✔ The talk answers the topic question.
✔ The point of view or position is clear.
✔ The talk is direct and well-organized.
✔ The sentences are logically connected.
✔ Details and examples support the main idea.
✔ The speaker expresses complete thoughts.
✔ The meaning is easy to comprehend.
✔ A wide range of vocabulary is used.
✔ There are only minor errors in grammar.
✔ The talk is within a range of 125–150 words.

EXAMPLE ANSWER FOR INTEGRATED SPEAKING QUESTION 3 "MEAL PLAN"

The man is glad that an alternative to the seven-day meal plan is now available for students who live in the dorms. He'll purchase the five-day meal plan, which provides three meals on weekdays and the option to buy meals on the weekends for $3 each. The new five-day meal plan is better for him because he likes to go home every other weekend, and when he's on campus, he likes to go out with his friends. So he wasn't taking advantage of the cafeteria on the weekends even though he was paying for it. The Student Union has fast-food as well as booths in the food court for Chinese or Mexican food or even a salad bar. Besides, if he wants to eat in the cafeteria on a weekend, he can buy a meal. He should save about $48 a month by using the new plan, and he can use that money to eat out.

Checklist 3

✔ The talk summarizes the situation and opinion.
✔ The point of view or position is clear.
✔ The talk is direct and well-organized.
✔ The sentences are logically connected.
✔ Details and examples support the opinion.
✔ The speaker expresses complete thoughts.

✔ The meaning is easy to comprehend.
✔ A wide range of vocabulary is used.
✔ Errors in grammar are minor.
✔ The talk is within a range of 125–150 words.

EXAMPLE ANSWER FOR INTEGRATED SPEAKING QUESTION 4 "ABORIGINAL PEOPLE"

The Aboriginal People are culturally and linguistically diverse, in part because the geography dictated both limitations and opportunities for their communities. So the establishment of identity as a member of the Aboriginal People because of appearance, language, culture, or geographical location is not considered accurate. The Department of Education suggests that the best means of identification is to be recognized and accepted by other members of the Aboriginal society. Um, according to the lecturer, even diverse groups have certain unifying beliefs that are passed down as oral tradition, called the "Dreaming." The stories associated with this tradition are used to teach ethical principles and spiritual lessons. It would probably be through knowledge of this shared oral history that Aborigines would identify each other.

Checklist 4

✔ The talk relates an example to a concept.
✔ Inaccuracies in the content are minor.
✔ The talk is direct and well-organized.
✔ The sentences are logically connected.
✔ Details and examples support the opinion.
✔ The speaker expresses complete thoughts.
✔ The meaning is easy to comprehend.
✔ A wide range of vocabulary is used.
✔ The speaker paraphrases in his/her own words.
✔ The speaker credits the lecturer with wording.
✔ Errors in grammar are minor.
✔ The talk is within a range of 125–150 words.

EXAMPLE ANSWER FOR INTEGRATED SPEAKING QUESTION 5 "SCHEDULING CONFLICT"

The man would like to visit his family over the weekend, but his friends are leaving before his economics class on Friday. He doesn't want to miss the class because he needs to bring his grade up. His friend suggests that he borrow the notes from the class. His roommate didn't have a problem lending him notes from that class earlier in the semester, but he's reluctant to do that. The other possibility that his friend mentions is for him to attend another section of the same class on Thursday night, but he isn't sure that the professor will give the same lecture. To find out, he would have to ask the professor. In my opinion, the man should stay for his economics class and take notes. It's hard to read someone else's notes, and besides, if he's in the class, he can ask questions. If he wants to visit his family, he should try to find a ride on Saturday or on Friday after the class.

Checklist 5

✔ The talk summarizes the problem and recommendations.
✔ The speaker's point of view or position is clear.
✔ The talk is direct and well-organized.
✔ The sentences are logically connected.
✔ Details and examples support the opinion.
✔ The speaker expresses complete thoughts.
✔ The meaning is easy to comprehend.
✔ A wide range of vocabulary is used.
✔ Errors in grammar are minor.
✔ The talk is within a range of 125–150 words.

EXAMPLE ANSWER FOR INTEGRATED SPEAKING QUESTION 6 "LABORATORY MICROSCOPE"

The two major systems of the laboratory microscope are the illuminating system and the imaging system. The illuminating system has a light source that can be controlled to let more or less light pass through the specimen you're viewing when you move a lever on the side of the microscope. The imaging system is actually a magnification feature, which can be calibrated by using the other lever to change powers. When you look through a higher power, the image appears to be larger, and conversely, when you look through a lower power, it appears to be smaller. What that really means is when you use a higher magnification, the image actually shows you a smaller part of the specimen because it's enlarged. Now when you switch powers, the lenses will focus automatically, but the big knob will allow you to make a rough adjustment, and the small knob will let you make a more detailed adjustment, if you want.

Checklist 6

✔ The talk summarizes a short lecture.
✔ Inaccuracies in the content are minor.
✔ The talk is direct and well-organized.
✔ The sentences are logically connected.
✔ Details and examples support the opinion.
✔ The speaker expresses complete thoughts.
✔ The meaning is easy to comprehend.
✔ A wide range of vocabulary is used.
✔ The speaker paraphrases in his/her own words.
✔ The speaker credits the lecturer with wording.
✔ Errors in grammar are minor.
✔ The talk is within a range of 125–150 words.

EXAMPLE RESPONSE FOR INTEGRATED ESSAY "SCHOOL ORGANIZATION"

Some writers begin with an outline and others begin with a map of their ideas. Only the essay will be scored.

Outline

Graded school system
Disadvantages

* Maturity
   First grade
      6 yrs old
   Intermediate
      Boys, girls
* Progress
   Standardized test
      Repeat concepts
      Penalizes capable
* Dropout rate
   Repeat all
   Learned part

Map

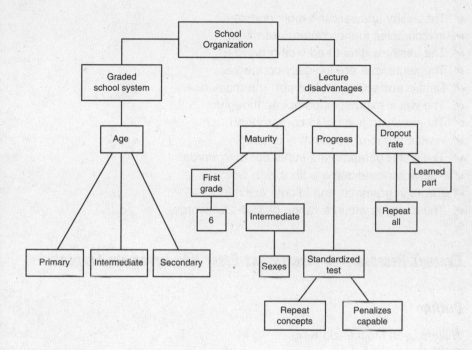

Example Essay

The graded school system, which groups students by age, is usually divided into primary, intermediate, and secondary grades. However, according to the lecture, there are several disadvantages to this type of system. In the first place, maturity is not considered. All students begin the first grade at six years old; however, many children are not mature enough to go to school at that age. In contrast, some younger children are ready for school before their sixth birthdays but are denied the opportunity to begin until they reach the required age of six. In addition, the disparity in the maturity of girls and boys is marked in the intermediate grades. Nevertheless, they are still scheduled for classes according to age, not maturity. Even more concerning is the problem of grade-level standards, which rely on testing to evaluate progress by age instead of by actual mastery on the part of individuals. The grade-level system is inefficient because it requires some learners to repeat concepts that they have already learned in order to master those that they still need to know. It also penalizes students who are capable of learning more material than the grade-level curriculum allows. Furthermore, research shows a correlation between low self-esteem and drop-out rates with the requirement that students repeat a calendar year because they have not learned part of the material for their grade.

Checklist for Integrated Essay

✔ The essay answers the topic question.
✔ Inaccuracies in the content are minor.
✔ The essay is direct and well-organized.
✔ The sentences are logically connected.
✔ Details and examples support the main idea.
✔ The writer expresses complete thoughts.
✔ The meaning is easy to comprehend.
✔ A wide range of vocabulary is used.
✔ The writer paraphrases in his/her own words.
✔ The writer credits the author with wording.
✔ Errors in grammar and idioms are minor.
✔ The essay is within a range of 150–225 words.

EXAMPLE RESPONSE FOR INDEPENDENT ESSAY "AN IMPORTANT LEADER"

Outline

William Lyon Mackenzie King
• Offices
    Parliament
    Head Liberal Party
    Prime minister
• Longevity
    21 years P.M.
    50 years public service
• Accomplishments
    Unity French + English provinces
    Represented all Canadians

Map

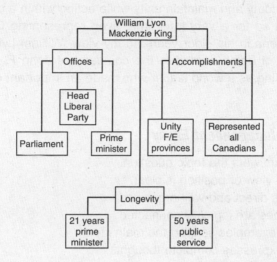

Example Essay

William Lyon Mackenzie King was a member of the Canadian parliament and head of the Liberal Party in the first half of the twentieth century. He held the office of prime minister for a total of twenty-one years, which is a longer period of time than that of any public servant in the history of Canada. Because his terms of office as prime minister were not consecutive, he held other positions of public service in many appointed and elected offices as well over a period of fifty years. Although it could be argued that he was an important world leader on the basis of longevity alone, I admire him because of his qualities of leadership. He was active in government during two world wars and the Great Depression and played a key role in guiding Canada during those very difficult years. He understood the importance of a unified nation and worked to bring various partisan groups together for the higher good of the country. Under his tenure in office, Canada became a participant in world affairs.

His three terms of office as prime minister were marked by compromise and often criticism, but he earned the respect of most Canadians for his political astuteness and his determination to unify Canada. In part because of his friendship with Wilfrid Laurier, he was able to preserve the unity between the French-speaking and English-speaking provinces, a negotiation that must be considered his greatest achievement. One biographer, John Moir of the University of Toronto, has identified a quality in King called "essential Canadianness." I understand this to mean that he was able to understand and represent all of the people of Canada.

King's methods were frustrating to some, but he was able to extend Canadian autonomy and maintain unity while acting within a difficult federal system. He did so for a very long time, even representing Canada in the international arena in his elder years. In my view, William Lyon Mackenzie King is worthy of being named in the company of John F. Kennedy and Martin Luther King as a world leader who made an important contribution to humanity.

Checklist for Independent Essay

✔ The essay answers the topic question.
✔ The point of view or position is clear.
✔ The essay is direct and well-organized.
✔ The sentences are logically connected.
✔ Details and examples support the main idea.
✔ The writer expresses complete thoughts.
✔ The meaning is easy to comprehend.
✔ A wide range of vocabulary is used.
✔ Various types of sentences are included.
✔ Errors in grammar and idioms are minor.
✔ The essay is within a range of 300–350 words.

MODEL TEST 2: PROGRESS TEST

➤ Reading

READING 1 "RESOURCES AND INDUSTRIALISM IN CANADA"

1. **B** "The building of the Temiskaming and Northern Ontario Railway led to the discovery of rich silver deposits." Choices A, C, and D are true, but they do not relate to the main point in paragraph 1, the resources in the western frontier.

2. **C** ". . . Sudbury became the world's largest nickel producer." Choice A is not correct because it is not mentioned directly in the paragraph. Choice B is not correct because Sudbury was a supplier, not a market for metals. Choice D is not correct because Sudbury is in Ontario, not in the Klondike.

3. **D** In this passage, *improve* is a synonym for "enhance." Context comes from the word "treasury" in the following sentence.

4. **B** ". . . the federal government created the Yukon Territory . . . in an effort to ward off the prospect of annexation to Alaska." Choice A is not correct because fortune-seekers were flocking there already. Choice C is not correct because the tales of lawlessness were told in popular fiction, but no effort to establish law and order was mentioned. Choice D is not correct because the legality of the mining claims was not mentioned.

5. **D** In this passage, *formerly* is a synonym for "previously." Context comes from the reference to "unsettled" for an area that was increasing in population.

6. **A** ". . . the tales [of the Klondike strike] . . . were immortalized through . . . the poetic verses of Robert W. Service." Choices B and C may have been true, but they were not mentioned in connection with the poetry of Robert Service. Choice D is not correct because the creation of the Yukon Territory, not the poetry, prevented the Klondike's annexation to Alaska.

7. **B** Choice A is mentioned in paragraph 3, sentence 2. Choice C is mentioned in paragraph 3, sentence 5. Choice D is mentioned in paragraph 3, sentence 4.

8. **D** In this passage, *Moreover* is a synonym for "Furthermore." Context comes from the addition of another way that the forest and water resources were exploited.

9. **C**   *Federal taxes* paraphrases "the high tariff policies" and *cheaper imported goods* paraphrases "lower-priced foreign manufactured goods." . . . *protecting domestic industries* paraphrases "protecting existing industries" and *supporting new businesses* paraphrases "encouraging the creation of new enterprises."

10. **C**   "To climb the tariff wall, large American industrial firms opened branches in Canada, and the governments of Ontario and Quebec aggressively urged them [American industrial firms] on by offering bonuses, subsidies, and guarantees to locate new plants." The pronoun "them" does not refer to Choices A, B, or D.

11. **A**   ". . . the governments of Ontario and Quebec . . . [offered] bonuses, subsidies, and guarantees to locate new plants within their borders." Choice B is true, but it is not the reason why British and American businesses opened affiliates. Choice C is not correct because the consumers in western Canada were eager to buy goods from eastern and central Canada, not from abroad. Choice D is not correct because British investors contributed to the construction of urban infrastructure.

12. **C**   Vocabulary reference is a transitional device that connects the insert sentence with the previous sentence. The connection is "Railway construction" and "discoveries of gold, silver, copper, lead, and zinc" to "The building of the . . . Railway" and "rich silver deposits."

13. **C, E, F** summarize the passage. Choices A and B are minor points that support major point C. Choice D is a minor point that supports major point E.

READING 2 "LOOKING AT THEATRE HISTORY"

14. **C**   ". . . the buildings in later periods became sources of stone for other projects and what remains is usually broken and scattered." Choice A is not correct because other theatres have been identified and many of them have been excavated. Choice B is not correct because the archeologists were not the ones who broke the stones. Choice D is not correct because concrete was not mentioned as construction material during early periods. The word "concrete" in the passage means "true" or "verifiable" in reference to "evidence."

15. **B**   ". . . many pieces are irrevocably lost." Choice A is not correct because drawings are conjectural. Choice C is not correct because the number of skenes that archeologists have excavated is not specified. Choice D is not correct because excavations did not begin until the late 1800s, not the early 1800s.

16. **B** In this passage, *important* is a synonym for "primary." Context comes from the phrase, "most concrete evidence."

17. **D** In this passage, *exact* is a synonym for "precise." Context comes from the contrast with the word "conjectural" in the same sentence.

18. **A** ". . . the myths on which dramatists drew were known to everyone, including vase painters, who might well depict the same subjects as dramatists." Choice B is not correct because reproductions were not mentioned. Choice C is not correct because the qualifications of scholars were not discussed. Choice D is not correct because thousands of vases have survived.

19. **B** In this passage, *debated* is a synonym for "controversial." Context comes from the phrases "easy to misinterpret" and "questionable assumption" in later sentences.

20. **D** ". . . these characters [women] often seem victims of their own powerlessness." Choice A is not correct because many plays featured strong female characters. Choice B is not correct because some critics have seen these plays [with women as victims] as rationalizations by the male-dominated culture and other critics have seen them as an attempt to examine this aspect of the culture. Choice C is not correct because plays featured numerous choruses of women.

21. **B** ". . . copies of plays had to be made by hand, and therefore the possibility of textual errors . . . was magnified." Choice A is not correct because the problem of sources was identified for archeological findings, not written evidence. Choices C and D are not mentioned as problems for written evidence.

22. **B** ". . . the majority of written references to Greek theatre date from several hundred years after the events they report. The writers seldom mention their sources of evidence, and thus we do not know what credence to give them [the sources]." The pronoun "them" does not refer to Choices A, C, or D.

23. **A** ". . . historical treatment of Greek theatre is something like assembling a jigsaw puzzle of which many pieces are missing." The reference to "missing pieces" is an analogy to the partial evidence for Greek theatre. Choice B is not correct because no comparison is made between written references and the paintings in paragraph 4. Choice C is not correct because the author does not use words and phrases that suggest justification. Choice D is not correct because the last sentence is a summary of the reading passage, not an opening sentence for a new topic.

24. **D** Because the author refers to the archeological evidence in vase paintings as "controversial," it must be concluded that there is dis-

agreement among scholars. Choice A is not correct because the oldest surviving manuscripts date from 1500 years after they were first performed. Choice B is not correct because they are easy to misinterpret. Choice C is not correct because the author does not mention the condition of the vases.

25. **C**   Vocabulary reference and contrast are two transitional devices that connect the previous and following sentences to the insert sentence. The connection is "theatres . . . have been excavated" in the previous sentence and "These excavations" in the insert sentence as well as the contrast with "Nevertheless, they" [the theatres or excavations of theatres] in the following sentence.

26. **B, D, C** summarize the passage. Choice A is a minor point that supports major point D. Choice E is a minor point that supports major point C. Choice F is reasonable, but it is not mentioned in the passage.

READING 3 "GEOTHERMAL ENERGY"

27. **A**   The author mentions geothermal power in 1904 in Italy, and then lists a number of countries worldwide that are using geothermal energy. Choice B is not correct because only successful production is mentioned. Choices C and D are discussed later in the passage.

28. **D**   ". . . at the global level, geothermal energy supplies less than 0.15% of the total energy supply." Choice A is not correct because geothermal energy was used as early as 1904. Choice B is not correct because Russia, Iceland, Mexico, and the United States are in the Northern Hemisphere. Choice C is not correct because several advantages of using geothermal power are noted, but the comparative cost was not mentioned.

29. **C**   In this passage *nearly* is a synonym for "approaching." Context comes from the number after the word.

30. **B**   "Some 40 million people today receive their electricity from geothermal energy at a cost competitive with that [the cost] of other energy sources." The pronoun "that" does not refer to Choices A, C, or D.

31. **D**   ". . . considered a nonrenewable energy source when rates of extraction are greater than rates of natural replenishment." Choices A, B, and C are true, but they do not explain the term "nonrenewable."

32. **A**   *High heat is the source of most of the geothermal energy* paraphrases ". . . most geothermal energy production involves the tapping of high heat sources," and *low heat groundwater is also used sometimes* paraphrases "people are also using the low-temperature geothermal energy of groundwater in some applications."

33. **B** "... areas of high heat flow are associated with plate tectonic bound-aries." Choice A is not correct because geothermal heat flow is very low compared with solar heat. Choice C is not correct because, in some areas, heat flow is sufficiently high. Choice D is not correct because geothermal energy is very practical along plate boundaries.

34. **A** In this passage, *large* is a synonym for "considerable." Context comes from the contrast with the phrase "not be as extensive" in the first part of the same sentence.

35. **B** "... geothermal energy does not produce the atmospheric pollu-tants associated with burning fossil fuels." Choice A is not correct because the pollution caused by geothermal energy was introduced before the discussion on atmospheric pollution. Choice C is not cor-rect because environmental problems caused by geothermal ener-gy are mentioned. Choice D is not correct because the author points out the problem of pollution, but does not suggest that the use of raw materials and chemicals be discontinued.

36. **A** Choice B is mentioned in paragraph 6, sentence 4. Choices C and D are mentioned in paragraph 6, sentences 5 and 6.

37. **C** "... known geothermal resources ... could produce ... 10% of the electricity ... for the western states. ... Geohydrothermal resources not yet discovered could ... provide ... [the] equivalent [of] the electricity produced from water power today." Choice A is not cor-rect because the author points out the disadvantages but argues in favor of using geothermal energy. Choice B is not correct because the author does not mention exploration as a prerequisite to further production. Choice D is not correct because the author cites the potential for geothermal energy to equal the production of water power, not to replace water power.

38. **C** Vocabulary reference is a transitional device that connects the insert sentence with the previous sentence. "One such region" is a phrase in the insert sentence that refers to "Oceanic ridge systems" in the previous sentence.

39. Fossil fuels: **C, H, I** Geothermal energy: **B, D, E, F** Not used: **A, G**

Reading 4 "Migration from Asia"

40. **D** In this passage, *particular* is a synonym for "distinctive."

41. **C** "... Stone Age hunter-gatherers were attracted by these animal pop-ulations [large animals]." Choice A is not mentioned. Choice B is not correct because the tools were made from the animals, not traded with other tribes. Choice D is not correct because the dogs accom-panied them.

42. **B**   In this passage, the phrase *Joined by* is a synonym for "Accompanied by." Context comes from the word part, "company."

43. **B**   "Because modern Asian populations include all three blood types, however, the migrations must have begun before the evolution of type B, which [evolution] geneticists believe occurred." The pronoun "which" does not refer to Choices A, C, or D.

44. **D**   ". . . the migrations must have begun before the evolution of type B." Choice A is not correct because the time frame was the same as the settlement of Scandinavia, but the origin of the migration was not Scandinavian. Choice B is not correct because almost no Native Americans have type B. Choice C is not correct because the blood typing was done with Native Americans and Asians, not Scandinavians.

45. **D**   ". . . glacial melting created an ice-free corridor along the eastern front range of the Rocky Mountains. Soon hunters . . . had reached the Great Plains." Choices A and C are not correct because the corridor was ice-free. Choice B is not correct because the hunters were looking for big game, but the game did not leave a migration path.

46. **B**   "The most spectacular find, at Monte Verde in southern Chile, produced striking evidence of tool making, house building . . . before the highway had been cleared of ice." Choice A is not correct because archeologists believe that migration in boats may have occurred, but no boats were found. Choice C is not correct because the footprints found there were human, not those of large animals. Choice D is not correct because no conclusions were made about the intelligence of the early humans.

47. **A**   In this passage, *In the end* is a synonym for "Eventually." Context comes from the phrase "The final migration" in the following sentence.

48. **A**   *Beringia was under water* paraphrases "Beringia had been submerged" and *the last people* paraphrases "The final migration."

49. **D**   Choice A is mentioned in paragraph 6, sentence 3. Choices B and C are mentioned in paragraph 6, sentence 5. Choice D is not true because the Yuptiks settled the coast of Alaska, not the Great Plains.

50. **D**   ". . . the most compelling support [for migration] . . . comes from genetic research." Choice A is not correct because oral traditions include a long journey from a distant place to a new homeland. Choice B is not correct because the author presents the evidence without commenting on the authenticity. Choice C is not correct because the author states that the Asian migration hypothesis is supported by most of the scientific evidence.

51. **C**   Chronological order and place reference are transitional devices that connect the insert sentence with the previous sentence. The date, 13,000 B.C.E. in the previous paragraph is a date that precedes 11,000 to 12,000 years old in the insert sentence. In addition, Washington State, California, and Peru in the insert sentence refer to the Pacific coast of North and South America in the previous sentence.

52. **E, D, C** summarize the passage. Choice A is a concluding point that is not developed with examples and details. Choice B is a minor point that supports major point E. Choice F is a minor point that supports major point D.

READING 5 "PHYSICAL AND CHEMICAL PROPERTIES AND CHANGES"

53. **C**   "They [characteristic properties] are subdivided into two categories: physical properties and chemical properties." Choice A is not correct because they are used to identify or characterize a substance, not to create a substance. Choice B is not correct because sugar and water are substances, but the physical and chemical properties of them are not identified in the paragraph. Choice D is not correct because the properties do not depend on the quantity of the substance.

54. **B**   In this passage, *relate* is a synonym for "pertain." Context comes from the word "relate" in the previous sentence.

55. **C**   ". . . some intensive physical properties include the tendency to dissolve in water, electrical conductivity, and density, which [density] is the ratio of mass to volume." The pronoun "which" does not refer to Choices A, B, or D.

56. **C**   ". . . to act as a poison or carcinogen (cancer-causing agent)." An explanation of a word or phrase often appears immediately after it in parentheses. Choices A, B, and D are not correct because they are intensive chemical properties that are mentioned before the reference to a carcinogen.

57. **B**   *The quantity of a substance* paraphrases "the amount present" in reference to extensive properties and *the characteristics of the substance* paraphrases "characterize a particular kind of matter" in reference to intensive properties.

58. **D**   "When a candle is burned, there are both physical and chemical changes." Choice A is not correct because only the example of the candle is mentioned. Choice B is not correct because the meaning is explained by example, not by definition. Choice C is not correct because the common characteristics were mentioned in previous paragraphs.

59. **A**   In this passage, *distinctive* is a synonym for "unique."

60. **B**   "This is a phase change (liquid to gas) which is a physical change." Because this example of a physical change is provided, it must be concluded that phase changes are sometimes physical changes. Choice A is not correct because the example is a physical change, not a chemical change. Choice C is not correct because the quantity of a substance (extensive properties) is not mentioned in the discussion on phase changes. Choice D is not correct because in a physical change the fundamental composition of a substance has not changed.

61. **B**   In this passage, *important* is a synonym for "critical."

62. **A**   "Has the fundamental composition of the substance changed? In a chemical change . . . it has, but in a physical change, it has not." Choice B is not correct because the quantity refers to extensive properties, not to the difference between physical or chemical properties. Choice C is not correct because both physical and chemical properties are intensive properties. Choice D is not correct because the apparent disappearance of a substance is not necessarily a sign that we are observing a chemical change.

63. **D**   "The following questions pertain to the chemical properties of a substance: '. . . Does it decompose . . . when heated?'" Choices A and B are mentioned as characteristic physical properties in paragraph 4. Choice C is mentioned as a characteristic physical property in paragraph 2 in the discussion of "viscosity."

64. **B**   Pronoun reference is a transitional device that connects the insert sentence with the previous sentence. The pronoun "It" in the insert sentence refers to "aluminum" in the previous sentence. The description of aluminum as "ductile" and "malleable" in the previous sentence means that this metal can be made into wire or shaped into flexible sheets as stated in the insert sentence.

65.   Physical properties: **A, D, E** Chemical properties: **B, C, F, H** Not used: **G, I**

➤ Listening

Model Test 2, Listening Section, CD 1, Track 1

LISTENING 1 "PROFESSOR'S OFFICE"

Audio Conversation

Narrator:	Listen to part of a conversation between a student and a professor.
Student:	Professor James. Do you have a minute?
Professor:	Sure. Come on in. What can I do for you?
Student:	Well, I did pretty well on the midterm . . .
Professor:	You sure did. One of the best grades, as I recall.

Q1 Student: But I missed a question, and I'd appreciate it if you could help me understand what I did wrong. I have the test right here, and I just can't figure it out.

Professor:	Okay. Fire away.
Student:	It's question 7 . . . the one on biotic provinces and biomes.
Professor:	Oh, that one. Um, quite a few people missed it. I was thinking that we should go over it again in class. But anyway, let's look at your answer.

Q2 Student: Thanks. Here's the thing. I said that a biotic province was a region with similar life, but with boundaries that prevent plants and animals from spreading to other regions. So an animal, for example, a mammal . . . it may have a genetic ancestor in common with another mammal. But a biome is a similar environment, an ecosystem really, like a desert or a tropical rainforest. So, in the case of a biome, well, the similar climate causes the plants and animals to evolve . . . to adapt to the climate, and that's why they look alike.

Q3 Professor: That's good, very good . . . as far as you went. But there's a second part to the question. Look, right here. "Include an explanation of convergent and divergent evolution." So . . . I was looking for a more complete answer. Next time, be sure to include both parts of a question . . . when there are two parts like this one. . . . Do you know how to explain convergent and divergent evolution?

Q4 Student: I think so. Isn't it . . . like when a group of plants or animals . . . when they're separated by mountains or a large body of water . . . then subpopulations evolve from a common ancestor and they have similar characteristics but their development diverges because of the separation, so that's why we call it divergent evolution.

Professor:	Right. Even when the habitat is similar, if they're separated, then they diverge. . . . How about convergent evolution then?
Student:	Well, that would be a situation where a similar environment . . . a habitat . . . it may cause plants and animals to evolve in order to adapt to the conditions. So a species that isn't really related can evolve with similar characteristics because . . . it can look like a species in another geographic region because of adaptation . . . and that would be convergent evolution?
Professor:	Right again. So temperature and rainfall, proximity to water, latitude and longitude all combine to determine the climate, and if we know the climate of an area, then we can actually predict what kind of life will inhabit it.
Student:	Okay. And I really did know that. I just didn't put it down. To tell the truth, I didn't see the second part. Not until you pointed it out to me.
Professor:	That's what I thought. Well, Jerry, it's a good idea to double-check all the questions on a test . . . not just my test . . . any test . . . to make sure you've answered each part of the question completely. Otherwise, you won't get full credit.
Student:	I see that. Well, live and learn.
Professor:	Jerry, you're one of my best students.
Student:	Thanks. I really like biology. In fact, I'm thinking of majoring in it.
Professor:	Good. That means you'll be in some of my upper-level classes.
Student:	And I'll be watching out for those two-part questions on your exams.
Professor:	And all the rest of your exams. I'll be honest with you. My questions usually have two parts so the students will have an insight into the grading system . . . and a lot of professors do that. In an essay question, it's difficult to know what to include and how much to write. Just read the question carefully, and be sure to include all the parts. There may be three or four in some essay questions. This is the way that the professor helps you organize your answer. I'm giving my students a hint about what I'm looking for by including several parts to the question. But if you miss one of the parts, then it lowers your score.

Student:	That makes sense. I think I was just trying to finish within the time limit, and I didn't read as carefully as I should have. On the final, I'll spend more time reading the questions before I start to answer them.
Professor:	Good plan.

Q5 (marginal note)

Audio	1.	Why does the man go to see his professor?
Answer	B	To clarify a question from the midterm

Audio	2.	Listen again to part of the conversation and then answer the following question.
Replay		"Thanks. Here's the thing. I said that a biotic province was a region with similar life, but with boundaries that prevent plants and animals from spreading to other regions."
Audio		Why does the man say this:
Replay		"Thanks. Here's the thing."
Answer	D	He is signaling that he will explain his problem.

Audio	3.	What did the man do wrong?
Answer	C	He did not answer one question completely. He did not see the second part.

Audio	4.	According to the student, what is *divergent evolution*?
Answer	C	A similar group that is separated may develop different characteristics.

Audio	5.	What will Jerry probably do on the next test?
Answer	A	To avoid the same problem that he had on the midterm, he will look for questions with several parts.

LISTENING 2 "ART HISTORY CLASS"

Audio Discussion
Narrator: Listen to part of a discussion in an art history class.

Professor:
Sorry about the tests. I don't have them finished. They just took longer to grade than I thought they would. So . . . I'll have them for you next time. Okay then. Let's begin our discussion of the ballet. . . . If you read the chapter in your text, you already know that uh . . . in 1489, a performance that was something like a dinner theater was organized to celebrate the marriage of the Duke of Milan, and . . . a dance representing Jason and the Argonauts

was performed just before the roasted lamb was served. By the way, it's interesting that the dance was called an *entree* and that name has been retained for courses in meals. Anyway, about the same time, outdoor entertainment, you know . . . parades and equestrian events . . . they were becoming more popular, and uh . . . we have evidence that they were referred to as "horse ballets."

Student 1:
So this . . . the horse ballet . . . was it the first time the term "ballet" was used?

Professor:
Right. The actual term in Italian was *balletti*, which meant "a dance done in figures." And it was characterized by the arrangement of the performers in various patterns. Actually, the balletti were staged versions of the social dances that were popular at court, and the steps . . . the basic movements . . . they were walking, swaying, and turning . . . so they combined in a variety of . . . of . . . sequences, each of which was named so that, uh, they could be referred to in the directions for individual dances. In fact, specific instructions for the placement of the dancer's feet probably provided the first, uh . . . the first record of the five positions of classical ballet. Question?

Q8

Student 2:
Sorry. I'm trying to get clear on the dancers. Um . . . could you explain what the book means about court dancing and, uh . . . I'm not saying this very well.

Professor:
I think I know where you're going. You see, the directions that were written down were intended as a reference for social dancing, but they were, uh . . . important in the history of ballet because uh . . . the theatrical dances or entertainments that preceded ballet were . . . not performed by professional dancers. Members of the court danced for the entertainment of society, and in general, the performances were in the central halls of castles and palaces with the audience seated in galleries above so that, uh, the floor figures could . . . could be seen when the people looked down. But back to your question . . . because of the limitations of the performers and the arrangement of the staging, well, the best way to impress the audience was to keep the steps simple enough for the amateur dancers but the geometrical patterns had to be, uh, . . . intricate and . . . and fresh . . . so the spectators would go away pleased because they'd seen something new.

Q9

Student 2:
Oh, I get it now. That makes sense, too, because everyone would be looking down at the dancers.

Professor:
Exactly. Now to continue that thought for a moment . . . by the middle of the sixteenth century, variety shows were being presented on a grand scale in Northern Italy. They included both indoor and outdoor entertainment, and most people called them *spectaculi*. And, uh . . . France had begun to make a significant contribution to the dance form that evolved into modern ballet.

But, to be precise, it was Catherine de Medici who used dance as part of her court entertainments and is, uh . . . credited with the use of the term *ballet*. In 1573 . . . I think it was 1573 . . . anyway, she organized a huge celebration to welcome the ambassadors from Poland who had arrived to, uh . . . to offer their country's throne to her son Henri. So she called it the *Polish Ballet*, and the production was staged on a landing at the top of a grand staircase. Sixteen ladies . . . and these would not have been dancers . . . just members of court . . . so they represented the sixteen provinces of France, and they performed a choreographed dance with a variety of floor figures. Afterward, the audience joined in court dances, similar to the ballroom dancing that evolved later. . . . So that's a long answer to your original question.

| 11 | Student 1: | Now *I* have a question. |

| | Professor: | Okay. |

Student 1:
You said that the *Polish Ballet* was the first ballet, but I thought that the book said the first ballet was *Queen Louise's Ballet*.

Professor:
Good question. Well, I said the *Polish Ballet* was the first use of the term *ballet* for a dance performance, but *Queen Louise's Ballet* is generally considered the first modern ballet. As you'll remember, from the book, the ballet was
10 performed before ten thousand guests, and it was five hours long. When I was doing the research for this lecture, I saw several references to the time, so . . . so I know that this is accurate, but I kept thinking, no one would watch a ballet for five hours. But it must be correct. I can only assume that other activities were going on simultaneously, like a banquet and conversation. Don't you think?

Anyway, what makes *Queen Louise's Ballet* so unique, besides the length, and why it's the first modern ballet, is that it was connected by a story line or, in technical terms, uh, it's called *dramatic cohesion*. Each scene was related to the tales of Circe, a Greek enchantress, who used her powers to battle with man and the gods. The triumph of good, portrayed by Jupiter, over evil, portrayed by Circe, was told in a . . . let's call it a unified production.

Audio   6.   What is the discussion mainly about?

Answer   C   All of the other choices are mentioned in relationship to the main topic: the development of the ballet.

Audio   7.   Listen again to part of the lecture and then answer the following question.

Replay   "So . . . I'll have them for you next time. Okay then. Let's begin our discussion of the ballet. . . . "

Audio   Why does the professor say this:

Replay   "Okay then."

Answer   A   To end his explanation and begin the lecture. Professors often use the word "Okay" as a transition from classroom management activities before the class to the beginning of their lectures.

Audio   8.   According to the professor, what does the term *balletti* mean?

Answer   C   A dance done in figures

Audio   9.   How did the early choreographers accommodate the abilities of amateur performers?

Answer   A   The steps were quite simple.

Audio   10.   Why does the professor mention that he checked several references about the length of *Queen Louise's Ballet*?

Answer   C   He wasn't sure that it was accurate.

Audio   11.   What can be inferred about the professor?

Answer   B   He encourages the students to participate.

LISTENING 3 "LINGUISTICS CLASS"

Audio Discussion

Narrator: Listen to part of a discussion in a linguistics class.

Professor: What comes to mind when I say the word *grammar*?

Student 1:   That's easy. English class and lots of rules.

Student 2:   Memorizing parts of speech . . . like nouns and verbs.

Student 3:   Diagramming sentences.

Professor:

Q12 Well, yes, that's fairly typical. But today we're going to look at grammar from the point of view of the linguist, and to do that, we really have to consider three distinct grammars for every language.

The first grammar is referred to as a *mental grammar*. And that's what a speaker of a language knows, often implicitly, about the grammar of that language. This has also been called *linguistic competence* and from that term *competence grammar* has become popular. I like to think of it, of mental or competence grammar, I mean . . . I like to think of it as an incredibly complex system that allows a speaker to produce language that other speakers can understand. It includes the sounds, the vocabulary, the order of words in sentences and . . . even the appropriateness of a topic or a word in a particular social situation. And what's so amazing is that most of us carry this knowledge around in our heads and use it without much reflection.

Q13 One way to clarify mental or competence grammar is to ask a friend a question about a sentence. Your friend probably won't know *why* it's correct, but that friend will know *if* it's correct. So one of the features of mental or competence grammar is this incredible sense of correctness and the ability to hear something that "sounds odd" in a language. Haven't you had the experience of hearing a sentence, and it stood out to you? It just wasn't quite right? For native speakers we can call this ability *native intuition*, but even language learners who've achieved a high level of competence in a second language will be able to give similar intuitive responses even if they can't explain the rules. So that's mental grammar or competence grammar.

Okay then, that brings us to the second type of grammar, and this is what linguists are most concerned about. This is *descriptive grammar*, which is a description of what the speakers know intuitively about a language. Linguists try to discover the underlying rules of mental or competence grammar and describe them objectively. So descriptive grammar is a *model* of competence grammar, and as such, it has to be based on the best effort of a linguist, and consequently, subject to criticism and even disagreement from *other* linguists. Because no matter how skilled a linguist is, describing grammar is an enormous task. In the first place, the knowledge is incredibly vast and complex; in the second place, the language itself is changing even while it's being described; and finally, the same data can be organized in different but equally correct ways in order to arrive at generalizations. And the ultimate goal of a descriptive grammar is to formulate generalizations about a language that accurately reflect the mental rules that speakers have in their heads.

But, getting back to what most people think of as grammar—the grammar that we may have learned in school. That's very different from either competence grammar or descriptive grammar because the rules aren't meant to describe language at all. They're meant to prescribe and judge language as good or bad. And this kind of grammar is called, not surprisingly, *prescriptive grammar* because of its judgmental perspective. Again, to contrast prescriptive grammar with descriptive grammar, just think of descriptive generalizations as accepting the language that a speaker uses in an effort to describe it and recognizing that there may be several dialects that are used by various groups of speakers and that any one speaker will probably choose to use different language depending on the formality, for example, of the situation. On the other hand, prescriptive rules are rigid and subject to enforcement. Prescriptivists want to make all speakers conform to one standard in all situations, and that tends to be a very formal level of language all the time.

Now which of these types of grammar do you think you were learning in school when you had to memorize parts of speech and rules and diagram sentences?

Student 2:   Sounds like prescriptive grammar to me.

Professor:
Precisely. But how did prescriptive rules get to be accepted, at least in the schools? And probably even more important, why are so many of these rules disregarded even by well-educated speakers in normal situations?

Student 1:   Did you say *disregarded*?   Q15

Professor:
I did. Some of you may recall that during the seventeenth and eighteenth centuries in Europe, Latin was considered the perfect language and was used by the educated classes. The argument for the perfection of Latin was   Q16 reinforced by the fact that Latin had become a written language and, consequently . . . Latin had stopped changing in the normal ways that spoken languages do, so the rules were also fixed, and for many writers of English during that period, the rules of Latin were held as a standard for *all* languages, including English. But the problem was that English had a different origin and very different constructions. For example, how many times have you heard   Q17 the prescriptive rule, "never end a sentence with a preposition?" This is a Latin rule, but it doesn't apply to English, so it sounds very formal and even strange when this Latin rule is enforced. Now, how many of you would say, "What are we waiting for?" I think most of us would prefer it to "For what are we waiting?" But as you see, this breaks the rule—the Latin rule, that is.

Student 2:
So we're really learning Latin rules in English classes. No wonder I was confused. But wouldn't you think that . . . well, that things would change? I mean, Latin hasn't been recognized as a world language for a long time.

Professor:
You're right. But the reason that prescriptive rules survive is the school system. Teachers promote the prescriptive grammar as the standard for the school, and consequently for the educated class. And "good" language is a requisite for social mobility, even when it's very dissimilar to the mental grammar or the descriptive grammar of a language.

Audio	12.	What is the discussion mainly about?
Answer	**B**	Different types of grammar

Audio	13.	How does the professor make his point about *native intuition*?
Answer	**A**	He explains how to perform an easy experiment. By asking a friend about a sentence, the students will understand the concept.

Audio	14.	What are two key problems for descriptive grammar?
Answer	**A**	The information is very complicated and subject to change.
	C	The language can be organized correctly in more than one way.

Audio	15.	Listen again to part of the lecture and then answer the following question.
Replay		"But how did prescriptive rules get to be accepted, at least in the schools?
		And probably even more important, why are so many of these rules disregarded even by well-educated speakers in normal situations?"
		"Did you say *disregarded*?"
Audio		Why does the student say this:
Replay		"Did you say *disregarded*?"
Answer	**B**	She is confirming that she has understood. Her tone is confused, not challenging.

Audio	16.	According to the professor, why were Latin rules used for English grammar?
Answer	**A**	Latin was a written language with rules that did not change.

Audio	17.	Why does the professor discuss the rule to avoid ending a sentence with a preposition?
Answer	**D**	It demonstrates the problem in using Latin rules for English.

LISTENING 4 "COLLEGE CAMPUS"

Audio Conversation

Narrator:	Listen to part of a conversation on campus between two students.
Man:	I didn't see you at the International Talent Show.
Woman:	No time for that kind of thing.
Man:	You mean you don't belong to the ISA?
Woman:	The ISA?
Man:	International Student Association.
Woman:	Oh, no. I don't belong to any clubs.
Man:	But this isn't like a regular club.
Woman:	How so?
Man:	Well, we have a house. You know, the brick house on fraternity row and . . .
Woman:	You live there, right?
Man:	Yeah. I moved in last year. It's really inexpensive because we take care of the house ourselves and we cook our own meals.
Woman:	That sounds like it would take a lot of time.
Man:	Not really. There's a list of chores posted every week, and you can choose something you like to do, so I usually put my name down for yard work. I like being outside so it's fun for me.
Woman:	But you have to cook too, right?
Man:	Okay, it's like this: twenty of us live there so every night two of the guys cook and two of the guys clean up, so you only have to cook about once a week and clean up once.
Woman:	What about breakfast and lunch?
Man:	Oh, well, you're on your own for that, but the dinners are just fantastic. It's like eating in a different ethnic restaurant every night. You know, because the guys are from different countries.
Woman:	That sounds good.
Man:	And it costs about half what it did to live in the dorm. But really, I'm doing it because it's a great experience living with people from so many different countries. My best friend in the house is from Korea. My roommate's from Brazil. And I've got friends from . . . well, just about everywhere.
Woman:	But you don't have to live in the house to belong to the club.
Man:	No, no. There are about a hundred members in the International Student Association. Only guys live in the house, but there are a lot of women in the association.

Q1

Q2

Woman:	I wish I had time to do it. It really sounds interesting.
Man:	You've got to relax sometimes. Anyway, we meet at the house the first Friday of the month from seven to ten. We have a buffet dinner and after that, we have a short meeting. That's when we plan our activities, like the talent show and picnics and dances. Then a lot of the people stay for music and a party, but some people leave after the meeting.
Woman:	So it's only a couple hours a month.
Man:	Right. Listen, why don't you come over next Friday for the meeting, as my guest, I mean. You have to eat anyway. And if you have a good time, you can think about joining.
Woman:	Next Friday? Well, I don't know . . . I usually study on Friday night, but . . . I could take a break . . . Sure I'll come over . . . but I might have to leave early.
Man:	Great.

Audio   18.   What is the purpose of this conversation?

Answer   C   The man is convincing the woman to join the International Student Association. He invites the woman to attend a meeting as his guest.

Audio   19.   What does the man imply about the house where he is living?

Answer   A   He is saving money by living at the house, but he prefers the house to the dorm because it is a great experience.

Audio   20.   How does the man feel about the International Student Association?

Answer   B   He enjoys meeting people with different backgrounds.

Audio   21.   Listen again to part of the conversation and then answer the following question.

Replay   "Then a lot of the people stay for music and a party, but some people leave after the meeting."
                   "So it's only a couple hours a month."

Audio   What does the woman mean when she says this:

Replay   "So it's only a couple hours a month."

Answer   D   Her tone indicates indecision. She is changing her mind about going.

Audio   22.   What does the woman agree to do?

Answer   C   Go to a meeting

LISTENING 5 "ZOOLOGY CLASS"

Audio Lecture

Narrator: Listen to part of a lecture in a zoology class. The professor is discussing coral reefs.

Professor:

Every ecosystem on Earth is unique, but the coral reef is perhaps the most unusual of all because it's the only ecosystem made by and made *of*—animals. All coral reefs are constructed by coral polyps, which are generally small, about the size of this pencil eraser. But, the structures themselves are, well, enormous. Astronauts have been able to identify the Great Barrier Reef in Australia from space. Can you believe that? And the diversity of species in large coral reefs is second only to the rainforest habitats. In fact, we estimate that for every species we've identified on a coral reef, there are probably a hundred times that number that remain to be classified and studied.

But how do these little polyps build such impressive reefs? Well, hard coral secrete a shell of calcium carbonate around their bodies. The polyp *isn't* hard, you see, but the shell *is*. And these shells are the material that forms a coral reef. So a coral reef is just a colony—millions and millions of coral animals whose shells are connected. And reproduction is really the basis for the construction of a large reef. You see, as each polyp matures, it converts the calcium and other minerals in ocean water to a hard limestone exoskeleton called a *corallite*. And this is fascinating. Although the polyps themselves don't appreciably increase in size, they continue to build new shells periodically, um, connecting them with . . . with partitions.

Now coral can reproduce sexually through an activity called mass spawning. During one night in the spring when the moon is full, coral polyps release egg bundles that contain both eggs and sperm. Most polyps have both male and female reproductive cells. The egg bundles are round, about half the size of marbles, I would say. They're brightly colored in orange or red or pink, and they float up to the surface to form a thick layer of, uh . . . well think of them as rather fragrant beads. So with the water so saturated with them, predators will only be able to devour a small number compared with the huge number that will survive and break open. The sperm cells swim away to fertilize the eggs from another bundle. So . . . once fertilized, the little egg begins to mature from a coral larva to a planulae, which can swim for a few hours, days, or even a few weeks. Ultimately it locates a hard surface on which to attach itself and from which it will *not* move for the rest of its life, except for the movement involved in the process of building a new, neighboring shell as . . . as it continues to mature.

But actually sexual reproduction isn't the way that coral reefs are really constructed. When a polyp matures on the site it's selected, the habitat is identified as being conducive to reef building. So the mature polyp doesn't just grow bigger, it actually replicates itself in a process called *budding*. After the genetic material is duplicated, then the polyp divides itself in half, and each half becomes a completely mature polyp. This budding process repeats itself, eventually producing thousands of asexually budded coral polyps connected by a tissue that grows over the limestone shells between the polyps. So, as you can imagine, budding will produce a large number of individual polyps, but they'll all have exactly the same genetic code as the first polyp. And this creates the beginning of a coral reef, but without the diversity that eventually populates the habitat. Wherever a coral reef is constructed, abundant sea life congregates. In fact, it's been estimated that about 25 percent of all ocean species can be found within the coral reefs.

Now most coral polyps eat plankton—single-celled microscopic organisms that float or swim very slowly in the ocean water in their habitat. But, um, a coral reef has such a high concentration of polyps, they can't rely solely on plankton to survive. So coral polyps have developed a symbiotic relationship with a single-celled algae called zooxanthella. Remember that to qualify as symbiotic, a relationship must be, um, mutually beneficial. So the zooxanthella produces food for the coral through the by-products of photosynthesis, and the coral provides a safe home for the zooxanthella, because it's hidden from predators that inhabit the coral reef.

Every species of coral grows at a different rate, some as much as six inches a year. But faster growing colonies are more prone to breaking apart either from their own weight or from the continuous force of the ocean waves. Some species tend to grow more slowly, but they may live as long as a thousand years. Even so, only the top portion of any reef is actually alive and growing and the lower structure is comprised of the skeletal remains . . . that's limestone corallite from coral that has died.

And what I find incredibly interesting about coral reefs is that each is a unique structure. But, of course, scientists need to classify, and so there's a classification system for coral reefs. A *fringing reef* grows around islands and the shorelines of continents and extends out from the shore. In order to flourish, fringing reefs must have clean water, lots of sunshine, and a moderately high concentration of salt. Some good examples of fringing reefs can be found around the Hawaiian Islands. Oh, yes, these are the most common and also the most recently formed class of coral reefs. Here's a drawing of a fringing reef.

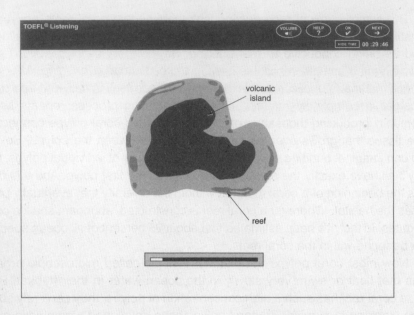

I think this is actually one of the Hawaiian reefs.

Now, *barrier reefs*—they're found further from shore, and they're usually separated from the shoreline by a shallow body of water, maybe a lagoon. As in the case of the Great Barrier Reef off the shore of Australia, the body of water can be miles wide, so the reef is miles away from the shoreline. And there may actually be a collection of coral reefs fused together. This is a drawing of a reef in the Great Barrier chain.

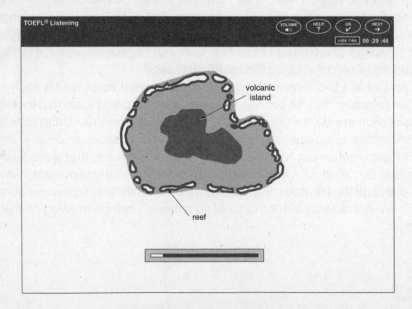

As I recall there are about twenty-five, or maybe even more individual coral reefs connected to form the Great Barrier Reef. As a general rule, barrier reefs are larger and older than fringing reefs.

Q27   But the oldest class of coral reef is the *atoll*, which is a ring-shaped reef with a lagoon in the middle and deep water surrounding the ring. These are scattered throughout the South Pacific, kind of like oasis settlements in the desert. And they abound with a diversity of sea life. This is one of the South Pacific atolls.

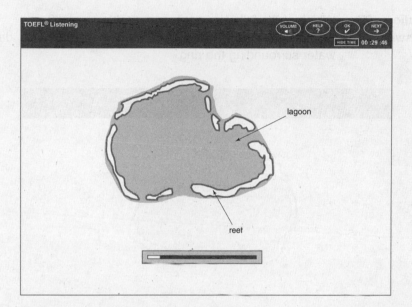

So, as we reflect on everything we've said about coral, we know that it's a relatively simple organism with a body ending in a mouth and tentacles. It reproduces both sexually and asexually by budding, and, um . . . it survives by forming a symbiotic relationship with zooxanthella. But none of this is very extraordinary. What is unique about coral in the animal kingdom is its ability to construct a variety of reefs, creating habitats that are absolutely unlike any others on Earth.

Audio   23.   According to the professor, how do coral reefs grow?
Answer   B   They connect corallite shells to build structures.

Audio   24.   Why are so many egg bundles released during mass spawning?
Answer   C   A number of the egg bundles will be eaten [by predators].

Audio   25. According to the professor, what is *budding*?
Answer   A The division of a polyp in half to reproduce itself.

Audio   26. What is the relationship between zooxanthella and coral polyps?
Answer   B The zooxanthella uses the coral for a shelter from enemies.
C The coral eats food produced by the zooxanthella.
The relationship is symbiotic.

Audio   27. Which of the following reefs is probably an atoll?
Answer   C A ring-shaped reef with a lagoon in the middle and deep water surrounding the ring.

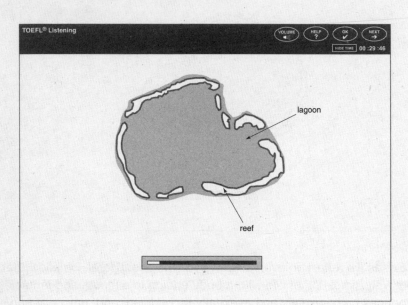

Audio   28. In the lecture, the professor explains coral reefs. Indicate whether each of the following is a true statement about coral reefs. Click in the correct box for each phrase.

		Yes	No
A	In general, the organism is quite simple.	✔	
B	The structure of a reef can be very large.	✔	
C	The living coral grows on top of dead shells.	✔	
D	Mass spawning is not very effective.		✔

LISTENING 6 "BUSINESS CLASS"

Audio Discussion

Narrator: Listen to part of a discussion in a business class.

Professor:

29 | Industry analysts report that multinational food companies are trying to use the same types of strategies that automobile and electronics manufacturers have found to be successful in the global marketplace. The problem is that general rules for products that tend to be traditional for national or even regional tastes . . . these products are very difficult to identify and sales aren't easy to project. But, the companies that tend to do best are those that are the most responsive to local tastes. And they spend development dollars on 30 | taste testing in the local markets before they formulate the final product. Can anyone recall any examples from the case studies in the text? Sandy?

Student 1:

McDonald's Big Mac has more mustard in the special sauce in Paris than it does in New York.

Professor: Because?

Student 1:

Because taste tests verified that people in the United States liked sweeter condiments than people did in France. In fact, I think the . . . the sugar content for export foods in general usually has to be modified when American products are taste tested overseas.

Professor:

Right you are. Probably the company that's adapted most to local tastes is Nestle. Can you believe that they produce more than 200 slightly different blends of Nescafe for export to different countries? Amazing but true. But sometimes taste is less a problem of ingredients and more a matter of the way a food product looks or feels. One case study that comes to mind is the one about the soft cookies that just don't sell as well in England as crisp cookies. So, you can see that taste extends way beyond just flavor. It's really ly a combination of flavor preferences and local expectations.

Look, here's another example of accommodation that had more to do with the expectation for a process than the flavor of the product. In this case study, it was cake. Remember when Betty Crocker cake mixes were introduced in England, they weren't accepted because the English homemaker felt more comfortable with convenience foods that required more than water to prepare them. Go figure. But that was the problem uncovered by extensive market research. So when the mix was reformulated without an egg, and the preparation included adding an egg with the water before mixing it, well, Betty Crocker cake mixes became very popular in England.

Any other examples come to mind? They don't have to be from the case Q3 studies in the book.

Student 2:   How about serving sizes?

Professor: Go on.

Student 2:
Well soft drinks for one. Just compare the serving sizes in the United States and many foreign markets where soft drinks are sold. The cans in foreign markets are much smaller because consumers expect it. But, uh, in the United States, well, super sizing is probably a consideration when a foreign company is trying to crack the American market.

Professor:
That's a great example. So the taste can be acceptable, but the packaging Q3 has to compare favorably with the competing brands and the public's expec-tations.

Student 3:
Yeah, but that makes products more expensive, doesn't it? I mean because you can't standardize the product or the packaging so that would make it more . . . more costly to produce, wouldn't it?

Professor:
Right you are, Chris. In fact, you've really gone to the heart of the issue. A compromise has to occur between the requirement that products be adapt-ed to please the taste and the expectations of local consumers and the pres-sure to standardize products for maximum cost effectiveness. Now, let's complicate that even further. Even the experts don't agree on the importance of how far to go in adapting products for local markets. A few years ago, Ted Levitt—he's the editor of the *Harvard Business Review*—Levitt predicted Q3 what he called a "pluralization of consumption." What he means is that at least in some areas, tastes are likely to converge, which makes sense when you think about the increased opportunities for travel and sampling of foods, as well as the continued global marketing efforts by multinational corpora-tions. So logically, it's smarter to simply identify the areas in which tastes are most likely to be the same, and concentrate efforts on those food products.

But there's also the issue of global marketing. How about the potential to create taste? I mean, selling the image that surrounds using a product. If consumers want to associate themselves with that image, won't they develop a taste for the product that does that for them? For example, there's some evidence that the popularity of products seen in movies and television spills into the foreign marketplace. This subtle brand association with the movie or the celebrities in it translates into high dollar deals for certain brands to be visibly displayed in widely distributed films.

Student 3:
Oh, right. I was reading about that. It was in a couple of the case studies. The bottle, a can, or . . . or a package appears as part of the character's persona, and if it's a character that audiences choose to identify with, then the taste for the product may follow, or at least that's what the marketing experts are betting on.

Professor:
And that includes foreign audiences. Anyone drink Starbucks coffee? Well, Starbucks began as a regional coffee in Seattle, Washington, and made the global leap in 2000, opening shops in China, a huge market surely, but also a traditionally *tea-drinking* society. So what's the attraction? Starbucks is marketing to the cosmopolitan consumer, the young trendy set looking for a modern image as well as a different taste.

Still, there have been some real surprises in the multinational dinner party. No one has really figured out why the Italians, Germans, and British love Kraft's Philadelphia cream cheese, and the Greeks simply don't buy it. And why did Perrier, a mineral water from France . . . why did Perrier take America by storm while other imported mineral waters . . . didn't? In short, success in the food export industry is probably a combination of the real taste . . . the flavor of the product, with some adaptation for the local markets, the satisfaction of certain expectations for the preparation and packaging, and the taste for the product created by images in the global marketing plan. Add to this mix the potential for a short shelf life or even perishable products and, well, you have a very challenging problem for the multinational food industry.

Audio	29.	What is the discussion mainly about?
Answer	**A**	The other choices relate to the main topic: the global marketing of food products.

Audio	30.	How does the professor organize the lecture?
Answer	**C**	He refers to case studies from the textbook.

Audio   31.   Listen again to part of the lecture and then answer the following question.

Replay   "Any other examples come to mind? They don't have to be from the case studies in the book."
"How about serving sizes?"

Audio   Why does the student say this:

Replay   "How about serving sizes?"

Answer   B   She is offering a possible answer to the professor's question. "How about" is a polite way to offer a possibility.

Audio   32.   What technique does the professor use to encourage student discussion?

Answer   A   He gives students positive reinforcement by praising their efforts.

Audio   33.   What did Ted Levitt mean by "the pluralization of consumption"?

Answer   D   More people will want the same products.

Audio   34.   What does the professor say about television and movie companies?

Answer   D   He points out that they are paid to display brand-name products.

➤ Speaking

 Model Test 2, Speaking Section, CD 1, Track 2

INDEPENDENT SPEAKING QUESTION 1 "A BIRTHDAY"

Narrator 2: Number 1. Listen for a question about a familiar topic. After you hear the question, you have 15 seconds to prepare and 45 seconds to record your answer.

Narrator 1: Explain how birthdays are celebrated in your country. Use specific examples and details in your explanation.

Narrator 2: Please prepare your answer after the beep.

Beep

[Preparation time: 15 seconds]

Narrator 2: Please begin speaking after the beep.

Beep

[Recording time: 45 seconds]

Beep

INDEPENDENT SPEAKING QUESTION 2 "COURSE REQUIREMENTS"

Narrator 2: Number 2. Listen for a question that asks your opinion about a familiar topic. After you hear the question, you have 15 seconds to prepare and 45 seconds to record your answer.

Narrator 1: Some students would rather write a paper than take a test. Other students would rather take a test instead of writing a paper. Which option do you prefer and why? Use specific reasons and examples to support your opinion.

Narrator 2: Please prepare your answer after the beep.

Beep

[Preparation time: 15 seconds]

Narrator 2: Please begin speaking after the beep.

Beep

[Recording time: 45 seconds]

Beep

INTEGRATED SPEAKING QUESTION 3 "HEALTH INSURANCE"

Narrator 2: Number 3. Read a short passage and listen to a talk on the same topic. Then listen for a question about them. After you hear the question, you have 30 seconds to prepare and 60 seconds to record your answer.

Narrator 1: A student is discussing the university's health insurance policy with the foreign student advisor. Read the policy in the college schedule printed on page 309. You have 45 seconds to complete it. Please begin reading now.

[Reading time: 45 seconds]

Narrator 1: Now listen to the foreign student advisor. He is explaining the policy and expressing his opinion about it.

Advisor:
I think it's very important for you to know that this policy wasn't instituted in order to increase fees for international students. In fact, the university doesn't make a profit from the sale of health insurance. The problem is that health care costs in this country are so high that it could be financially disastrous for the family of an international student who needed more than just a simple visit to the doctor's office. A trip to the emergency room at the hospital could cost thousands of dollars without health insurance! Most families abroad just don't realize how costly it is. As for foreign health insurance providers—well, it was just too difficult to validate their coverage for medical services, and the local doctors and hospitals simply stopped accepting them. So . . . to be sure that our students are protected, we're offering low-cost health insurance through the school.

Narrator 1: The foreign student advisor expresses his opinion of the policy for health insurance. Report his opinion and explain the reasons that he gives for having that opinion.

Narrator 2: Please prepare your answer after the beep.

Beep

[Preparation time: 30 seconds]

Narrator 2: Please begin speaking after the beep.

Beep

[Recording time: 60 seconds]

Beep

INTEGRATED SPEAKING QUESTION 4 "ANTARCTICA"

Narrator 2: Number 4. Read a short passage and listen to part of a lecture on the same topic. Then listen for a question about them. After you hear the question, you have 30 seconds to prepare and 60 seconds to record your answer.

Narrator 1: Now read the passage about Antarctica printed on page 310. You have 45 seconds to complete it. Please begin reading now.

[Reading time: 45 seconds]

Narrator 1: Now listen to part of a lecture in a geography class. The professor is talking about Antarctica.

Professor:
With the increasing pressure to replace raw materials that are being consumed in other parts of the world, Antarctica and the waters offshore could become a stage for international conflict in the future. During the eighteenth and nineteenth centuries, hunters decimated huge populations of whales and seals, and the race to reach the South Pole resulted in national claims by explorers from a variety of countries, which finally resulted in the partitioning of pie-shaped sectors radiating away from the center at the pole. So today several claims overlap, and only one sector remains unclaimed. Virtually all of these claims are covered by an ice sheet about two miles thick, but the question is, what's beneath the ice? Scientific experiments indicate that proteins, fuels, and minerals exist in abundance, and that means that in spite of the difficulties and challenges involved in the exploitation of these natural resources, the countries with claims haven't demonstrated an intention to relinquish their stake in the area. While resources are available in more convenient sites, the remote areas in Antarctica appear to be relatively safe from exploitation. In addition, as the reading passage suggests, global self-interest may engender international cooperation in this crucial environmental system.

Narrator 1: Explain why many countries have staked claims in Antarctica, and why national interests have not been pursued.

Narrator 2: Please prepare your answer after the beep.

Beep

[Preparation time: 30 seconds]

Narrator 2: Please begin speaking after the beep.

Beep

[Recording time: 60 seconds]

Beep

INTEGRATED SPEAKING QUESTION 5 "EXTRA MONEY"

Narrator 2: Number 5. Listen to a short conversation. Then listen for a question about it. After you hear the question, you have 20 seconds to prepare and 60 seconds to record your answer.

Narrator 1: Now listen to a conversation between a student and her friend.

Student:	I need to earn some extra money. My budget's just out of control.
Friend:	I hear you. I had the same problem last semester.
Student:	So what did you do?
Friend:	I got a job at the cafeteria. I don't really like the work, but the good thing is that you get free meals.
Student:	Really? Are they hiring?
Friend:	I don't know, but I could ask. The pay isn't great though. See, the meals are the thing.
Student:	Oh. Still, that would cut down on the grocery bill.
Friend:	Yeah . . . Or, you know what? You could rent that extra room in your apartment. I'll bet you could get $250 a month, at least.
Student:	I've been thinking about that. It would help with the rent and the utilities, and I wouldn't have to work so I could use my time for my classes, but, I keep thinking, what if my roommate doesn't pay on time, or what if there's a lot of noise.
Friend:	Well, you'd have to have a deposit and a contract . . . something in writing so you could keep the deposit if there were problems, and you could break the contract if it didn't work out.

Narrator 1: Describe the woman's problem, and the two suggestions that her friend makes about how to handle it. What do you think the woman should do, and why?

Narrator 2: Please prepare your answer after the beep.

Beep

[Preparation time: 20 seconds]

Narrator 2: Please begin speaking after the beep.

Beep

[Recording time: 60 seconds]

Beep

INTEGRATED SPEAKING QUESTION 6 "RESEARCH REFERENCES"

Narrator 2: Number 6. Listen to part of a lecture. Then listen for a question about it. After you hear the question, you have 20 seconds to prepare, and 60 seconds to record your answer.

Narrator 1: Now listen to part of a lecture in a sociology class. The professor is discussing the criteria for using older research references.

Professor:
Well, first of all you have to understand that there's no hard and fast rule for deciding when a research reference is too old. But that doesn't help you much. So, I'll try to give you a couple of guidelines, and then you'll just have to use good judgment. Okay, let's just say for our purposes, that the research is thirty years old. Then the next thing to think about is whether any changes have occurred in society to call the data into question. For example, in a study that looks at diet, we know logically that many changes have occurred in eating patterns over the past thirty years, so this study would probably be out of date. But a study of, say, uh, language development may be okay because the way that babies learn their native language hasn't changed much in the same period of time. So, what I'm saying is . . . the date is less important than the potential for change. Okay, then the second criteria to consider is whether the citation is a *finding* or an *opinion*. If you have a study that indicates, uh, for example, that college students are drinking more, that's a *finding*, but if you have a statement by the researcher that drinking is the most serious problem on campus, then you have an *opinion*. And opinions are accurate over the years as long as they're attributed to the person and the date is cited. But the finding for an older study may be too old. In that case, it's probably better to use a more recent study.

Narrator 1: Using the main points and examples from the lecture, describe the two criteria for using an older research reference presented by the professor.

Narrator 2: Please prepare your answer after the beep.

Beep

[Preparation time: 20 seconds]

Narrator 2: Please begin speaking after the beep.

Beep

[Recording time: 60 seconds]

Beep

➤ Writing

INTEGRATED ESSAY "THE TURING TEST"

First, read the passage on page 315 and take notes.

 Model Test 2, Writing Section, CD 1, Track 3

Narrator: Now listen to a lecture on the same topic as the passage that you have just read.

Professor:
Philosopher John Searle has challenged the validity of the Turing Test because it's premised on behavior rather than on thought. To prove his argument, he's suggested a paradox, which he refers to as the Chinese Room. If a monolingual English-speaking person receives questions on a computer terminal from a Chinese person in another room, naturally the English-speaking person won't understand the questions. However, if there's a large reference that can be accessed, and if the reference is detailed and comprehensible, then the English speaker could, conceivably, break the code. For example, if a sequence of Chinese characters are received, the reference could indicate which sequence of Chinese characters would be expected in response. In other words, the behavior would be correct, although the English speaker wouldn't be thinking at a level that included meaning. The person would be manipulating symbols without understanding them, or, as Searle suggests, the person would be *acting* intelligent without *being* intelligent, which is exactly what a computer could be programmed to do.

Therefore, at least theoretically, a computer could be designed with complex input that would allow it to provide adequate behavioral output without being aware of what it's doing. If so, then it could pass the Turing Test. But the test itself would be meaningless because it doesn't really answer the most basic question about artificial intelligence, which is, can the computer think?

➤ Example Answers and Checklists for Speaking and Writing

 Model Test 2, Example Answers, CD 1, Track 4

EXAMPLE ANSWER FOR INDEPENDENT SPEAKING QUESTION 1 "A BIRTHDAY"

In my country, birthdays are celebrated every year but the most important birthday for a young girl is the *quinceañera*, the birthday when she's fifteen. This is celebrated with a church service. The girl wears a white dress, kind of like a wedding dress, and several attendants accompany her to the altar where the priest talks with her about becoming an adult woman. After the service, the whole family celebrates with friends. And there's music and dancing and food. Traditionally, only relatives and close friends are invited to the church service, but many more people attend the party afterward. Um, in the old days, the ceremony presented the girl to society for marriage proposals . . . but now she's considered the appropriate age to begin dating.

Checklist 1

✔ The talk answers the topic question.
✔ The point of view or position is clear.
✔ The talk is direct and well-organized.
✔ The sentences are logically connected.
✔ Details and examples support the main idea.
✔ The speaker expresses complete thoughts.
✔ The meaning is easy to comprehend.
✔ A wide range of vocabulary is used.
✔ There are only minor errors in grammar.
✔ The talk is within a range of 125–150 words.

EXAMPLE ANSWER FOR INDEPENDENT SPEAKING QUESTION 2 "COURSE REQUIREMENTS"

I prefer to write a paper instead of taking a test because I know exactly what the topic is when I'm researching a paper, but there are a large number of possibilities for questions on a test and that makes it much more difficult to prepare for. Besides, in my experience, some teachers aren't very straight-forward about their tests, and even though I've studied and understand the subject, well, sometimes the questions that you would expect to see aren't on the test and some obscure information is tested instead. But probably the most important reason for my preference is that I get very nervous when I'm taking a test, and that can affect my performance. Writing a paper doesn't cause me the same level of anxiety.

Checklist 2

✔ The talk answers the topic question.
✔ The point of view or position is clear.
✔ The talk is direct and well-organized.
✔ The sentences are logically connected.
✔ Details and examples support the main idea.
✔ The speaker expresses complete thoughts.
✔ The meaning is easy to comprehend.
✔ A wide range of vocabulary is used.
✔ There are only minor errors in grammar.
✔ The talk is within a range of 125–150 words.

EXAMPLE ANSWER FOR INTEGRATED SPEAKING QUESTION 3 "HEALTH INSURANCE"

The foreign student advisor agrees with the policy that requires international students to purchase health insurance from the university at registration. He assures students that the university isn't trying to increase fees for international students by doing this. He explains that health care is very expensive. For example, a visit to the emergency room can be a financial burden to a family who doesn't have medical insurance. He says that most families of international students don't expect the costs to be so excessive. And the reason that the university doesn't allow students to substitute other health care providers is because the local medical community has had problems with validation for health insurance plans from abroad and now refuses to accept them. So, um, in order to protect the students, the school doesn't make any exceptions to the policy.

Checklist 3

✔ The talk summarizes the situation and opinion.
✔ The point of view or position is clear.
✔ The talk is direct and well-organized.
✔ The sentences are logically connected.
✔ Details and examples support the opinion.

✔ The speaker expresses complete thoughts.
✔ The meaning is easy to comprehend.
✔ A wide range of vocabulary is used.
✔ Errors in grammar are minor.
✔ The talk is within a range of 125–150 words.

EXAMPLE ANSWER FOR INTEGRATED SPEAKING QUESTION 4 "ANTARCTICA"

Many countries have staked claims in Antarctica because the natural resources in other areas are being depleted and, uh, research indicates that minerals, fuels, and even some sources of protein are probably under the ice in large quantities. So, the implication is that as raw materials are exploited in areas that are relatively easy to reach, nations will think about taking advantage of their claims. For the time being, the location and climate have discouraged exploitation, and so have the treaties that protect the environment and encourage scientists to collaborate. It's also worth mentioning that Antarctica is vitally important to the balance that's maintained in the environment worldwide. So, in addition to all the difficulties that would have to be overcome to take advantage of the resources in their claims, individual nations also recognize the danger to the global environment and, at least for now, they're not pursuing their national interests.

Checklist 4

✔ The talk relates an example to a concept.
✔ Inaccuracies in the content are minor.
✔ The talk is direct and well-organized.
✔ The sentences are logically connected.
✔ Details and examples support the opinion.
✔ The speaker expresses complete thoughts.
✔ The meaning is easy to comprehend.
✔ A wide range of vocabulary is used.
✔ The speaker paraphrases in his/her own words.
✔ The speaker credits the lecturer with wording.
✔ Errors in grammar are minor.
✔ The talk is within a range of 125–150 words.

EXAMPLE ANSWER FOR INTEGRATED SPEAKING QUESTION 5 "EXTRA MONEY"

The woman needs additional income to meet her expenses so her friend suggests that she get a job at the cafeteria. Even though the salary isn't very high, the free meals are helpful. He isn't sure whether there's a job available but he agrees to find out. He also recommends that she rent the second bedroom in her apartment for a minimum of $250 a month, which would subsidize the rent and utilities. The problem she points out is that roommates can be disruptive, and sometimes they aren't financially responsible. But, she would have more time to study if she didn't have to work and her friend reminds her that she could require an agreement in writing, along with a deposit. Okay, in my opinion, she should try to get a job either in the cafeteria or someplace else on campus because if she lives alone, she can maintain a quiet environment for study, and she won't have to worry about a contract that could be difficult to enforce.

Checklist 5

✔ The talk summarizes the problem and recommendations.
✔ The speaker's point of view or position is clear.
✔ The talk is direct and well-organized.
✔ The sentences are logically connected.
✔ Details and examples support the opinion.
✔ The speaker expresses complete thoughts.
✔ The meaning is easy to comprehend.
✔ A wide range of vocabulary is used.
✔ Errors in grammar are minor.
✔ The talk is within a range of 125–150 words.

EXAMPLE ANSWER FOR INTEGRATED SPEAKING QUESTION 6 "RESEARCH REFERENCES"

According to the lecturer, there are two major criteria for using an older research reference. First, she mentions, and I'm quoting here, the "potential for change." For example, research on diet may be too old after thirty years because many changes have occurred in dietary practices during that time, but research on language development may be okay because fewer changes have taken place in language acquisition in the same number of years. The other criteria requires that you first identify the research as a conclusion or an opinion. Because, uh, in general, a conclusion may be outdated when a newer study is published, but an opinion credited to a person with the date of the opinion in the citation, um, that's correct over time. In other words, there's no exact number of years to decide whether a reference is acceptable so the date isn't as significant as the criteria. So, an older study can be used if changes in the research haven't taken place or if the results are worded as opinions with the dates cited.

Checklist 6

✔ The talk summarizes a short lecture.
✔ Inaccuracies in the content are minor.
✔ The talk is direct and well-organized.
✔ The sentences are logically connected.
✔ Details and examples support the opinion.
✔ The speaker expresses complete thoughts.
✔ The meaning is easy to comprehend.
✔ A wide range of vocabulary is used.
✔ The speaker paraphrases in his/her own words.
✔ The speaker credits the lecturer with wording.
✔ Errors in grammar are minor.
✔ The talk is within a range of 125–150 words.

EXAMPLE RESPONSE FOR INTEGRATED ESSAY "THE TURING TEST"

Some writers begin with an outline and others begin with a map of their ideas. Only the essay will be scored.

Outline

Turing Test—1950

* People interact w/ something
   In another room
   Questions microphone or computer
   Response voice synthesizer or text
* Evaluate
   Person or computer
   Wrong or can't decide →
   Machine passed Turing Test

Lecturer
* Premised on behavior, not thought
* Chinese Room—John Searle
   Questions in Chinese
   Reference
   Correct behavior
   Symbols w/o comprehension

Map

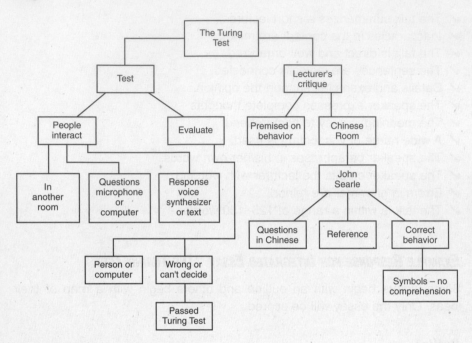

Example Essay

The Turing Test, developed in 1950, allows subjects to interact with a person or a computer in another room by speaking into a microphone or typing questions onto a computer. When they receive an answer by voice synthesizer or by text on their computer screens, subjects must determine whether they have been communicating with a computer or with a human being. If they think that they have been interacting with a person or they are unable to decide, then the computer has passed the Turing Test, proving that the machine is actually capable of higher-level thought processes similar to those of a human brain.

According to the lecture, however, a machine can be programmed to produce responses that appear to be intelligent without the awareness required for thought. In John Searle's Chinese Room, an English-speaking person is able to respond to questions in Chinese by referring to source material that allows him or her to break the code without comprehending the underlying meaning of the symbols. The person can behave correctly without the higher-level thought required to process the meaning. Therefore, a computer could pass the Turing Test if it were programmed to generate behavioral output but the Turing Test itself would be flawed. The experiment would not prove that a computer can think.

Checklist for Integrated Essay

✔ The essay answers the topic question.
✔ Inaccuracies in the content are minor.
✔ The essay is direct and well-organized.
✔ The sentences are logically connected.
✔ Details and examples support the main idea.
✔ The writer expresses complete thoughts.
✔ The meaning is easy to comprehend.
✔ A wide range of vocabulary is used.
✔ The writer paraphrases in his/her own words.
✔ The writer credits the author with wording.
✔ Errors in grammar and idioms are minor.
✔ The essay is within a range of 150–225 words.

EXAMPLE RESPONSE FOR INDEPENDENT ESSAY "FAMILY PETS"

Outline

Outline
Agree that pets should be treated like family members
* Children—learn how to care for brother, sister
* Couple—substitute for babies
* Disabled, elderly—help, caring like family members
* Every stage in life

Map

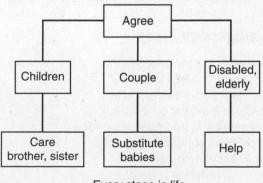

Every stage in life

Example Essay

Although the argument has been made that money spent on pets could better be directed to programs that provide assistance for needy people, I agree that pets should be treated like family members because they live in our homes and interact with us like family members do. Often parents allow children to have pets in order to teach them to be responsible. By feeding, walking, and grooming a dog, children learn to be dependable and kind. Parents expect their children to take care of the pets as if they were members of the family in order to learn these valuable lessons. For many children, a dog or a kitten is also a best friend and a wonderful way to learn how to treat a new brother or sister when the family expands.

Besides the friendship that children enjoy with animals, pets can substitute for the absence of other family members. Sometimes a couple who is unable to have children will adopt pets and treat them like babies. They shower the love on their cats that they might have provided a child, and receive affection and companionship in return. Many people who are living alone enjoy the companionship of a pet instead of loved ones who are at a distance or have passed away. The pet becomes a family member for these people and deserves the same kind of treatment that a family member would receive.

Many articles have appeared in the popular press citing the benefits of pets to the disabled and the elderly. In addition to the usual services that pets may provide, such as bringing objects to their owners or helping a vision-impaired owner to walk in unfamiliar surroundings, there is evidence that pets actually extend the life expectancy of their owners. In a real sense, these pets are caring for their owners like family members would, and for this reason, they should be treated like family.

At every stage in life we interact with our pets in the same ways that we interact with family. Children, young married couples, and elderly people have reason to treat their pets like family members.

Checklist for Independent Essay

✔ The essay answers the topic question.
✔ The point of view or position is clear.
✔ The essay is direct and well-organized.
✔ The sentences are logically connected.
✔ Details and examples support the main idea.
✔ The writer expresses complete thoughts.
✔ The meaning is easy to comprehend.
✔ A wide range of vocabulary is used.
✔ Various types of sentences are included.
✔ Errors in grammar and idioms are minor.
✔ The essay is within a range of 300–350 words.

MODEL TEST 3: PROGRESS TEST

➤ Reading

READING 1 "EXOTIC AND ENDANGERED SPECIES"

1. **C** ". . . exotic species . . . a resident of an established community that was deliberately or accidentally moved from its home range and became established elsewhere." Choice A is not correct because it refers to an endangered species, not an exotic species. Choice B is not correct because exotic species are moved from their communities. Choice D is not correct because an exotic species becomes established, unlike most imports, which fail to thrive outside of their home range.

2. **D** "Unlike most imports, which can't take hold outside their home range, an exotic species permanently insinuates itself [the exotic species] into a new community." The pronoun "itself" does not refer to Choices A, B, or C.

3. **B** In this passage, *connect* is a synonym for "bond." Context comes from the result at the end of the same sentence. ". . . they started to import familiar animals."

4. **C** ". . . no natural predators . . . was the reality." Choice A is not correct because it refers to a solution for the problem, not why the plan failed. Choice B is not correct because Australians imported rabbits because they liked the familiar species. Choice D is not correct because it refers to the reason that the rabbits were introduced, not to why the plan failed.

5. **C** The rabbits create deserts by eating the vegetation, but they were not moved to deserts. Choice A is mentioned in paragraph 4, sentence 6. Choice B is mentioned in paragraph 4, sentence 7. Choice D is mentioned in paragraph 4, sentence 9.

6. **B** "Biting insects, mainly mosquitoes and fleas, quickly transmit the virus from host to host." Choice A is not correct because South American rabbits are the normal hosts for the myxoma virus. Choice C is not correct because it is the *O. cuniculus* rabbit that dies when infected. Choice D is not correct because resistant populations of *O. cuniculus* rabbits, not fleas, have an immunity to the virus.

7. **C** ". . . researchers are now questioning whether . . . it can . . . infect animals other than rabbits (such as humans)." Choice A is not correct because insects were not mentioned in the Spencer Gulf

experiment. Choice B is not correct because the purpose of the experiment was to kill the rabbits. Choice D is not correct because 80 to 95 percent of the rabbits are being killed, but the small number with immunity is not identified as dangerous.

8. **C**   In this passage, *results* is a synonym for "consequences." Context comes from the logical connection between researchers "questioning" and the phrase "long-term," which describes the "consequences."

9. **D**   The farm and processing plant will manufacture products from kudzu, which will offer partial solutions. Choice A is not correct because kudzu was imported to control erosion, not for manufacture. Choice B is not correct because no argument is presented in defense of the decision. Choice C is not correct because it grows in Asia already.

10. **A**   In this passage, *surpasses* is a synonym for "exceeds." Context comes from the logical relationship between "demand" and "supply."

11. **D**   "When you hear someone bubbling enthusiastically about an **exotic species**, you can safely bet the speaker isn't an ecologist . . . they [exotic species] make native species **endangered species**." This introduction establishes the author's opinion that exotic species are often disruptive to the ecology.

12. **C**   Vocabulary reference is a transitional device that connects the insert sentence with the previous sentence. The connection is the reference to "starch" in both the insert sentence and the previous sentence.

13. **E, B, C** summarize the passage. Choice A is a minor point that refers to major point C. Choice D is a detail that is not developed as a major point. Choice F is an important fact, but it is not a major point because is it not developed.

READING 2 "PALEOLITHIC ART"

14. **C**   ". . . the remoteness and difficulty of access . . . suggest[s] . . . magical properties . . . rituals or dances." Choice A is not correct because they were probably used for rituals. Choices B and D are not mentioned or implied in the passage.

15. **D**   Choice A is mentioned in paragraph 1, sentence 7. Choice B is mentioned in paragraph 1, sentence 8. Choice C is implied in paragraph 1, sentences 5 and 7.

16. **A**   In this passage, *admission* is a synonym for "access." Context comes from the contrast with "remoteness" and "difficulty" in the same sentence.

17. **C** In this passage, *assist* is a synonym for "facilitate." Context comes from the contrast of "destruction" and "survival" in the same and following sentences.

18. **C** "A central problem for both the . . . theories is that the animals that seem to have been diet staples of Old Stone Age peoples are not those [animals] most frequently portrayed." The pronoun "those" does not refer to Choices A, B, or D.

19. **B** In this passage, the phrase *not believed* describes "discredited." Choice A describes *distracted*. Choice C describes *discouraged*. Choice D describes *disorderly*. Context comes from the parts of the word. The prefix *dis* means "not." The root *credit* means "believe."

20. **A** *It is true* paraphrases "cannot . . . be doubted" and *the paintings were meaningful* paraphrases "the paintings did have meaning."

21. **B** "Several observers have seen a primitive writing form in these representations of nonliving things." Choice A is not correct because they accompany the pictures of animals. Choice C is not correct because they may have had some other significance. Choice D is not mentioned or implied.

22. **C** "Some scholars have argued that the 'spots' which appear both within and without the horses' outlines, are painted rocks thrown at the animals." Choice A is true, but it is not the reason that the spots may represent a hunting scene. Choice B is not correct because the spots are drawn on the wall, not attached to it. Choice D is not correct because an interpretation of the geometric lines and figures in words is not mentioned.

23. **B** "Some scholars have considered them [positive imprints] 'signatures' of cult or community members, or . . . individual artists." Choices A and C are not correct because they are not mentioned or implied. Choice D is not correct because the author states that the "handprints . . . must have had a purpose."

24. **C** Because the author presents several different theories and does not offer a strong argument for any of them, the author's opinion is probably that the exact purpose of cave paintings is not known. Choice A is not correct because the author also presents the food-creation theory and the mythology theory as alternatives to the hunting ritual theory. Choice B is not correct because the mythology theory is not the only possibility discussed. Choice D is not correct because the author suggests several reasons why this theory cannot explain the narrow range of subjects or the inaccessibility of many of the paintings.

25. **B** Example is a transitional device that connects the insert sentence with the general statement in the previous sentence. The connec-

tion is between the general statement "animals that seem to have been diet staples . . . are not . . . portrayed" and the example that "red deer, not bison were eaten."

26. **B, D, A** summarize the passage. Choice C is true, but it is a minor point that is mentioned as evidence for Choice B. Choice E is not mentioned in the passage. Choice F is true, but it is a point that is used to develop the ideas in Choice A.

READING 3 "GROUP DECISION MAKING"

27. **A** "Groups accumulate more information, knowledge and facts . . . and often consider more alternatives." Choice B is not correct because a group tends to view a problem in more than one way. Choice C is not correct because making recommendations instead of decisions is not mentioned or implied in the passage. Choice D is not correct because each person has experience, but the experience of a group is not mentioned as a reason why a group is chosen to participate.

28. **B** ". . . people will . . . be more committed to a decision in which they have had a say than to a decision made for them." Choice A is true, but more ideas do not explain why the decisions are successful. Choice C is not correct because the help provided by a large number of people is not mentioned in the passage as an advantage during implementation. Choice D is not correct because implementation is successful in group decisions, but the decisions themselves may or may not be successful.

29. **B** In this passage, *significant* is a synonym for "considerable." Context comes from the reference to the "time required to make a decision" as a "disadvantage."

30. **D** In this passage, *As a result* describes "Consequently." Context comes from the conclusion that follows the word "Consequently."

31. **B** "One obvious disadvantage of group decision making is the time required to make a decision." Choice A is not correct because the implication is that sometimes a decision could have been made as effectively by an individual. Choice C is not correct because the "cost" refers to the time, not to the pay for group members. Choice D is not correct because groups tend to avoid disagreements.

32. **B** "All group members need to be encouraged and permitted to contribute." Choice A is not correct because the group should have goals, and personal goals by one member [the leader] should not dominate the discussion. Choice C is not correct because it is considered a disadvantage when an individual such as the group leader dominates the group. Choice D is not correct because

expectations are not mentioned as a responsibility of the group leader.

33. **B**   In this passage, *debatable* is a synonym for "controversial." Context comes from the contrast with "social pressure . . . to conform."

34. **A**   "It occurs when groups are highly cohesive, have highly directive leaders, are insulated so they have no clear ways to get objective information, and—because they lack outside information—have little hope that a better solution might be found than the one [solution] proposed by the leader or other influential group members." The phrase "the one" does not refer to Choices B, C, or D.

35. **C**   ". . . a group may try too hard to compromise . . . to maintain friendships and avoid disagreements." Choice A is not correct because the group may not make optimal decisions when the members try too hard to compromise. Choice B is not correct because groupthink requires agreement rather than compromise. Choice D is not correct because helping one member to reach a personal goal or win an argument would be the opposite of compromise.

36. **B**   ". . . self-appointed 'mind guards' . . . bring pressure on dissenters." Choice A is not correct because people who conform will not necessarily pressure others. Choice C is not correct because "mind guards" use force to exert influence and may not be the most ethical members. Choice D is not correct because "mind guards" do not disagree with the group.

37. **C**   ". . . decisions . . . are made without consideration of . . . alternative options." Choice A is not correct because the group exerts pressure on dissenters, but dissenters do not exert pressure on the group. Choice B is not correct because it is neither mentioned nor implied in the passage. Choice D is not correct because when groupthink takes place, poor decision making and wrong decisions occur.

38. **A**   Generalization and example is a transitional device that connects the insert sentence with following sentences. "In fact, the traditional group is prone to a variety of difficulties" provides a general statement that introduces the disadvantages developed in the following sentences. Choices B, C, and D would interrupt the examples by inserting the generalization.

39.   Advantages: **C, D, H**   Disadvantages: **A, B, E, F**   Not used: **G, I**

READING 4 "FOUR STAGES OF PLANETARY DEVELOPMENT"

40. **B**   "The moon, for example, is much like Earth, but its evolution has been dramatically altered by its smaller size." Choice A is not correct because the four stages are explained in the following para-

graphs. Choice C is not correct because the Moon and all the terrestrial planets have passed through the same stages. Choice D is not correct because exploration is not mentioned in the passage.

41. **A** "A meteorite hitting Earth at high velocity converts most of its [the meteorite's] energy of motion into heat." The pronoun "its" does not refer to Choices B, C, or D.

42. **A** *The Earth was probably liquid* paraphrases "Earth may have been molten," and *the heat collected faster than it dissipated* paraphrases "this heat would have accumulated much more rapidly than it could leak away." In addition, *if the formation took place quickly* paraphrases "If Earth formed rapidly."

43. **B** In this passage, *broken into small parts* describes the word "pulverized." Context comes from the reference to "battered."

44. **B** Because radioactive elements continued to "warm and soften the rock layers," it must be concluded that radioactive matter generates intense heat. Choice A is not correct because all traces of early lava flooding caused by radioactive heating have been destroyed. Choice C is probably true, but the relative importance of the stages is not mentioned in the passage. Choice D is not correct because the heating, not the fracturing, is caused by radioactive decay.

45. **D** In this passage, the phrase *most important* describes the word "dominant." Context comes from the contrast with the phrase "still occasionally" earlier in the sentence.

46. **B** ". . . water fell as rain, filling the deepest basins to produce the first oceans." Choices A, C, and D are true, but they do not describe how the oceans formed.

47. **B** ". . . this process [the presence of living matter] seems to be totally missing from other worlds in our solar system." Choice A is not correct because the author does not express doubt in her opinion. Choice C is not correct because she gives her opinion in the final sentence. Choice D is not correct because she states that living matter is "totally missing."

48. **A** According to the passage, *cratering* is the second stage and *flooding* is the third stage. Choice B is not correct because slow surface evolution is the fourth stage, after *flooding*. Choice C is not correct because *differentiation* is the first stage, which comes before, not after *cratering*. Choice D is not correct because it is not a stage, although it is an important process.

49. **B** "We do not know how the presence of living matter [which is peculiar to Earth] has affected the evolution of Earth." Choice A is mentioned in paragraph 1, sentence 1. Choice C is mentioned in paragraph 1, sentences 1 and 2. Choice D is mentioned in paragraph 4, sentence 8.

50. **D**   Addition is a transitional device that connects the insert sentence with the previous sentence. The reference to the way that the "mountains" and "continents" are "changing" in the previous sentence introduces the way that "air and water erode the surface and wear away geological features [like mountains and continents]" in the insert sentence. Choices A and B are not correct because they refer to flooding, not to the processes in slow surface evolution such as erosion. Choice C is not correct because the sentence does not include a reference to erosion and cannot introduce an additional sentence about erosion.

51. **A**   In this passage *different* is a synonym for "peculiar." Context comes from the phrase "On the other hand," which signals a contrast with the previous sentences that show similarities between Earth and the other planets.

52. **E, F, B** summarizes the passage. Choice A is not correct because the stages are the same. Choice C is true, but it is a minor point that refers to major point E. Choice D is true, but it is a minor point that refers to major point F.

READING 5 "SPEECH AND WRITING"

53. **B**   In this passage, the phrase *come close to* is a synonym for "approximate." Context comes from the words "imperfectly" and "ideals" in the same sentence.

54. **D**   "When linguists study language, they take the spoken language as their best source of data and their object of description." Because they use the spoken language, researchers must prefer speech samples. Choice A is not correct because when researchers study Latin, they must make an exception [use written samples]. Choices B and C are not mentioned in the passage.

55. **A**   ". . . the majority of the Earth's inhabitants are illiterate." Choice B is not correct because illiterate populations are quite capable of spoken communication. Choice C is not correct because the majority of the Earth's inhabitants in the modern world are illiterate. Choice D is not correct because it is not mentioned in the passage.

56. **D**   *Both simple and complex writing systems* paraphrases "Writing systems [that] vary in complexity," and *require direct instruction* paraphrases "must all be taught."

57. **B**   In this passage, *thought* is a synonym for "deliberation." Context comes from the contrast with "spontaneous and simultaneous formulation of ideas" later in the sentence.

58. **C**   ". . . the association of writing with the standard variety is not a necessary one, as evidenced by the attempts of writers to transcribe faithfully the speech of their characters." Choice A is not correct because the speech of their characters is transcribed [written down]. Choice B is not correct because the examples are transcriptions of speech, not writing styles. Choice D is not correct because examples of the two varieties are not provided and could not be contrasted.

59. **B**   In this passage, *temporary* is a synonym for "transient." Context comes from the contrast with writing, which tends to "last."

60. **D**   "Writing could also change if it were made to follow the changes of speech. The fact that people at various times try to carry out spelling reforms amply illustrates this possibility [writing could change to follow the changes in speech]." Choice A is not correct because examples of British and American spelling are different. Choice B is not correct because pronunciation in British and American English is not compared. Choice C is not correct because spelling changes because of pronunciation, but pronunciation does not change because of spelling.

61. **A**   "The fact that people at various times try to carry out spelling reforms amply illustrates this possibility [writing could also change]." The phrase "this possibility" does not refer to Choices B, C, or D.

62. **C**   "It is a widely held misconception that writing is more perfect than speech." This opening statement expresses the author's opinion, which is developed in an essay with argument and persuasion. Choice A is not correct because the history of writing begins 1,200 years later than that of speech. Choice B is not correct because the author says that "the association of writing with the standard variety is not a necessary one." Choice D is not correct because the author points out that "Writing could also change if it were made to follow the changes of speech."

63. **C**   The author organizes the passage as a persuasive argument by explaining the reasons why speech is primary and then demonstrating why people have the "misconception" that writing is more perfect than speech. Choices A, B, and D are included as part of the argument.

64. **C**   Reference is a transitional device that connects the insert sentence with the previous sentence. *The Sumerians* in the insert sentence refers to "Sumer" in the previous sentence.

65. .   Speech: **B, C, E, I**   Writing: **D, F, G**   Not used: **A, H**

➤ Listening

 Model Test 3, Listening Section, CD 2, Track 1

LISTENING 1 "PROFESSOR'S OFFICE"

Audio Conversation

Narrator: Listen to a conversation between a student and a professor.

Student: Hi Dr. Davis. I'm a little early. Should I wait outside?
Professor: No. Come on in. I'm free. What did you want to talk about?
Student: Well, I've read the first couple of books you had on my list . . .
                 the reading list for my independent study . . . and I was just
                 wondering how you want me to report them to you. We
                 didn't really talk about that.
Professor: Well, I'm glad you stopped by. Let me think . . . didn't you
                 have a project to do in addition to the reading list?
Student: Yes. You said it could be a research paper or I could come
                 up with a proposal for a different kind of project.
Professor: That's right. So, the reading list is . . . background informa-
                 tion then. Why don't you just come in when you finish the
                 first part of the list. I think it was divided in two distinct parts
                 . . . so just come in, and we'll talk about the readings.
Student: You mean I should prepare a synopsis of each book and . . .
                 and kind of report to you on each one?
Professor: No, no. Nothing as formal as that. I was thinking more along
                 the lines of a conversation. As I recall, the list has a focus,
                 doesn't it?
Student: Definitely. All of the books are novels and plays from the
                 second half of the twentieth century.
Professor: The Post Modern Period then. And all North American nov-
                 elists and playwrights.
Student: Right.
Professor: So we should be able to find some common threads then.
                 Remember, though, Post Modernism is very difficult to
                 define precisely. Maybe we could start with a discussion of
                 the themes that emerge in the collection of literature from
                 that period.
Student: That sounds interesting.

Q1

Q4

Professor:	I think so, too. And by the time you get through with the second half of the reading list and we get together again, maybe we can figure out whether we're looking at a logical extension of Post Modernism or whether there's actually a new movement there . . . in the readings on the second part. If you'll notice, there are quite a few minority writers represented, so you might want to think about what that means.
Student:	I noticed that in the list. The first part of the list has the usual North American writers and, of course, a good representation of women writers as you would expect, but the second part of the list includes a number of African-American authors, several Hispanic-American writers, and a few Oriental-Americans. **Q2**
Professor:	It's a multiethnic mix.
Student:	Yeah.
Professor:	Good. So have you decided whether you want to do a paper or . . . something else perhaps?
Student:	To tell the truth, I'd really like to do something a little more creative. Maybe bring in some visuals on the computer as part of the . . . I don't know . . . I suppose you would call it a mixed media report. But I've never done anything like that before.
Professor:	But that's what an independent study is designed to do. It's an opportunity to experiment and to have some one-on-one time with a professor.
Student:	But a research paper is easier in some ways. At least I know that I can do a decent job. The computer project is unknown territory.
Professor:	True. But remember, it's unknown territory for all of us. I think I've heard some references to *Cybermodernism*, if you want to investigate some of the work that's being created in, as you call it, mixed media literature. **Q3**
Student:	Cybermodernism? Wow!
Professor:	I think you'd find it interesting. Anyway, it's up to you. It's your project.
Student:	Thanks. I'm really excited about doing this independent study. Actually, I'm spending more time on it than on any of my other classes.
Professor:	I've found that students usually invest more time and energy in a class that they can design. That's why I like to direct them. Oh, and Terry, if you run into any problems, don't wait until you're halfway through your reading list. Just stop by **Q**

during my office hours. Maybe I can give you some references or at least a sounding board.

Student: Thanks. This is better than I even expected.

Audio 1. Why does the man go to see his professor?
Answer C To ask about the professor's requirements

Audio 2. How is the second part of the reading list different from the first part?
Answer A More minority authors are represented.

Audio 3. Listen again to part of the conversation and then answer the following question.
Replay "I think I've heard some references to *Cybermodernism*, if you want to investigate some of the work that is being created in, as you call it, mixed media literature."
"Cybermodernism? Wow!"
Audio What does the man mean when he says this:
Replay "Cybermodernism? Wow!"
Answer B His tone expresses interest and excitement.

Audio 4. What will the man probably do before the next meeting?
Answer D Prepare to talk with the professor

Audio 5. What can be inferred about the professor?
Answer B She is willing to help her students.

LISTENING 2 "ENVIRONMENTAL SCIENCE CLASS"

Audio Lecture
Narrator: Listen to part of a lecture in an environmental science class. The professor is talking about wind power.

Professor:
Today I want to talk with you about another renewable source of energy . . . wind power. This isn't a new concept. In fact, wind has been used for centuries to pump water and launch sailing vessels. But more recently, wind power has been used to generate electricity.

By the year 2000, California was using, maybe 15,000 wind turbines to produce about 400 megawatts of electricity. And that was happening at a cost that would be considered competitive with coal or nuclear power. And, although California currently leads the United States in harnessing wind power, there are several other areas that also hold considerable potential for increased production. Texas and the Dakotas alone have enough wind potential to power the nation, but, since the winds there are so variable, well, wind power alone would be unreliable as a primary source of continuous energy. Nevertheless, it could be used as a secondary resource, along with fossil fuels. The strong and steady winds of the Pacific Northwest, especial-   **Q7** ly in the Columbia River Basin . . . these winds would be ideal as a supplement to hydroelectric power when the river is experiencing periods of low water levels. Studies by the U.S. Department of Energy indicate that wind power generated from the Great Plains in the middle of the country could supply the continental United States with almost . . . 75 percent of the electricity required for the region.

In another section of the same report, it was noted that wind power is the world's fastest growing energy source. Since 1998, the capacity for wind energy has increased by more than 35 percent worldwide. And improvements in wind turbine technology in the past couple of decades has improved efficiency, cutting the cost dramatically, from roughly 40 cents to about 4 cents per kilowatt hour, and a new turbine design is being tested with a lower torque, so that may actually move the price closer to 3 cents.

Europe currently accounts for over 17 . . . Oh, sorry that's 70 . . . seven-   **Q8** zero percent of the world's wind power. India, China, Germany, Denmark, Italy, and Spain have published plans for major increases in wind-generated electricity projects in the next few years, and recent interest and exploration have been initiated in the United Kingdom and Brazil. Remote areas, especially islands, and other regions at a distance from electrical grids are vigorously exploring wind options. Clearly, the global implications not only for cheap energy but also for clean energy could be enormous. And, in some areas, the consumers are even willing to pay a subsidy for the pollution-free energy that wind provides their communities. In Colorado, for instance, through a program called Windsource, about 10,000 customers pay an additional $2.50 per month for every 100-killowatt hours of wind power. Legislation in several states in the United States now requires utility companies to guarantee that a percentage of their electricity will be generated from renewable sources like wind power.

Of course, there are some problems associated with wind power that do need to be considered. The blades on the turbines present a hazard to   **Q9** migrating birds. In some cases, the vibrations interfere with television reception in the area. And, there have been objections to wind farms because they produce noise and because they're not visually appealing to residents nearby. So, in addition to the studies to improve turbine design and energy efficiency, some of the attendant problems also require research and development. Regarding the noise, let me mention that design modifications, basically modifying the thickness of the turbine blades and making adjustments to the orientation of the turbines . . . these modifications have diminished the noise substantially in a number of sites. As for visual appeal, some creative ways to share the land to create a more attractive wind farm are being piloted.

So that brings us to the issue of storing wind power. And, although wind energy can be stored temporarily as battery power, the real challenge for wind power exploration will be how to level out the energy source. Alternatives for storage will be critical because, even in an area with steady winds, wind is still not totally reliable. But, the Tellus Institute has released promising results from studies to investigate the problem of intermittent wind. This is what they did. By dividing the wind turbines from one farm into two smaller farms with geographical separation, the capacity of the pair of farms increased by 33⅓ percent over the efficiency of the larger farm with the same number of turbines. So, by taking advantage of the slightly different wind patterns, a more continuous supply of wind power can be generated.

So where are we with all of this? Well, the research that will make wind power a viable option is underway but we need to continue to study . . . in order to solve some of the problems . . . before we can use wind power as a primary source of energy, globally.

| **Audio** | 6. | What aspect of wind power is the lecture mainly about? |
| **Answer** | **D** | Wind as a renewable energy option |

Audio	7.	Which two regions of the United States have the greatest potential for supplying wind power?
Answer	**B**	The Midwestern Plains
	D	The Pacific Northwest

Audio	8.	Listen again to part of the lecture and then answer the following question.
Replay		"Europe currently accounts for over 17 . . . Oh, sorry that's 70 . . . seven-zero percent of the world's wind power. India, China, Germany, Denmark, Italy, and Spain have published plans for major increases in wind-generated electricity projects in the next few years, and recent interest and exploration have been initiated in the United Kingdom and Brazil."
Audio		Why does the professor say this:
Replay		"Europe currently accounts for over 17 . . . Oh, sorry that's 70 . . . seven-zero percent of the world's wind power."
Answer	**C**	He is correcting a previous statement.

Audio 9. In the lecture, the professor identifies several problems associated with wind power. Indicate whether each of the following is one of the problems mentioned. Click in the correct box for each phrase.

Answer

	Yes	No
A Poor television reception	✔	
B Noisy turbines	✔	
C Expensive operating costs		✔
D Remote areas		✔
E Dangerous blades for birds	✔	

Audio 10. How did the Tellus Institute solve the problem of intermittent wind?

Answer D By separating one wind farm into two locations

Audio 11. What is the professor's opinion about the future of wind power?

Answer A He thinks that wind power will require more research before it becomes practical.

LISTENING 3 "PHILOSOPHY CLASS"

Audio Discussion

Narrator: Listen to part of a discussion in a philosophy class.

Professor:

The earliest Greek philosophers, also known as the pre-Socratic philosophers, they were very interested in determining the nature of the universe. Initially, Thales proposed that water was the original material from which all other material was derived, and by that he was referring not only to things on Earth but also in the heavens. He observed that life sprouts from a moist ground, unlike death that dries and shrivels into dust. The fact that water could transform itself into a solid as it does when it freezes into ice or it could change into air as it does when heated into steam, well, this convinced him

Q1

that everything had originated as water and would eventually return to water. He believed that all things are living things, including rocks and metals, and so literally everything would transform itself into the original material, water, in a logical pattern of change.

A little later, Anaximander, and he was a student of Thales, so Anaximander was set on a path that involved questioning which of the elements was the most basic or fundamental. But he suggested that the universe was not originally made up of water as Thales had reasoned, but was a living mass, which he called the *infinite.* The word in Greek actually means "unlimited" but most translators have used the term *infinite* since it probably captures the meaning a little better in English. So Anaximander put forward what some believe is the first theoretical postulate . . . that the infinite was constantly in motion . . . up and down, back and forth. So, although the infinite had begun as a whole, the motion had caused pieces to be broken off to form all of the elements of the universe . . . the Earth, the Sun, stars. Then he speculated that as the oceans had begun to evaporate, the first sea plants and animals had formed, and from them their descendants, the birds and land animals evolved, until finally, mankind was created.

Student 1:   That sounds a lot like evolutionary theory.

Professor:
Yes, it does. Probably the first instance of evolutionary theory among Europeans, although the Chinese philosophers had discussed this possibility earlier. Okay, so what do you think he postulated about the continued motion of the universe? Anyone?

Student 2:
I remember that part. He thought that all of these separate elements would eventually be put back together into the original infinite mass.

Professor:
Precisely right. But good students think for themselves, and some years later, Anaximander's student Anaximenes, criticized his teacher's view. He deduced that the original element of the universe was air, which was timeless and boundless, and in fact, alive. Because mankind and all the animals must breathe air in order to survive, he believed, therefore, that air had been transformed into blood, bone, and flesh. He also concluded that air was the origin of water, stone, and earth, and I think you can see the analogy with the parts of the body there. Furthermore, he contended that the solid condensations of air constituted the body of the world, but the ethereal quality of air constituted the spirit of the world, and it was the spirit that remained alive forever.

Now these three philosophers . . . Thales, Anaximander, and Anaximenes . . . they were all residents of Miletus, and were very active beginning about 600 years before the Christian Era. So they were called the Milesian philosophers. And they all had different views, but they also had something in common.

Student 1:
Do you mean that they were all materialists? Because they were trying to explain the universe in terms of perceivable elements like water and air?   Q14

Professor:
Good observation. Let's take that a step further. They all attempted to explain the unknown in terms of the familiar instead of looking to the current mythologies or to a divine presence. And that's what is truly extraordinary about these pre-Socratic philosophers. A naturalistic account of the cosmos was profoundly different from the myths and legends of gods and goddesses that had been the basis for explaining the origin of the universe.   Q15

Student 2: So what do you mean by naturalistic?

Professor:
I mean that they tried to use scientific arguments, and this marked a very new way of thinking. Unlike the exciting narratives of superhuman beings with the powers to create and change the universe, they proposed that the universe was made up of something very basic, and that it was constantly undergoing *natural* changes. The Milesians made a major contribution . . . and they did this by moving beyond the old mythologies and folktales, and some scholars even suggest that they were responsible for the beginnings of Western philosophy as we know it. Now when we talk about philosophy, it's important to point out that for many centuries philosophy was *not* a separate discipline from other areas of thought and knowledge. In fact, early philosophers were mathematicians, physicists, chemists, and biologists before any of these sciences were identified as separate, uh, . . . subjects, or . . . fields of study. So the pre-Socratic philosophers were trying to discover a scientific basis for the universe long before the scientific method and the technologies were available to support their investigations. But, really, many scholars argue that these philosophers *did* initiate the process at least, and the process eventually resulted . . . years later . . . as the beginning of the physical sciences.   Q1

Okay, all of this appears on the surface to be very positive, right? But at the time, many philosophers as well as ordinary citizens were feeling much less comfortable with the very sparse tenants of emerging science than they had been with the rich and complicated stories that had explained the   Q1 universe for them. Remember that this is all before Socrates, Aristotle, and Plato who were . . . by then . . . well, more able to expand on protoscientific thought and produce a massive and elaborate scientific alternative to the ancient beliefs.

Audio	12.	What is the discussion mainly about?
Answer	**C**	The nature of the universe

Audio	13.	Why does the student mention evolutionary theory?
Answer	**D**	He is comparing evolution to Anaximander's theory.

Audio	14.	Listen again to part of the discussion and then answer the following question.
Replay		"Do you mean that they were all materialists? Because they were trying to explain the universe in terms of perceivable elements like water and air?" "Good observation. Let's take that a step further."
Audio		Why does the professor say this:
Replay		"Good observation. Let's take that a step further."
Answer	**C**	She is going to expand on the comment. To "take a step further" means to "elaborate" or "provide details."

Audio	15.	What view did the three Milesian philosophers share?
Answer	**B**	They introduced a scientific approach to explaining nature.

Audio	16.	What can be inferred about the early Greek philosophers?
Answer	**A**	They were exploring the physical sciences.

Audio	17.	Listen again to part of the discussion and then answer the following question.
Replay		"Okay, all of this appears on the surface to be very positive, right? But at the time, many philosophers as well as ordinary citizens were feeling much less comfortable with the very sparse tenants of emerging science than they had been with the rich and complicated stories that had explained the universe for them."
Audio		What does the professor mean when she says this:
Replay		"Okay, all of this appears on the surface to be very positive, right?"
Answer	**B**	She is introducing doubt.

LISTENING 4 "PROFESSOR'S OFFICE"

Audio Conversation

Narrator:	Now listen to a conversation between a student and a professor.
Student:	Excuse me, Professor Jones. I was wondering whether I could talk with you for a minute? If you're busy now, though . . .
Professor:	Sure, Anne. What's up?
Student:	Well, I've been working on my research project. I'm doing it on decaffeinated beverages.
Professor:	Oh, I remember. That's going to be interesting. How's it going?
Student:	Good. I've got all the data, but the report is turning out to be fairly short. It took such a long time to do the research, I thought I'd have a lot more to write about.
Professor:	Well, how long will it be, do you think?
Student:	Probably five or six pages, and that includes a couple of pages with charts in them.
Professor:	That sounds about right.
Student:	It does?
Professor:	Yes. Of course, it depends on what you included in the five pages. The issue here is whether the research design was well thought out, and whether you have all of the information in your report that you need to explain what you did . . . the approach . . . and the results that you found.
Student:	Okay. I have a short introduction . . . just a few paragraphs really . . . so that's about caffeine, and then I talk about the benefits of decaffeination, and several ways to do that.
Professor:	Unhuh. What else?
Student:	Well, I explain my research design . . . and that's sort of a problem too because I'm not sure whether to make this sound like a book, you know, the way the studies are explained in our textbook, or whether I should just write it up as clearly as I can so that anyone would understand what I did.
Professor:	I'd go for that option. In fact, why don't you ask a few friends to read it before you turn it in? If your friends get it, that's a good indication that you've explained it well, but if they have a lot of questions, then maybe you need to do some rewriting. And Anne, it's even better if your friends aren't chemistry majors like you are.

Q18

Q1

Student:	Well, I would never have thought of that.
Professor:	Then I'm glad I suggested it. By the way, did you include references at the end of your study?
Student:	Just two. That's all I used.
Professor:	Okay. Good. Just as long as you cite the references you used.
Student:	Well, thanks. This is the first time I've ever done my own research. It was hard because I didn't have any experience, but it was fun, too. I was thinking about trying to get a part-time job as a lab assistant next year.

Q20 Professor: I think you'd be a good candidate. In fact, why don't you write up a draft of that report, and I'll look it over for you before you hand in the final copy.

Q21 Student: That would be perfect. I could bring it in on Monday since that's when you have your usual office hours. Would that be okay?

Professor: Yes, but that would only give you one day before the report is due.

Student: Oh right.

Professor: Okay then. Why don't you bring it to class on Friday?

Student: That would be great.

Professor: And Anne, if you're really serious about that lab assistant position, I can give you some information about that when I see you.

Student: I can't thank you enough.

Q22 Professor: Not at all, Anne. You've got a lot going for you. I'm glad to help.

Audio	18.	Why does the woman want to talk with her professor?
Answer **C**		She has some questions about the report she is writing.

Audio	19.	What advice does the professor give the woman?
Answer **A**		Have some friends read the research

Audio	20.	What does the professor offer to do?
Answer **A**		Read a draft of the report before the woman submits it

Audio	21.	Listen again to part of the conversation and then answer the following question.
Replay		"I could bring it in on Monday since that's when you have your usual office hours. Would that be okay?"
		"Yes, but that would only give you one day before the report is due."
		"Oh right."

Audio		Why does the professor say this:
Replay		"Yes, but that would only give you one day before the report is due."
Answer	A	His tone expresses reluctance because he realizes that she won't have time to revise the report.

Audio	22.	What is the professor's opinion of the woman?
Answer	B	He is very impressed with her attitude.

LISTENING 5 "BIOLOGY CLASS"

Audio Lecture

Narrator: Listen to part of a lecture in a biology class. The professor is talking about bacteria.

Professor:

Bacteria is the common name for a very large group of one-celled microscopic organisms that, we believe, may be the smallest, simplest, and perhaps even the very first forms of cellular life that evolved on Earth. Because they're so small, bacteria must be measured in microns, with one micron measuring about 0.00004 inches long. Most bacteria range from about 0.1 microns to about 4 microns wide and about 0.2 microns to almost 50 microns long. So how can we observe them? I'll give you one guess. Under the microscope, of course. As I said, bacteria are very primitive and simple. In fact, they're unicellular, which means that they're made up of a single cell. Q25 We think they probably evolved about three and a half billion years ago. Some of the oldest fossils are bacterial organisms. They've been found almost everywhere on Earth, including all the continents, seas, and fresh water habitats, and in the tissues of both plants and animals.

Well, since they're so prevalent, you might ask, how do they reproduce? Okay, they grow in colonies and can reproduce, quite rapidly, in fact, by a Q2. process called *fission*. In fission, the cell, and remember, there's only one in bacteria, one cell. So the cell increases in size and then splits in two parts. Fission is also referred to in your text as *asexual budding*. Now you'll also read about *conjugation*, and that's when two separate bacteria exchange pieces of DNA, so there are two ways that reproduction can occur, but we think that fission is more common.

Okay. Bacteria were virtually unknown until about 1600 when microscopes were introduced, and at that time, bacteria were observed and classified into three main types according to their shapes, and that classification hasn't really changed that much over the years. So that's what I want to talk about today—the main types of bacteria. The slides that I'm going to show you are enlargements of bacteria that I observed under the microscope in the lab earlier today. Now, this first slide is an example of *bacilli*.

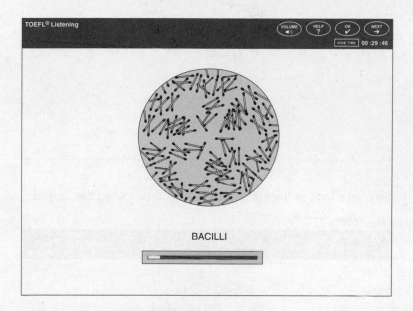

The bacilli are a group of bacteria that occur in the soil and air. As you can see, they're shaped like rods, and if you were to see them in motion, they'd be rolling or tumbling under the microscope. Of course, you can't see that because this is a still visual, but later, when you go into the lab, you'll see that rolling motion in examples of bacilli. These are kind of a greenish blue, but some are yellow. So don't try to identify them by their color. Look at the shape. These bacilli are largely responsible for food spoilage.

Okay, the next slide is a very different shape of bacteria. It's referred to as the *cocci* group, and it tends to grow in clusters or chains, like this example. This specimen is one of the common streptococci bacteria that cause strep throat.

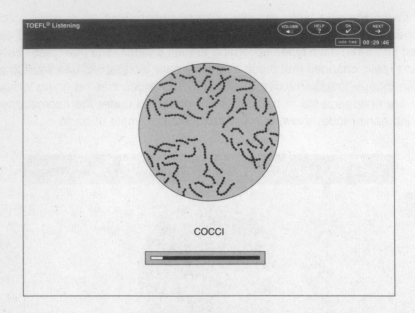

COCCI

Finally, let's look at the spiral-shaped bacteria called the *spirilla*.

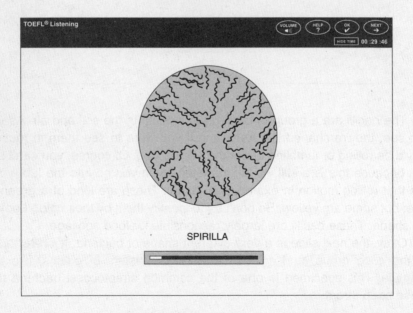

SPIRILLA

This is the spirilla. They look a little like corkscrews, and they're responsible for a number of diseases in humans. But I don't want you to get the wrong idea. It's true that some species of bacteria *do* cause diseases, but for the most part, bacteria are benign.

There's a lot of bacteria in this room in fact. We all have it on us. They live harmlessly on the skin, in the mouth, and in the intestines. In fact, bacteria are very helpful to researchers because bacterial cells resemble the cells of other life forms in many ways, and may be studied to give us insights. For example, we have a major research project in genetics here at the university. Since bacteria reproduce very rapidly, we're using them to determine how certain characteristics are inherited.

Okay, now, let me review these three types with you . . . cocci are spheres, bacilli are rods, and spirilli are spirals. One of my students came up with a way to remember them. Just try to visualize the first letter in the name of each of the different types: Cocci starts with *C* like the shape of half a sphere. Bacilli starts with a straight line on the *B*, and a rod is straight. Spirilla starts with *S*, and that's a spiral shape. If it helps you, use it.

In any case, although I want you to know the three major classifications, within these basic groups there are virtually hundreds of variations that make them somewhat more difficult to identify and classify than the rather straightforward specimens that I showed you a minute ago. Because, you see, bacteria can join in chains, clusters, pairs. And sometimes, more than one type of bacteria may be found together in a specimen. I think you get the picture.

Okay then, in addition to identifying bacteria by their shape, which we now know isn't really a very good method for distinguishing them easily, if we really want to identify what type of bacteria we're dealing with, it's better to study the biochemistry or genetic structure of the specimen. They have one chromosome of double-stranded DNA in a ring, which we can analyze fairly easily.

Audio   23.   What aspect of bacteria is this lecture mainly about?
Answer   D   The three major types of bacteria

Audio   24.   Which of the following slides contain cocci bacteria?
Answer   B   The cocci bacteria are shown in this slide.

Audio   25.   Which two characteristics are common in bacteria?
Answer   A   They have one cell.
             C   They reproduce quickly.

Audio   26.   Why are bacteria being used in the research study at the university?
Answer   C   Bacteria are similar to other life forms.

Audio   27.   How does the professor help the students to remember the types of bacteria?
Answer   C   He uses the first letter to represent the shape.

Audio   28.   Listen again to part of the lecture and then answer the following question.

Replay   "Because, you see, bacteria can join in chains, clusters, pairs. And sometimes, more than one type of bacteria may be found together in a specimen. I think you get the picture."

Audio   Why does the professor say this:

Replay   "I think you get the picture."

Answer   **D**   To "get the picture" means "to understand." He thinks that the information is very clear.

LISTENING 6 "HISTORY CLASS"

Audio Lecture
Narrator: Listen to part of a lecture in a history class.

Professor:

Frontier home design in the United States was greatly influenced by the provisions of the Homestead Act of 1862. The legislation gave settlers the right to open land but mandated that homesteaders build a structure that was at least ten by twelve feet and included at least one glass window, and they had to live on their homestead and improve the land for five years before their claim was recognized. Of course, when they first arrived, most homesteaders lived in their wagons or pitched tents until they filed claims and planted crops. And even then, knowing that fully half of the homesteaders wouldn't make it through the five years required to complete their claims, homesteaders tended to view the construction of their homes as semi-permanent dwellings . . . more likely they'd build something better later or try to improve on what they'd built initially if they made it through the first five years. So, in addition to the requirements in the Homestead Act, the settlers needed a home that was easy to build, cheap, and maybe even disposable.

Well, the log cabin is the construction that comes to mind when we think of Western settlements, but the plains and the prairies had so few trees that log construction was almost impossible. So the sod house was a practical solution for homesteaders on flat, treeless land. So how do you build a sod house? Well, first you wait for a rain that makes the earth soft, then you use a sod cutter to form sod bricks about two or three feet square and a few inches thick. Then, you stack the bricks to form walls, and weave branches or twigs and grass into a roof that's finally covered with sod as well. Now, there were tremendous advantages to this type of construction. In the first place, it was very cheap . . . there are journals from the 1800s that document construction prices at about $2.50, and most of that was for the glass window. And, it took very little time to build, probably a day or two. And the thick walls actually kept the house quite cool in the summer and fairly warm in the winter. If a better home could be built later, the sod house would simply dissolve into the soil. But there were serious disadvantages as well. Even well-built roofs leaked onto the dirt floors, forming mud puddles, and sometimes the roof even collapsed from the water weight. Or, in dry spells, the dirt crumbled from the roof into the home. Not to mention the infestations of insects and even snakes that inhabited the dirt walls.

Q31   So, those settlers who arrived in wooded areas opted to build log cabins instead of sod homes. Like the sod construction, the log cabin could be built in a few days, using simple tools, often only an axe. But it was much more comfortable. There's evidence that the first log cabins were introduced by Swedish settlers as early as the 1700s but other immigrant settlers quickly
Q34 adopted the construction. First, you build a foundation of rocks to keep the logs away from dampness that might cause them to rot. Then, you cut down the trees and square off the logs, cutting notches in the top and bottom of each end so they could fit together when they were stacked at the corners and it also had the advantage of assuring structural integrity. And there were several types of notching techniques that were used, depending on the skill of the builder. In any case, with notching, no nails were required and that was good since nails had to be shipped into towns and then transported out to
Q34 the new settlements. But there were gaps in the walls so these had to be filled by a technique called *chinking*. In *chinking*, grass, hay, moss and mud were worked into rolls about a foot long and maybe four inches wide and then they were inserted into the cracks between the logs. These rolls were commonly referred to as *mud cats* and were very effective in keeping out the cold and keeping in the heat. Of course, the tighter the logs, the fewer chinks were required, and that's important because the chinks were the weakest part of the cabin, and with the expansion and contraction that resulted from freezing and thawing, well, chinking tended to deteriorate and needed constant maintenance and repair.

   Okay, there was usually a stone or brick fireplace along one wall. And the roof was usually made of wood shingles. So you can imagine, this was quite an improvement over the sod house. The advantages were that the home could be kept clean. Even though the floor was usually dirt or gravel because flat boards were difficult to obtain, it was still an effective shelter to keep out the rain and dust.

33   Later, at the end of the 1800s, when the railroads brought materials such as asphalt shingles, tar paper, and finished boards to the frontier, the sod house was abandoned for one-room board shanties, covered with tar paper. Whether this was an improvement is subject to debate. For one thing, since they were often built without foundations, the harsh winds of the prairies literally blew the shanties away. Still, many settlers considered the shacks

preferable to the old soddies even though they weren't as easy to heat and cool. To go back to the log cabin for a minute, the effect of new construction materials on the log cabin was . . . aesthetic . . . as well as practical. The logs were often covered on the outside by finished boards and on the inside with plaster, which gave the cabins a more finished look and improved insulation. And by this time the old one-room ten-by-twelve was also being replaced with larger homes with several rooms. The frontier settlers had weathered the hardships of their first five years, they'd received their claims, and they and their homes were a permanent part of the great western expansion.

Audio 29. What is the lecture mainly about?

Answer C Frontier homes in the West

Audio 30. How does the professor organize his lecture?

Answer D He contrasts several types of homes in the West—log cabins, sod houses, and board shacks.

Audio 31. What does the professor imply about construction materials for early homes?

Answer A Settlers used the materials from the natural environment.

Audio 32. What is the evidence for the inexpensive price of a sod home?

Answer D Personal records and accounts—journals

Audio 33. Listen again to part of the lecture and then answer the following question.

Replay "Later, at the end of the 1800s, when the railroads brought materials such as asphalt shingles, tar paper, and finished boards to the frontier, the sod house was abandoned for one-room board shanties, covered with tar paper. Whether this was an improvement is subject to debate."

Audio Why does the professor say this:

Replay "Whether this was an improvement is subject to debate."

Answer B To demonstrate uncertainty

Audio 34. In the lecture, the professor identifies attributes for different frontier homes. Indicate whether each attribute refers to a sod house or a log cabin. Click in the correct box for each phrase.

Answer

	Sod House	Log Cabin
A A mud roof	✔	
B A rock foundation		✔
C Chinked walls		✔
D Notching techniques		✔
E Thick brick insulation	✔	

➤ Speaking

 Model Test 3, Speaking Section, CD 2, Track 2

INDEPENDENT SPEAKING QUESTION 1 "A GOOD SON OR DAUGHTER"

Narrator 2: Number 1. Listen for a question about a familiar topic. After you hear the question, you have 15 seconds to prepare and 45 seconds to record your answer.

Narrator 1: In your opinion, what are the characteristics of a good son or daughter in a family? Use specific examples and details to explain your answer.

Narrator 2: Please prepare your answer after the beep.

Beep

[Preparation time: 15 seconds]

Narrator 2: Please begin speaking after the beep.

Beep

[Recording time: 45 seconds]

Beep

INDEPENDENT SPEAKING QUESTION 2 "JOB OPPORTUNITIES"

Narrator 2: Number 2. Listen for a question that asks your opinion about a familiar topic. After you hear the question, you have 15 seconds to prepare and 45 seconds to record your answer.

Narrator 1: Some people are attracted to jobs that include a great deal of travel. Other people prefer jobs that allow them to return to their homes every evening. Which type of job opportunity would you prefer and why? Use specific reasons and examples to support your opinion.

Narrator 2: Please prepare your answer after the beep.

Beep

[Preparation time: 15 seconds]

Narrator 2: Please begin speaking after the beep.

Beep

[Recording time: 45 seconds]

Beep

INTEGRATED SPEAKING QUESTION 3 "EXCUSED ABSENCE"

Narrator 2: Number 3. Read a short passage and listen to a talk on the same topic. Then listen for a question about them. After you hear the question, you have 30 seconds to prepare and 60 seconds to record your answer.

Narrator 1: The professor's attendance policy is published in the course syllabus. Read the policy in the course syllabus printed on page 372. You have 45 seconds to complete it. Please begin reading now.

[Reading time: 45 seconds]

Narrator 1: Now listen to a student who is talking with friends about the policy.

Student:
On the one hand, it's good that you can be absent once without explaining why, but on the other hand, you can't be absent more than one time without

getting a lower grade, so, I'd rather have the option of explaining my problem to the professor if I need to be absent, and then try to figure out a way to make up the work. Look, if I'm sick for two weeks, I don't think it's fair for the professor to lower my grade as long as I keep up with the class. Or, if you have a legitimate reason not to be there—like a family emergency or something. I don't think you should have to choose between your health or your family and your grade in the class.

Narrator 1: The student expresses his opinion of the professor's policy for excused absences. Report his opinion and explain the reasons that he gives for having that opinion.

Narrator 2: Please prepare your answer after the beep.

Beep

[Preparation time: 30 seconds]

Narrator 2: Please begin speaking after the beep.

Beep

[Recording time: 60 seconds]

Beep

INTEGRATED SPEAKING QUESTION 4 "INSECTS"

Narrator 2: Number 4. Read a short passage and then listen to part of a lecture on the same topic. Then listen for a question about them. After you hear the question, you have 30 seconds to prepare and 60 seconds to record your answer.

Narrator 1: Now read the passage about insects printed on page 373. You have 45 seconds to complete it. Please begin reading now.

[Reading time: 45 seconds]

Narrator 1: Now listen to part of a lecture in a biology class. The professor is talking about insects.

Professor:

Strictly speaking, a spider is not an insect. True, it is an invertebrate and an arthropod, but it belongs to a class identified as *arachnids*. Arachnids are not included in the insect world because their body structure is very different. The bodies of spiders are divided into two parts—the . . . a head with a fused thorax, which is all one structure, and the second part is a separate abdomen joined to the large head-thorax part by a narrow stalk. The head contains what many researchers now believe is a highly developed brain. There are no antennae, but four pairs of eyes and eight legs covered with fine, sensitive hairs more than compensate for the absence of the antennae. These hairy legs and feet explore the environment sending sensory messages back to the brain. Okay . . . the abdomen—remember that's the second part of the spider—it includes not only the digestive and reproductive systems but also the silk glands that allow spiders to spin their webs. So, as you see, even though spiders and insects are commonly grouped together as bugs, they are really not the same. An oversimplification is that spiders have too many legs and not enough wings. In reality, the entire body structure is quite different.

Narrator 1: Describe the structure of an insect and explain why a spider is not strictly considered an insect.

Narrator 2: Please prepare your answer after the beep.

Beep

[Preparation time: 30 seconds]

Narrator 2: Please begin speaking after the beep.

Beep

[Recording time: 60 seconds]

Beep

INTEGRATED SPEAKING QUESTION 5 "MEETING PEOPLE"

Narrator 2: Number 5. Listen to a short conversation. Then listen for a question about it. After you hear the question, you have 20 seconds to prepare and 60 seconds to record your answer.

Narrator 1: Now listen to a conversation between a student and his friend.

Student:	Can you believe that I've been here almost a whole semester, and you're the only friend I've made.
Friend:	No. How can that be?
Student:	I don't know. You know me better than anyone here at school. I thought maybe you could give me some advice.
Friend:	Sure. Um, well, do you belong to any clubs or any organizations on campus? That's always a good way to meet people.
Student:	No. I don't have a lot of time to, you know, go to meetings.
Friend:	Neither do I, but I do play inter-mural sports.
Student:	What's that?
Friend:	It's just a group that meets regularly to play basketball. Of course, there are lots of other teams, besides basketball, I mean. You could join a football team, or soccer . . . uh baseball, volleyball. Just go over to the Recreation Center and sign up. They'll put you on a team. You could use some time away from the books.
Student:	I'd like to do that, but . . .
Friend:	Well, since you don't want to take time away from your studies, why don't you join a study group, or get one going in one of your classes? That way, you wouldn't feel like you are wasting time, and besides, the people you meet will be serious students, so maybe they would be better friends for you anyway.

Narrator 1: Describe the man's problem, and the two suggestions that his friend makes about how to handle it. What do you think the man should do, and why?

Narrator 2: Please prepare your answer after the beep.

Beep

[Preparation time: 20 seconds]

Narrator 2: Please begin speaking after the beep.

Beep

[Recording time: 60 seconds]

Beep

INTEGRATED SPEAKING QUESTION 6 "SKINNER BOX"

Narrator 2: Number 6. Listen to part of a lecture. Then listen for a question about it. After you hear the question, you have 20 seconds to prepare, and 60 seconds to record your answer.

Narrator 1: Now listen to part of a lecture in a psychology class. The professor is discussing the Skinner Box.

Professor:
There have been several references to the Skinner Box in your textbook because a lot of behavioral modification experiments still use similar devices, even today, so let's just take a few minutes and make sure that everyone understands exactly what a Skinner Box is and how it works. The box which was named for B. F. Skinner, the American psychologist who developed it . . . it was used in Skinner's original experiment in 1932, and its construction hasn't changed much from that time. It's just a small, empty box, really, except for a bar with a cup underneath it. So picture this: In Skinner's experiment, a rat that had been deprived of food for twenty-four hours was placed in the box. As the animal began to explore its new environment, it accidentally hit the bar, and a food pellet dropped into the cup. The rat ate the pellet and continued exploring for more food. After hitting the bar three or four times with similar results, the animal started hitting the bar with intention instead of by accident. It had learned it could get food by pressing the bar. In other words, the food stimulus reinforced the bar pressing response. So . . . many psychology experiments were modeled after Skinner's original research. Um, various animals have been placed in modified Skinner Boxes and presented with conditions that will result in a reward—food or some other desirable object or experience. In most of the behavior modification experiments in your book, you'll see a citation for Skinner's classic study.

Narrator 1: Using the main points and examples from the lecture, describe the Skinner Box, and then explain how the device is used in psychology experiments.

Narrator 2: Please prepare your answer after the beep.

Beep

[Preparation time: 20 seconds]

Narrator 2: Please begin speaking after the beep.

Beep

[Recording time: 60 seconds]

Beep

➤ Writing

INTEGRATED ESSAY "PRIMORDIAL SOUP"

First, read the passage on pages 378–379 and take notes.

Model Test 3, Writing Section, CD 2, Track 3

Narrator: Now listen to a lecture on the same topic as the passage that you have just read.

Professor:
Most textbooks that have been published within the past fifty years include the Miller-Urey experiment because it was such a groundbreaking discovery at the time, and researchers honestly believed that they were on the verge of discovering the origin of life. But the current view of the Miller-Urey experiment is, let's say, skeptical. And there are several serious objections that we really need to deal with before we move on. First, the laboratory atmosphere that Miller and Urey created was charged with continuous electrical energy, but even though the atmosphere of early Earth was subjected to frequent electrical storms, they were probably not continuous. So, some scientists argue that, although amino acids and other organic compounds may have been formed in the early history of Earth, they probably would not have been produced in the amounts seen in the experimental environment. Some scientists are also concerned about the fact that oxygen was reduced from the atmosphere in the Miller-Urey experiment. What if the premise that the mixture of gases simulated that of early Earth were false? Then, of course, everything else in the experiment is flawed.

And here's another problem. Because several meteorites have fallen to Earth since the publication of the Miller-Urey experiment, there has been interest in analyzing them for amino acid content, and amino acids have been found in them. Well, that proves that amino acids are able to survive in severe conditions in space. So what does that mean? Some scientists think that the early Earth was similar to asteroids and comets that contain amino acids so they may have been present from the moment that the Earth was formed. Others point to the possibility that organic compounds escaped from within meteorites in impact sites where they hit the surface of the newly forming planet Earth.

The truth is that we just don't know how the first cell was formed, and we really aren't sure how that cell reorganized into larger living structures. So, although the Miller-Urey experiment is interesting, it probably does not hold the promise of unlocking the mystery of life on our planet.

➤ Example Answers and Checklists for Speaking and Writing

 Model Test 3, Example Answers, CD 2, Track 4

EXAMPLE ANSWER FOR INDEPENDENT SPEAKING QUESTION 1 "A GOOD SON OR DAUGHTER"

The role of a good son or daughter changes over the years. Initially, being an obedient child is probably all that a parent requires. But when a child grows up and begins to become independent, then a good son or daughter is a person who has good character—who does well in school or succeeds in a career and demonstrates the personal qualities that the parents have tried to teach. Um . . . a good son or daughter is also a good parent when they have children of their own. When parents see their grandchildren being brought up well, uh, they know that they have provided a good example. And . . . and when the parents become old and need care, a good son or daughter won't be too busy to spend time with them and provide them with help.

Checklist 1

✔ The talk answers the topic question.
✔ The point of view or position is clear.
✔ The talk is direct and well-organized.
✔ The sentences are logically connected.
✔ Details and examples support the main idea.
✔ The speaker expresses complete thoughts.
✔ The meaning is easy to comprehend.
✔ A wide range of vocabulary is used.

✔ There are only minor errors in grammar.
✔ The talk is within a range of 125–150 words.

EXAMPLE ANSWER FOR INDEPENDENT SPEAKING QUESTION 2 "JOB OPPORTUNITIES"

Although a job that involves travel seems glamorous to people who spend day after day in an office, it really isn't for me. For one thing, traveling for business usually means going to the same places repeatedly and staying in the same, tired hotel rooms. Besides that, the pace of a business trip doesn't allow much time to see anything besides the inside of an office building and the road to the airport. And eating in restaurants isn't that healthy, and traveling all the time is exhausting. No, I'd rather have a job opportunity that . . . that would let me sleep in my own bed and, uh, eat my own cooking. Um . . . but ideally, the job would also include a three-week paid vacation so . . . I could travel to a destination of my choice and relax.

Checklist 2

✔ The talk answers the topic question.
✔ The point of view or position is clear.
✔ The talk is direct and well-organized.
✔ The sentences are logically connected.
✔ Details and examples support the main idea.
✔ The speaker expresses complete thoughts.
✔ The meaning is easy to comprehend.
✔ A wide range of vocabulary is used.
✔ There are only minor errors in grammar.
✔ The talk is within a range of 125–150 words.

EXAMPLE ANSWER FOR INTEGRATED SPEAKING QUESTION 3 "EXCUSED ABSENCE"

According to the professor's policy, students can be absent from one class without explaining unless there's a test scheduled and then the professor expects students to go to her office to give her an explanation for being out of class and arrange for making up the test. Also, being absent more than once could mean that your grade could be lowered by one letter for each time you miss class. The student doesn't agree with the excused absence policy because he thinks that his grade shouldn't be affected by absence if he makes up the work. Um . . . from his point of view, a valid reason for absence, uh, like an emergency, a family problem, or illness, uh, that shouldn't jeopardize his grade unless he fails to keep up with the class or his work's unsatisfactory.

Checklist 3

✔ The talk summarizes the situation and opinion.
✔ The point of view or position is clear.
✔ The talk is direct and well-organized.
✔ The sentences are logically connected.
✔ Details and examples support the opinion.
✔ The speaker expresses complete thoughts.
✔ The meaning is easy to comprehend.
✔ A wide range of vocabulary is used.
✔ Errors in grammar are minor.
✔ The talk is within a range of 125–150 words.

EXAMPLE ANSWER FOR INTEGRATED SPEAKING QUESTION 4 "INSECTS"

Insects are arthropods with a three-part body structure—a head, a thorax, and an abdomen. The head has a pair of eyes and a pair of antennae, and three pairs of legs and two pairs of wings are usually attached to the thorax. Now, although a spider is also an arthropod, it isn't considered an insect, uh, because, um, because it only has a two-part body structure. The head and the thorax are joined together on a spider and attached to its abdomen by a thin stem. And a spider doesn't have antennae but it does have four pairs of eyes. Instead of six legs, it has eight, hairy legs that are used kind of like an insect uses its antennae to explore the environment. A spider doesn't have wings. It has a unique glandular system that allows it to spin its webs. So, because of this very different body structure, a spider is not really an insect.

Checklist 4

✔ The talk relates an example to a concept.
✔ Inaccuracies in the content are minor.
✔ The talk is direct and well-organized.
✔ The sentences are logically connected.
✔ Details and examples support the opinion.
✔ The speaker expresses complete thoughts.
✔ The meaning is easy to comprehend.
✔ A wide range of vocabulary is used.
✔ The speaker paraphrases in his/her own words.
✔ The speaker credits the lecturer with wording.

✔ Errors in grammar are minor.
✔ The talk is within a range of 125–150 words.

EXAMPLE ANSWER FOR INTEGRATED SPEAKING QUESTION 5 "MEETING PEOPLE"

The man's problem is that he hasn't been very successful meeting people and making friends. He's been on campus for an entire semester, and the woman's the only friend he has. She suggests that he participate in some clubs, but he's reluctant to spend the time required for meetings. The woman plays inter-mural basketball. She says that there are a lot of sports options at the Recreation Center. Another possibility that she recommends is for the man to join a study group. That way, he'd meet some serious students and he'd still be using the time to study for classes while he was getting to know people. I think that the man should join a group to play sports for an hour twice a week because he probably needs the exercise, and he should also try to get into a study group because he'll probably have more in common with the people who are using their time to study for their classes.

Checklist 5

✔ The talk summarizes the problem and recommendations.
✔ The speaker's point of view or position is clear.
✔ The talk is direct and well-organized.
✔ The sentences are logically connected.
✔ Details and examples support the opinion.
✔ The speaker expresses complete thoughts.
✔ The meaning is easy to comprehend.
✔ A wide range of vocabulary is used.
✔ Errors in grammar are minor.
✔ The talk is within a range of 125–150 words.

EXAMPLE ANSWER FOR INTEGRATED SPEAKING QUESTION 6 "SKINNER BOX"

A Skinner Box is a small box that's empty except for a cup and a bar. When the bar over the cup is depressed, a food pellet drops into the cup. An animal that's placed in a Skinner Box will explore the environment for food, and at some point, will accidentally hit the bar, releasing the pellet. So . . . after the animal hits the bar about three or four times and it's rewarded with food, then it learns how to find food, using the bar, and it begins to hit the bar on purpose. The Skinner Box, or something like It, it's commonly used in psychology experiments that involve behavior modification. By presenting a sub-ject with the opportunity for a reward, the behavior that produces the reward is reinforced. In the case of the classic experiment, the subject's opportunity for a reward is a food pellet, and the behavior that's reinforced is pressing the bar, but many types of rewards and behaviors have been used.

Checklist 6

✔ The talk summarizes a short lecture.
✔ Inaccuracies in the content are minor.
✔ The talk is direct and well-organized.
✔ The sentences are logically connected.
✔ Details and examples support the opinion.
✔ The speaker expresses complete thoughts.
✔ The meaning is easy to comprehend.
✔ A wide range of vocabulary is used.
✔ The speaker paraphrases in his/her own words.
✔ The speaker credits the lecturer with wording.
✔ Errors in grammar are minor.
✔ The talk is within a range of 125–150 words.

EXAMPLE RESPONSE FOR INTEGRATED ESSAY "PRIMORDIAL SOUP"

Outline

Summary reading

- Miller-Urey
- Create conditions life in E's atmosphere
    Water, methane, hydrogen, ammonia
    Heat + electrical charges
- Weeks amino acids
- Posited
    Simple life forms in oceans
    Comets + meteorites amino acids
- Referred to as "primordial soup"
    Living structures on E ← natural evolution atmosphere

Lecture
Criticism → procedure + conclusions

- Procedure
    Constant electrical stimulation
    Acids more concentrated
    Amount oxygen reduced → incorrect proportions
- Conclusions
    E similar to meteorites = amino acids from beginning
    Acids deposited meteorite crash on landmasses

Map

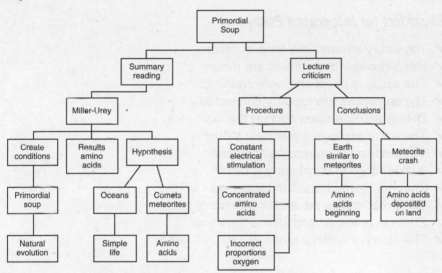

Example Essay

The Miller-Urey experiment was an attempt to recreate the conditions under which life may have evolved in the Earth's atmosphere. First, water, methane, hydrogen, and ammonia were heated and electrical charges were administered to simulate strong electrical storms that were probably part of early conditions. At the end of a few weeks, amino acids were identified in the liquid. Miller and Urey posited that simple life forms could have been nurtured in the early oceans, and furthermore, that comets and meteorites could have added more amino acids to the oceans. The mixture, referred to as "primordial soup," seemed to suggest that living structures on Earth could have developed from the natural evolution of the atmosphere.

Recent criticism of Miller and Urey calls into question both the procedure for the experiment and the conclusions. First, the mixture was subjected to constant electrical stimulation; however, storms in the early atmosphere were probably not continuous. Second, the amino acids that were created in the laboratory were probably more concentrated than those produced in the natural environment. Third, there is some question about the amount of oxygen that was reduced from the experimental mixture, a serious concern since the proportions would have to be the same for a simulation to be achieved. Finally, some researchers suggest the possibility that early Earth was similar to meteorites, and consequently, may have contained amino acids from the beginning or amino acids may have been deposited when meteorites crashed into the landmasses of a young planet Earth.

Checklist for Integrated Essay

✔ The essay answers the topic question.
✔ Inaccuracies in the content are minor.
✔ The essay is direct and well-organized.
✔ The sentences are logically connected.
✔ Details and examples support the main idea.
✔ The writer expresses complete thoughts.
✔ The meaning is easy to comprehend.
✔ A wide range of vocabulary is used.
✔ The writer paraphrases in his/her own words.
✔ The writer credits the author with wording.
✔ Errors in grammar and idioms are minor.
✔ The essay is within a range of 150–225 words.

EXAMPLE RESPONSE FOR INDEPENDENT ESSAY "LEARNING A FOREIGN LANGUAGE"

Outline

Advantages own country

- Teacher has similar experience—can use L1
- Cheaper than foreign travel
- Less stressful

Advantages foreign country

- Natural speech—accent + idioms
- Cultural context—behaviors
- Opportunities

My opinion—intermediate proficiency own country + advanced abroad

Map

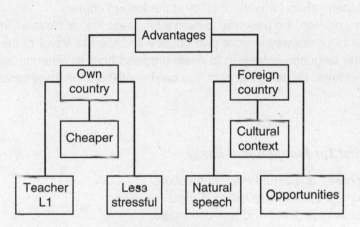

Intermediate own country
Advanced abroad

Example Essay

There are many advantages to learning a language in your own country. In the first place, it is quite a lot cheaper than it would be to travel to the country where the language is spoken. The cost of airfare, living accommodations, food, and tuition at a foreign school can be prohibitively high. In addition, there is less stress involved in learning in a familiar environment. Studying abroad requires that you speak the foreign language all the time to accomplish basic activities. Although it is an opportunity to use the language daily in a real setting, it can be very wearing. Finally, it is advantageous to have teachers who speak your native language because they have gone through the same stages of learning the foreign language that you are experiencing, and they know how to explain the new language by relating it to the native language.

Nevertheless, an argument can be made for learning a language in the country in which it is spoken. Only there can you truly hear the accent and idioms of natural speech. Being surrounded by the foreign language allows you to acquire nuances that elude the classroom. It is also beneficial to learn the language within the context of the culture so that you can learn the behaviors that accompany language. For example, learning how to order in a restaurant when you are right there with native speakers will also let you see how to behave in a restaurant in the foreign country. Finally, there are often opportunities that occur while you are in another country. Friendships can result in invitations to spend time with native speakers in their homes, and possibilities can present themselves for work or study in the foreign country.

In my opinion, the best way to learn a language is to achieve an intermediate level of proficiency in your own country and then to travel to the country where the language is spoken to make progress from the intermediate to the advanced level. By using this plan, you can benefit from the advantages of both options.

Checklist for Independent Essay

✔ The essay answers the topic question.
✔ The point of view or position is clear.
✔ The essay is direct and well-organized.
✔ The sentences are logically connected.
✔ Details and examples support the main idea.
✔ The writer expresses complete thoughts.
✔ The meaning is easy to comprehend.
✔ A wide range of vocabulary is used.
✔ Various types of sentences are included.
✔ Errors in grammar and idioms are minor.
✔ The essay is within a range of 300–350 words.

8

SCORE ESTIMATES

IMPORTANT BACKGROUND INFORMATION

It is not possible for you to determine the exact score that you will receive on the TOEFL® iBT. There are three reasons why this is true. First, the testing conditions on the day of your official TOEFL will affect your score. If you are in an uncomfortable room, if there are noisy distractions, if you are upset because you arrived in a rush, or if you are very nervous, then these factors can affect your score. The administration of a model test is more controlled. You will probably not be as stressed when you take one of the tests in this book. Second, the model tests in the book are designed to help you practice the most frequently tested item types on the official TOEFL. Because they are constructed to teach as well as to test, there is more repetition in TOEFL® iBT model tests than there is on official TOEFL® iBT tests. Tests that are not constructed for exactly the same purposes are not exactly comparable. Third, the TOEFL scores received by the same student will vary from one official TOEFL examination to another official TOEFL examination by as many as twenty points, even when the examinations are taken on the same day. In testing and assessment, this is called a standard error of measurement. Therefore, a TOEFL score cannot be predicted precisely, even when two official tests are used. But, of course, you would like to know how close you are to your goal. To do that, you can use the following procedure to estimate your TOEFL® iBT score. An estimate is an approximation.

PROCEDURE FOR SCORING

The official TOEFL® iBT tests have either a longer Reading section or a longer Listening section. The extra part on each test contains experimental questions that will not be graded as part of your score. You will need to do your best on all of the questions because you will not know which questions are experimental. The model tests in this book have either a longer Reading section or a longer Listening section. Use the procedure below with the charts on the following pages to determine your score estimate for each TOEFL® iBT model test.

1. Count the total number of correct answers for the Reading section Parts I and II.
2. Count the total number of correct answers for the Reading section Parts I and III for the model tests with a long Reading section.
3. Add the two totals for the Reading section and divide by 2 to calculate the Reading section average for the model tests with a long Reading section.
4. Count the total number of correct answers for the Listening section Parts I and II.
5. Count the total number of correct answers for the Listening section Parts I and III for the model tests with a long Listening section.
6. Add the two totals for the Listening section and divide by 2 to calculate the Listening section average for the model tests with a long Listening section.
7. Rate each question for the Speaking section on a holistic scale 0–4.
8. Add the six scores and divide by 6 to calculate the Speaking section average.
9. Rate each essay for the Writing section on a holistic scale 0–5.
10. Add the two scores and divide by 2 to calculate the Writing section average.
11. Refer to the reference charts on the following pages to find the scaled scores for each section *average*.
12. Finally, add the scaled scores for all four sections.

REFERENCE CHARTS

Reading

Correct Answers	Scaled Score
39	30
38	29
37	29
36	28
35	27
34	27
33	26
32	25
31	24
30	23
29	23
28	22
27	22
26	21
25	20
24	20
23	19
22	19
21	18
20	18
19	17
18	17
17	16
16	16
15	15
14	15
13	14
12	13
11	12
10	11
9	10
8	9
7	8
6	6
5	5
4	4
3	3
2	2
1	1
0	0

Listening

Correct Answers	Scaled Score
34	30
33	29
32	28
31	28
30	27
29	26
28	25
27	25
26	24
25	23
24	22
23	22
22	21
21	21
20	20
19	19
18	19
17	18
16	17
15	17
14	16
13	15
12	15
11	14
10	13
9	13
8	12
7	11
6	9
5	8
4	6
3	5
2	4
1	2
0	0

Speaking

Holistic Rating	Scaled Score
4.0	30
3.5	27
3.0	23
2.5	19
2.0	15
1.5	11
1.0	8
0	0

Writing

Holistic Rating	Scaled Score
5.0	30
4.5	28
4.0	25
3.5	22
3.0	20
2.5	17
2.0	14
1.5	11
1.0	8
0	0

EXAMPLES FOR SCORING MODEL TESTS

Example of iBT Model Test with Long Reading Section

Reading Section	Correct Answers	Scaled Score
Reading Parts I and II	37	
Reading Parts I and III	35	
Average number of correct answers	36	28

Listening Section		
Listening Parts I and II	30	
Listening Parts I and III	N/A	
Average number of correct answers	30	27

Speaking Section	Holistic Rating	
Speaking Question 1	4	
Speaking Question 2	4	
Speaking Question 3	3	
Speaking Question 4	3	
Speaking Question 5	4	
Speaking Question 6	3	
Average number of ratings	3.5	27

Writing Section		
Integrated essay	4	
Independent essay	5	
Average number of ratings	4.5	28

TOTAL
Add scaled scores for all sections   110

Example of iBT Model Test with Long Listening Section

Reading Section	Correct Answers	Scaled Score
Reading Parts I and II	36	
Reading Parts I and III	N/A	
Average number of correct answers	36	28

Listening Section		
Listening Parts I and II	29	
Listening Parts I and III	31	
Average number of correct answers	30	27

Speaking Section	Holistic Rating	
Speaking Question 1	4	
Speaking Question 2	4	
Speaking Question 3	3	
Speaking Question 4	3	
Speaking Question 5	4	
Speaking Question 6	3	
Average number of ratings	3.5	27

Writing Section		
Integrated essay	4	
Independent essay	5	
Average number of ratings	4.5	28

TOTAL
Add scaled scores for all sections   110

FEEDBACK

A new feature of the TOEFL score report is feedback. A general analysis of your strengths and weaknesses will be included with the numerical score. The computer program on the CD-ROM in the larger book provides feedback along with an automatic score report at the end of each model test.

OPTIONS FOR PERSONAL EVALUATION

SPEAKING

➤ Speak Up!

Speak Up! is a teacher-based evaluation, using the same criteria that raters use to score the official TOEFL Speaking section.

For more information on *Speak Up!*, visit *www.teflprep.com*.

WRITING

➤ Score It Now!

Score It Now! is an Internet-based essay evaluation using E-rater, a computerized scoring program that provides immediate scores for essays on a scale of 5–1 and general suggestions for improving essay writing skills. For a fee of $10, you can select from several authentic TOEFL essay topics, submit two essays, and receive two scores. Although the essays are not timed, you should complete them within thirty minutes in order to simulate a TOEFL writing experience. You should also take the time to read the sample essays that received scores of 5.

For more information on *Score It Now!*, visit *www.ets.org/scoreitnow*.

➤ Write Now!

Write Now! is a teacher-based evaluation, using the same criteria that raters use to score the official TOEFL essays.

For more information on *Write Now!*, visit *www.teflprep.com*.

9

RESOURCES

GLOSSARY OF CAMPUS VOCABULARY

academic advisor   n.   a person who helps students make decisions about their academic programs
Example: Dr. Jones is the *academic advisor* for the engineering students.
Suggestion: You should see your *academic advisor* before you decide.
Assumption: Dr. Jones is your *academic advisor*?
Problem: I can't see my *academic advisor* until Friday.

ace   v.   to receive a grade of A
Example: I *aced* that exam.
Suggestion: Find someone who *aced* the course to help you.
Assumption: Kathy *aced* her computer science class?
Problem: If I don't *ace* the final, I'll get a B in the class.

admissions office   n.   the administrative office where students apply for admission to a college or university
Example: I have an appointment at the *admissions office* to review my application.
Suggestion: Why don't you go over to the *admissions office*?
Assumption: You mean you couldn't find the *admissions office*?
Problem: I need to get to the *admissions office* before five o'clock.

all-nighter   n.   a study session that lasts all night
  Example: We had to pull an *all-nighter* to get ready for the final exam.
  Suggestion: If I were you, I wouldn't pull another *all-nighter*.
  Assumption: So you did pull another *all-nighter*.
  Problem: I have to pull an *all-nighter* in order to be ready for the final exam.

article   n.   a publication about an academic subject
  Example: We read six *articles* in addition to the reading in the textbook.
  Suggestion: You had better read the *articles* that were assigned.
  Assumption: You read the *articles* already?
  Problem: I need to read the *articles* again.

assignment   n.   work that must be done as part of the requirements for a class
  Example: The *assignment* was to read two chapters in the textbook.
  Suggestion: You had better read the *assignment* before class.
  Assumption: So you did read the *assignment* after all.
  Problem: I can't finish the *assignment* before class.

assistant professor   n.   a college or university teacher who ranks above a lecturer and below an associate professor
  Example: Dr. Green is an *assistant professor*.
  Suggestion: Why don't you find out whether he is a lecturer or an *assistant professor*?
  Assumption: You mean Dr. Green isn't an *assistant professor*?
  Problem: I need to find out whether Dr. Green is an *assistant professor*.

assistantship   n.   an opportunity for a graduate student to teach or do research in exchange for a stipend
  Example: Terry got an *assistantship* from State University.
  Suggestion: If I were you, I would apply for an *assistantship*.

Assumption: So you did get an *assistantship* from State University.

Problem: The *assistantship* doesn't pay as much as I thought it would.

associate professor n. a college or university teacher who ranks above an assistant professor and below a professor

Example: Dr. Peterson is an *associate professor* now, but she will be promoted to a full professor at the end of the year.

Suggestion: You could ask the secretary if Dr. Peterson is an *associate professor*.

Assumption: Dr. Peterson isn't an *associate professor*, is she?

Problem: If Dr. Peterson is an *associate professor*, I used the wrong title in my letter to her.

audit v. to attend a course without credit

Example: It usually costs as much to *audit* a course as to take it for credit.

Suggestion: You could *audit* the course if you don't need the credit.

Assumption: You mean you are *auditing* the course?

Problem: If I *audit* the course, I won't get credit for it.

bear n. a difficult class

Example: That computer science course was a *bear*.

Suggestion: I heard that Dr. Young's class is a real *bear*, so I would advise against it this semester.

Assumption: Your roommate thought this class was a *bear*?

Problem: Two of the classes I am in are real *bears*.

be behind v. to be late; to have a lot of work to do

Example: I *am behind* in my physics class.

Suggestion: You *are behind* in your psychology class so you should study.

Assumption: Bill *is behind*?

Problem: I can't go to the party because I *am behind* in my classes.

bike   n.   an abbreviation of the word *bicycle*
   Example: Many students ride their *bikes* on campus.
   Suggestion: You could park your *bike* outside the student union building.
   Assumption: Your *bike* was locked?
   Problem: I can't ride my *bike* to the pizza parlor because there isn't any parking for it.

bike rack   n.   the metal supports where bicycles are parked
   Example: That *bike rack* is full, but there is another one by the library.
   Suggestion: If I were you, I would use the *bike rack* closest to the door.
   Assumption: The *bike rack* was moved from in front of the library?
   Problem: The *bike racks* at my dormitory will not hold all of the students' bikes.

blackboard   n.   the writing surface in the front of the classroom
   Example: Dr. Mitchell always writes the important words on the *blackboard*.
   Suggestion: You had better copy everything the instructor writes on the *blackboard*.
   Assumption: You mean you copied all of the material that was on the *blackboard*?
   Problem: I can't see what is written on the *blackboard*.

book   n.   a written work
   Example: The *books* for this class cost eighty dollars.
   Suggestion: You shouldn't wait too long to buy your *books*.
   Assumption: You didn't buy all of your *books*?
   Problem: I can't buy all of my *books* with only fifty dollars.

book bag   n.   a bag in which to carry books and school supplies
   Example: This *book bag* is very heavy.
   Suggestion: Why don't you buy a sturdy *book bag* so it will last longer?
   Assumption: Your brand new *book bag* fell apart?
   Problem: I can't carry all of my books at one time because my *book bag* is too small.

bookstore n. the store on campus where students buy their
textbooks
Example: The *bookstore* opens at seven in the morning.
Suggestion: You should be at the *bookstore* before it opens so
that you can get a used book.
Assumption: You mean that you were at the *bookstore* early
and there were still no used books?
Problem: The *bookstore* is too far from my apartment for
me to walk.

break n. a pause in work or study
Example: Let's take a *break* after we finish our homework.
Suggestion: If I were you, I would take a *break* before I began
a new project.
Assumption: You mean you're taking a *break* right now?
Problem: I can't take a *break* until I complete this section of
the problem.

bring up v. to improve
Example: If Jack doesn't *bring up* his grades, he won't get
into graduate school.
Suggestion: If you want to *bring up* your grades, you will have
to study more.
Assumption: You *brought up* your grades without studying?
Problem: If I don't study more, I won't be able to *bring up*
my grades.

cafeteria n. a restaurant where students can select food from
several choices and carry their meals on trays to their tables
Example: Let's order a pizza instead of going to the *cafeteria*.
Suggestion: Why don't we meet in the *cafeteria* before going
to see our advisor?
Assumption: You mean you like the food in the *cafeteria*?
Problem: I can't meet you in the *cafeteria* because I have to
speak with my professor after class.

call on v. to acknowledge in class; to invite to speak
Example: The professor *calls on* students who sit in the
front more often than those who sit in back.

Suggestion: If you want the professor to *call on* you frequently, then sit in the front of the room.

Assumption: You sat in the front of the room and weren't *called on*?

Problem: I didn't know the answer when the professor *called on* me.

call the roll v. to read the names on a class roster in order to take attendance

Example: Some professors don't *call the roll*, but Dr. Peterson always does.

Suggestion: You should always find out whether or not the professor *calls the roll*.

Assumption: You mean you weren't there when Dr. Peterson *called the roll*?

Problem: I need to get to class earlier so that I will be there when Dr. Peterson *calls the roll*.

campus n. the buildings and grounds of a college or university

Example: State University has a beautiful *campus*.

Suggestion: You should see the *campus* before you decide to apply to school here.

Assumption: You mean you walked the entire *campus* by yourself?

Problem: I can't go with you to see the *campus* if you go this afternoon.

campus security n. the police on campus

Example: In an emergency, call *campus security*.

Suggestion: You had better call *campus security* to report that your bicycle is missing.

Assumption: The *campus security* is understaffed, isn't it?

Problem: Carol had to call *campus security* to help her get her car started.

carrel n. a private study space in the stacks of the library

Example: There are never enough *carrels* for all of the graduate students.

Suggestion: You should go to the library early in the evening if you want a *carrel*.

Assumption: You mean the *carrels* are free?
Problem: There aren't enough *carrels* in the library.

chapter   n.   a division in a book
Example: The professor assigned three *chapters* in the
textbook.
Suggestion: If I were you, I would set aside several hours to
read all of the *chapters* assigned today.
Assumption: So you did allow enough time to finish the
chapters.
Problem: I have to go to the lab, and I am in the middle of a
chapter.

cheat   v.   to act dishonestly
Example: Students who *cheat* may be expelled from the
university.
Suggestion: You should not *cheat* because the penalty is
serious.
Assumption: Gary was expelled because he *cheated*?
Problem: I know that some of my friends *cheated*, but I
don't know what to do about it.

cheating   n.   a dishonest act
Example: Sharing answers on an exam is *cheating*.
Suggestion: You could sit alone during the exam so that the
professor knows you are not *cheating*.
Assumption: You consider copying a few sentences from a
book *cheating*?
Problem: Should I report it to the professor if I see some-
one *cheating*?

check out   v.   to borrow
Example: You must have a library card to *check out* books.
Suggestion: If you want to *check out* books for your research
paper, you had better go to the library soon.
Assumption: So you didn't go to the library to *check out* the
books you needed?
Problem: I need a new library card to be able to *check out*
books.

class   n.   the meeting place and the content of a course
Example: We have three *classes* together this term.
Suggestion: You could arrange your schedule so that you have three *classes* on the same day.
Assumption: So you wanted your *classes* to be on Friday.
Problem: I have to work on Tuesdays and Thursdays, so I can't have *classes* on those days.

class discussion   n.   an exchange of ideas during a class
Example: Dr. Green often has *class discussions* instead of lectures.
Suggestion: If I were you, I would prepare for a *class discussion* in tomorrow's class.
Assumption: You prepared for the *class discussion*, didn't you?
Problem: I am not ready for the *class discussion* today.

closed out   adj.   to be denied access to a class
Example: Register early so that you aren't *closed out* of the classes you want.
Suggestion: Why don't you plan to register tomorrow before you are *closed out* of the classes you need to graduate?
Assumption: Sue registered early to avoid being *closed out* of her classes?
Problem: I was *closed out* of the English class I needed.

coed   adj.   an abbreviation for *coeducational,* which is a system of education in which both men and women attend the same school or classes
Example: Most of the schools in the United States are *coed*.
Suggestion: If I were you, I would live in a *coed* dormitory.
Assumption: You mean you don't attend a *coed* school?
Problem: My parents don't want me to live in a *coed* dormitory.

college   n.   a school that grants a bachelor's degree; an undergraduate division or a school within a university
Example: Steve applied to the *college* of business at State University.

Suggestion: You need to apply to the *college* of nursing early.

Assumption: So you did apply to several *colleges* after all.

Problem: The *college* of education requires three letters of recommendation.

commencement n. a graduation ceremony

Example: Larger colleges and universities usually have *commencement* more than once each year.

Suggestion: You had better be early for *commencement* because it starts on time.

Assumption: So you did attend last year's *commencement* exercises.

Problem: I don't have a cap and gown for *commencement*.

committee n. a group of professors who guide a graduate student's program and approve the thesis or dissertation

Example: Bill's *committee* signed his dissertation today.

Suggestion: You should be prepared before you meet with your *committee*.

Assumption: Your *committee* didn't approve your dissertation topic?

Problem: I need to do more research before I meet with my *committee*.

computer n. a programmable electronic machine that calculates, processes, and stores information

Example: At some universities, students must bring their own *computers* with them to school.

Suggestion: If I were you, I would purchase a *computer* before going to college.

Assumption: You mean you don't know how to use a *computer*?

Problem: I need to have my *computer* repaired.

computer disk n. a magnetic disk on which computer data is stored

Example: It's a good idea to save a copy of your papers and projects on a *computer disk*.

Suggestion: You should always have extra *computer disks*.

Assumption:	You mean you didn't save your work on a *computer disk*?
Problem:	I can't print my paper until I find my *computer disk*.

counselor n. a person who gives advice, often of a personal nature

Example:	See your advisor for academic advice and a *counselor* for personal advice.
Suggestion:	Why don't you speak with your *counselor* about the problems with your roommate?
Assumption:	You mean you have to make an appointment before seeing your *counselor*?
Problem:	I can't see my *counselor* until tomorrow.

course n. a class

Example:	How many *courses* are you taking this semester?
Suggestion:	If I were you, I would take fewer *courses* this semester.
Assumption:	You registered for your *courses* already?
Problem:	I need to take *courses* that apply to my major.

course request (form) n. a form used to register for a class

Example:	A student's academic advisor usually signs a *course request* form.
Suggestion:	You should pick up a *course request* form from the registrar's office today.
Assumption:	So you did pick up your *course request* form.
Problem:	I need to speak with my advisor about my *course request* form.

cram v. to study at the last minute

Example:	Nancy always *crams* for the quizzes in her math class.
Suggestion:	Why don't you study each night instead of *cramming* the night before the test?
Assumption:	You mean you *crammed* for the biology final?
Problem:	I need to be more organized so I won't have to *cram* for my tests.

credit   n.   a unit of study

Example:	I have thirty *credits* toward my master's degree.
Suggestion:	Why don't you check your *credits* with your advisor?
Assumption:	You mean you have enough *credits* to graduate?
Problem:	I have to take thirty more *credits* in my major area.

credit hour   n.   the number that represents one hour of class per week for one term

Example:	This course is three *credit hours*.
Suggestion:	You could take eighteen *credit hours* this semester.
Assumption:	So you did complete fifteen *credit hours* last summer.
Problem:	I can't take enough *credit hours* to graduate this semester.

curve   n.   a grading system that relies on the normal curve of distribution, resulting in a few A grades, the majority C grades, and a few failing grades

Example:	Grading on the *curve* encourages competition.
Suggestion:	Forget about the *curve*, and just do your best.
Assumption:	Dr. Graham grades his tests on the *curve*?
Problem:	Since the exams were graded on the *curve*, a 95 was a B.

cut class   v.   to be absent from class, usually without a good excuse

Example:	My roommate *cut class* on Monday because he didn't come back to campus until late Sunday night.
Suggestion:	You had better not *cut class* on Thursday.
Assumption:	You *cut class* to sleep in?
Problem:	I can't *cut class* because I have too many absences.

dean   n.   an administrator who ranks above a department chair and below a vice president

Example:	The *dean* called a meeting with the department chair.

Suggestion: You should meet with the *dean* about your problem.
Assumption: So you did speak with the *dean*.
Problem: Vicki has to prepare a presentation for the *dean*.

dean's list n. the honor roll at a college or university
Example: You must maintain a 3.5 grade point average to be on the *dean's list*.
Suggestion: You had better improve your grades if your want to make the *dean's list*.
Assumption: Jack made the *dean's list* last semester?
Problem: I can't make the *dean's list* this semester.

declare v. to make an official decision about a major field of study
Example: Most students *declare* their major in their third year at the university.
Suggestion: If I were you, I would *declare* my major before I take any more classes.
Assumption: You mean you *declared* your major last year?
Problem: Joe needs to *declare* his major soon.

degree n. an academic title awarded to a student who completes a course of study
Example: The three most common *degrees* are a bachelor's, a master's, and a doctorate.
Suggestion: You should get your *degree* before you get married.
Assumption: So you did graduate with a *degree* in music theory.
Problem: I can't get a good job without a *degree*.

department n. a division of a college or university organized by subject
Example: The English *department* offers classes for international students.
Suggestion: Why don't you check the *department's* phone number again?
Assumption: So you worked in the English *department* office.
Problem: I can't find the list of the *department* offices.

department chair   n.   a university administrator for a division of a
college or university
Example: The professors in a department report to the
               department chair.
Suggestion: You could speak to the *department chair* about
               auditing the class.
Assumption: You mean Dr. Carlson is the new *department
               chair*?
Problem: I can't meet with the *department chair* until after
               registration.

diploma   n.   the certificate of completion for a degree
Example: Students receive their *diplomas* at the graduation
               ceremony.
Suggestion: You should get your *diploma* framed.
Assumption: So you did show your family your *diploma*.
Problem: I need to mail this form and pay my fees before I
               can get my *diploma*.

dissertation   n.   a thesis that is written in partial fulfillment of the
requirements for a doctorate.
Example: Dr. Green wrote his *dissertation* on global warming.
Suggestion: If I were you, I would consider several ideas
               before selecting a *dissertation* topic.
Assumption: You mean you already started your *dissertation*?
Problem: I can't find enough research on my *dissertation*
               topic.

distance learning   n.   courses organized so that students can
complete the requirements by computer, or other media, often
without going to campus
Example: There are several *distance learning* opportunities
               for working adults.
Suggestion: Why don't you sign up for that course through
               distance learning?
Assumption: So you did take that *distance learning* class.
Problem: I can only take three *distance learning* classes.

division   n.   a group of departments in a college or university

Example: The *division* of modern languages includes both the Spanish department and the French department as well as the German department.

Suggestion: Why don't you go to the *division* of math and sciences to find more information about biology instructors?

Assumption: You mean you've already spoken to Dr. Conrad about the entrance exam for the *division* of social sciences?

Problem: I need to find out what opportunities the *division* of modern languages offers for foreign study.

doctorate   n.   the degree after a master's degree awarded to an academic doctor

Example: Karen will receive her *doctorate* in the spring.

Suggestion: You should meet with your academic advisor to discuss a *doctorate.*

Assumption: So you did receive your *doctorate* from State University.

Problem: I must complete my dissertation before I get my *doctorate.*

dorm   n.   an abbreviation for *dormitory*

Example: Living on campus in a *dorm* is often cheaper than living off campus.

Suggestion: You should live in a *dorm* for at least one year.

Assumption: You lived in a *dorm* for four years?

Problem: Sue needs to apply now for a room in the *dorm.*

draft   n.   a preliminary copy of a paper or other written document

Example: A good student does not turn in a first *draft* of a paper.

Suggestion: You should edit each *draft* on the computer.

Assumption: You wrote the first *draft* in one night?

Problem: I can't turn in my essay because I have only the first *draft* written.

drop   v.   to withdraw from a course

Example: If you *drop* a course early in the term, you may get a partial refund.

Suggestion: If I were you, I would *drop* the class immediately.

Assumption: You mean you *dropped* the class because it was too hard?

Problem: Bill needs to *drop* one of his classes because he is taking too many credit hours.

drop out   v.   to withdraw from a college or university

Example: Mark *dropped out* because he needed to work full-time.

Suggestion: You could *drop out* and then reenter next semester.

Assumption: Diane *dropped out* after her junior year?

Problem: I have to *drop out* because I don't have enough money for tuition.

due   adj.   expected on a certain date

Example: The assignment is *due* on Friday.

Suggestion: Why don't you turn in the paper before it's *due*?

Assumption: You mean the project is *due* this week?

Problem: I can't complete the assignment by the *due* date.

elective (course)   n., adj.   an optional academic course

Example: In the junior year, most students are taking *elective* courses as well as requirements.

Suggestion: Take some *elective* classes in your areas of outside interest.

Assumption: So you did take an *elective* in art appreciation.

Problem: I can't take any *elective* classes this semester.

enroll   v.   to register for a course or a university program

Example: Only a few students *enroll* in seminars.

Suggestion: Why don't you *enroll* early before the class fills up?

Assumption: You mean you didn't *enroll* in the computer class?

Problem: I can't *enroll* in that class without taking the introductory class first.

essay   n.   a short composition on a single subject, usually presenting the personal opinion of the author
    Example: An *essay* is often five paragraphs long.
    Suggestion: If I were you, I would make an outline before writing the *essay*.
    Assumption: So you did get an A on the *essay*.
    Problem: I have to write an *essay* for my class on Friday.

exam   n.   an abbreviation for *examination*
    Example: The professor scheduled several quizzes and one *exam*.
    Suggestion: You had better prepare for the *exam* in chemistry.
    Assumption: You studied for the physics *exam*?
    Problem: I have to meet with my study group before the *exam*.

excused absence   n.   absence with the permission of the professor
    Example: Dr. Mitchell allows every student one *excused absence* each semester.
    Suggestion: You could take an *excused absence* in your Friday class so we could leave early.
    Assumption: You mean you have two *excused absences* in biology?
    Problem: I already have one *excused absence* in Dr. Mitchell's class.

expel   v.   to dismiss from school
    Example: Gary was *expelled* because he cheated on an exam.
    Suggestion: You should avoid getting *expelled* at all costs.
    Assumption: Gary was *expelled* from the university?
    Problem: I would be *expelled* if I helped you.

extension   n.   additional time
    Example: We asked Dr. Peterson for an *extension* in order to complete the group project.
    Suggestion: You should organize your time so that you will not have to ask for an *extension*.

Assumption:	You mean your request for an *extension* was denied?
Problem:	I need to meet with my professor to discuss an *extension*.

faculty member   n.   a teacher in a college or university

Example:	Dr. Baker is a *faculty member* at State University.
Suggestion:	Why don't you ask a *faculty member* for directions?
Assumption:	You didn't meet any of the new *faculty members* when you visited the campus?
Problem:	I don't know the other *faculty members* in my department very well.

fail   v.   to receive an unacceptable grade

Example:	If Mary gets another low grade, she will *fail* the course.
Suggestion:	You had better complete the project or you will *fail* the class.
Assumption:	You mean you *failed* the exam?
Problem:	I have to study tonight, or I will *fail* the test tomorrow.

fee   n.   a charge for services

Example:	You must pay a *fee* to park your car on campus.
Suggestion:	If I were you, I would pay my *fees* before the late penalty applies.
Assumption:	You mean there are *fees* for using the recreational facilities?
Problem:	I need to go to the business office to pay my *fees*.

field trip   n.   a trip for observation and education

Example:	The geology class usually takes several *field trips* to the museum.
Suggestion:	You should wear sturdy shoes on the *field trip*.
Assumption:	You didn't sign up for the *field trip* to the art gallery?
Problem:	I have to go on a *field trip* Saturday morning, but my boss won't let me off work.

fill-in-the-blank (test) n., adj. an objective test in which the student completes sentences by writing in the missing words

Example: Dr. Stephens always gives *fill-in-the-blank* tests during the semester, but he gives short-essay finals.

Suggestion: You had better study the definitions for the *fill-in-the-blank* portion of the test.

Assumption: You mean the test was all *fill-in-the-blank*?

Problem: Kathy needs to do better on the *fill-in-the-blank* questions.

final (exam) n. the last examination of an academic course

Example: The *final* will include questions from the notes as well as from the textbook.

Suggestion: You should use both your notes and the text to review for the *final exam.*

Assumption: You finished your *final* in an hour?

Problem: I have to prepare for two *final exams* on the same day.

fine n. a sum of money paid for violation of a rule

Example: The *fine* for keeping a library book after the due date is one dollar per day.

Suggestion: You should move your car to avoid a *fine.*

Assumption: You mean you were charged a *fine* for parking there?

Problem: I need to pay my *fines* before the end of the semester.

fraternity n. a social organization for male college students

Example: Bill is going to join a *fraternity*.

Suggestion: You could join a professional *fraternity*.

Assumption: You were invited to join three *fraternities*?

Problem: I can't afford to join a *fraternity*.

fraternity row n. a street where many fraternity houses are located

Example: I live on Fifth Street, near *fraternity row*.

Suggestion: Why don't you walk down *fraternity row* to look at the homecoming decorations?

Assumption: Isn't Ken going to live on *fraternity row* next year?

Problem: I can't find a place to park on *fraternity row*.

freshman n. a first-year college student

Example: Most of the students in Manchester Hall are *freshmen*.

Suggestion: You should establish good study habits while you are a *freshman*.

Assumption: Didn't you live in a dorm when you were a *freshman*?

Problem: The *freshmen* have to take requirements.

full-time adj. the number of hours for standard tuition at a college or university, usually 9 hours for a graduate student and 12–15 hours for an undergraduate student

Example: Tom is a *full-time* student this semester.

Suggestion: If I were you, I would register as a *full-time* student this semester.

Assumption: You mean the scholarship is only available to *full-time* students?

Problem: I need to register as a *full-time* student to be eligible for a loan.

get behind v. to be late or off schedule

Example: I am *getting behind* in my math class.

Suggestion: You had better study this weekend or you will *get behind* in English.

Assumption: Ken *got behind* in his classes?

Problem: I *got behind* in French, and now my class is really confusing.

get caught up v. to bring up to date

Example: We are going to *get caught up* in our classes this weekend.

Suggestion: Why don't you *get caught up* in English before you start your next project?

Assumption: Sue *got caught up* over vacation?

Problem: I need to *get caught up* before final exams.

G.P.A. n. abbreviation for grade point average
    Example: Kathy's *G.P.A.* as an undergraduate was 4.0, but she isn't doing as well in graduate school.
    Suggestion: You should be concerned about your *G.P.A.*
    Assumption: Laura's *G.P.A.* dropped last semester?
    Problem: I can't raise my *G.P.A.* if I take calculus.

grade point average n. a scale, usually 0–4, on which grades are calculated
    Example: If students' *grade point averages* fall below 2.0, they will be placed on probation.
    Suggestion: If I were you, I would speak to my academic advisor about your *grade point average.*
    Assumption: You mean your *grade point average* is more important than work experience?
    Problem: I need to improve my *grade point average.*

grades n. a standard number or letter indicating a student's level of performance
    Example: We will get our *grades* in the mail a week after the semester is over.
    Suggestion: You should check the *grades* that the professor posted.
    Assumption: Our *grades* are already in the mail?
    Problem: I have to have better *grades* to get into the college of business.

graduate school n. a division of a college or university to serve students who are pursuing masters or doctoral degrees
    Example: I would like to apply to *graduate school* after I complete my bachelor's degree.
    Suggestion: Why don't you work a year before applying to *graduate school*?
    Assumption: So Tracy did get accepted to *graduate school.*
    Problem: I have to get letters of recommendation to apply to *graduate school.*

graduate student   n.   a student who is pursuing a master's or doctorate

Example:	*Graduate students* must maintain higher grades than undergraduate students.
Suggestion:	You had better work with the other *graduate students* on this project.
Assumption:	You mean only *graduate students* are allowed to take this class?
Problem:	All of the students in the class are *graduate students* except me.

grant   n.   funds for research or study

Example:	Carol received a *grant* for her research in psychology.
Suggestion:	You should apply for a summer *grant.*
Assumption:	You mean there are *grants* available for undergraduate students?
Problem:	Bill needs to write a proposal before Tuesday if he wants to be considered for a *grant.*

group project   n.   an assignment to be completed by three or more students

Example:	I prefer to work on *group projects* instead of on assignments by myself.
Suggestion:	You should select your *group project* before midterm.
Assumption:	You've chosen your *group project* already?
Problem:	The *group project* will take more time than I thought.

hand back   v.   return an assignment

Example:	Dr. Graham always *hands back* our assignments the next day.
Suggestion:	You had better be there when Dr. Mitchell *hands back* your exam.
Assumption:	Dr. Mitchell hasn't *handed back* your exam yet?
Problem:	I can't find the exam that he *handed back.*

handout   n.   prepared notes that a teacher provides to the class
    Example: Dr. Stephen's *handouts* are always very helpful.
    Suggestion: You had better save all of your *handouts.*
    Assumption: You lost the *handouts*?
    Problem: I need to organize all of my *handouts* before I
                    start to study for the final.

head resident   n.   the advisor for a dormitory
    Example: The *head resident* can help you resolve problems
                    with your roommate.
    Suggestion: If I were you, I would introduce myself to the *head*
                    resident.
    Assumption: So you did speak with the *head resident.*
    Problem: I can't find the *head resident.*

health center   n.   the clinic on campus to provide basic health
care for students
    Example: We are going to the *health center* for a free eye
                    examination.
    Suggestion: You had better go to the *health center* for that
                    cough.
    Assumption: You mean the *health center* is closed?
    Problem: I am too sick to go to the *health center.*

health insurance   n.   protection for students who may need
medical attention
    Example: *Health insurance* is required on most campuses.
    Suggestion: You need to purchase *health insurance* through
                    the university.
    Assumption: You don't have *health insurance*?
    Problem: I have to earn some more money to pay for my
                    health insurance.

hit the books   v.   to study very hard
    Example: I have to *hit the books* tonight and tomorrow to
                    get ready for the midterm.
    Suggestion: You had better *hit the books* for Dr. Sheridan's
                    exam.

Assumption: You mean you didn't *hit the books* for the psychology exam?

Problem: My friends have to *hit the books* this weekend so they can't go to the party with me.

homework n. schoolwork done at home

Example: If I do my *homework* every day, I understand the lectures better.

Suggestion: Why don't you do your *homework* before dinner?

Assumption: There wasn't any *homework* last night, was there?

Problem: I have to do my *homework* in order to be prepared for the class discussion.

honors adj. special recognition for exceptional students

Example: Jane is an *honors* graduate.

Suggestion: You could live in an *honors* dorm.

Assumption: So you did enroll in the *honors* program.

Problem: The courses in the *honors* program are much harder than the regular courses.

housing office n. an administrative office for residence halls and off-campus rentals

Example: Let's go over to the *housing office* to ask about apartments near the campus.

Suggestion: If I were you, I would check at the *housing office* for a dorm application.

Assumption: You mean the *housing office* closed early?

Problem: I need to speak with someone in the *housing office* about my application.

incomplete n. a grade in a course that allows students to complete requirements the following term

Example: I asked Dr. Young for an *incomplete* in his class.

Suggestion: You should request an *incomplete* at least two weeks before the end of the term.

Assumption: Bill took an *incomplete* in sociology last semester?

Problem: I can't ask Dr. Young for another *incomplete*.

instructor   n.   a college or university teacher who ranks below an assistant professor
Example: My *instructor* for math is from Hawaii.
Suggestion: You should check with the *instructor* to see if there is room in the class.
Assumption: The *instructor* was absent?
Problem: I can't seem to get along with my *instructor*.

interactive television (course)   n.   a distance learning course that is taught on two-way television connections
Example: The instructor for our *interactive television course* is on a campus about fifty miles away.
Suggestion: You could take that *course* on the *interactive television.*
Assumption: Dr. Stephen's *course* is offered on *interactive television?*
Problem: *Interactive television courses* make me uncomfortable.

interlibrary loan   n.   a system that allows students on one campus to borrow books from other libraries on other campuses
Example: It takes at least a week to receive a book by *interlibrary loan.*
Suggestion: You could see if the book is available through *interlibrary loan.*
Assumption: Your *interlibrary loan* books arrived in time?
Problem: I can't seem to find the desk for *interlibrary loans.*

internship   n.   a training opportunity for an advanced student or a recent graduate
Example: Bill got an *internship* at the University Hospital.
Suggestion: You should apply for an *internship* very early.
Assumption: You are getting paid for your *internship?*
Problem: I need to serve a two-year *internship.*

junior   n., adj.   a third-year college student
Example: When I am a *junior*, I plan to study abroad for a semester.
Suggestion: You could concentrate on your major your *junior* year.

Assumption: A *junior* can study abroad?
Problem: I need to carry eighteen credit hours both semesters of my *junior* year.

keep grades up   v.   to maintain a good grade point average
Example: If Joanne doesn't *keep her grades up*, she will lose her scholarship.
Suggestion: You need to study harder if you want to *keep your grades up*.
Assumption: Kathy didn't *keep her grades up* this semester?
Problem: I can't *keep my grades up* and work full-time.

lab   n., adj.   abbreviation for laboratory
Example: The course includes a five-hour *lab*.
Suggestion: You had better allow sufficient time for your biology *lab*.
Assumption: You missed the last *lab* session?
Problem: I need to find a partner for my psychology *lab*.

lab assistant   n.   a graduate student who helps in the lab
Example: Bill is Dr. Peterson's *lab assistant*.
Suggestion: You could ask the *lab assistant* for help.
Assumption: You are the *lab assistant*, aren't you?
Problem: I need to speak with the *lab assistant* before class.

laboratory   n.   a classroom equipped for experiments and research
Example: The physics *laboratory* at State University is very old.
Suggestion: You could meet your biology study group in the *laboratory*.
Assumption: The *laboratory* isn't closed Saturday, is it?
Problem: I have to get directions to the *laboratory*.

lab report   n.   a written description of the laboratory activities
Example: Our *lab reports* are due every Friday.
Suggestion: If I were you, I wouldn't wait to start my *lab report*.
Assumption: You mean the *lab reports* have to be typed?
Problem: I have to turn in my *lab report* tomorrow.

learning assistance center   n.   an area used for tutoring and special programs to help students with their classes

Example: I have to meet my tutor at the *learning assistance center* at four o'clock.

Suggestion: You should go to the *learning assistance center* for help in the morning.

Assumption: So Nancy did go to the *learning assistance center* for tutoring.

Problem: The tutors at the *learning assistance center* are all juniors and seniors, so I don't qualify.

lecture   n.   a presentation for a class, delivered by the professor

Example: The *lectures* are really interesting, but I don't enjoy the labs as much.

Suggestion: You should take more notes during Dr. Mitchell's *lectures*.

Assumption: The *lecture* is canceled for today?

Problem: I can't keep up with the *lectures.*

lecturer   n.   a college or university teacher, usually without rank

Example: Mr. Lewis is only a *lecturer*, but his classes are very good.

Suggestion: If I were you, I would speak with the *lecturer* about your questions.

Assumption: The *lecturer* isn't here?

Problem: I can't take notes because the *lecturer* speaks too fast.

library   n.   the building on campus where books and other research materials are kept

Example: Vicki has a job in the *library*.

Suggestion: Your study group could reserve a study room in the *library*.

Assumption: You mean the *library* is within walking distance?

Problem: I need to return my books to the *library*.

library card   n.   an identification card that permits the holder to borrow books and materials from the library

Example: Without a *library card*, you can't borrow books here.

Suggestion: You should get a *library card* right away.
Assumption: So you did bring your *library card* with you.
Problem: I can't use my *library card* because I owe a fine.

library fine   n.   a payment for returning books and materials after the due date
Example: You can't get your grade report unless you pay your *library fines*.
Suggestion: You should pay your *library fines* immediately.
Assumption: You owe ten dollars in *library fines*?
Problem: Nancy needs to pay her *library fines* before she checks out any more books.

lost and found   n.   an area on campus where items are kept for their owners to reclaim
Example: Maybe someone picked up your book and took it to the *lost and found*.
Suggestion: Why don't you check at the *lost and found* for your backpack?
Assumption: You mean Sue's wallet wasn't at the *lost and found*?
Problem: Sue needs to fill out a report at the *lost and found*.

lower-division (course)   adj.   introductory-level courses for first- and second-year students
Example: Seniors don't usually take *lower-division* courses.
Suggestion: You should take *lower-division* classes your first year.
Assumption: You mean all of the *lower-division* classes are full?
Problem: I have to take a *lower-division* class before I can take the advanced course.

major   n.   a field of study chosen as an academic specialty
Example: My *major* is environmental studies.
Suggestion: You should declare your *major* by your junior year.
Assumption: You mean you have to declare a *major* to graduate?
Problem: I have to tell my advisor my *major* tomorrow.

makeup test   n.   a test taken after the date of the original administration

Example:	Dr. Stephens usually allows her students to take a *makeup test* if there is a good reason for being absent.
Suggestion:	You could speak with Dr. Stephens about taking a *makeup test*.
Assumption:	Dr. Peterson let you take a *makeup test*?
Problem:	Dana needs to take a *makeup test* before spring break.

married student housing   n.   apartments on or near campus for married students

Example:	There is usually a waiting list to be assigned to *married student housing*.
Suggestion:	If I were you, I would get an application for *married student housing* today.
Assumption:	You mean there are no vacancies in *married student housing*?
Problem:	We need to pick up an application for *married student housing*.

Mickey Mouse course   n.   a very easy course

Example:	This is a *Mickey Mouse course,* but it is on my program of study.
Suggestion:	Why don't you take one *Mickey Mouse course* this semester just for fun?
Assumption:	You thought physics was a *Mickey Mouse course*?
Problem:	I have to take this *Mickey Mouse course* to fulfill my physical education requirement.

midterm   n.   an exam that is given in the middle of the term

Example:	I got an A on my *midterm* in accounting.
Suggestion:	Why don't you study with your study group for the music theory *midterm*?
Assumption:	You mean Sue failed her economics *midterm*?
Problem:	I have three *midterms* in one day.

minor   n.   a secondary area of study
    Example: With a major in international business, I decided to do my *minor* in English.
    Suggestion: You should *minor* in economics since you're studying prelaw.
    Assumption: You mean you've completed all of your *minor* classes?
    Problem: I need one more class to complete my *minor*.

miss (class)   v.   to be absent
    Example: My roommate is *missing* a lot of classes lately.
    Suggestion: If I were you I wouldn't *miss* Dr. Mitchell's class today.
    Assumption: So you did *miss* class last Friday.
    Problem: I can't *miss* any more of Dr. Mitchell's classes, or my grade will be lowered by one letter.

multiple-choice test   n.   an objective test with questions that provide several possible answer choices
    Example: We usually have *multiple-choice tests* in Dr. Graham's classes.
    Suggestion: You had better study very carefully for Dr. Graham's *multiple-choice test*.
    Assumption: It was a *multiple-choice test*?
    Problem: I don't usually do well on *multiple-choice tests*.

notebook   n.   a bound book with blank pages in it for notes
    Example: I lost the *notebook* with my biology notes in it.
    Suggestion: You should make sure that your *notebook* is well organized.
    Assumption: You lost your *notebook*?
    Problem: I need to organize my *notebook* this weekend.

notebook computer   n.   a computer the size of a notebook
    Example: Joe has a *notebook computer* that he uses in class.
    Suggestion: Why don't you use my *notebook computer* to see whether you like it?
    Assumption: So you did purchase a *notebook computer*.

Problem: I can't possibly afford a *notebook computer* right now.

notes n. a brief record of a lecture to help students recall the important points

Example: We didn't take *notes* in class today because most of the lecture was from the book.

Suggestion: You should copy Tracy's *notes* before the next test.

Assumption: You mean you lent your *notes* to someone?

Problem: I need to recopy my *notes* this evening.

objective test n. a test with questions that have one possible answer, usually presented in a multiple-choice, matching, or true-false format

Example: The final exam will be an *objective test*, not an essay test.

Suggestion: You should probably prepare for an *objective test* in math.

Assumption: The final exam was an *objective test*?

Problem: I have to study harder for *objective tests*.

off campus adj. not on university property

Example: There are some very nice apartments just *off campus* on State Street.

Suggestion: You should come to campus early unless you want to park *off campus*.

Assumption: You mean Carol doesn't want to live *off campus*?

Problem: I need to live *off campus* to save money.

office n. a place for university faculty and staff to meet with students and do their work

Example: Mr. Lewis has an *office* in Madison Hall.

Suggestion: Most of the advisors' *offices* are in Sycamore Hall.

Assumption: So you did find Mr. Lewis's *office* before he left for the day.

Problem: I have to go to the business *office* tomorrow to ask about my bill.

office hours   n.   a schedule when faculty are in their offices to meet with students
Example: *Office hours* are usually posted on the door of the professor's office.
Suggestion: You should write down the instructor's *office hours* in your notebook.
Assumption: You don't know Dr. Miller's *office hours*?
Problem: I can't find my copy of Dr. Miller's *office hours.*

online course   n.   a course taught on the Internet
Example: There is a separate list of *online courses* this semester.
Suggestion: Why don't you consider an *online course* in economics?
Assumption: Joe took an *online course* last year?
Problem: I need a computer to take an *online course.*

on probation   prep. phrase   experiencing a trial period to improve grades before disciplinary action
Example: Kathy is *on probation,* so she will probably be studying this weekend.
Suggestion: You had better keep up your grades or you will end up *on probation.*
Assumption: Sue couldn't be *on probation* again.
Problem: I can't let my parents find out that I am *on probation.*

on reserve   prep. phrase   retained in a special place in the library, usually for use only in the library
Example: Dr. Young always puts a lot of books *on reserve* for his classes.
Suggestion: You could check to see if the book is *on reserve.*
Assumption: You mean the articles are *on reserve*?
Problem: I have to find out which books are *on reserve.*

open-book test   n.   a test during which students may consult their books and notes
Example: *Open-book tests* are often longer than other tests.
Suggestion: You should still prepare even though it is an *open-book test.*

Assumption: You mean you didn't know it was an *open-book test*?

Problem: I can't find my notes for the *open-book test*.

orientation   n.   a program for new students at a college or university during which they receive information about the school

Example: I missed the first day of *orientation*, so I didn't get a map.

Suggestion: You should sit near the front during *orientation*.

Assumption: So you did go to freshman *orientation*.

Problem: I have to go to *orientation* tomorrow evening.

override   n.   permission to enter a class for which the student does not qualify

Example: Dr. Stephens will usually give you an *override* if you need the class.

Suggestion: You should speak to the professor about getting an *override* for that class.

Assumption: You mean your request for an *override* was denied?

Problem: I need to get an *override* so that I can take that class.

paper   n.   a research report

Example: The *papers* for this class should be at least ten pages long.

Suggestion: You had better follow Dr. Carlyle's guidelines for this *paper*.

Assumption: Laura turned in her *paper* late?

Problem: I can't print my *paper* because I need an ink cartridge for my printer.

parking garage   n.   a structure for parking, usually requiring payment

Example: The *parking garages* are too far away from the classrooms.

Suggestion: You had better get a parking permit for the *parking garage*.

Assumption: You mean you don't know which *parking garage* you used?

Problem: I have to find a *parking garage* with a vacancy.

parking lot   n. an area for parking
    Example: This *parking lot* is for students only.
    Suggestion: You should avoid leaving your car in the *parking lot* overnight.
    Assumption: You mean your car was towed from the *parking lot*?
    Problem: I have to leave early to get a spot in the *parking lot* beside the dorm.

parking permit   n. permission to park in certain parking lots or garages
    Example: Your *parking permit* expires at the end of the month.
    Suggestion: If I were you, I would get a *parking permit* when you register.
    Assumption: My *parking permit* has expired?
    Problem: I need to pay my fines before they will issue me another *parking permit*.

parking space   n. a designated area for one car
    Example: There is a car in my *parking space*.
    Suggestion: You should not use a reserved *parking space*.
    Assumption: So you did park in someone else's *parking space*.
    Problem: I can't find a *parking space*.

parking ticket   n. notice of a fine due for parking in a restricted area
    Example: If you don't take care of your *parking tickets*, you won't be able to register for classes next semester.
    Suggestion: You could avoid getting *parking tickets* by using the student parking lots.
    Assumption: You mean Carol got a *parking ticket* because she didn't have a permit?
    Problem: I have to save money to pay my *parking ticket*s.

part-time   adj. less than the full work day or school day
    Example: Laura has a *part-time* job after school.
    Suggestion: Why don't you get a *part-time* job to pay for your books?

Assumption: You applied for a *part-time* job on campus?

Problem: I need to find a *part-time* job this summer.

pass back v. to return tests and assignments to the owner

Example: Dr. Young is going to *pass back* our quizzes today.

Suggestion: You should ask Dr. Young for an appointment after he *passes back* the tests.

Assumption: Dr. Young didn't *pass back* the papers?

Problem: I have to get my paper from Dr. Young because I wasn't there when he *passed them back*.

placement office n. the office where students receive assistance in locating employment

Example: Several companies are interviewing students at the *placement office* this week.

Suggestion: Why don't you check the interview listing in the *placement office* on Monday?

Assumption: Joe got his job through the *placement office*?

Problem: I need to schedule an interview in the *placement office*.

plagiarize v. to use someone else's written work without giving that person credit

plagiarizing n. the use of someone else's work without giving that person credit

Example: To avoid *plagiarizing*, always cite the source.

Suggestion: If you change this sentence, it will keep you from *plagiarizing*.

Assumption: You mean you know someone who *plagiarized*?

Problem: The professor thought that I had *plagiarized* a report.

pop quiz n. a quiz that is given without notice

Example: We had a *pop quiz* in our sociology class today.

Suggestion: You should always be prepared for a *pop quiz*.

Assumption: You passed all of the *pop quizzes*?

Problem: I have to be on time to class in case there is a *pop quiz* at the beginning of class.

post (grade) v. to publish a list and display it in a public place

Example: The grades for the exams are *posted* on Dr. Graham's door.

Suggestion: You should see if the grades have been *posted* yet.

Assumption: The assignments aren't *posted* yet, are they?

Problem: I can't get to campus to see if the grades are *posted*.

prerequisite n. a course required before a student is eligible to take a higher-level course

Example: This English class has two *prerequisites*.

Suggestion: You should check the *prerequisites* before seeing your advisor.

Assumption: You took the *prerequisites* last year?

Problem: I have to pass the *prerequisites* before I can register for the next class.

presentation n. a lecture, speech, or demonstration in front of the class

Example: Your *presentation* in our anthropology class was very interesting.

Suggestion: You could use more pictures in your *presentation*.

Assumption: You mean your *presentation* is fifty minutes long?

Problem: I need to get over my fear of public speaking before I give my *presentation*.

professor n. a college or university teacher who ranks above an associate professor

Example: Dr. Baker is a *professor* of English.

Suggestion: Why don't you speak with your *professor* about the project?

Assumption: The *professor's* office hours are posted, aren't they?

Problem: I need to speak to my *professor* before class on Friday.

program of study n.   a list of the courses that a student must take to fulfill the requirements for graduation

Example: If you want to change your *program of study*, you must see your advisor.

Suggestion: Why don't you review your *program of study* in your catalog?

Assumption: The *program of study* is a four-year plan, isn't it?

Problem: I need to become familiar with my *program of study*.

project n.   an assignment that often involves the application of knowledge

Example: We can do the *project* by ourselves or in a group.

Suggestion: Why don't you and your study group do the *project* together?

Assumption: You did the *project* that everyone is talking about?

Problem: I have to present my *project* to the class.

quarter n.   a school term that is usually ten to twelve weeks in length

Example: This *quarter* has gone by very quickly.

Suggestion: You could take fewer classes next *quarter*.

Assumption: You mean you have to finish your thesis this *quarter*?

Problem: I need to study harder next *quarter*.

quiz n.   an evaluation that is usually shorter and worth fewer points than a test

Example: We have a *quiz* in our algebra class every week.

Suggestion: You should always be prepared for a *quiz*.

Assumption: The *quiz* doesn't include last night's reading, does it?

Problem: We have a *quiz* in chemistry this week.

registrar n.   a university official in charge of keeping records

Example: You need to see the *registrar* about your grade change.

Suggestion: If I were you, I would check with the *registrar* about your transcript.

Assumption: So you did file a change of address with the *registrar*.

Problem: The *registrar* is unavailable until next week.

registration   n.   the process for enrolling in courses at a college or university

Example: *Registration* always takes longer than I think it will.

Suggestion: You should meet with your advisor before *registration*.

Assumption: You mean that early *registration* is available for graduate students?

Problem: I can't get to *registration* before noon.

report   n.   a written or oral presentation of results, either of research or experimentation

Example: Ken gave an excellent *report* in our management class today.

Suggestion: If I were you, I would allow more time for my next *report*.

Assumption: So you did listen to Ken's *report*.

Problem: I have to do five oral *reports* for speech class.

research   n.   investigation or study

Example: Dr. Peterson is going to give a lecture about her *research* on cross-cultural interaction.

Suggestion: You could use my class for your *research*.

Assumption: Your *research* is complete, isn't it?

Problem: I need more sources for my *research*.

research assistant   n.   a research position under the supervision of a faculty member

Example: The *research assistants* get to know the faculty better than the other graduate students do.

Suggestion: You could apply to be a *research assistant* next year.

Assumption: You mean Ken's a *research assistant*?

Problem: I need to speak to the *research assistant* who works in the psychology lab.

research paper   n.   a written report based on research
Example: Use at least ten references for your *research papers*.
Suggestion: You had better go to the library soon if you want that book for your *research paper*.
Assumption: You mean we have to present our *research paper* to the class?
Problem: I can't get started on my *research paper*.

resident advisor   n.   an advisor who lives in a dormitory in order to provide supervision and counseling for the students
Example: We call our *resident advisor* the "head resident."
Suggestion: Why don't you speak to the *resident advisor* about your problem?
Assumption: You live next door to the *resident advisor*?
Problem: I need to speak with the *resident advisor* regarding the desk in my room.

review session   n.   a study meeting to review material before a test, often led by the professor
Example: I'm on my way to a *review session* for my art appreciation class.
Suggestion: You could schedule a *review session* with your study group.
Assumption: The *review session* was productive?
Problem: I can't meet Thursday afternoon for the *review session*.

room and board   n.   fees for room rent and meals
Example: *Room and board* goes up every year.
Suggestion: You should plan to include the price of *room and board* in your budget.
Assumption: You mean your scholarship covers *room and board* ?
Problem: I need to find a part-time job to pay for *room and board*.

roommate   n.   a person who shares a room or rooms
   Example: I think Diane is looking for a *roommate*.
   Suggestion: Why don't you and Diane get another *roommate*?
   Assumption: You mean you're looking for another *roommate*?
   Problem: I need a *roommate* to share my rent.

schedule   n.   a list of courses with days, times, and locations
   Example: My *schedule* this semester allows me to work in
                  the afternoons.
   Suggestion: With your *schedule*, you could get a job at school.
   Assumption: Your *schedule* doesn't include evening classes?
   Problem: I can't fit that class into my *schedule*.

scholarship   n.   a grant awarded to a student
   Example: Tracy got a *scholarship* to attend a special sum-
                  mer course abroad.
   Suggestion: Why don't you apply for a *scholarship*?
   Assumption: There aren't any *scholarships* available for interna-
                  tional students, are there?
   Problem: I have to turn the application in tomorrow to be
                  eligible for the *scholarship*.

section   n.   one of several options for the same course
   Example: Everyone wants to take the *section* that Mrs.
                  McNiel teaches.
   Suggestion: You could ask Mrs. McNiel to let you into her
                  section.
   Assumption: You mean there are no *sections* open in the
                  morning?
   Problem: I can't get into that *section* because it is closed.

semester   n.   a school term that is usually fifteen to eighteen
weeks in length
   Example: When the *semester* is over, I am going to visit my
                  family.
   Suggestion: You could sign up for more classes this *semester*.
   Assumption: This *semester* ends before winter break, doesn't
                  it?
   Problem: I need to take eighteen credit hours next *semester*.

senior   n.   a fourth-year student
    Example: Laura will be a *senior* next semester.
    Suggestion: If I were you, I would take that class as a *senior*.
    Assumption: You mean Dana is a *senior*?
    Problem: I have to take five classes when I'm a *senior*.

short-essay test   n.   a test with questions that require a written response of one sentence to one paragraph in length
    Example: I would rather take a *short-essay test* than an objective test.
    Suggestion: You had better study your notes for Dr. Mitchell's *short-essay test*.
    Assumption: You think a *short-essay test* is easier than an objective test?
    Problem: I have three *short-essay tests* in that class.

shuttle   n.   a bus that has a short route around the campus area
    Example: Carol has a car, but she still uses the campus *shuttle* most of the time.
    Suggestion: If I were you, I would take the *shuttle* at night.
    Assumption: You mean there's no *shuttle* on Sundays?
    Problem: I need to leave early to catch the *shuttle*.

sign up (for a class)   v.   to enroll (in a class)
    Example: Let's *sign up* for the same geology class.
    Suggestion: You should *sign up* for Dr. Brown's music theory class.
    Assumption: So you did *sign up* for the field trip.
    Problem: I can't *sign up* for that class because it conflicts with my schedule.

skip class   v.   to be absent
    Example: Nancy has been *skipping class* again.
    Suggestion: If I were you, I wouldn't *skip class* this week.
    Assumption: Ken *skipped class* yesterday?
    Problem: Bill *skipped class* on the day of the test.

snack bar   n.   a small restaurant area where a limited menu is
available

Example: We usually meet at the *snack bar* for a quick
lunch.

Suggestion: You could meet me at the *snack bar*.

Assumption: So you did go to the *snack bar* after class.

Problem: I need to go to the *snack bar* between classes
because I don't have a break for lunch.

social security number   n.   a nine-digit number that is often used
for student identification as well as for employment purposes

Example: What is your *social security number*?

Suggestion: You should memorize your *social security
number*.

Assumption: Your *social security number* is on your license,
isn't it?

Problem: Anna doesn't have a *social security number*.

sophomore   n.   a second-year college student

Example: A full-time student is usually a *sophomore* by the
third semester.

Suggestion: You had better complete your general education
classes by the end of your *sophomore* year.

Assumption: You mean Bill is only a *sophomore*?

Problem: I can't take advanced psychology because I am
only a *sophomore*.

sorority   n.   a social organization for female college students

Example: About a dozen *sororities* are on campus.

Suggestion: You should consider joining a *sorority*.

Assumption: So you did join a *sorority*.

Problem: *Sororities* require a lot of time.

spring break   n.   a short vacation in the middle of the spring
semester

Example: Some of my friends are going to Florida for *spring
break*.

Suggestion: Why don't you visit your family over *spring
break*?

Assumption: You got your research paper done over *spring break*?

Problem: I have to work during *spring break*.

stacks n. the area of the library where most of the books are shelved

Example: At a small college, the *stacks* are usually open to all of the students.

Suggestion: You should look in the *stacks* for that book.

Assumption: The librarian let you go up in the *stacks* to look for your own book?

Problem: I need to find a carrel in the *stacks*.

student n. one who attends a school

Example: State University has more than fifty-thousand *students* enrolled on the main campus.

Suggestion: If you tell them that you are a *student*, maybe you will get a discount.

Assumption: You mean you aren't a *student*?

Problem: I need to find five *students* to complete my study.

student I.D. number n. a number used for identification at a college or university, often a social security number

Example: Your social security number is your *student I.D. number*.

Suggestion: You should write your *student I.D. number* on all of your papers.

Assumption: Pat has a *student I.D. number*?

Problem: I can't seem to remember my *student I.D. number*.

student services n. an administrative branch of a college or university that provides noninstructional support services for students

Example: I have to go over to *student services* to meet with a financial aid advisor.

Suggestion: You had better go to *student services* to check on your dorm application.

Assumption: The *student services* office is open during registration, isn't it?

Problem: I have to go to the *student services* office before
              the end of the day.

student union n.   a building on campus where students can relax
Example: There is a movie at the *student union* tonight.
Suggestion: You could meet Ken in the *student union* before
              the concert.
Assumption: You mean the *student union* is closed over the
              holidays?
Problem: The *student union* closes at 10:00 P.M.

studies n.   research investigations
Example: Many *studies* have been conducted here at State
              University.
Suggestion: Why don't you speak with Dr. Mason about her
              studies?
Assumption: So you did begin your *studies*.
Problem: I have to complete my *studies* by the end of the
              semester.

study v.   to acquire knowledge or understanding of a subject
Example: I have to *study* if I want to get a good grade in
              this class.
Suggestion: Why don't you plan to *study* at my house this
              weekend?
Assumption: You mean you *studied* for that test?
Problem: I need to allow more time to *study*.

study date n.   a date in which the activity is studying
Example: Joe and Diane have *study dates* most of the time.
Suggestion: You could arrange a *study date* with Jack before
              the test.
Assumption: You mean you don't have a *study date* tonight?
Problem: I have to meet Jack at the library for our *study
              date*.

study lounge n.   a quiet area of a dormitory where students can
go to study
Example: Even the *study lounge* is noisy in this dorm.

Suggestion: Why don't you meet me in the *study lounge* this
               evening?
Assumption: Did you say that the *study lounge* is quiet?
Problem: I can't concentrate in the *study lounge*.

subject   n.   an area of study
Example: Math is my favorite *subject*.
Suggestion: Why don't you ask Tracy for help with the *subjects* she tutors?
Assumption: You can get tutoring in all of the *subjects* taught at
               the university?
Problem: I have to take a lot of classes in *subjects* that I
               don't really like.

summer school   n.   the summer sessions, which are usually
June through August
Example: *Summer school* starts the second week of June
               this year.
Suggestion: Why don't you take the art appreciation course in
               summer school?
Assumption: You mean you've gone to *summer school* every
               summer?
Problem: I can't go to *summer school* this year.

T.A.   n.   an abbreviation for teaching assistant
Example: Laura has applied to be Dr. Graham's *T.A.*
Suggestion: You should see the *T.A.* if you have questions
               about the lecture.
Assumption: So Bill did apply to be a *T.A.*
Problem: I have to find Dr. Graham's *T.A.* before class
               tomorrow.

teaching assistant   n.   a graduate student whose teaching duties
are supervised by a faculty member
Example: We have a *teaching assistant* for the discussion
               session of this class.
Suggestion: You had better speak with the *teaching assistant*
               before the next lab session.
Assumption: You mean you haven't spoken with the *teaching
               assistant*?
Problem: The *teaching assistant* is really difficult to understand.

tenure   n.   an academic rank that guarantees permanent status
    Example: Professor Peterson has *tenure*, but Mr. Lewis
                    doesn't.
    Suggestion: Why don't you request the requirements for
                    tenure?
    Assumption: You mean Dr. Peterson has *tenure*?
    Problem: Mr. Lewis will have to get his Ph.D. to qualify for
                    tenure.

term   n.   a time period when school is in session, usually a quarter
or a semester
    Example: Dana needs two more *terms* to graduate.
    Suggestion: Dana had better take statistics next *term*.
    Assumption: Nancy passed all of her classes last *term*?
    Problem: I have to complete my dissertation in three *terms*.

test   n.   an evaluation that is usually longer and worth more
points than a quiz but shorter and worth fewer points than an
exam
    Example: You will have a *test* every week in this class.
    Suggestion: If I were you, I would work with my study group
                    before the *test*.
    Assumption: You mean you forgot about the *test*?
    Problem: I have to study for two *tests* next week.

textbook   n.   a book that is used for a course
    Example: The *textbooks* can be purchased at the bookstore
                    or ordered over the Internet.
    Suggestion: You could purchase used *textbooks* for some of
                    your classes.
    Assumption: You mean you had to buy new *textbooks*?
    Problem: I can't find good used *textbooks* anywhere.

thesis   n.   a written research report in partial fulfillment of a
graduate degree
    Example: Tracy isn't taking any courses this semester
                    because she is writing her *thesis*.
    Suggestion: You should get the handbook at the graduate
                    school before starting your *thesis*.

Assumption: Tracy isn't writing her *thesis* this semester, is she?

Problem: I need to allow at least one semester to write my *thesis*.

transcript n. a printed copy of a student's grades

Example: The admissions office requires two *transcripts* with every application.

Suggestion: Why don't you request an extra copy of your *transcript*?

Assumption: You mean you still haven't received your *transcripts*?

Problem: I have to have those *transcripts* by next Monday.

transfer v. to change schools

Example: It is better to *transfer* at the beginning of the third year.

Suggestion: If I were you, I would *transfer* as soon as possible.

Assumption: Dana *transferred* to State University?

Problem: I can't *transfer* colleges because I would lose credits.

tuition n. fees for instruction at a school

Example: The *tuition* is different from school to school.

Suggestion: You should check the *tuition* before deciding on a college.

Assumption: *Tuition* at private colleges is more?

Problem: I need a scholarship to pay my *tuition*.

tuition hike n. an increase in the fees for instruction

Example: There is a *tuition hike* every year at State University.

Suggestion: You should sign the petition protesting the *tuition hike*.

Assumption: You mean you graduated before the *tuition hike*?

Problem: I can't afford another *tuition hike*.

turn in v. to submit an assignment

Example: Please *turn in* your homework before you leave.

Suggestion: You had better *turn in* your paper before the end of the day.

Assumption: You mean I could have *turned in* my paper tomorrow?

Problem: I have to *turn in* the paper by Friday or I will get an F.

tutor n. a private instructor, often another student

Example: I have to meet my *tutor* at the library.

Suggestion: Why don't you get a *tutor* for your accounting class?

Assumption: You mean Jack is your *tutor*?

Problem: I can't afford to hire a *tutor*.

tutoring n. private instruction

Example: Nancy needs some *tutoring* in this class.

Suggestion: You could earn extra money *tutoring* for math.

Assumption: So you did get the *tutoring* job.

Problem: *Tutoring* takes a lot of time.

undergrad n., adj. abbreviation for undergraduate

Example: I think that Dana is an *undergrad*.

Suggestion: You could still enroll for *undergrad* classes while you are waiting to hear from the graduate school admissions office.

Assumption: You mean you're an *undergrad* ?

Problem: I need to apply for an *undergrad* scholarship.

undergraduate (student) n., adj. a student pursuing a bachelor's degree

Example: Some *undergraduates* require five years to complete a four-year program.

Suggestion: You should look at more than one *undergraduate* program.

Assumption: You mean you completed your *undergraduate* courses in three years?

Problem: I can't complete my *undergraduate* degree before we move.

upper-division (course)   adj.   advanced courses for third- and fourth-year students

Example:	Most of the *upper-division* courses are numbered 400 or above.
Suggestion:	Why don't you take an *upper-division* music class?
Assumption:	You mean grammar is an *upper-division* course?
Problem:	Dana needs to take an *upper-division* math class.

withdraw   v.   to leave school

Example:	My roommate *withdrew* from school.
Suggestion:	You should *withdraw* so that you won't have failing grades on your transcript.
Assumption:	You mean your parents want you to *withdraw* from school?
Problem:	I have to *withdraw* from school at the end of the semester.

work-study   adj.   a special program that allows study time when there is nothing to do on the job

Example:	There are several *work-study* positions open in the finance office.
Suggestion:	Dana should apply for the *work-study* program next semester.
Assumption:	You mean Vicki's library job is a *work-study* position?
Problem:	The *work-study* students couldn't answer my questions.

Xerox (machine)   n.   a copy machine

Example:	There is a long line at the *Xerox* machine.
Suggestion:	You could use the *Xerox* machine in the library.
Assumption:	You mean there are only three *Xerox* machines on campus?
Problem:	I need to find a *Xerox* machine.

More TOEFL Test Prep Titles from BARRON'S

How to Prepare for the TOEFL iBT, 12th Ed.

w/CD-ROM or Audio CDs
Pamela Sharpe, Ph.D.

The TOEFL (Test of English as a Foreign Language) is now offered as an internet-based test, or iBT, and the new edition of Barron's TOEFL manual and accompanying software has been revised to reflect the new format. The manual presents seven full-length model TOEFL iBT tests with explanations or examples. The author also offers general orientation to the new TOEFL iBT and a review of language skills—listening, speaking, reading, and writing. The optional CD-ROM presents seven on-screen TOEFL iBT exams that simulate actual test conditions. The optional audio CDs—which may be purchased together with the manual or separately—present audio prompts for the Listening, Speaking, and Writing sections of all tests in the book.

Book w/CD-ROM: ISBN-10: 0-7641-7905-5, $16.99, Can$24.50, paper, 740 pp., ISBN-13: 978-0-7641-7905-1

Book w/Audio CDs: ISBN-10: 0-7641-7917-9, $34.99, Can$49.99, ISBN-13: 978-0-7641-7917-4

Audio CD Package: ISBN-10: 0-7641-7918-7, $24.99, Can$35.99, ISBN-13: 978-0-7641-7918-1

Pass Key to the TOEFL iBT, 6th Ed. w/2 Audio CDs
Pamela Sharpe, Ph.D.

This shorter version of Barron's full-size TOEFL iBT test prep manual has also been revised to prepare students for the new internet-based test. It presents three model TOEFL iBTs, all with explanations or example answers, an overview of the new test format, and extensive test-taking advice. The audio CDs present audio prompts for the Listening, Speaking, and Writing sections in the book's practice tests.

ISBN-10: 0-7641-7919-5, $18.99, Can$25.99, paper w/2 audio CDs, 512 pp., ISBN-13: 978-0-7641-7919-8

Practice Exercises for the TOEFL, 5th Ed.

w/Optional Audio CDs
Pamela Sharpe, Ph.D.

This manual's practice exercises consist of more than 1,000 items with explanatory answers and example answers that prepare students for the Listening, Speaking, Structure, Reading, and Writing sections of the TOEFL. A TOEFL practice test with evaluation is also included. The book can be purchased alone or with a set of five audio CDs offering practice in pronunciation and listening comprehension.

Book only: ISBN-10: 0-7641-2046-8, $16.95, Can $24.50, paper, 400 pp., ISBN-13: 978-0-7641-2046-6

Book w/audio CDs: ISBN-10: 0-7641-7512-2, $29.95, Can $43.50, ISBN-13: 978-0-7641-7512-1

Audio CD Package: ISBN-10: 0-7641-7740-0, $21.95, Can $31.95, ISBN-13: 978-0-7641-7740-8

TOEFL WordMaster
Steve Matthiesen

Three hundred basic English words that TOEFL test-takers need to recognize are presented in this set of 56 flash cards. A viewing window in the container box shows the word to be learned and its part of speech. Users slide the card slightly to see its definition, and then to see it used in a sample sentence taken from an actual TOEFL exam. All 300 words are indexed on the set's last four cards, enabling students to find specific words and meanings quickly.

56 Flash Cards in case, ISBN-10: 0-7641-7907-1, $11.99, Can$17.50, ISBN-13: 978-0-7641-7907-5

BARRON'S
www.barronseduc.com

Barron's Educational Series, Inc.
250 Wireless Blvd., Hauppauge, NY 11788
Order toll-free: 1-800-645-3476 Order by fax: 1-631-434-3217
In Canada: Georgetown Book Warehouse
4 Armstrong Ave., Georgetown, Ont. L7G 4R9
Canadian orders: 1-800-247-7160 Fax in Canada: 1-800-887-1594

prices are in U.S. and Canadian dollars and subject to change without notice. Order from your bookstore—or directly from Barron's adding 18% for shipping and handling (minimum charge $5.95). New York, New Jersey, Michigan, Tennessee, and California residents add sales tax to total after shipping and handling.

CHOOSING A COLLEGE

For every question you have, Barron's guides have the right answers.

BARRON'S COLLEGE GUIDES

AMERICA'S #1 RESOURCE FOR EDUCATION PLANNING.

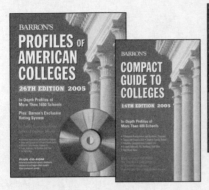

PROFILES OF AMERICAN COLLEGES,
26th Edition, w/CD-ROM
$26.95, Can. $38.95, (0-7641-7575-0)

COMPACT GUIDE TO COLLEGES
14th Edition
$9.95, Can. $14.50, (0-7641-2311-4)

BARRON'S BEST BUYS IN COLLEGE
EDUCATION, 8th Edition
Solorzano
$18.95, Can. $27.50, (0-7641-2310-6)

BARRON'S GUIDE TO THE MOST
COMPETITIVE COLLEGES, 4th Edition
$18.99, Can. $27.50, (0-7641-3197-4)

PROFILES OF AMERICAN COLLEGES:
THE NORTHEAST, 16th Edition
$16.95, Can. $24.50, (0-7641-2312-2)

THE ALL-IN-ONE COLLEGE GUIDE
Marty Nemko, Ph.D.
$10.95, Can. $15.95, (0-7641-2298-3)

BARRON'S HEAD START TO COLLEGE
PLANNING
Susan C. Chiarolanzio, M.A.
$11.95, Can. $17.50, (0-7641-2697-0)

BARRON'S EDUCATIONAL SERIES, INC.
250 Wireless Blvd., Hauppauge, NY 11788
In Canada: Georgetown Book Warehouse
34 Armstrong Ave., Georgetown, Ont. L7G 4R9
$ = U.S. Dollars Can.$ = Canadian Dollars

Prices subject to change without notice.
Books may be purchased at your
bookstore, or by mail from Barron's.
Enclose check or money order for total
amount plus 18% for postage and
handling (minimum charge of $5.95).
New York, New Jersey, Michigan,
Tennessee, and California residents
add sales tax to total. All books
are paperback editions. Visit us at
www.barronseduc.com

(#8) R 3/06

Barron's TOEFL Compact Disks

The compact disks in the back of this book can be used in your compact disk player to provide the audio for TOEFL® iBT model tests 2 and 3 in this book. You should hear audio only. If you want to simulate the Computer-Based TOEFL, with both audio and visuals, you need a CD-ROM, not a compact disk. The CD-ROM is available from Barron's Educational Series, Inc. The CD-ROM has seven model tests on it.

Telephone: 800-645-3476
FAX: 631-434-3723
E-mail: customer.service@barronseduc.com
Web site: *http://www.barronseduc.com*